Conversion Chart

Liquid Conversions

U.S.	Metric
1 tsp.	5 ml
1 tbsp.	15 ml
2 tbsp.	30 ml
3 tbsp.	45 ml
¼ cup	60 ml
⅓ cup	75 ml
⅓ cup + 1 tbsp.	90 ml
⅓ cup + 2 tbsp.	105 ml
½ cup	120 ml
⅔ cup	155 ml
¾ cup	180 ml
¾ cup + 2 tbsp.	210 ml
1 cup	240 ml
1 cup + 2 tbsp.	270 ml
1 ¼ cups	295 ml
1 ⅓ cups	315 ml
1 ½ cups	355 ml
1 ⅔ cups	395 ml
1 ¾ cups	415 ml
1 ¾ cups + 2 tbsp.	445 ml
2 cups (1 pint)	475 ml
2 ½ cups	590 ml
3 cups	710 ml
4 cups (1 quart)	945 ml

1,000 ml = 1 liter

Weight Conversions

U.S.	Metric
½ oz.	14 g
1 oz.	28 g
1 ½ oz.	43 g
2 oz.	57 g
2 ½ oz.	71 g
3 oz.	85 g
3 ½ oz.	100 g
4 oz.	113 g
5 oz.	142 g
6 oz.	170 g
7 oz.	200 g
8 oz.	227 g
9 oz.	255 g
10 oz.	284 g
11 oz.	312 g
12 oz.	340 g
13 oz.	368 g
14 oz.	400 g
15 oz.	425 g
1 lb.	454 g

Oven Temperatures

°F	Gas Mark	°C
250	½	120
275	1	140
300	2	150
325	3	165
350	4	180
375	5	190
400	6	200
425	7	220
450	8	230
475	9	240
500	10	260
550	Broil	290

Vérane Frédiani

TASTE THE WORLD IN MARSEILLE

Translation: Alexis Steinman

MARSEILLE CUISINE BY THE MARSEILLAIS

FRANCE'S NEW FOOD MECCA • RESTAURANTS

• PEOPLE • RECIPES • CHEFS • STORIES •

Éditions
de La Martinière

WHY MARSEILLE?

Marseille is my hometown.
I grew up here, on the sunny shores of the Mediterranean, close, yet so far, from the Côte d'Azur, frolicking in this less-chic part of Provence, with Paris at my back, far north behind our hills. It felt like a corner of the world, disconnected from the rest of France and despised by it. The oldest city in France, once rich but now poor, opens its arms to all the Mediterranean and beyond. Marseille is a city where one ends up after fleeing misery, hunger, unemployment, war . . . One arrives on the quays with somewhat empty pockets but with the will to start again, to work, to study . . . the city benefits from this tenacious energy and creative rage.
My family came from Italy and Corsica. As everybody else here, I am the product of migrations. In Marseille, we are all from elsewhere and yet we are all Marseillais and proud of it.

The Marseille of my childhood – from Boulevard Chave and Les Cinq-Avenues to La Plaine – didn't interest anyone 20 years ago, and, admittedly, for years, all it took was a gust of the mistral wind or a football match for everyone to stay in. Marseille wasn't a gastronomic city and Marseillais ate at home or at their Italian, Vietnamese, Armenian, Lebanese, Jewish, and Arab friends' and family's places. On nights that we couldn't be bothered to cook, we'd go to a pizza truck (*camion à pizza*) or our favourite pizzeria if we were in a celebratory mood.

Ironically, as it always is, I became a food documentary filmmaker. A few years ago, my research led me to *A Considerable Town* by the famously gastronomical MFK Fisher. Written when I was three years old, in 1977, it's an entire book about Marseille, a city that Mary Frances held to be 'considerable'! She probably wished to counterbalance the snobbish criticism that had been repeatedly flung at Marseille. As she was a well-known fan of elegant Aix-en-Provence, I was surprised by her enthusiasm for turbulent Marseille but I feel MFK's naughty side couldn't help but find Marseille alluring . . .

'*I myself have a different definition of the place, which is as indefinable as Marseille itself* – insolite. *There seems to be no proper twin for this word in English; one simply has to sense or feel what it means. Larousse says "it is contrary to what is usual and normal" . . . inwardly I know that it means mysterious, unknowable, and in plain fact undefinable.*'

This book stuck with me and when I moved to London eight years ago, I began to see Marseille through some sort of foreign eyes. I started seeing Marseille's multicultural food mix as like that in London or Berlin and considering this unique cultural tapestry as a pattern that makes sense, and a source of inspiration. Marseille was founded 2,600 years ago by Greek sailors coming from Phocaea, looking for a new colony. They annexed this quiet *calanque* to become a new trading port. Hence from the beginning Marseille has been both international and its own little self.

Problems exist, like in all big global cities, but Marseille's particularity is that in terms of cooking and eating, we always come together.
Here, more than anywhere else in France, food is more than food. It's our history, our love, our generosity, our largesse, our common language, our links to others, but also our struggle. As we eat together around a table, we do what we like the most . . . we argue! Yes, Marseillais get worked up easily but nothing is ever too serious. We mostly consider life as some sort of comedy show.

Only a few writers had tried to sink their teeth into '*le manger marseillais*' or the 'Marseille culinary heritage', as some intellectuals of the plate like to say. But in 2013, Marseille was chosen as the European Capital of Culture, which had a huge impact on the dynamic of the city. Marseille was reinventing itself one more time. I felt it was about time to document this movement through food. I started photographing and interviewing chefs in 2019 and went on until 2023. While rediscovering my own town, the book I wrote became a testimony of an era. My personal inquiry bumped into a culinary revolution.

Another delicious revolution

Today I dare think that the future of French gastronomy is being written here, in Marseille. French cuisine always needed foreign influences and in recent decades – due to living in something of a vacuum – it has been running out of steam. The free and uninhibited Marseille mix is just the gusto it needed.

From 2013 onwards, the *magnifique* Mucem, new hotels with a view, the arrival of heaps of tourists and of ambitious chefs from everywhere – because experimenting is cheaper here, the Michelin stars that started raining down on restaurants, the willpower of many female cooks to become cheffes . . . All of these elements together gave Marseille the much-needed oomph to wake up and reassert its melange of cultures, its codes, its atmosphere, and its curiosity for others, above all, in its professional kitchens.

In 2019, the Marseille-Provence-Gastronomy festival (MPG) and their sold-out *Dîners Insolites* in atypical settings were born. The bar was set high, and since then, everyone here in gastronomy is trying to keep up.

The high-quality, once-introverted culinary diversity is now bursting into the public realm at food events and restaurants for everyone to share, discover, and celebrate.

Facts are that here you can still own your restaurant, your menu can be as personal as you want, and no one will look down on you if you didn't train with famous chefs or attend a prestigious private culinary school.

We dream less about fine dining than about mouthwatering hearty food. In Marseille, restaurants and healthy food remain unfussy and affordable. Chefs and waiters are chatty and casual, their character and their wackiness define their eateries. We eat seasonally without even thinking about it, vegetables grow easily and nature is close by.

In Marseille, many chefs are self-taught, children of very good female home cooks. All of them are recovering nostalgics. They've filled their suitcases of memories with scents, flavours, and tastes, but their strength is in how they blend them together. Fiercely turned towards the present, everyday life, the ephemeral, the seasons, the sun, the sea, but also the Garlaban massif, the Rhône delta and wild Camargue . . . they are obliged to look straight ahead and not back. So, at a time when gourmets of every persuasion are turning away from highbrow gastronomy and seeking to give meaning to their culinary curiosity, the Marseille restaurant model offers an accessible, modern, inclusive and intelligent alternative (mind you, I'm not talking about the cookie-cutter *moules frites* on the Vieux-Port).

Marseille cooks the world and its history . . . Reading this book, drinking apéro at a local's home or strolling through our food-laden neighbourhoods will allow you to truly size up the concentration of cultures and stories that every generation reinterprets and embellishes with new ones.

Embrace Marseille's philosophy through food. What's in this book is what we, Marseillais, consider 'considerable'. I want you to feel connected to us, close to us. Marseille uses no filter, and there is nothing to be ashamed of about our outspoken ways, our rebellious attitude, and, more importantly, our lack of means and money. Marseille is one of the few big cities that depicts the present state of the world, its reality and its political history. Parisians, who looked down on us for ages, now think we're trendy.

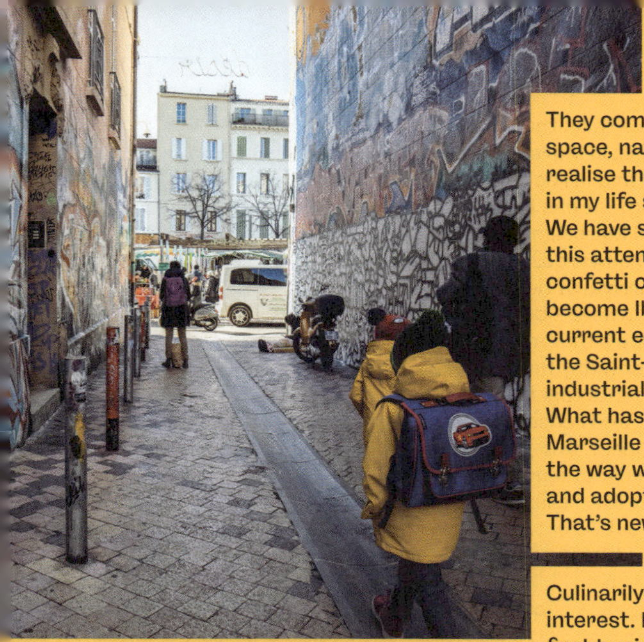

They come here for holidays and many move here for more sun, space, nature, the sea, and cheaper properties. Covid helped them realise they needed that. (I too realised I needed more of Marseille in my life since Covid.)
We have somewhat adapted to our new trendiness, even if all this attention won't change Marseille much. Michelin stars and confetti can be showered upon us, but Marseille won't ever become Ibiza! We happily prevail as the ultimate outsider city. The current economic fuss happened before, in the 19th century, when the Saint-Charles train station and the Suez Canal opened. Rich industrials came but the Marseille '*esprit*' didn't change.
What has changed is our self-confidence. Suddenly in France Marseille matters beyond football and rap music. The way we live, the way we mix cultures, the way one calls oneself a Marseillais and adopts this identity very fast, the way we talk and eat matter. That's new.

Culinarily speaking, there is a real upside to arousing international interest. Having young cooks come to Marseille to open their first business boosts the city's chefs, restaurateurs and entrepreneurs. Chaos is still the rule of thumb but Marseille has never been so *tarpin* (very) *belle*.
I spent hours, days, months, walking in my city, chatting with the chefs, eating and cooking with them, capturing our uniqueness in my photos. I wanted them to share their experience with Marseille and offer another point of view on France's second largest city. A positive and unifying look to inspire other towns.
In this book, Marseillais are talking straight to you and they were all super enthusiastic about it. The recipes have been written by the chefs themselves or by my family members. It is rare you get to read their culinary language. Most chefs don't write their own cookbooks.
I never felt so connected with my hometown. My friends in London thought I would never return but I always had in mind that one day, I'd travel with the book . . . I am not Ms. Fisher, Julia Child, Richard Olney nor Alice Waters – Francophile Americans I admire so much – but I am Marseillaise. This book is me, it's us, translated with care. Alexis Steinman, a radiant American writer living in Marseille, and Nicole Foster in London, tackled the huge task of translating my love letter to Marseille into English. It took hours of lively conversation to find the right words en *anglais* that maintained the spirit of the local way of expressing ourselves. I also had my views on English matters . . . and rewrote part of the book just for you, my dear friends in the United K.
Remember, Marseille is neither cute nor charming, it is a vibrant and uplifting place. When in Marseille, be over-adventurous. You will be welcomed for it. And when cooking our recipes, keep in mind what famous French chef Alain Chapel wrote, '*La cuisine, c'est beaucoup plus que des recettes.*' ('Cooking is a lot more than recipes.')

So, is Marseille redefining what a food city should be?

It's your call . . .

— Vérane Frédiani

CONTENTS

**'Marseille or New York?
The winner is obvious! I choose Marseille!
Because it's a true cosmopolitan city'**

— Words of Marseillais, Nouredine Azzouk

MARSEILLE ITINERARIES FOR CURIOUS BELLIES

Belsunce and La Canebière

My cousins' grandparents, Dédé and Paulette Michel, were coffee roasters in the neighbourhood on Rue Nationale. When the Michels would go out on delivery, they entrusted their shop to the district's prostitutes, who gladly kept an eye on it. At the end of their career, in 1979, the Michels sold their business, Les Cafés Eldorado, to then-unknown Henry Blanc who wanted to start his own outfit. So, the emblematic coffee magnate of Marseille also got his start here. When it comes to beautiful stories, in Belsunce, there are many and, in Marseille, we all have a bit of Belsunce in us. Here you can eat organic vegetarian fare at Le Grain de Sable; grab a seat at Coco Velten, an incubator for culinary projects, pay-what-you-can meals, and lunch *suspendus*; buy *pâtisseries orientales* (in French, *oriental* refers to North Africa and/or the Middle East, not the Far East, and is widely used when talking about cuisine from that region) at Délices Pâtisserie d'Aix at the start of Rue d'Aix; and do a bit of shopping at Little Asia.

On La Canebière, the Champs-Elysée of Marseille, and Boulevard d'Athènes, try to imagine how prestigious these avenues were in the 19th century. Magnificent hotels like Hôtel Noailles or Hôtel des Empereurs earned their reputation welcoming the most important people in the world. Rumour has it that in the back of the C&A department store (formerly Hôtel du Louvre et de la Paix) , there are rooms as resplendent as Le Train Bleu at Paris's Gare de Lyon. Grand Hôtel de Russie et d'Angleterre, at 31 Boulevard d'Athènes, became the Hôtel Splendide at one point and that's where American Varian Fry settled in 1940. In the 19th century, La Canebière was also home to not-to-miss cafés with sumptuous décor, like the Café Turc. Incidentally, the first café in France opened in Marseille, the city where the stimulating beans first disembarked in France.

Afterwards, our Canebière, immortalised in Marseille composer Vincent Scotto's song, lost its elegance. Personally, I remember when the first McDonald's opened in Marseille. It ironically replaced a café on La Canebière in 1982. It was a major event. Everybody in town wanted an American burger!

Today, the somewhat-roguish boulevard is relaunching with a huge new movie house, Artplexe, and its super-welcoming rooftop terrace. The Allée Gambetta is also getting its gourmand on thanks to the lovely teams at Golda, Petit Tamky and nearby Petit Dugo. Undoubtedly promising, our Cane . . . Cane . . . Cane . . . Canebière!

Longchamp, Cinq-Avenues and La Friche la Belle de Mai

I spent my adolescent years in these neighbourhoods, at the Collège Longchamp, followed by the Lycée Saint-Charles, but at that time, there weren't restaurants to lunch at on these quiet streets. We'd pick up giant American-style sandwiches (I can't disown these beloved baguettes stuffed with frites and minced meat) that we'd eat in the sun on Palais Longchamp's lawn. No one would have had the inkling to brunch here on the weekends. In 2007, the new tram laid tracks down the Boulevard Longchamp and habits changed. Rue Consolat and Boulevard de la Libération were next to be revitalised and there now are good, affordable spots galore everywhere in this sloped part of town: Ashourya, Romain et Marion, the community canteen Casa Consolat, Jéjé barbu's restaurant, Les Eaux de Mars, Le Longchamp Palace, Le Bar à Pain and L'Épicerie Yasmine Al Cham. The arrival of a new branch of Bricoleurs de Douceurs pâtisserie at the gates of Parc Longchamp officially sealed the deal that this district is primed for food-lovers.

I gladly include a part of the Belle de Mai *quartier* here, unjustly cut off from the centre of Marseille by the railway lines that extend from the Gare Saint-Charles. Amazingly, once you're at the top of Boulevard Longchamp, you're not so far from La Friche, its *expos*, its farmers' market, Les Grandes Tables restaurant and its brilliant roof top. Here, the north and south of Marseille rub shoulders and move forward together. As you make your way to Belle de Mai, pop into the Belleville-sur-Mer bistro. Even for a quick apéro, it's lovely.

From Noailles to Cours Julien by way of Rue d'Aubagne

The epicentre of *bobo* (bourgeois-bohemian) tourists is nonetheless authentic. The beauty of Noailles is its encounters. You must sit down and talk with everyone. Noailles displays the conviviality of cookery every day. When touring this incredible open-air food court, fittingly nicknamed the 'belly of Marseille' for its foodstuffs and central location, you must take the time to observe. Eclecticism is de rigueur. From the best couscous in Marseille at Le Fémina to Au Grand Saint-Antoine – Baussens' charcuterie beside the Capucins food market – , passing by Maison Empereur (a theme park for kitchen-utensil lovers) one can eat Algerian, Tunisian, Senegalese, Vietnamese and Sicilian in this maze of roads. . .

Up until the Cours Lieutaud cleaved through the districts in 1789 then 1864, the Rue d'Aubagne and Cours Julien/Notre-Dame du Mont were one and the same. So it's logical to find a sort of second open-air food hall, further up Rue d'Aubagne, between Cours Julien, Rue des Trois Rois, Notre-Dame du Mont, Rue Fontange and La Plaine. Super lively, even exuberant, it is stuffed to the gills with good spots for filling up your shopping basket with even more deliciousness!

‘Belsunce, jewel of the Phocaean quarters,
Stuck between the train station and the Vieux-Port
We’re not the ones to take pity on.
Whether at home or away
We crack down on cockroaches like Baygon.’

‘Belsunce Breakdown’
— Bouga, sample from the soundtrack to
Comme un Aimant, a film by Kamel Saleh and Akhenaton

A summer's evening on the Vieux-Port

From Place Sébastopol to La Plaine via Boulevards Chave and Eugène-Pierre

This is the neighbourhood of my childhood that is directly linked to Noailles by a tunnel and a tram (before WWII, there were a hundred or so tram lines in Marseille). It used to be a quiet and familial area with a mix of middle-class and rather low-income families and up until ten years ago, it wasn't a foodie destination at all. Today, Boulevards Chave and Eugène-Pierre are the stars of the food show. Young families have refurbished a good chunk of the flats and houses and even the *cavistes* (wine sellers) are livening things up. The metamorphosis happened thanks to mini clusters of local restaurateurs like the team behind Le Parpaing Qui Flotte (Bambino, Gigi, Les Danaïdes, etc.), the bistrot Georges (same owners as Golda), Trois-Quarts, Les Mains-Libres boulangerie, La Brûlerie Mokä café and roaster, La Cuisine de Gagny, and Cheffe Sarah Chougnet's Regain. Most recently, Bouillon has caused a sensation with Cheffe Auregan Dean, a meat and natural-wine lover. Yes, that does exist!

This is also the quarter of bubbly Cheffe Marie Dijon (Caterine restaurant). With 20 years between us, we both played in the school playground at École Chave, a former prison that staged executions by guillotine from 1912 to 1934. The day that you learn this fact, you don't enter your Year 6 classroom in the same way!

Back to food. This quarter is home to two essential markets: La Plaine, the square where bar and café terraces take it easy today, and the marché at Place Sébastapol. This square and the streets that stem from it are in the early stage of gentrification but grandmas and grandpas are still kings and queens here. The indestructible Corsican épicerie U Mio Paese (which was already there when I lived in the area) that provisions us with authentic *brocciu* and charcuterie is a must go-to, the Royaume de la Chantilly makes us happy for many edible reasons and will do the same to you, the poissonnier Chez Yves will teach you how to cook *galinettes* (a local cheap and excellent fish), Josiane, her rotisserie chicken and *pieds paquets* will satisfy your need for Provençal cuisine, Les Délices de Granoux boulangerie will surprise you, and new spots like Bar Marylou on Rue Granoux or Monsieur Madame Café on Avenue Foch are places to relax or party or both!

Le Panier and the Vieux-Port

I'm always surprised to see the extent at which Le Panier retains its share of authenticity and culinary surprises despite the waves of tourists that swell each year. It's here that Massalia was founded, as well as what we called 'La Petite Naples' and the prostitutes' quarter, nicknamed 'Le Quartier Réservé'. These old, winding streets have always welcomed an influx of communities. Here, the most diverse refugees, the Mafia and WWII resistants cohabited, up until January 1943, when the German SS (and Vichy French regime forces) demolished half of the quarter, with a strong desire to remove it from the maps. Once again, someone wanted to clean up Marseille . . .

First there was the round-up that evacuated 20,000 people from the neighbourhood, of which 6,000 were imprisoned and 2,000 were deported (including Jews, Gypsies, homosexuals, former prisoners, the homeless, foreigners without papers, and members of the Resistance). Then, they blew up 1,500 buildings, just like that. All that remains today is the 'haut du Panier', above the Rue Caisserie.

As for the Vieux-Port as a lunch and dinner destination, I urge you to be wary . . . but there are good addresses like Chez Madie Les Galinettes and La Caravelle for the revelry. Another good tip to pick up a pizza at La Vieille Pelle or at Pizzeria Saint-Jean and eat it on a portside bench. At any hour, day or night, the lively street scene can't be beat. Surely, I'm exaggerating . . . but this port's show is too mad to not stand and gawk here for hours. In the summer of 2020, between two Covid-19 lockdowns, Marseille was bursting at the seams and at 10pm on the port, you would have thought that our OM team had won the UEFA Champions League once more! There was such a good ambiance . . . with everybody! This spirit lives on, summer after summer.

Around La Bonne Mère, Vauban, Endoume and Roucas-Blanc

Still more neighbourhoods perched on hills, and it's here where the living is easy. There are countless good spots for lunch, dinner or an afternoon snack, wine merchants, pizzerias and épiceries. Here, Charlotte Crousillat has her ambitious café-épicerie Carlotta With; La Bonne Mère (the pizzeria, not the monument) slings one of the best pizzas in Marseille; Mijoba cooks gastronomic goodness; Emki Pop pretties popsicles with natural ingredients; a pétanque court, next to Chez Francette épicerie, offers a peaceful haven; and the adorable Hako+ makes authentic Japanese. Eat your way up to Notre-Dame de la Garde Basilica (aka La Bonne Mère) on foot through le Bois Sacré. The view and the restaurant up there are worth the effort. Then, redescend to the sea, La Corniche and its rocks and valleys. It's truly enchanting here. You feel like you're elsewhere, the houses sprouting willy-nilly catch your eye. After spending a bit of time here, it's hard not to peruse the real estate ads.
A lesser-known stroll: in Samatan (um, where's that? Even Marseillais don't know), the little, calm streets overlook the city and provide breathtaking views of the sea. As you head up the Rue d'Endoume, you can choose between good pizza, good café and good cakes . . . Leave from Bar de L'Avenir or Bar de la Relève, head up the hill, turn right, climb again, have a rest at tiny Place Saint Eugène, explore and then give your legs a break as you descend into Vallon des Auffes, La Malmousque or Les Catalans. Good for getting the heart rate up!

La Malmousque, for picnics paired with seaside views

The southern beaches to Les Goudes

Marseille's Corniche is our Highway 101 (according to fans of California and its Pacific Coast Highway). La Corniche is often bottlenecked, but that's because everyone is looking at the view rather than their steering wheel! Many of us cruise with music blasting while others pretend to jog or cliff dive into the sea to impress passers-by. All of us meet up for rustic apéros on the rocks between Vallon des Auffes and Malmousque. Sometimes, we stretch all the way to Pointe-Rouge, where it smacks of vacation all year long. And if you go even further, it's a top-notch escape . . . to the *cabanons* of Marseille. Montredon quarter and Chez Paulette in particular are my favourite spots (a sunset apéro that you'll never forget), yet, nonetheless, I strongly encourage you to keep on down the road to get lost in Les Goudes and Baie des Singes. Here, on the southern tip of the city, you'll have the impression that you've left planet Earth. You'll be tired but happy. Swim wherever you like, with or without a swimsuit, you're free here! At this exact moment, you'll get a sudden craving for a good bouillabaisse or *soupe de poissons* and, on that subject, everything you need can be found in Les Goudes or Callelongue. But don't forget to reserve your table in paradise beforehand.

From La Préfecture to the Stade Vélodrome via Castellane and Le Prado

Rue Saint-Fé is no longer. It's been ages since a Marseillais institution stood at №18, Le Café Peutabin-Boudoul, founded in 1798. Its speciality, bouillabaisse, could be shipped in bottles across France and abroad. In the 19th century, after this street had already housed elegant shops for almost a century, the first *grands magasins* opened. It was, as one said at the time, the centre of 'Marseillais high life'. In the 1990s, I'd still spend Saturday afternoons there in the flamboyant Virgin Megastore. Nowadays, the big brands have made Saint-Férreol bland and barren, but the new co-working space Babel Community, and its Le Ciel rooftop have put some flavour back to the adjacent streets, Rue Haxo, Rue Venture and Rue Francis Davso. Cantoche, Howard, À Moro, Libala/Kin . . . so many we don't know where to dig in! It's a veritable lab of good lunch spots and terrasses. We needed some streets like this in Marseille. This particularly culinary fervour has also popped up around the Préfecture, up to Castellane. Explore Rue d'Italie peppered with an atypical La Femme du Boucher and a Korean épicerie. Walk up Rue Edmond Rostand (Oh Faon! pâtisserie) and keep going until you reach the upper part of Rue Breteuil/Rue Paradis where you'll love the artisanal *chocolaterie* La Baleine à Cabosse, and the joyful bistronomy of Maëlyss Vultaggio and Éric Maillet, the chef/couple behind Mama Kyuna and Cédrat. At some point drink a pint at Brasserie Zoumaï near Place Castellane, then keep strolling until the end of the wide Avenue du Prado, before it hangs a right towards the beach, to dine at Michelin-starred Coline Faulquier's or collide with Planet Alexandre Mazzia.

From Opéra to Catalans via Rue Grignan, Rue Sainte and Saint-Victor Abbey

Friends of good eats and drink, you have two prime districts here. First, the Opéra neighbourhood, which has tidied up the escort bars and moved the score-settling elsewhere. The roads around the Opéra are pedestrianised and jam-packed (*cafi* as we say here) with new *bonnards* (delightful) restaurants and a dashing Maison Marrou café (cult Marseille deli). The vibe is relax, and shopping is good too. It feels a bit like Soho NY. I'm getting a bit carried away, but, frankly, you're not that far from a noshing Disneyland in this area.
And then, as you head up Rue Sainte, nicknamed 'restaurant row', or Rue Grignan, about to become its twin sister, stop by Mouné for a Leabanese lunch or Ourea when you're craving a good gastronomic table, at Maison Ferroni's Atelier du Rhum to improve your booze know-how, before getting your bearings at Gaspard for a cocktail later that eve. Beforehand, you could buy cheese at La Laiterie Marseillaise, then continue straight to the Saint-Victor quarter and its iconic Abbey. It's the meeting place for people who finish their workday early, for those who look on the bright side of life and who have the time to watch the sun set from Café de l'Abbaye, to lunch at Bar de la Relève, to talk food with the La Fabriquerie team a bit further down on Avenue de la Corse, or who have the insouciance to leave their babysitter hanging while lingering at L'Abri. This is the area where Julia Child lived and let loose, first on the Vieux-Port at 28A Quai de Neuve, then at 113 Boulevard de la Corderie.
While you're at it, keep going until Les Catalans. And if, at that moment, you want to reflect on your life while looking over the horizon, the Pharo Palace, Napoleon III and Eugénie's gift to Marseille, will welcome you with open arms. Perched above the Vieux-Port, you can watch the ferries depart for Corsica, Algeria, or Tunisia. You will feel untouchable! Finally, stay the night at Hôtel les Bords de Mer and think of me when you open your windows at daybreak.

'Va te jeter aux Goudes!'
(literally, 'go throw yourself in Les Goudes',
figuratively, ' get lost! ')
This is my favourite insult.

— Vérane

From Mucem to L'Estaque

The 2013 Marseille European Capital of Culture programme and investments shook up this edge of northern Marseille that we used to only frequent to take a ferry to the other side of the Mediterranean. Do Marseillais willingly visit this quarter now? Half-heartedly, partly because we have a hard time changing our habits. Museums, international shops, and restaurants are all here, but in Marseille, we are also wary of the extravagant. We find the Mucem museum beautiful, but we never go inside. Instead kids jump from the rocks around it into the sea, the grown-ups climb the stairs to the roof and cross the skybridge to admire the view and the horizon. The marriage of ancient and modern is *magnifique*, but, for a Marseillais, it's like a free fall and a step towards the unknown that we mostly only take once in our lives, when we first arrive in Marseille. Nevertheless, Mucem's intention is good, and the exhibits constantly try to connect communities with each other and tell the city's history. Mucem does its job. The new replica of the Cosquer cave, Les Terrasses du Port shopping centre and the rehabilitated docks are initiatives that we never dared to dream of. They give Marseille big-city swagger. Hopefully the local sulking about it won't last long. It's frankly unjust. As for L'Estaque . . . it remains L'Estaque. Either you live there, and you love it, or you go there on Sundays to gobble up chichis and panisses and you love it! Even if you don't spend much time in Marseille, take a spin there. Boat rides from the Vieux-Port to L'Estaque are a blast in the summer.

The population of Marseille amounted to around 900,000 souls in 1936, 1975 and 2020. In the meantime, we ended up with only 600,000 in 1946 after WWII, then we jumped to 780,000 after Algeria became independent from France. In the 80s and 90s, Marseille's population shrank by 100,000 – Marseillais would just leave the city they felt was too problematic and often bought houses in nearby villages like Allauch, Aubagne, La Ciotat, Aix . . .
But since 2000, the trend has reversed. Marseille gained 100,000 inhabitants in 20 years and this time the upward curve should last . . .

01

FORGET PASTIS, START WITH A PIZZA ON THE ROCKS!

Without doubt, pizza, or 'pitze' as we say here, is the most typical Marseillais dish. It's our common denominator. Many of us have only eaten bouillabaisse once or twice in our lives, but each Marseillais has their own history with pizza and there's nothing better than eating it on the rocks in front of the sea.

As a kid, my parents and I were regulars at (the now closed) pizzeria Chez François in the Noailles district but on Saturdays, for lunch, we would go to La Galiotte on the Vieux-Port. In those pizza meccas, I would willingly burn my tongue on slices dripping with mozzarella.

We also had our favourite 'camion à pizza' for football-on-TV nights and Sunday nights. In 1962, Jean Méritan invented the pizza truck based on the *frites* shacks in northern France. True gathering places for locals, these trucks still play an indispensable role in the social life of each neighbourhood, and even more so on Sunday evening. Everyone has their regular pizza truck to whom they remain incredibly loyal. It's hard to change. Ours was the one at Place Sébastopol.

We lived nearby. As did my maternal grandmother. One doesn't easily move between neighbourhoods in Marseille and, very often, one lives where one's family settled many generations before.

Oui, this tomato pie symbolises the influence Neapolitans have had on Marseille, but Marseille pizza is not really Neapolitan anymore. Like all somewhat reckless teenagers trying to find their own footing, many of us went against the grain, and in this case, against mozzarella! Marseille invented the '*moit-moit*', half anchovy and half Emmental, which supplanted the Italian standard.

The Emmental vs mozzarella battle remains vivid today. I have come to realise what team I'm on: no oily Emmental on my pizza. I am from a mozzarella family. But this club does not yet have many members in Marseille.

However, each culture has put its own stamp on the classic: the Armenian pizza has meat, the Corsican comes with figatelli sausage and brousse sheep cheese, the Lebanese with za'atar, and so on . . .

FOCUS

Where to eat pizza in Marseille?

I'm going to try and draw up a list of the best Marseille pizzas based on my palate and those of the chefs I've interviewed on the matter. This is risky business since every Marseillais has very strong opinions on their favourites - so I'm bound to be criticised. Like all good Marseillais and Marseillaises, I follow @marseille_en_bouche, @legrandpastis and @lovespots_marseille, who each rate Marseille pizzas with a mix of seriousness and humour. I cross-referenced their reviews with mine and, it turns out, we're often on the same page. Phew!

LA BONNE MÈRE: Where the Parisians go.
If you're on your way down from La Bonne Mère basilica, up in Vauban, stop here for a pizza made with top ingredients but no need to exhaust your heart and your friends to climb the hill just for it.

L'EAU À LA BOUCHE: This place surprised me the most. Their thin pizza won't please everyone (but lovers are numerous). It's worth the detour on the Corniche, even with the haphazard parking, to eat one on the Malmousque beach boulders as the mistral blows and the sun sets.

CHEZ ÉTIENNE: You simply need to go there. Cult restaurant in Le Panier where the *moit-moit* (half anchovy, half cheese) arrives at your table even before you order. The pizza is as Marseille as it gets - wood-fired, garlicky sauce, oozy cheese. In Marseille 'cult' means 'look before you speak'. Follow the lead of the table beside you and order a pizza to share as a starter. It's how it's done in Marseille. Then, follow it up with garlicky squid, wood-fired meats or aubergine parmigiana. And yes, you need to finish your plate! Think 'Rosanna Arquette eating pasta in *The Big Blue*...'

LA VIEILLE PELLE: An historic address between Le Panier and the Vieux-Port. The mozzarella melts in your mouth as it should, as does the house gnocchi that I highly recommend for your main course. The pizza is the starter, to be shared with your friends and family.

PIZZA LE SAINT-JEAN (OPPOSITE LA VIEILLE PELLE): This new pizzeria is serious about great ingredients.

THE PIZZA TRUCK AT THE END OF BOULEVARD BAILLE, NEAR CASTELLANE: This pizza truck is friendly, well placed, and serves good pizzas. It belongs to the pizzeria across the street, La Cantine de Jeanine.

L'OSTERIA DU PRADO: An efficient pizza in an authentic Italian restaurant.

MIA NONNA: A super-warm welcome and original, thoughtful recipes. During the Covid lockdown, I often ordered here. FYI, Takeaway only.

SCUDERIA: Between Saint-Victor and Endoume. When you try it, you'll say to yourself, 'Oh, so that's what good tomato sauce on a pizza tastes like!'

CHEZ NOËL: The cult pizzeria on La Canebière. The true pizza 'à la marseillaise'.

DI VENEZIA, PRACTICALLY ON THE VIEUX-PORT: The pizzaiola has a strong personality, the room is full of loud-talking regulars (scriptwriter friends, this is the place to go to take notes), and the authentic pizza oven dates back to when the address was a bakery, a very long time ago. Just the combo you want in a pizzeria.

BAMBINO: All the chefs talk about this pizzeria. It belongs to the owners of the trendy bar Parpaing Qui Flotte, just down the street. The pizzeria is part of the Chave district's booming food scene and adds conviviality to Boulevard Eugène-Pierre.

PAPÀ FREDO: One of the rare true Neapolitan pizzas in Marseille. This pizza will leave make an impression.

LUNA PIENA: Located in the neighbourhood where I grew up – Sébastapol. A good *pizzéria du quartier* that only does takeaway.

LA FRICHE LA BELLE DE MAI: Pizza during the summer. They even have a real wood-fired oven outside . . . Mamma mia! A great spot for l'apéritif!

LA BELLA PIZZA: Notre Dame du Mont, between Rue de Lodi and Cours Julien, has become a great spot for meating up with hungry friends. As far as pizza goes, this new place does the job, with its laid-back atmosphere, enthusiastic team, and a young boss whose Sicilian great-great-grandmother opened one of the first pizzerias in Marseille in 1924. A menu of classics and originals that aren't nonsensical neo-pizzas.

PIZZA NOSTRA: For curious ones. Explore the back country between the Rue Fontange and Rue de Lodi, stumble across this pizzaiolo – alone in front of his wood-fired oven, and take away a great margherita that doesn't impose 5cm crusts on you, all for less than 10 euros. I ate mine in front of the new Parisian-transplant Tripletta to show my local pride.

LE VESUVIO (IN THE VILLAGE OF ALLAUCH): My Allaudian cousins are huge fans and love the view that spans all of Marseille. Me too.

ETNA: A Sicilian family as the name suggests. Between the up-and-coming residential districts of St Barnabé and Montolivet. Like a pizzeria in an Italian village, tucked away in a charming street. Excellent pasta dishes too that Madame cooks.

LA LOCO À CASSIS: In front of the train station, far from everything else, the joyful team will make you feel at home and they also make the best pasta in Marseille!

The pizza truck at the end of Boulevard Baille, where my dad often waits for a pizza.

Emmanuel Salze

Even though it looks like a tiny *cabanon* (beach hut) perched above Malmousque, the reputation of this pizzeria greatly extends beyond the limits of the Endoume quarter. So many of us buy pizza here to share with friends on the rocks right under the restaurant, at lunch time or for an aperitif at sunset. Jumping into the sea afterwards is a local must-do. Don't forget the rosé. The new owner, Emmanuel, a naturally cheerful (that counts!) Marseillais, has brought together an ultra-motivated and upbeat team who continue to uphold the tradition of this unique pizza. The pizzaioli, including the boss, roll out the dough by hand with a rolling pin. Some of the toppings are added after cooking to preserve their flavours and textures. What's the secret to how this ultra-thin dough is both crispy and chewy? Fermentation time. The dough rests for a minimum of 24 hours. This allows for light pizzas (yes, it's possible), with high-quality toppings (including the olives), fine 00 Italian flour, and original combinations like the Angelina, their number one pizza!

A FEATHER IN THE MISTRAL

An addictive original pizza from a full-throttle team

120 Corniche du Président John-Fitzgerald-Kennedy 13007 Marseille

Interview with Emmanuel in La Pointe Rouge with his friend from Le Bar des Amis, Ivan:

The story of L'Eau à la Bouche started with a chef who had worked at Ducasse's Louis XV in Monaco and at the Tour d'Argent in Paris: Marseillais Rodolphe Bodikian. He was originally a patissier, then he joined his sister who worked in Venice hotels. That's where he first touched pizza. Back in Marseille, he bought this pizzeria from a slightly older gentleman who only sold takeaway. At the time, I had a pizzeria a little further up the neighbourhood, Place Saint-Eugène, so I know the story well. Initially, Rodolphe wanted to make gourmet plates to-go, but he only had a pizza oven! And customers came in asking for pizzas. He couldn't afford to upgrade the kitchen, so he continued to make pizza. People always asked for their pizzas with a bowl of *salade à l'ail* (garlic salad) or a bowl of onion-lemon salad and that annoyed him. He thought to himself, 'in Venice, we put the salad on the pizza,' so he decided to do the same here. In 17 years, the salad pizza has become a classic. As for me, I bought this pizzeria four years ago. My son was a pizzaiolo here for six years. At first, I wanted to open a second L'Eau à la Bouche elsewhere in Marseille because I was afraid of not feeling at home at Rodolphe's institution. But, after working with him for a year and soaking up the pizzeria's atmosphere, I ended up buying the place from Rodolphe, who was fed up with making pizza. I kept the pizzaiolo Giovanni who had been working here since 2011 and Rodolphe bought another restaurant to cook traditional food.

What is your background in the restaurant industry?

I began as a bartender and waiter. My grandparents already had establishments. My family isn't Italian but there are Corsicans on my mum's side. At 24 years old, I set up shop at Place Saint-Eugène in Endoume with a chef friend who had 10 years of experience in a big Marseillais brasserie where we had met. We made daily specials and pizza. It was a huge success! We made a lot of pizzas, and I liked it! We had a pizza oven, and we only made the classics. We didn't invent anything! But in the end, we had 60 covers every day at lunch. It was crazy.

What do we need to know about L'Eau à la Bouche pizzas?

Ingredients-wise, we order mozzarella and Parmesan from Italy and Emmental from the Savoie. There is nothing better. Low-quality Emmental becomes incredibly oily when you bake it. And when black olives are cheap, they are way too salty. My pizza dough is not at all greasy. I add the equivalent of 4 teaspoons of sunflower oil to 23kg of dough. I put in the least amount of oil that is necessary for cooking.

An addictive original pizza
from a full throttle team

120 Corniche Président
John-Fitzgerald-Kennedy
13007 Marseille

Low-quality Emmental
becomes incredibly oily
when you bake it.

And when black olives are cheap,
they are way too salty.

LA PIZZA ANGELINA

INGREDIENTS FOR 1 PIZZA

1 x 215–250g ball of pizza dough
Tomato sauce
Dried oregano
A few black olives
1 handful of mesclun
Baby spinach
1 small head of Little Gem (baby Romaine)
½ sweet onion, finely chopped
Olive oil
Juice of ½ lemon
1 or 2 thin slices of Serrano ham
Parmesan

1. Prepare the pizza dough and let it rest for 24 hours covered in plastic wrap at 3–4°C (in the refrigerator). Roll it out with a rolling pin until you have a very thin dough. If the dough has rested long enough, it will not become holey. Make sure to roll it out by hand, not with a machine, as we do in the restaurant. This removes the air so that it cooks better.

2. Spread tomato sauce on the dough and sprinkle with oregano and black olives. The oven temperature at L'Eau à la Bouche is 380°C. The cooking time won't be more than a few minutes. Keep a close eye on your pizza.

3. Once you remove the pizza from the oven, top it with mesclun and other salad leaves plus a little sweet onion. ('We use mesclun, baby spinach and 10% of baby Romaine, which is less flat, to add a little volume to the pizza.')

4. Drizzle with olive oil and a bit of freshly squeezed lemon juice. Add Serrano ham and big slivers of just-cut Parmesan. Drizzle with more olive oil and a little lemon juice.

A little tip: if necessary, this pizza can be reheated in a pan. When the pan is quite hot, turn off the heat, put the pizza in the pan, then turn the heat to medium. Don't cover!

M R S
Cours Julien

Faiza Bougheraba and Fredo Boubessla

Vera Neapolitan pizza and a Sunday brunch spot

56 Cours Julien
13006 Marseille

VERA PIZZA NAPOLETANA

This young couple are marvellous. Instilled with an incredible desire to do things well, the Alsatian and Marseillaise decided to up the level of pizza in Marseille by serving real Neapolitan pizza. Grazie! The rest of the menu is Italian, as is the weekend brunch. This is a truly fantastic place.

Fredo studied at the state-run culinary school in Guebwiller and trained with starred chef Philippe Bohrer in Alsace. Faiza grew up in Le Panier in Marseille. Three of her brothers – Ali (won a Molière, the French national theatre prize in 2017), Ichem and Redouane Bougheraba – are successful in the theatre and stand-up world. So, it's not surprising that Faiza has the gift of the gab. I first met the young lovebirds seated at Chez Romain et Marion, the Afghani restaurant on Boulevard de la Libération. We spoke about football – PSG had just lost in the Champions League finals. For them, me, and all of Marseille, it felt like a victory, since Paris Saint-Germain is our one and only rival (think Man City vs Arsenal).
A few weeks later, Sophie Ferjani mentioned the couple and their restaurant when I interviewed her for the book, so I grew even more eager to try their pizza. I went to taste it during lockdown when restaurants were only allowed to sell takeaway. For pizzerias, and we have many in Marseille, this was almost business as usual! Faiza and Fredo were in great spirits since they had just been awarded the famous Neapolitan label 'Vera Pizza Napoletana', which is rarely bestowed by the Neapolitan association.
In France, only eleven pizzerias have the official AVPN label. Let's face it. Italians don't like it when French chefs make pizza. There are one in Paris, two in Toulon, and now one in Marseille. Amazing, no? When I entered the restaurant, Faiza and Fredo were getting ready to participate in the first international pizza marathon! An online 24-hour master class with pizzaiolos from all four corners of the world, each in their proper restaurant. So, the mood was understandably festive.

Fredo, when did you begin your restaurant career?
FREDO: I was 14 years old and I began in French gastronomy. I worked in restaurants in Alsace, then Cannes, Saint-Tropez, Toulouse, Geneva, and Cape Town in a French restaurant. Then, I opened my first business in Alsace in 2013. I made gourmet burgers with homemade bread, real steak, and high-quality ingredients. This was the beginning of the era of good burgers in France. That's why I'm a chef and a pizzaiolo. What is interesting about pizza is that, before, it was somewhat of a poor man's dish, but today it is more sophisticated and there is more technique. The ingredients also make our pizza stand out. These are very high-quality ingredients that we source ourselves. Even the tomato sauce! The tomatoes are pressed by hand like in Naples. And the Petra flour comes from Italy.

Where did the idea come from to open an Italian restaurant?
FREDO: We met in Alsace. Faiza came to see a friend.
FAIZA: I succeeded in convincing him to move to Marseille. I mean, everyone likes the sun and the sea!
FREDO: We got married and had a little girl, then we decided to open a restaurant. Faiza always had business in her blood and I had sold my restaurant in Alsace to move to Marseille. Consequently, I was working at a theatre/café run by one of her brothers, L'Antidote in La Blancarde. It's a rather unique place to have a restaurant. Then, we found this space in front of Espace Julien where her brothers often performed. So, for us, Cours Julien embodied both family and Marseille. It's a cosmopolitan neighbourhood, a real melting pot. We are both Muslim. All the ingredients we use are halal.
In fact, we are the first halal restaurant that is certified 'Vera Pizza Napoletana' in France. We worked for two years to get this label. It's savoir-faire that you have to earn. You adjust to humidity level in the room, and you have to source the right ingredients.

In Marseille, Italian restaurants are often started by people who have no Italian heritage, which might sound crazy . . .
FREDO: When we opened our restaurant, we first did bistronomy with burgers but it didn't catch on. We saw that Italian restaurants do well, so we began to make Italian food: antipasti, lasagne, pasta, aubergine parmigiana, but not pizza. Yet, one of my daughter's first words was 'pizza'!

What is interesting about pizza is that, before, it was somewhat of a poor man's dish, but today it is more sophisticated and there is more technique.

Crazy, no? Our restaurant housed a pizzeria thirty years ago. Apparently, the pizzas were so good that customers would line up for them. In 2018, a year after our opening, we decided to order a pizza oven from Naples and I trained in Paris with Guillaume Grasso, the one chef there with the Neapolitan label. He is in the 15th district. At the beginning, it was a bit stressful . . . and now it is our flagship dish. We make the dough 24 hours in advance as they do in Naples. That makes it easier for digestion. The Marseillais are used to putting Emmental on their pizza! Here, Emmental is forbidden!
FAIZA: This mentality must be changed!
FREDO: We must educate palates! It's the same with *huile piquante* [chilli oil]. I love eating really spicy food and we make a pizza with spicy Italian sausage, but to drench this pizza with *huile piquante* is a real travesty! That's why you won't find *huile piquante* on the table here, just as gastronomic restaurants don't have salt and pepper on the table. You must eat our pizzas as they are.

Fredo, what were your first impressions of Marseille?
FREDO: The mix of cultures. It's only in Marseille that you have many religions mix together and it isn't a problem. Look, we have a halal restaurant without forcing it on anyone. I want to have an open mind. That's why we sell alcohol, cocktails, Italian wines . . . and anyone can come here to eat our high-quality ingredients. We keep our religion at home. At the restaurant, we serve halal because we want to bring people together. Pizza is the ultimate shared dish! We even tried to cook kosher, but it was very complicated.
FAIZA: Our goal is to bring everyone together. And it was time for halal not to be confined to snack bars, fast food and couscous. We searched for the finest halal charcuterie, and now you can find it in Italy, Spain, and even one of my brothers makes his own.
Once a year, during Ramadan, it feels strange to make money selling alcohol, so instead we cook a break-the-fast buffet at sundown: traditional North African and Middle Eastern dishes, Algerian *chorba*, Moroccan *harira*, Tunisian tajine (it's thick like an omelette), *briks*, and Comorian *samoussas*. It's a culinary melting pot. There is also lasagne, pizzas and citronnade [lemonade]. There's something for every person and palate. These are unforgettable moments of sharing.

How did you create the pizza whose recipe is in this book?
FREDO: It's truly a pizza that resembles us. When we make soup for our two kids, we like to use butternut squash. We make it thick and like to eat it all the time with bresaola. So, we said, 'Why not put them together on a pizza?' It's a way to make kids eat their vegetables.

What are your childhood memories, culinarily speaking?
FAIZA: The large tables during Ramadan! I'm from a large family, the only daughter amongst six children! It's really lively!

How would you describe the evolution of restaurants in Marseille?
FAIZA: The Marseille food scene is evolving very slowly but we are in the right direction! The lack of proper training of kitchen staff has been an issue. Sometimes we would hire a pizzaiolo and my toddler could knead dough better than him! So, it's good to see Parisians and Alsatians coming to work here!

Where do you eat out in Marseille?
FAIZA: We often go to Petit Pernod in the Vieux-Port. And before making our own pizza, we'd go to La Bonne Mère for pizza.
FREDO: It isn't Neapolitan pizza but it's excellent. They're the best.

Faiza, what are your childhood memories of Le Panier?
FAIZA: There were Sicilians, Corsicans, and Chez Étienne pizzeria and its many fans! When the old Dad Étienne Cassaro was still there, everyone went for the atmosphere. You would sit down, and they would serve you food without ordering. The bill was written on the paper tablecloth. The first Ferrari that I ever saw

in my life was in front of Chez Étienne. I was 14 years old. It was the footballer Bixente Lizarazu's car. Zidane would eat there also. Today, the Rue de la République has lost its soul. There was a certain dynamic that the tram ruined. You could double-park to pop into a market or buy bread. Now, there are no more local shops. A Monoprix supermarket replaced the Asian restaurant that always had a queue in front of it. They used to hang lacquered ducks in the window. Their ducks were exceptional! And, also, there was La Bonbonnière. When I was young, we'd go there to buy sweets after school. It was just next to where the Sophie Ferjani boutique is now. There was a butcher, a boulangerie. There was 'Pizza à Gogo'. It was lively! Me, I didn't want to leave this quarter. I lived on Rue des Phocéens. We were somewhat forced to leave when North American pension funds bought and refurbished the buildings, evicting locals and raising the rents to lure rich investors from elsewhere.

Vera Neapolitan pizza and a Sunday brunch spot

56 Cours Julien 13006 Marseille

BUTTERNUT CREAM, MOZZARELLA AND BRESAOLA PIZZA WITH PANISSES

INGREDIENTS FOR 4 PIZZAS

For the Neapolitan pizza dough:
412g water
21g salt
687g flour
2.44g yeast

For the toppings:
About 1.6kg butternut squash
15g butter
1 large onion, finely chopped
Turmeric
200ml double cream
Mozzarella
Grated Parmesan
Fresh basil
Datterini tomatoes (yellow and red mini-plum tomatoes)
Panisse dough from l'Estaque or homemade (*Author's note: you can find the recipe in a few pages. It's a very Marseillais snack but you rarely find it on pizzas, so that's why this recipe rocks.*)
Beef bresaola
Vegetable oil
Salt and pepper

1. In a large bowl, mix the water and salt. Add a quarter of the flour and mix well. Mix the yeast in a little water then pour into the bowl. Mix everything together. Incorporate the rest of the flour in thirds, kneading well after each addition. Then remove the dough from the bowl and knead for 10 minutes.

2. Shape into a ball and put back in the bowl. Cover with a tea towel and leave to rest for 2 hours in a warm place.

3. Then, separate the dough into four balls, putting each one in a separate bowl, covered, and leave to rise for at least 8 hours.

4. Peel the butternut and cut into big cubes. Bring lightly salted water to the boil then cook the butternut for 10–20 minutes. Drain.

5. Melt the butter in a pan and lightly brown the onion with some turmeric. Add the squash, salt and pepper, then put the mixture in a blender. Incorporate the cream and blend until creamy.

6. Preheat the oven to the highest temperature (usually 240°C/gas mark 8 at home).

7. Roll out each of the dough balls. Garnish first with butternut cream, like you would do with tomato sauce on a classic pizza. Cut mozzarella in slices and place them on the cream. Sprinkle with Parmesan, add a few basil leaves. Bake for 15–20 minutes.

8. While it's cooking, halve tomatoes lengthwise. Slice panisse into rounds. Fry the panisse rounds for a few minutes in 5cm of hot vegetable oil.

9. Remove the pizzas from the oven, top with the tomatoes and panisse rounds, then bresaola, and a few more basil leaves. All that's left to do is enjoy!

FOCUS

Marseille: an Italian city

We eat the best Italian dishes again and again, in our own homes or at friends'.

In 1881, there were 57,900 Italians living in Marseille, where the total population was around 360,000. These Italians came from Naples, Genoa, Piedmont and Tuscany. Neapolitans were fishermen and lived around Place de Lenche near the Vieux-Port while the Tuscans and the Piedmontese were working in factories and lived mainly in the northern part of the city, including L'Estaque. In the early 20th century, Italian families also settled in the Eastern part of Marseille where new factories were set up.

In 1911, Marseille's Italian community represented almost a quarter of the city's population and four-fifths of the city's foreigners: 100,000 Italians out of 550,000 residents. In 1912-13, half of factory workers in Marseille were Italians. And this didn't include the many naturalisations at the end of the 19th century which occurred because of the hostility and violence towards Italian immigrants. As cheap and docile workforce, the local industrialists and the port authorities unscrupulously exploited them to break the strikes and ignore the demands of French workers. 'The babas [old Marseille slang for Italians] are eating our bread [taking our jobs]' was an 1881 refrain which was unfortunately adopted for other migration waves. Between the two world wars, migration towards Marseille began to diversify. Decimated by war or preferring not to return to a city that didn't accept them, Italian workers were in short supply and the need for labour was great.

The 1920s saw the arrival of Russian, Greek and Armenian political refugees in Marseille and the start of immigration from African colonies. The ongoing large Corsican migration is difficult to differentiate from the Italian one because the family names are often similar (don't tell the Corsicans! They really don't see themselves as Italians . . .). These new arrivals often lived in the same districts, Le Panier and around the Saint-Charles train station. Jamaican-American writer Claude McKay was there - he captured this colourful era in his book *Banjo*.

Greg Mandonato and his partner, Greg Hessmann

Two or three generations later, the reputation of Italians has changed dramatically. Today, one out of three Marseillais have Italian heritage and they are proud of it. I am one of them, so is our current mayor, Benoît Payan, who speaks Italian fluently.

But, when it comes to cuisine, Italians complain it is hard to find good Italian food in Marseille. They are exaggerating, but there's some truth to this. Culinary clichés have it easy here and we like to reduce foreign cuisines to a few simple dishes.

So the best Italian cuisine in Marseille is the one you cook at home or the one your Italian friends cook for you. For ingredients, Chez Enzo beneath the Palais Longchamp holds the upper hand, but as I write these lines, Enzo is angry, the Historic Preservation Society have made him demolish his storefront . . . so if Enzo packs up, get an unlimited subscription to La Sicile Authentique which, contrary to its name, actually sells all of Italy. If your tummy is crying out for fresh pasta, the aptly named Ravioli et Pâtes Fraiches shop on Rue St Michel run by Harut Harutyunyan, a robust Italian-Armenian, is worth the detour (buy some arancini while you're at it), Coquillettes and Fusilli in Vauban is up to the task and the legendary Moutte on Boulevard Chave is no longer legendary but will not disappoint you.

If you really want to eat Italian food in a restaurant, sure-fire bets are Le Vésuvio in Endoume until chef Anne-Marie Gargiulo retires, and La Sicile Authentique on Friday night in Liliane Casteldaccia's home-turned-restaurant, but I must admit my heart belongs to L'Atelier Renata, a supper club run by Italian chef Erika Blu, and La Loco restaurant in Cassis.

For lunch, there's À Moro, a newcomer who cooks Italian seriously in bistro fashion in the budding 'where to lunch on a terrace' quarter around Rue Haxo. In Cours Julien, I prefer Papà Fredo to La Cantinetta. Really, hear me out. If you are in the mood for rubbing shoulders with *bobos* (*bourgeois-bohèmes*, aka French hipsters), then try Otto or Jéjé Barbu's Il Capriolo. Both serve transalpine flavours *à la française* but we like that here and we can all play *bobos* for a day. It's Ok.

If you get lost near Château Gombert, find the south at Sapori di Napoli, a deli steeped in Italia which has tables for lunch. When you've run out of mojo, shopping at Marseille's Géant Casino super-supermarket or Ikea in La Valentine, dig into a real carbonara accompanied by an extravagant dessert for pleasure-seeking grown-ups. At Babbo, you'll be stuffed for the entire weekend!

Finally, my favourite pasta recipe in Marseille. It comes from Chef Greg Mandonato of festive Bar de la Relève. With Neapolitan roots, Mandonato's family founded beloved Marseillais patisseries all over town. Greg's recipe is later in this chapter. It's surprisingly delicious, as an unexpected mix of ingredients can be.

M R S
Saint-Julien

Liliane Casteldaccia

FOR MAMMA

Familial Italian cuisine

36 Impasse du Maroc
13012 Marseille

Almost every quarter has their Italian épicerie, often generic and lazy, but Marseille also has a few gems. In the middle of the residential neighbourhood of Saint-Julien, la signora Liliane has opened her shop of delicacies in her garage. This is an adventure with a whiff of the unique Marseille as we like it, the one that proves to us that nothing is impossible here. You just need an idea and some folly.
Liliane's parents came from Sicily in 1965 and her husband's family, also Sicilian, first moved to Algeria before landing in Marseille. Liliane decided to drop everything and change paths when her mother fell ill. She didn't want to lose her mum's flavours. Of course, at the start, her husband, Barthélémy, did not believe in the project at all!
Today, the whole family works in this paradiso of pinsa, colatura di alici, cannoli, and pasta alla norma. You can buy all of Italy here and you can even have lunch here and dinner on Friday evening. The place is reminiscent of the unassuming trattorias typical to small Italian roads at which one arrives by accident. Everything is good here, without pretence, and it is always full.

I'll explain... my daughter was little, I worked as a medical secretary at the hospital, I didn't like what I was doing at all, my boss hated me. One evening when I couldn't take it anymore, my husband told me, "You don't need to work, I'll manage." My parents were sick. I quit and for eight years I took care of my parents and my children. I wondered what I was going to do when my mum passed away. One day, we had a family celebration in the garage, and I complained about not being able to find an épicerie in Marseille like the ones in Italy where they sold everything. My family said to me, "Why don't you open one? You have room here." I thought to myself, "Who will come all the way here?" To which they answered, "Try it and if it doesn't work, you'll eat what you don't sell!" It all started from there. At the beginning, one of my relatives took care of the purchases, and my cousin who has a store in the centre of Sicily came for three days to set up the shop for me. It's a profession that I didn't know at all . . . hence the "authentic" in the name. I have no rules! I opened it in 2010 and Mum passed away in 2012.

What is your family's Marseille history?

My parents came to Marseille following in the footsteps of my mother's brothers. They arrived one by one. When my grandmother passed away, my parents came to Marseille to visit her brothers. In Marseille, there was a lot of work at that time and my uncles asked my dad to work with them. They would go to work and when they returned home, their wives had cooked dinner, they were as happy as clams! My parents lived in the Beaumont district, then they bought a big parcel in the 11th near Éoures with my mum's four brothers, which they divided into five. Each one built their own nest, and we all grew up together. Me, I was born in 1968. For 10 years, my dad didn't want to stay in France, and we went back and forth. As a kid, I had my home here and my home in Sicily. Then, my parents bought this land in Saint-Julien, my dad built this house, but we didn't live here because my mum wanted to remain with her brothers! When I got married, they offered us the house to live in.

What are your culinary memories from childhood?

I grew up in Marseille. I ate Italian food at home. We never went to restaurants. My mum was very economical. The recipes from my childhood were baked pastas, pasta with vegetables, fish involtini, a lot of fried things.

And in terms of scents linked to your childhood?

Everything that simmers. In the morning, I would wake up to aromas from the kitchen. As soon as my mother woke up, she would put on an apron, and started cleaning and cooking. I began to cook only when I launched this adventure. Before, I never had, my mum cooked for us. When she passed away, I had to do it. My mum's cousin, Gaetana, took me under her wing. She still helps me when I ask how my mum did this or that . . . When I realised that people had to taste the products I sold to buy them, I added tables in front of the grocery store. In the kitchen, my sister, Filipina, is with me. We serve up to 40 customers.

The clientele in Marseille is becoming more and more demanding, but I don't have a problem with that, I'm proud of my products. I work with small producers, I go to salons in Italy to find them thanks to the Italian Chamber of Commerce in Marseille and I've learned a ton... Alba truffles, Italian caviar and balsamic pearls. You think my mum would have cooked with truffles?

CALAMARATA, MUSSELS, GORGONZOLA, SAUSAGES
(recipe by Bar de la Relève)

At Bar de la Relève, Chef Greg Mandonato is partnered with Greg Hessmann, the star of Marseille bistronomy. Cheffe Laëtitia Visse once made a name for the cuisine of this magnificent bar in the heart of Saint-Victor, home of sunset-kissed apéros. Today, it's Mandonato that mans the menu. A child of the quarter, he worked for 24 years in the family-run Pâtisserie Saint-Victor that his Italian grandfather bought with his grandmother in 1956. The shop was finally sold in 2020 but the family still has several patisseries in town and their *gâteau des rois* is still one of the best in Marseille.

INGREDIENTS FOR 4

300g Italian sausage
100g gorgonzola
50ml double cream
400g calamarata pasta (that you can buy at La Sicile Authentique or at Chez Enzo)
350g prepared mussels
2 garlic cloves, chopped
½ preserved lemon, chopped
Olive oil
½ bunch of parsley, finely chopped
Piment d'Espelette
Guérande salt and freshly-ground pepper

1. Bake the sausage in the oven at 190°C/gas mark 5 for 15 minutes.
2. Melt the gorgonzola and cream together. Cook the pasta *al dente* in a pan of boiling salted water, reserving the cooking water.
3. In another saucepan, open the mussels over high heat. Remove the mussels, keep their broth, but best to filter it to avoid sandy bits.
4. In a large pan, brown the garlic and preserved lemon in olive oil. Slice the sausage, add to the pan, brown for 2 or 3 minutes, then add the pasta, melted gorgonzola mixture, mussels, and their broth.
5. Sauté the mix for a few minutes and, if necessary, add a bit of reserved pasta water.
6. Serve with finely chopped parsley, pepper, piment d'Espelette and salt.

LA FOCACCIA DE LAURA MILIANI
(an Italian patissière who lived in Marseille while I was making this book)

INGREDIENTS FOR 1 FOCACCIA

For the focaccia:
5g yeast
225g room-temperature water
1 pinch of sugar
250g T65 flour
50g T80 flour
1 tbsp extra-virgin olive oil
8g salt

For the topping:
1 tbsp extra-virgin olive oil
1 tbsp water
Coarse salt or fleur de sel (optional)

1. It takes patience to make good focaccia. Plan on 5 or 5 ½ hours. In a stand mixer bowl, dissolve the yeast in the water, add the sugar and mix well. Then incorporate both flours using the hook attachment. Work the dough at medium speed.

2. When the dough begins to thicken (be careful, this recipe is 75% hydration, so the dough will be a little runny, but you must resist the urge to add more flour), add the olive oil. You must give the dough time to absorb the oil before incorporating the salt. Knead for 10–15 minutes - you can increase the speed to 3–4, until you get a smooth ball that easily pulls away from the sides of the bowl.

3. Lightly flour the work surface, wet your hands (to avoid adding too much flour), and work the dough by stretching and gently folding it over itself, turning it 90° after each fold. Shape into a ball and put back in the lightly oiled bowl. Leave to rise for 3 hours, covering with a damp kitchen towel or cling film (during summer it will take about 2 hours).

4. After 2 or 3 hours, prep a baking sheet with parchment paper and a generous amount of olive oil. Still with very little flour on the work surface and wet hands, give two simple turns to the dough, being careful not to flatten small air bubbles. Stretch out the dough on the baking sheet without spreading it out too much. Leave to rise for another hour, then, with wet fingertips, spread the dough to the edges of the baking sheet. Let rise for 20 minutes, then spread it out a bit more.

5. To help the focaccia rise, put it in a warm place or in the oven with only the light on. Let rest for 30 minutes before heating the oven to 230°C/gas mark 8 (if focaccia is inside, you must remove it before heating!).

6. While waiting for the oven to heat up, mix the topping ingredients and gently make holes on top of the focaccia, always with wet fingers, then spread the topping across the top using a spoon or brush.

7. Bake for about 15 minutes, then check for doneness. Normally focaccia will be nicely browned on top, so you will have to move it to your oven's lowest rack to brown the bottom for 5–7 minutes. Then, it's ready!

Cédric Rubini

Another fanatic! Camille Garcin, the full-throttle coordinator of Les Grandes Tables, told me about Cédric. She lent him a kitchen at the Monticole café in Les Quartiers Nord so he could start working while opening his focacceria near Le Panier. I went there in the early morning (how beautiful the view is when driving above the Grand Littoral shopping centre!) and I fell literally and figuratively - with my camera and my appetite - on the fellow in full-on work mode.
Cédric has two passions: Marseille's OM football club and Italy.
As a child, when he drove south in the car to see his father's family in Puglia, he always managed to pester Papa to make a pit stop near Genoa and satisfy his love for focaccia Genovese. After 11 years in Barcelona, as a sports journalist and then in a law firm (he studied law in Aix), Cédric returned home to change careers. His project: to open the FIRST MARSEILLAISE FOCACCERIA. A motivated *fada* (Marseillais for 'mad') is worth two *fadas*! As a result, his focaccia vera is so addictive that I swallowed up a whole slab.
It could be a landmark moment for Italian cuisine in Marseille. Back to fundamentals. With Cédric, I realised how much we must explore and leave to come back better. This is valid for all cultures, countries, cities and families. The Marseille stew today is acquiring its unique flavour thanks to this.

FOR PAPA

Cédric: When it comes to Italy, I'm not objective. I like it too much. I'm crazy. I want to eat good pasta, drink good coffee . . . I really think that I should have been born in Italy. At the same time, I've had a rather eccentric journey in life.
Vérane: Like many Marseillais?
Cédric: Not really, because Marseillais adore their city. They usually don't budge. I have plenty of friends who have never moved. We love it too much here! The Italians move around. Not us. Me, I'm so happy to be back. I think our bay is as beautiful as Rio's! Look, when you leave here, from Plan d'Aou, the view you have of the sea and the islands . . . That doesn't normally exist in a city. Plus, here, people still talk to each other. Compared to the rest of France, that's incredible. It's unique.
Vérane: What do you think of Marseille now that you're living it with new eyes?
Cédric: Barcelona is a super-urbanised city that has lost its personality and its charm. Marseille is wild. It always has been. But I admit at the moment, I'm a little afraid that Marseille is becoming like Barcelona, Venice, Florence . . . It's hard because there's good in the change too. It brings money to the city and businesses.
Vérane: Good Italian places are rare in Marseille.
Cédric: We agree! A school friend with Neapolitan roots, who is also

obsessed with Italy, told me that La Sicile Authentique is one of the only good spots she's found in Marseille. I love Etna in Montolivet. That restaurant is madness. Plus, I like that they aren't necessarily super friendly at first sight. You must earn their respect. It felt like I was in Italy. So Etna to the max. Salvatore and Anne Marie's Vésuvio as well.

Vérane: In which neighbourhood did you grow up?

Cédric: In Chave-Jeanne d'Arc like you. We must have crossed paths. Later, I went to the private Chevreul secondary school. When I was a kid, there was nothing on Boulevard Chave. Lots of brocken souls . . . Le Dernier Métro was my *café*. I'm still a regular there. When I returned from Spain, I couldn't believe my eyes when I saw how lively the quarter had become.

Vérane: Introduce me to your focaccias . . .

Cédric: I trained with Rosario Bisanti, the vice president of the baking association in Genoa. It was *trop bon* (very good). I couldn't have asked for a better teacher! For Easter, I did a pilgrimage to Recco, of course, for the focaccia di Recco with cheese and then I discovered the village of Camogli – incredible. It's like the Cassis of Genoa but more working class. An unfussy Portofino. Cars are banned. I loved it. Pure extravagance! And Revello's focaccia in Camogli is incredible! It drives you crazy. Me, I'm only making the classics. Above all, I don't want to French it up. I do the opposite of bakeries that stuff them to the gills. I make them plain, with peppers, tomatoes, black Italian Taggiasche olives, or with cheese. Potato is also a classic, but I don't make it. It's not the one I fancy the most. The problem with Italian cuisine in France is that when you go to a meeting run by the association of Italian chefs in France, you realise that they are all sponsored by the same wholesaler – Carniato. So, they all use the same Italian products. And it really gets me mad when I see restaurateurs like Splendido who make money on Disneyland-like versions of Italy or those who use frozen focaccias to make their sandwiches!

Vérane: Where do you feast in Marseille?

Cédric: The best Chinese place for me is Lilin on Rue Sainte. Pure mouthwatering madness. Last weekend, I had their lacquered duck! The chef is the former chef of the Chinese consul in Marseille. When the consul finished his mandate, the chef set up his restaurant and he makes the best dumplings in Marseille. By far. I also like Bouillon on Boulevard Chave. The female chef has a charcuterie training like La Femme du Boucher. At the bottom of Boulevard Notre Dame, in the same spirit, there is Le Bec du Coq. I like it a lot and the owners are very *sympathiques*. In terms of patisserie, Oh Faon! is mad good! I went to secondary school with the pastry chef and co-owner Jérome, I also worked in his lab. I know him well. He is very serious. For a kebab, I go to Tombiq on Rue Saint Saëns or Au Falafel. I don't like things that are overly marketed. In Marseille, in fact, we're lacking in good finger food that isn't too expensive. But it's starting to change.

Vérane: How did you find your place for your focacceria?

Cédric: If I could have chosen, I would have settled down on Boulevard Chave but the leases have become too expensive. In the end, City Hall put me in contact with the social landlord Marseille Habitat. They came to see me at the Docks in La Joliette where I was part of the FoodCub (*author's note: the first gastronomic incubator in Marseille where each participant tested their concept in a food court*). They loved the project so they let me use one of their ground-floor spaces. I'm just renting it out.

Vérane: And it's working out?

Cédric: Yesterday, I made focaccia for 16 hours! My first client was a greengrocer on Boulevard National. Les Grandes Tables order for their Salle des Machines café at La Friche. Dwish makes his sandwiches with my focaccia. Bakers do not have time to flatten each sheet of dough by hand in oil, to *'schiacciare'* [squash] them as Italians say. Each sheet, I flatten each one three times, every 20 minutes. First a little abruptly then more and more gently to keep out air bubbles. It's a long process and it takes practice. You must be passionate. It takes time to learn. It's a feeling. I think I belong now . . . and I have never been so 'fit' in my entire life!

'Estaque
arbour

FOCUS

On the chickpea route

When we say 'chickpea' in Marseille, we immediately think of our panisses fritters. Without a doubt. The panisses are not socca pancakes you eat in Nice! Don't you dare. . . but the truth is they were both brought to France by Italian migrants and both are made with chickpea flour. In Marseille, Italians worked in the many factories in L'Estaque and the north part of town in the 19th century/early 20th. And even now, these addictive round, flat, fried delights are to be eaten hot in L'Estaque harbour as an afternoon snack. Some trendy restaurants cut them like fries but that is not the official way of serving panisses. I know it shouldn't bother me, yet it makes me sad to see our panisses suffer such a makeover. So chickpeas here mean panisses but not only. . . I immediately think also about the best hummus in town at the Lebanese restaurant Mouné, or about a savoury Algerian flan made with chickpea flour that Faiza from Papà Fredo introduced me to. At Chez Charly in the Noailles market and at many bakeries along the Rue Longue des Capucins, they make this calentica or karantika. Faiza recommends, 'Open your baguette and put it inside with a little harissa. In Algiers, in the Casbah, you buy this. . . and it's hard not to bite your fingers off! It's excellent.'

This Algerian street food staple originates in Oran and is believed to have Spanish roots. That seems really possible since Spaniards occupied the city of Oran for almost three centuries, and with my limited Spanish, I know that 'hot' is 'caliente' in the streets of Madrid. My wise and famous food critic friend Estérelle Payany had told me many times about the chickpea route, but seeing how much Marseille is one of its crossroads struck me at that time. I went to Noailles to try calentica. Then, one weekend, with Francky, my husband, we challenged ourselves to make our own calentica. Eating and cooking all of Marseille, that was my discipline while creating this book. We devoured our calentica with a twinkle in our eyes, so I'm sharing our recipe with you.

Come to think of it, Marseille's cement, this strong link between so many communities, is perhaps the chickpea, whose cultivation has sadly disappeared around Marseille... It has been planted across the Med for thousands of years. Hot weather and poor-quality soil are enough for the chickpea to thrive. So. . .

GROW SOME CHICKPEAS, FOR GOODNESS SAKE!

Panisses and chichis booth in L'Estaque harbour

Panisses

CALENTICA WITH CREAM CHEESE

INGREDIENTS

200g chickpea flour
1 egg
25cl whole milk
1 tbsp strong mustard
2 tsp olive oil
2 wedges of Vache qui rit® (or Philadelphia® cream cheese)
Cumin
Harissa, to serve
Salt

1. Mix the chickpea flour and 2 pinches of salt in a large bowl. Add 1 litre of water and mix.

2. In another bowl, whisk the egg and milk together well.

3. Pour the egg-milk mixture into the large bowl and incorporate the mustard, olive oil and cheese. Mix again, cover, and leave to rest 1 hour.

4. Preheat the oven to 220°C/gas mark 7. Oil the bottom and sides of a glass or metal gratin dish and pour in the mixture. Sprinkle with cumin. Bake for 25 minutes.

5. Serve hot with top-quality harissa in 2 slices of a good baguette. The aim is to have two textures in the same bite, a flan with a crispy top.

For the harissa, Julia Sammut at l'Épicerie L'Idéal makes a fantastic one and Marseillais William Lellouche has created a taste bomb under the brand Tava Hada Pilpelta. Not for delicate palates!

PANISSES

INGREDIENTS

2 tsp salt
70ml olive oil
750g chickpea flour
Frying oil
Fleur de sel
Freshly ground pepper

1. Bring 2 litres of water to the boil with the salt and olive oil, then remove the saucepan from the heat. Add the chickpea flour. Whisk with an electric whisk ('When the batter takes its last breath, I finish with a wooden spoon,' explains Céline, the chef at Boîte à Sardine). The final consistency should be like a pâte à choux (choux dough); the spoon should stand up straight in the batter.

2. Spoon the batter into a rectangular baking tin. Of course, this is when you can feed your sentimental side and put the batter in a cylindrical tin (which Marseillais buy at Maison Empereur in Noailles).

3. Chill for at least 12 hours. Then cut the hardened dough into fries (of a good thickness) or round discs.

4. Quickly fry them in 180°C oil until they are just browned. Place the piping-hot treasures on paper towels. Sprinkle with fleur de sel and a turn of the pepper mill.

5. Panisses must be devoured when they are hot!

Céline Bonnieu

'I can't keep my eyes on the pans all the time, so I listen to them. I can hear the calamari! They call to me when I need to flip them.'

CATCH OF THE DAY

MY MARSEILLAIS CHILDHOOD

I grew up in the Quartiers Nord of Marseille, in the 15th, between Saint-Antoine and the Hôpital Nord. At that time, the area was still mostly countryside. My grandparents lived near Cinq Avenues, and I loved going 'into town' to see them. They took me to the movies, to the sandy Plage des Catalans beach, and to Napoleon III's grandiose Palais Longchamp, which felt really chic to me.

MY CHILDHOOD INGREDIENT

Thyme. My mother and my grandmother put it in all their dishes. As for a smell that reminds me of my childhood, it's the smell of the countryside and that of the chimney fire that perfumed the *cabanon* [cottage]. *Le Sud* [the South] is in each one of my dishes – olive oil, or garlic or herbs. And my dishes must remind me of my childhood memories to bring pleasure to those who eat them.

THE MARSEILLE FOOD SCENE ...

Young, feminine, gourmand. I'm happy to see more female entrepreneurs in the restaurant industry now. As for a dish that symbolises Marseille today, for me, it is aioli, which connects the sea to the land.

Best fish & seafood spot

2 Boulevard de la Libération
13001 Marseille

For a panisses recipe, I camped out in the kitchen of Cheffe Céline Bonnieu, the quiet force behind the gastro-fishmonger La Boîte à Sardine. Without her, this spot above the La Canebière wouldn't be the best fish joint in the city. Even during the Covid lockdown, Céline did not stop! With her business partner, Fabien Rugi, and Chef Lionel Levy, they parked the Fishe and Shipe food truck in front of the (also closed) InterContinental Hotel in Le Panier and invited Marseille chefs to come and sell take-out menus. They warmed our palates and our hearts all winter long, even inventing a 16-hand *oursinade* (sea urchin feast) with 8 chefs, pastry chefs and even a fromager. Bravo Céline! You dedicated countless hours to helping Marseille's food industry. On top of that, I added a little homework for you: share your Fishe and Shipe recipe with me.

Shipe marseillaise,
or panisse in bars

FISH AND CHIPS MARSEILLAIS

To stick with the theme, Céline replaces mayo with a 'family-style' aioli. Here is her formula.

INGREDIENTS

Whiting or mullet fillets
Flour
Frying oil
Panisses in the shape of fries (see recipe earlier in this chapter)

For the aioli:
5 garlic cloves
300ml sunflower oil
3 egg yolks
2 tbsp mustard
300ml olive oil
Fresh coriander
Fresh chives
Fresh parsley

1. For the aioli, peel and crush the garlic cloves. Mix the garlic and 2 tablespoons of the sunflower oil in a food processor until you get an ointment-like purée. Add egg yolks and mustard. Mix everything together.

2. Whip the aioli in the food processor with the rest of the sunflower oil, then add the olive oil.

3. At the end, Céline also adds coriander, chives and parsley. All herbs must be fresh and chopped by hand.

4. For the fish, you can use whiting fillets. Céline also likes mullet (whose eggs are used to make the famous bottarga in Martigues).

5. Dust the fish fillets with flour. Fry them in 180°C oil.

6. Add some Britishness back and plate fish, panisses and aioli in a cardboard box as if you were in North London, on a match night near Arsenal's stadium...

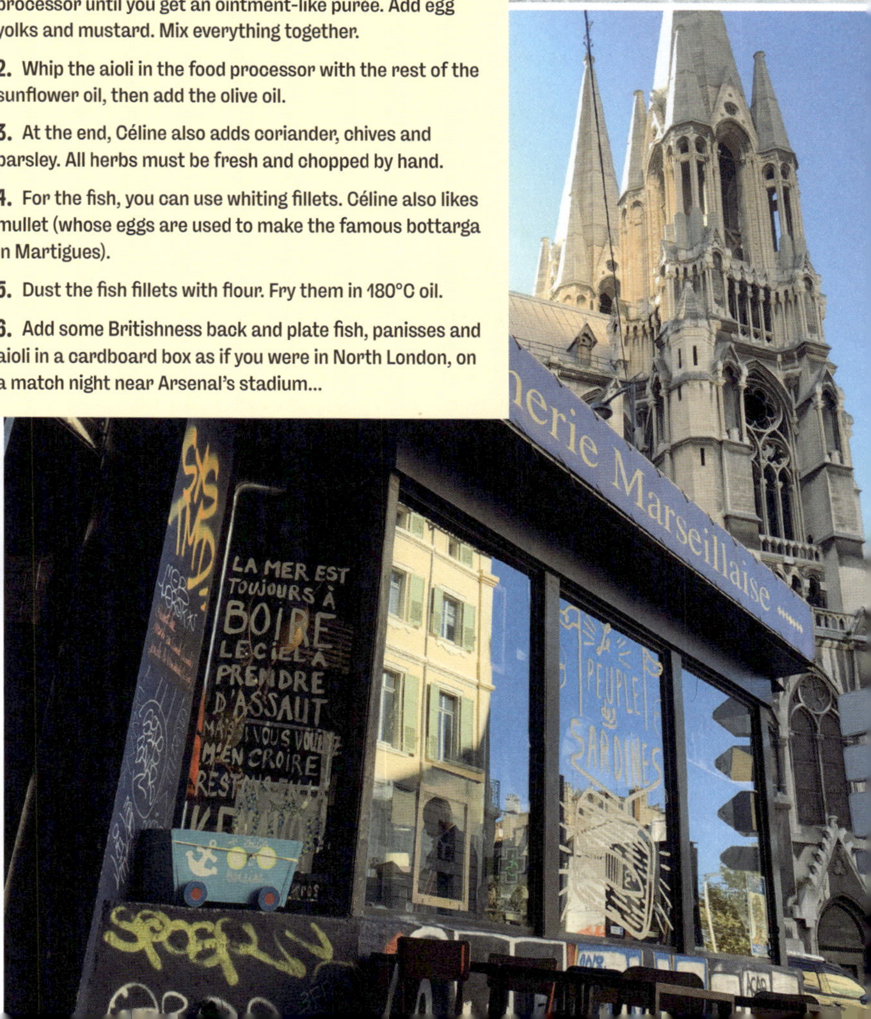

Sophie Ferjani

A DIFFERENT VIEW

Interior designer Sophie Ferjani moved her whole family, her energy, and her talent to Marseille in 2017. 'Madame Déco' on French TV station M6, notably alongside the very media-savvy Stéphane Plaza, Sophie is one of the newcomers who has chosen Marseille to express their creativity. Moreover, Sophie's challenge, mission really, behind opening her home décor boutique, La Sélection, was to revive a very peculiar Marseille artery, Rue de la République – known as Rue de la Rep and formerly Rue Imperiale – which Napoleon III had imperially pierced through old Marseille in the middle of the 19th century. The fact of the matter is that this street has been imposed on Marseillais again and again.
A few years ago, the neighbourhood's renovation had masterfully sanitised the street by forcing its cosmopolitan population and working-class shops to look elsewhere. Today, the return of independent businesses is giving the street a renewed interest. But there is still a long way to go.
Sophie and Baligh, an inspiring couple, don't want to change Marseille but rather to teach her how to better handle her tremendous potential. Glued to Le Panier, the shop is surprising, even grandiose. You want to live in it and dine at its large, magnificently set table. In Marseille, we remain fiercely attached to our grannies' old, mismatched plates, but let's admit that a touch of *Elle Déco* in our homes wouldn't hurt.

Where did you grow up?
I grew up in a small town in Loir-et-Cher, in Mesland, in the centre of France. A small village where nothing exceptional happens but which instilled deep and sincere work and family values in us.

Why did you open your shop in Marseille?
We were looking for a place to call home and set up our project: to open a home decoration concept store.

How did you choose the Rue de la République?
This district was somewhat of a given to me because for years we had been visiting Marseille as tourists, then afterwards with a professional perspective when we were looking to set up shop. And Rue de la République, a large artery that is 25 metres wide and 1.2 kilometres long, and which starts from the Vieux-Port and joins the docks and the 'newer' port of La Joliette, is the only 100% Haussmann boulevard in Marseille [Haussmann is the famous architect who designed all of Paris's grand boulevards]. From an architectural point of view, it had won. Then, strategically, one out of three trams pass in front of my shop and stops there. And, finally, because everyone told me not to come to Rue de la République. I like to go where no one expects me to go and listen to my inner voice. I am not stubborn, but I know what I want and how to succeed! This street, which was totally redesigned more than 10 years ago, has not found its DNA, but I'm convinced that brands like mine will breathe new life into it.

How would you describe the neighbourhood?
It's an emerging neighbourhood even though it's a few metres from Le Panier, the oldest quarter in Marseille and France. It has a connection with La Joliette, which has sprung up like crazy, a new

face of Marseille where everything can be done and where everyone can create their own place. On the Rue de la République, we are surrounded by people like us: entrepreneurs with young minds and full of ideas, with enthusiasm to spare.

What is your first memory of Marseille?
One of my earliest memories of Marseille was this rare feeling of having salt in my hair and smelling the sea air as I walked through a big city among old buildings. It is this very strong relationship between nature and urbanism that I like here. We don't have to choose – we have everything close by!

How did you get to know this city?
One can feel like you've quickly made the rounds of very disparate neighbourhoods which are juxtaposed with such different stories and souls. But, if you dig a little deeper and take the time to really discover each of these neighbourhoods, you then realise that it takes a long time to grasp their contours! Sizewise, this city is so extensive. You go from a hipster district to a fishing port... to a secluded countryside... to the hills of Marcel Pagnol... to a cove in the Calanques. I love this variety of landscapes and their accompanying mentalities. You never get bored!

Which district of Marseille do you have a particular attachment to?
Beside the République district, I am profoundly attached to the little port of Les Goudes on the southern edge of town. You know that unique feeling when time stands still and all you need to do is touch the hill to put the dots on the I's and remind you that you're not much. It helps you to review your priorities in life! This place does me so much good and makes me deeply happy.

What is your first culinary memory in Marseille?
I think it was a plate of *supions* [squid] in Les Goudes with an unpretentious white wine.

Have you found culinary happiness in Marseille?
I love cuisine that takes me on a journey, and that surprises me no matter where it's from. But I must admit that Italian cuisine (I'm not talking about pizza) particularly resonates with me. If I had to choose just two restaurants, it would be Il Cuoco, which my neighbour and friend Michel Zeraibi helms, and Il Capriolo, on Boulevard Longchamp, run by Chef Jéjé le Barbu. Recently, I've really enjoyed the Les Réformés restaurant on the rooftop at the Artplexe cinema, Bistrot Mimi behind City Hall, and the Senegalese restaurant Marafiki in Le Panier.

If you had the choice, which restaurant's décor would you (re)do in Marseille?
I wouldn't want to make any enemies! But if I could, I would redo Une Table au Sud. I find that the décor of this restaurant does not really go with the cuisine of Chef Ludovic Turac, nor with the image I have of this young entrepreneurial couple who own it! Chez Étienne also, I would at least change the tables and chairs but I might get mailed a small coffin for that comment?!

Where do you eat in Marseille?
We have our regular spots around Boulevard Longchamp, a neighbourhood that we really like because we lived there for three years. It was easy for us to go there for dinner during the week on a terrace. But we also love Cours Julien, a very cosmopolitan area where children also can enjoy themselves when we spend time at the table and frolic in the alleys. Our friends Fred and Faiza helm Papà Fredo pizzeria in Cours Julien. Our favourite little pleasure is to drink aged rum at the Rhumerie, watch the sunset, and nibble on tapas at the Escale Borély beach with our feet in the sand. And when I really need to recharge my batteries, we take the car and drive to Les Goudes to L'Auberge du Corsaire where Thierry always reserves his best table for us among the boats on the quay. It's true joy, simple and surrounded by what we love!

One of my earliest memories of Marseille was this rare feeling of having salt in my hair and smelling the sea air as I walked through a big city among old buildings.

For you, Marseille is...
When you walk around Belsunce, or along the Marché des Capucins, and all the streets behind it in Noailles, you can savour so many flavours and smell so many different aromas. For me, that's what Marseille is: this stew of cultures and tastes!

OUR HILLS ARE ALIVE

Sea fennel

02

Freedom rules in our hills. Between the Marseille village of La Treille, the surrounding towns of Aubagne and Allauch, and the famous Garlaban hills, Marseille plunges into an 8,000 hectare massif where children still frolic like in the days of little Marcel Pagnol (1895–1974), the beloved local writer famous for capturing Provence and Marseille spirit in his books and films. We even coined the term 'pagnolesque' to describe funny situations that mirror his films. I know that a lot of you don't get why we laugh and cry watching his black and white films or read his autobiographical books again and again, but American chef Alice Waters named her iconic Chez Panisse restaurant in Berkeley after a key character in his Marius/Fanny/César trilogy, Honoré Panisse. So I am going to let her try to explain: *'Many of his films are about that longing for nature and a kind of rhythm and concerns about the change in the way people were living their lives.*

'It's the way I felt. How do we get back to that other place where everyday life is meaningful?' Alice Waters in SFGATE, Aug 2011.

Getting lost in the hills (*les collines*) is our version of fun! We smell and spot thyme, rosemary, mushrooms, *cousteline* salad, dandelion greens, and wild asparagus. Those who are even more in the know go mad crazy harvesting many other edible wild things, such as wild rocket, diplotaxis ('false rocket' as we like to call it), plantain, precious phytoestrogen-rich clary sage, wild leeks, burnet, false clover, ground ivy, mallow, and the round, strawberry-like fruit on the *arbousier* trees! It's a free consumable feast! Start with collecting wild fig tree leaves and cook your fish in them . . . you are on the verge of new flavour territory here. In the Marseille region, the biotope is generous and we were hills-to-table by necessity way before it became chic . . .

To stuff some Pagnol in your lives, I spent time with Célia Broussegoutte, who walks in and around Marseille for anyone who wants to learn about edible plant foraging, and chef Sébastien Cortez, who invents recipes for every season with wild plants he finds on Marseille's Corniche.

I could have lingered over the knockoff Herbes de Provence sold almost everywhere on the planet and whose only link to the south of France is by name, but I preferred to highlight the positive because our hills are far from empty and our knowledge of them is becoming too weak.

So, head out on a Sunday, go for a walk, and *mange ze* hills. This chapter is just an appetiser.

Sébastien Cortez

Crazy about cooking with the bounty of the hills and the sea, Chef Sébastien, a bit of a dreamer, invents his dishes based on what the sun, the rain and the moon give him. This Marseillais doesn't helm from afar, he's from Hyères, and he brilliantly cultivates the rebellious spirit of Marseille.
His love for wild plants is fittingly coupled with a passion for the cuisine of ancient Rome, which strongly influenced Provençal cuisine. A Roman dinner conceived by Sébastien and Chef Emmanuel Perrodin would be to die for.
In the meantime, cooking with Sébastien gave me an opportunity to meet another Sébastien, Sébastien Richard, a chef with a thousand ideas, who fell into the culinary magic potion at a very young age. It is to him that we owe the solidarity restaurant Le République, nicknamed LE REP. Sébastien Cortez has been part of this innovative adventure from the start. Both Sebs cook for the Rep supper club. This is where we met to cook a Marseillais gargouillou. Acidity, bitterness, gourmandise . . . all that a good recipe needs.

Cuisine from the hills and the sea

1 Place Sadi-Carnot
13002 Marseille

WILD PLANT

How was the foraging this morning?
It's November and all the springtime plants have already arrived in the hills! It's going to be a disaster come spring if the seeds endure a big cold snap afterwards.
I work with non-cultivated plants. Many chefs work with select wild plants and flowers that are actually greenhouse-grown. I don't want to work with pumped-up flowers. The borage flowers that the hipsters are sprinkling on their plates taste like oysters, their leaves have a pronounced cucumber taste, but in reality, in nature, borage has a much lighter and finer flavour. With rocket, it's the opposite. You can't eat a salad of wild rocket, its taste is 10 times stronger in its wild state. I use it like wasabi.
These local plants symbolise the flavours of our territory. When you speak of the garrigue, you think of thyme and rosemary but it's a very arid soil, quite hard, and wild rocket embodies that. She has the strength of our soil in her stems. The same goes for lesser calamint, which represents our region's union between the forest and the sea with its fresh and camphoric side.
I chose to do simple, refined cooking with a few ingredients, so that they are legible. Consequently, I push the flavour of each product to the max. For the recipe in this book, I used plants that are easy to find and are hard to mess up. We have cornflower (purple flower), diplotaxis – false rocket (white flower), some pale stonecrop (a sedum-succulent plant, it's super good), dandelion, and sea fennel that we're going to cook tempura-style. Be careful, you must not pick it in the Calanques, it is strictly forbidden. Gleaning should be respectful. I gather it below Passédat's place, Le Petit Nice, on the Corniche and there are some on the side of the road in Les Goudes. I also found sea alyssum, which tastes like nectar. Quite fragile, it can be found all over the Calanques. When you see this plant, you know the soil is pretty clean. Today, despite the industrial past of Marseille's southern quarters and beaches, where there were factories like in Saména, you're starting to see alyssum and that's a very good sign. All these plants that we're going to cook with today clean the soil. Diplotaxis, for example, is often found on the side of the road. It needs CO_2 and slightly damaged soil to play its part.
In general, I gather plants in the *Quartiers Nord* (the nothern quarters) of Marseille, or along the Corniche in the southern part, and around the village of Gémenos near Aubagne, in abandoned fields, because land regeneration follows several steps and different wild plants arrive along the way. At the start, there are thistles, which re-aerate the soil, then wild carrots (white, almost transparent, very bitter . . . they allow you to return to carrots' original taste by breaking down the sugar a bit), fennel and diplotaxis. Ground ivy,

clover and wild sage with large leaves come later. In Côtes de Provence vineyards, the land is set aside for four years when the vines are too old, but in four years, the land barely regenerates. You're just getting to the plants with big roots. The revered Domaine d'Ott waits nine years when plants with 'weak' roots break down. There the soil is aerated and alive again.
With flowers and plants, I don't like cooking them a lot since they are fragile in terms of taste. I touch them as little as possible, apart from the sea fennel that we're going to cook tempura-style. It makes it more supple. If it was spring, I would have picked the young sea fennel shoots, they are flexible and firm at the same time, and you can eat them raw. The rest of the year, you can only take the tips, the tops. The reddened parts are too bitter. For this dish, we are also going to make an oil from the diplotaxis leaves and we'll keep some of them to put on the plate at the end, to add a bit of piquancy. Diplotaxis flowers are very pretty, very fine. I put in a lot of leaves too, and dandelions at the very end.

How would you define Marseille cuisine today?
It's blowing up! It's finally freeing itself from the bad touristy cooking that had killed our gastronomy. Mediterranean cuisine is very rich, but we made it into a commercial cuisine. We had lost its very essence, with moules frites, prawns flambéed with pastis, farmed sea bass grilled with fennel. We want to get rid of that. It's a disservice to us. Today, we have young chefs who have arrived here, who have reclaimed Mediterranean cuisine. They are breaking the dogmas of French gastronomy. We are re-teaching everything to our customers. It will take time for people to actually eat wild plants and not treat them like decoration only, but in the years to come, we will have real Marseille gastronomy that will have a real identity, a real strength.

What are your sure-fire addresses in Marseille?
For lunch, Opéra Zoizo with their new chef, Charles Pinoteau. It's great bistro-style cooking.
I also go to Maëlyss Vultaggio, who worked at Zoizo previously and created Mama Kyuna at the restaurant Cédrat. She's a fantastic chef. She was my sous-chef during the Covid lockdown.
Caterine, I was there yesterday. Cheffe Marie Dijon is incredible.
The Vietnamese canteen Nguyen-Hoang. My favourite.
And I love Chez Étienne in Le Panier, getting yelled at by the servers and being forced to drink a bottle of rosé even before I sit down! I go for the spectacle.
I never eat in the Vieux-Port except at Chez Madie Les Galinettes.
I order the *alibofis* [lamb testicles!]. It's my Monday restaurant. And for shellfish platters, I go to Entre Terre et Mer in Le Panier.
I like apéro spots, like the Lebanese-Egyptian tapas bar Mina in La Plaine. I can let my daughter play on the square.
At night, I take my time in a gastronomic restaurant. I really like La Mercerie, Ekume, and Le Petit Nice remains a mythical spot. Chef Passédat's book *Des Abysses à la Lumière* was my cooking bible at one time.

'This is a dish that I make year-round and that evolves according to my gleanings. It's never the same. It really is my identity. The base remains constant: a plant, a bouillon or an oil, a garum [a fermented fish sauce used in ancient Roman times] and a lightly cooked fish.
I have almost one variation per month, but can one say that a creation is ever finished? My tastes change, my sensibility evolves, my technique progresses, and the dish will continue to develop. I still have a lot to learn.'

JOLIE BALADE EN COLLINE
(a nice walk in the hills)

Garum

'For this recipe, I use my garum made with Mediterranean galère (a cross between a prawn and a langoustine). I follow the ancient method (Roman and Greek), it is not a sanitised "Noma" style garum that is made in a week in a fermentation chamber. It takes 2 months for galère garum to be ready. The other one I make with anchovies takes a month and a half. Then I filter them and refine them. I remove the salt crust as I go. For the advanced ageing, I use an amphora (ancient Greek container). I push them far. I have one that is two and a half years old for another ancient condiment preparation that I use a lot, aillatum. It gives a nice strength to the dishes.
There is never a rotten taste in garum. The fermentation isn't that violent. (*Author's note: when I stuck my nose in the old garum, my nostrils were pushed to the limits! Sébastien asked me 'Do you get the taste of shellfish, of bisque? This hasn't been cooked at all.' I couldn't answer . . .*)
At first, I keep the jar closed, it blocks the fermentation a little. That provides an exceptional fishy taste, complex but not aggressive. The salt in my dish comes from this. I even tried to make a garum with violets (a Mediterranean sea snail) but I felt like I was . . . dunking my head in the sea! It's super briny. I expected that with the violets but I had cut it with mussels to give it a bit more flavour. I'm still trying to figure out how to use it. I've been trying to get my customers to "dunk their heads" for years, but this may be a bit too much!
The equivalent of garum today in Italian colatura.'

INGREDIENTS FOR 4

A whole dentex (a Mediterranean fish that is a bit fatty), about 1.5kg
'At the morning Vieux-Port fish market, there are still three or four real fishermen, three with small *pointus* [traditional wooden fishing boats], one that only does conger and moray eel, and I work with another that has a tiny trawling net and targets very little. So, he sells 8–10 different fish. Fish are like wild plants, people here only know sea bream, mackerel, sea bass and tuna. We must eat the rest of them.'
Olive oil
Juice and zest of 1 lemon
Shellfish (*galère*) garum or colatura
'Either you are passionate about ancient Greece or Rome, especially Apicius, and you have a jar of homemade garum that has perfumed your kitchen for months, or you buy a bottle of colatura.'

Foraged plants and flowers:
Diplotaxis
Sea alyssum
Mallow
Dandelion (*pissenlit*)
Pale stonecrop (*orpin de Nice*)

For the tempura:
150g plain flour
250ml very cold sparkling water
Sea fennel (*criste marine*)
Salt

For the aillatum:
100g ground almonds
4 or 5 garlic cloves, crushed
6 tbsp fish garum or colatura
Olive oil (quantity depends on the texture you want)

Kitchen utensils needed: blender, kitchen blowtorch, flat kitchen brush, tea towel

1. Blend diplotaxis leaves, juice from 1 lemon, and olive oil until you get a very smooth purée. Strain the mixture through a tea towel.

2. Fillet the dentex and marinate in olive oil and juice from 1 lemon for 15 minutes. Lightly crisp the skin with a blowtorch. 'Work the dentex a bit like for an aguachile, raw, just with a quick blowtorch on the skin to melt it a bit. You don't have to char it, just heat the fish a little.'

3. Brush shellfish (*galère*) garum on each fillet, sprinkle with lemon zest for seasoning and leave it to marinate.

4. For the tempura, mix flour, salt and sparkling water until the batter has a consistency to coat the back of a spoon. Coat sea fennel tops in the batter and fry. 'For the tempura batter, I don't use egg because it makes the batter stickier and more pillowy. That isn't the point of this recipe, where I'm looking for finesse and crispiness.'

5. For the aillatum, mix ground almonds, crushed garlic, olive oil and fish garum until you get a lightly briny and garlicky batter.

6. To serve: Place three slices of fish, 1cm thick, at the centre of the plate. Add two dots of aillatum per fish slice. Place flowers and sprouts harmoniously on top of the fish. Add a large tablespoon of diplotaxis oil and a few drops of shellfish (*galère*) garum.

FOCUS

LE RÉPUBLIQUE and Sébastien Richard

LE RÉPUBLIQUE

1 Place Sadi-Carnot
13002 Marseille

'I'm originally from Tours in the north of France, I ran a Michelin-starred restaurant for 18 years in nearby Istres, then I was the private chef for the Saadé family, owners of the Marseille shipping company CMA-CGM (*author's note: the world's third largest, we're proud to say!*). Before the Covid pandemic, I had a table d'hôte in Le Panier.

During the lockdown, I realised that in Marseille, we lacked a solidarity restaurant like Italian chef Massimo Bottura's Refettorios. I wanted to create one, but to my knowledge, the different types of diners at Refettorios do not mix. At lunch, it's businessmen and in the evening, the restaurant transforms into a canteen where you give food to people in need. Me, I wanted to have different social classes come together. In Marseille, this is extremely important. More than 60 chefs are members. Nadia Sammut, Georgiana Viou, Sébastien Cortez . . . they come to create dishes or do four-hand dinners.

Everyone thought I was crazy for wanting to mix the "rich" and the "poor" in this magical setting, but for me, the vocation of a restaurant is not just to nourish. I wanted this place. One of my clients at the table d'hôte was a director of the group that owns this building. I got the keys, a bank lent me 300,000 euros, Saadé helped us, and I went looking for investment subsidies. City Hall gave us aid but not monetarily. The Region helped us financially when I banged my fists on the table. We also have a professional insertion component, which allows us to get additional funding. And I asked Mucem's architect, Rudy Ricciotti, to lend a hand. The reality is our customers are from all walks of life. It is a gastronomic restaurant, but certain customers only pay 1 euro for their meal. We have signed agreements with 80 associations, both national and local. They are members and reserve seats. Today, we give 32% of the seats to these associations. The average bill for the other 68% of customers is 28–30 euros. We have a lot of women who come to lunch here. Inclusion is a real hot topic, incidentally. As are job training and placement for women.

The story has just started. I'm finalising a charter. Other cities, like Strasbourg, want to set up the same kind of place. I am also sinking my teeth into training so that we can have a culinary school for all, a real campus in Marseille. I want to find people who would not have previously chosen the restaurant industry for fear they wouldn't fit in. At the same time, we've opened a private chef's table at Le Rep with Chef Sébastian Cortez and myself manning the stoves. I also won a bid from the city to create a residence for Mediterranean chefs on the Rue Saint Saëns, near the Vieux-Port, and there also, in terms of price, I want us to stay in the fabric of the city centre. We must not go any further with the disparity between Marseille's prices (because it's becoming a hotspot) and what the Marseillais can afford.'

Sébastien Richard, Chef and 'President' of Le République

R
M ╳ S
Longchamp

Célia Broussegoutte

Célia is a fount of natural science knowledge who knows brassicas like the back of her hand. She didn't know Marseille, however, so when she moved here from Nice, she met hearty duo Caroline Decque and Camille Gasnier. The founders of Bigoud' collected edible natural treasures, flowers and plants for Marseille chefs and makers of artisanal spirits until they handed over their nature-fed business to Retour de Cueillette's Joffrey Nicoletti. After having worked some time with the team, Célia, an environmental educator by trade, created rustic walks within Marseille, along the Jarret river and the housing estates, in the pretty Parc Longchamp, or in the Pagnol hills behind the Château de La Buzine. She offers them to all those eager to learn to identify and pick plants in the wild. We first set off together in the middle of winter behind the huge La Valentine shopping centre for some wild, and free, shopping. We harvested mallow and diplotaxis, aka 'false rocket'. An intrigued local walker we met along the way said, 'Ah, my grandmother used to do many things in the kitchen with mallow but, me, I don't know what to do with it!' We are losing it my friends . . .
A year later, we met again in troubled, lively La Rose and I photographed the quarter's bucolic side. The young people hanging out between the estates and a supermarket couldn't believe that the wild plants they were sitting on could be handy. Coding is maybe not the most precious thing that we could learn at school . . .

URBAN FORAGER

When did you arrive in Marseille?
In February 2016, for a civic service volunteer job in an organisation focused on protecting the environment [France Nature Environnement]. Afterwards, once I was hired by them, I settled down here for good.

When did you first become interested in wild plants?
It was first in the summer of 2018 during a hiking, camping and yoga retreat in the mountains. The mountain guide, a local, explained how people in the valley make use of the various edible and medicinal plants. In the evening, we garnished our dishes with plants that we had picked.
Then, when I was unemployed in October 2018, I decided to get involved in urban farming and permaculture associations. I met Bigoud', an association that foraged and grew edible leaves and flowers which they were selling to the best restaurants in Marseille. This is where I really realised we have everything we need at our feet and my growing need to reconnect with nature. I admire Caroline and Camille from Bigoud' because they introduced me to this passion that I now share, and they are two really great people.
Having gained enough knowledge, I wanted to pass it on so that everyone could rediscover this forgotten know-how and gain autonomy. I also organise workshops and trainings to put what people learn during the walks into practice (cooking wild plants and making remedies or natural cosmetics). It felt essential to offer walks in an urban or semi-urban setting in order to re-evaluate these 'weeds' – which are not weeds at all – as well as the natural spaces which shelter them (parks, hills, rivers, etc.). These are real resources that need to be preserved. What's more, it is really important for me to show that we can find everything we need without having to go far, which allows our participants to be more autonomous. It doesn't make any sense to travel kilometres to show them plants that they will never see again, when in town, you can discover a plant's heritage.

What are your usual routes and how did you discover them?
I discovered the places on my walks by searching and feeling around, sometimes finding myself stuck in a wasteland with grass taller than me or crossing through garrigue bushes that scratched my legs along the way. It turns out there are many green spaces in Marseille, but they are not well developed.
I discovered that near La Rose metro station you could wander along the small Jarret river. Not a lot of Marseillais know that this tiny river that runs under our city centre is in the open air around here.
I also really like the Parc Longchamp walk. In this urbanised space, there is a real density of plants that you can use in cooking or making natural remedies. The park is easy to access and known by many people.

What is the advantage of wild plants?
These plants grow by themselves, so they are heartier. They had to draw from the earth to develop, so consequently, they are bursting with nutrients. What's more, if you spot a plant in one place, you can come back to the same place to find it. It will grow back on its own.

What are the rules when picking wild plants?
Once you have properly identified the plant, it is necessary to ensure that the place where you pick is not polluted, particularly by road traffic, but also by animal waste or pesticide treatments. Better to stay away from paths for pets and waterways for bacteria. If in doubt, cook the plant or at least rinse it with white vinegar. Generally, we try not to pick the parts of plants that directly touch the ground because they are less safe and hygienic.
It is also necessary to respect the plant, to not pull out the whole roots, to not take a single or poorly developed plant, to always leave two-thirds of an area intact, and, of course, to not pick protected species or those found in natural reserves (like in the Calanques). Then, it makes sense to pick the leaves of a plant before the flower stage, and to pick the roots when there are no more flowers or seeds.

Mallow

What are the wild edible plants that symbolise Marseille for you?
Wild rocket, lesser calamint, hackberry, rosemary, everlasting [helichrysum], wild fennel and Sicilian sumac.

What's the most surprising edible wild plant you've easily found within reach?
The fact that they manage to find the conditions necessary for their development in the city's hostile environment, the fact that they can grow through concrete or on dry ground, without anyone watering them or bringing them fertilisers, makes all the wild plants remarkable to me, whether they're edible or not.

Today, what things surprise you about Marseille?
The nature that is so present and so close, the protected areas (classified Natura 2000 or others), and restaurants which are gradually starting to use wild plants to enhance dishes and no longer just as garnish.

Which Marseille quarter do you have a particular attachment to?
The Cinq-Avenues quarter. Its park, Longchamp, where I lead a bunch of my walks, appealed to me immediately: a large green space in the heart of the city is rare in Marseille! In addition, I was surprised to discover that even though the park is maintained, the wild has found its place there: many plants grow spontaneously and birds, bats, insects all find refuge in the park.

Is there a restaurant in Marseille that you are fond of?
La Cuisine de Gagny. We eat well, the staff are really welcoming, and I sometimes find edible flowers on my plate!

Which recently discovered restaurant in Marseille has surprised you?
Entre Terre et Mer in Le Panier. As a huge fan of seafood, I did not leave disappointed.

Do you feel Marseillaise now?
Yes, it's been seven years since I moved here, and you could say that I feel like a Marseillaise. It's a heterogeneous city; here, everyone comes from elsewhere and it is not easy to meet 'pure' Marseillais. Moreover, it is such a large city, that was formed by connecting different villages together, so it displays great disparities.
What makes you feel Marseillais or not is whether you feel attached to the city. And I feel attached to Marseille. I have always heard that either one loves Marseille, or one hates it and would do anything to leave. There is rarely a happy medium between the two.

Diplotaxis, aka 'false rocket'

What the Marseillais generally overlook about their territory . . .
That acorns can be eaten! As well as the oak bark, stems and leaves. Acorns have a somewhat bitter taste. They contain tannins in very large quantities. You must bite into them to test their bitterness, then slit them, boil them, discard the water, remove the thick skin, and boil them again in clean water. Sometimes you must change the water five or seven times to get rid of their bitterness.
They can be used like chestnuts – dried and made into flour. Acorns are much more nutritious than chestnuts, which only contain carbohydrates. The acorns also contain protein. You have to gather them from under the tree or pick them when they unhook without resistance from their cup. In Marseille, we don't have chestnuts, so acorns could replace them.

By the small river le Jarret, on the road to Plan de Cuques and Allauch

'Lamb's quarters, whose leaves are shaped like bird feet and have a kind of white powder on the back of their leaves (hence the plant's other name "white goosefoot"), is very nutritious. The leaves are smooth and hairless, unlike those of stinging nettle. They're like wild spinach. This plant is found near the city centre, it is invasive . . . It is better to cook the leaves, blanch them, and then prepare them like spinach, in quiches, samoussas, soups, omelettes . . . You'll want to pick the young leaves. You can also pick the young stems at the top of the plant, which are very tender, and cook them like asparagus. For the soft stalks, you can boil them, and they taste really good. Like spinach, when you have kidney stones, you shouldn't overdo it. Lamb's quarters contains oxalic acid.'

'The figuier is the ultimate Mediterranean tree. You don't need to wait for a fig tree to bear fruit to cook with it. Infusing the tender leaves in a little milk enables you to make a slightly aromatic dessert cream, in which you dip very ripe strawberries. But they are like bay leaves, you don't eat them.'

'Garlic mustard can climb very high. The leaves have a heart or kidney shape. As they grow, the new leaves are more pointed. You need to look at the bottom of the plant to recognise the leaves. Take them and rub them in your hands, they will release a strong garlicky aroma, but a mellow garlic. You can cook the upper leaves and use them in hummus instead of garlic and you can make a flavour bomb of a pistou with just olive oil, pine nuts or almonds or walnuts. You can also eat the white flowers and the small seeds when they're still fresh.'

'Lichwort, you see it everywhere, on the edge of sidewalks or in low walls since it breaks through rock – hence the name "casse-pierre / rock-breaker". Logically, it is widely used in herbal teas to break up kidney stones. It is appealing to chefs because it tastes like fresh cucumber. You do a Velcro test to recognise it because it is very hairy. So, it easily clings to your clothes. And it has reddish stems. You pick the buds when they haven't yet flowered. You can eat them raw or cooked, but remember, they are very hairy! And if you're allergic to pollen, be careful, there's a lot of pollen!'

'Calamint has small flowers shaped like snapdragons, I love its minty, peppery smell. It goes great with butter or rolled in cream cheese. Personally, I think it pairs really well with chocolate, like in a chocolate dessert cream or fondant. I love it!'

We finished our walk with a rare find, some wild borage. It's delicious and chefs love it. They put it on fish. The flowers have a briny taste, subtly reminiscent of oysters.

Now get out there! You could get lucky too . . .

Lichwort

Wild borage

Lamb's quarters

Calamint

Garlic mustard

'I like to show that you don't have to be a chef to discover the flavours of wild plants. Simply incorporate them into recipes, replacing or complementing the ingredients you usually use.
Here are two simple recipes that require few ingredients, recipes that everyone knows but that take on a whole new dimension when enlivened by wild plants. You can make them your own and adapt them as you wish, depending on what you find near you and the season. Many have tasted pesto, but few know its flavour when it is prepared with wild rocket. Make it with plantain, stinging nettle, wild radish, *ail des ours* – wild garlic . . .'

MALLOW AND FRESH GOAT CHEESE SAMOUSSAS

1. Roughly chop the mallow leaves. Sauté them in a little olive oil. Crumble in fresh goat cheese then add spices, salt, and pepper to taste.

2. Make samoussas using *brik* pastry sheets (2 samoussas per sheet).

3. Spread the mallow mixture on the *brik* pastry sheets and fold them into triangles. Fry samoussas in a little olive oil. 5 minutes will do.

4. You can also substitute plantain leaves for mallow, but in this case, you must add lemon juice and a bit of brown sugar to balance the bitterness of the plantain.

INGREDIENTS FOR 16 SAMOUSSAS

A few handfuls of wild mallow (the mallow leaf has 5 lobes like a hand and a red dot at the base while the pink flowers have 5 fused and dark-ribbed petals)
Olive oil
500g fresh goat cheese
Cumin or a mix of couscous spices (ras el-hanout)
8 *brik* pastry sheets
Salt and pepper

WILD PESTO

INGREDIENTS FOR 4

80g wild rocket (yellow flower with 4 petals) or diplotaxis/false rocket (white flower with 4 petals)
1 garlic clove
4 tbsp olive oil (don't skimp on olive oil)
70g sunflower seeds, pine nuts or hazelnuts
Lemon juice
Salt and pepper

1. Rinse the rocket leaves and dry thoroughly.

2. Place all the ingredients in a blender, blend, and adjust quantities of each ingredient for taste. Careful – garlic tends to mask the flavour of plants.

3. Pesto is great for an apéro on slices of toasted bread, or you can use it in pasta.

FOCUS

Urban agriculture and social ties

'50 years ago, Marseille was more than 90% self-sufficient for fruits and vegetables. Today, it's not even 5%. When you talk to the older folk in the neighbourhood, they say that here, there was a farm, and next to it, there was a dairy farm, etc. Today, we have 'waterproofed' the land with concrete.

I spent six years in Berlin before returning to Marseille where I had grown up. There, so many places inspired me. There was a real reclamation of public space, of abandoned spaces filled with mixed-use projects, and a significant mix of audiences. I wanted to recreate that here. We had the opportunity to rehabilitate this piece of land, but we decided to go with a very specific angle: edible plants. How to make a third place with something that connects us all? Well, no matter where you come from, or how much you earn, we are all interested in food. We all eat three times a day. It is ultimately an entry point for everything, for entertainment, education, ecology, biodiversity, social ties, and interculturality. The mix of uses and audiences is very dear to us. We also wanted to show that the project could support itself economically and create jobs, in addition to having a strong social and environmental impact. We have 540 square metres of usable agricultural area, and with that we manage to pay one person. Usually, it is said that it takes 6 hectares to be able to live off it!

> When we arrived here, we were taken for oddballs who wanted to change the world and throw seed bombs everywhere like the Green Guerrillas.
>
> Valentin Charvet
> Co-founder of community urban farm *Le Talus*

The land belongs to the State, who has lent it to us. The L2 motorway passes below our feet and, overground, we are next to the railways. Here, it was an empty base for a worksite, then a rubble dump. There were lots of mounds. It was a lot of work since we had to sort and clear the metal, concrete, plastic, and make everything flat. We brought 600 tonnes of organic matter to recreate living soil as quickly as possible and turn it into an organic farm.

Thanks to partnerships, we are even at more than 1,000 tonnes today. We were a pilot project, so we didn't have any comparable feedback. We went from a landfill in April 2018 to an organic space in less than three years. Now it's growing well! The land benefits from scientific monitoring by academics and researchers on soil microbiology. We regularly take readings of the earthworm density: we have increased it by more than 400%.

Our main role models came from third places in Berlin and North America, where people like urban farmer Curtis Stone used plots of home gardens to produce food. They realised that this system works very well, in small spaces, very close to consumption basins. There is also the farmer and writer Jean-Martin Fortier, in Quebec. In fact, the foundation for urban agriculture started in Cuba. Cubans put planters in the parking lots at the bottom of buildings. They really needed to eat. The State put potting soil in the planters and then left people to fend for themselves. Cuba inspired Berlin and Berlin, the rest of the world.

When we arrived here, we were taken for oddballs who wanted to change the world and throw seed bombs everywhere like the Green Guerrillas. But there were also people who wanted to talk about all these issues. It was a key moment in French society. Frédéric Denel who set up our association also co-financed the successful French documentary film *Tomorrow* by Cyril Dion and actress Mélanie Laurent. Thanks to the film, we realised that, in ecology, there were concrete things that seemed to work. All the solutions were there, but it's true that in France, we hadn't done much, especially in the southern half of the country. So, it had to be done!

The idea was to show what was possible with already proven models. In Marseille, there was reluctance for sure! We were quickly told that it would never work, that we were next to a rough, poor neighbourhood,

603 Rue Saint-Pierre
13012 Marseille

that the soil was disgusting . . . The goal was to show that where there is a will, there's a way. All you need to do is to start working on it. Now that we've done it, everyone wants to do the same. It was also our goal to have a project that inspires others.
We are not a farm because a farm (*une ferme*) is closed off (*fermé*). Here, we wanted to succeed in getting everyone on board. So, we had to offer something for everyone. It is a community project. You can come here just to have a drink, have a bite to eat, take a walk, some just come to see the chickens, others come to our parties because we play music and organise open mic rap sessions. You don't have to participate directly in the project, but by coming here, you are an active member who keeps this place alive. Some pick vegetables with us, buy a crate of products, others come for the participatory worksites because they want to do some gardening or DIY repair of objects and recycling. There are people from the neighbourhood who come for educational work camps, there are training courses. Everyone comes for different reasons but meets to discuss quality of life and food. These are common concerns. On the other hand, we wanted people who know about healthy food and sustainable agriculture to have a place to share their knowledge.
The interest around the environment, better eating and better living, is not only for *bobos* [*'bourgeois-bohémes'*, aka hipsters]. We are wrong to think that people with limited means do not care about ecology. In reality, these are issues that they know very well because many of them were connected to the agricultural world not so long ago (in a former job or in the country where they were born) and they are very interested.
We also try to experiment with new varieties in the region. With global warming, it has become a favourable territory for certain species. For example, when we planted fruit trees, we included guava trees. They grow very well here nowadays even though it is a fruit found in the Caribbean and other islands. We also have varieties of Japanese mustard that people didn't know about. Now they are asking for it.
We plant a lot of leafy vegetables, there are plenty to discover. The terroir must now be transformed. Provence is not just lavender, olives and vines. By the way, we have done too much single-crop farming, which has led to diseases. The changing of our land because of global warming will change our local history of food.
In the kitchen, we are also experimenting with how to eat quality, varied products at a lower cost and with the least ecological impact possible. Today, we manage to make meals for 1.10 euros throughout the week to feed the whole team. It is possible to cook cheaper than McDonald's.'
Today, Valentin has handed Le Talus over to a new team who organise DIY workshops and trainings in compost, tree grafting, tree pruning . . . and you can buy your greens there or stop by to eat your lunch on Wednesdays and Saturdays.

'If we managed to bring this land back to life here, in Marseille, starting from a construction site dump beside housing projects, in the blazing sun, you can do it almost anywhere'

Valentin Charvet

FOCUS

Where to feast on a good couscous in Marseille?

FAIZA AND FREDO
PAPÀ FREDO

At my mum's house! Or at Le Fémina in Noailles. What's more, I just learned that we have family ties with the owner, Mustapha!

MYRIAM RAHMAN EBADI
CHEZ ROMAIN ET MARION

Actually, in Afghan the word 'cous' refers to a vagina. One of the first times that my grandmother came to Kabul, she brought couscous to cook it for us. This story was spread around Kabul. My grandmother was a pied-noir [a European descendant born in Algeria, Morocco or Tunisia during colonial rule who moved to Europe post-independence] from Algeria. She made an excellent batch. It was really good. Since we liked it, she wanted to make it again for us when we arrived in Marseille. So, couscous was my first culinary memory in Marseille! Nowadays, I eat couscous at La Goulette near the Vieux-Port. Otherwise, I cook it myself.

MARIE JO ORDENER
LES GRANDES TABLES

Sur le Pouce . . . Nostalgia from when I was 26 years old in 1990, and for six months ate their vegetarian couscous every day. We lived at the end of Rue des Convalescents and Rue Nationale and I was pregnant with Benjamin. Each day, Mohamed asked me if he could touch my belly to bring him luck! At that time, you could eat there for 5 francs (less than 1 euro!) This is also where I told my parents that I was expecting my first child. So, Sur le Pouce until my days are done!!!

SOPHIE FERJANI
LA SÉLECTION

For couscous, no question, you must go to La Kahena at the bottom of Rue de la République: an exceptional Tunisian couscous!

NICOLE FERRONI

When I'm in Marseille, and I think many people have said the same thing, I go to Sur le Pouce in Belsunce, and before, I used to go to Saf Saf not very far from La Canebière. But right now, my favourite address is the Alpine butcher's shop in Aubagne, run by a rather unique couple. Abrahim is Moroccan, his wife is Russian.
They called their *boucherie* 'Alpine' but when you go there, you'll quickly see that there is nothing from the Alps in this place. I fell in love with this couple. The butcher's became a restaurant and they gradually added more and more tables. Today, they operate around their two specialities, tajines and couscous.

SARAH CHOUGNET
REGAIN

Sur le Pouce on Rue des Convalescents in Belsunce.

VÉRANE FRÉDIANI

Many Marseillais answered my question with a big smile, 'at my place' or 'at my mother's'! Truth is, you can eat good couscous out for less than 10 euros or so, like at Le Soleil or Sur le Pouce in Belsunce and at La Fontaine in Castellane. And for those who can spend a little more, there are very good reasons to dine at Le Fémina or La Kahena.

COUSCOUS MANIA

Many often confuse couscous as both the name of the dish and the grain with which it's made. In Marseille, in France, and in North Africa, the couscous we love and eat as much as our body can take is the king and queen of comfort food. It refers to the 'full monty', a hearty dish with meat (could be lamb, chicken, meatballs, fish, even merguez - a slightly spicy beef and lamb sausage), cooked vegetables, chickpeas, lots of semolina (the grain made from wheat or sometimes barley), lots of sauce and some harissa.

One of the major culinary symbols of the city, couscous has its own festival in Marseille. Every year, at the end of August and the beginning of September, everyone gathers in the evening on the roof of the Friche la Belle de Mai cultural centre for a big fiesta where different kinds of couscous are served, each more original than the next. Many neighbourhood restaurants throughout the city also participate in this celebration of 'true culinary pleasure' and serve their own take on couscous for a week or two, mixing the idea of couscous with their own culinary lexicon. Now that this dish is part of UNESCO's Intangible Cultural Heritage list, even more chefs from Marseille are reworking it . . .

Are your stomachs ready for pure happiness?

03

Mustapha Kachetel

OPEN YOUR HEART

Mustapha and his dad

Barley couscous restaurant, founded in 1921

1 Rue du Musée
13001 Marseille

Mustapha Kachetel is a man who alone symbolises Marseille. His restaurant, Le Fémina, celebrated its 100th anniversary in 2021. This Noailles figure maintains the neighbourhood's memories; he has seen Marseille regulars, newcomers and tourists drop by his restaurant for decades and welcomes them all with the same enthusiasm. I even think this restaurant should be your first stop when arriving in town, just to make sure Mustapha gives you all the news and tips.
Mustapha is a man of action and during the prolonged closure of restaurants in the pandemic, he recorded funny live streams on social media one after another and delivered his couscous all over Marseille. Each time I went to Le Fémina to pick up dinner, it took me two days to finish my flavourful couscous 'royal'.
The secret to his generous Berber couscous with barley semolina is the heart that the family puts into it – Mustapha's mum passed away in early 2022 but her savoir-faire was passed on to Mustapha and the various members of the family who have worked or work in the kitchen. From father to sons, from mother to daughters, and newcomers too that Mustapha is training . . .
For this book, I took some pictures during the Kouss-Kouss festival. One day each year, the street in front of the restaurant is all about Kachetel's couscous, and everybody sits at the same long table as one big couscous family!

Where did you grow up?
In Marseille.

How many generations have worked before you at this restaurant?
Three. I'm the fourth generation.

What is the aroma of cooking that whisks you back to your childhood?
The smell of couscous. It's my childhood.

You have written on the façade 'from father to sons and mother to daughters'.
From father to sons because my father, grandfather and great-grandfather worked at the restaurant, but there was also my mother, my grandmother and my sisters with me. I am from a family of nine and I am the only boy. And I only had girls.
Up until five years ago, my sisters worked here with me, but they stopped because they had kids. They're taking a break, maybe they'll come back. I always save a place because there are also my daughters.

Does one of them want to be a chef?
There is one who likes to cook. She loves it, but I don't wish this for her. It's tough, it's a tough job. We work with fresh ingredients, so we have to get up early and go to bed late. Twice a week, I leave the house at half past two in the morning, even though I only just got back at midnight. We use regional produce, and we only work with farmers. That makes considerable demands on your time.

How old were you when you started working at the restaurant?
I have always been here. I was born in Algeria, in Kabylie. I was conceived behind the ovens. My sisters and I were all born in Algeria. Even though my parents lived here, we were born in Algeria. I don't know why. I asked my parents the question, but they didn't have an answer. It was by accident that we were all born there. I stayed for four years in Algeria, and then I came back to Marseille. I went back and forth and, from the age of six, I did my schooling here. I would do my homework in the restaurant, and it soon became the canteen for my school friends!

What are your first memories of Noailles?
The 1980s, 1978 to be exact. Noailles is the belly of Marseille, the heart, the lungs. My first memories are of all the shops that were here: the first Royaume de la Chantilly dairy shop opened here on the Rue Longue des Capucins in 1917 and closed in 2004, the first Cantini-Flandin butcher shop started on the same street in 1909, there was also the pizzerias François and Sauveur, and Toinou seafood. I saw him start with a wheelbarrow. Toinou closed a few years ago and the shop has just been sold to another family of restaurateurs.

How has Noailles evolved since then?
There have been several eras in the Noailles neighbourhood. There was a rough patch when it was quite dodgy. For the past 15 years we have started to return to our former heyday. Actually, all of Marseille is beginning to take on another dimension across the planet. Now, everyone wants to come to Marseille. People come to see us from all over the world.

Do you also see this with your clientele?
Absolutely. In relation to the clientele, but also with the interviews that we do for Australian TV, CNN, Canal 7

Australia, Jakarta. I have done them in French and in English. I also did some for Quebec. Lately there have been articles about Marseille and its cuisines in the *Guardian*, in the *New York Times* . . .

Have you always used the same couscous recipe?
I try to stick to the same recipe, that of my great-great-grandmother, which my mum and sisters taught me. A recipe that I will try to preserve for as long as possible, as long as I am alive. I am in the process of passing it down, but it's always me who gives the finishing touch. It takes heart and passion to learn and preserve a recipe. You must be passionate about this dish. I am passionate about couscous.

When did you eat your first one?
The first one? I think I was in my mum's belly when I started eating couscous.

What did your mum think of your recipe?
My mum, she always felt it was missing something. That's totally normal since she is the one who passed the recipe down to me. I accept this. My mother came to visit us every day. If not in the morning, it was in the evening. There was always something missing. You know what's missing? It's her hands. I would tell her, 'Your hands are still missing, I admit it.' Couscous is made with your hands. Everything is worked with the hands. Except that currently, we wear gloves. We respect the preventative Covid measures, but couscous is made with the hands and the heart.

What kind of couscous do you make here?
It's Berber couscous. It comes directly from the mountains of Kabylie. The difference from other couscous is the barley – the taste, the texture. Barley semolina is much lighter and easier to digest. You can eat two plates of it, and you won't be bloated. Once cooked, it no longer swells, whether on the plate or in the stomach. Wheat semolina continues to ferment on the plate. We serve the two semolinas. But our speciality is barley. It is much more fragrant, and the vegetables are not the same. The recipe is not the same, the cooking method is not the same. Barley semolina is prepared over two days. The couscous you eat today began to be prepared yesterday. Tomorrow's is prepared today. We work like in the Middle Ages.

Barley couscous restaurant, founded in 1921

1 Rue du Musée
13001 Marseille

I also make fish couscous with grouper. An Israeli gave me the recipe. He came to make it with me and now I add my personal touch to it!

When you eat out in Noailles, where do you go?
There are interesting new restaurants that opened a few years ago like La Mercerie and L'Épicerie L'Idéal. All these restaurants are contributing to the evolution of Noailles. We all know each other. Generally, when new owners arrive, they come to eat here, or I go to meet them.
I have links with all the restaurateurs who are in this neighbourhood. The couple who owns Pastels World are among the young people who have recently arrived. They are good people.
I was afraid during Covid that things would go wrong for them, but, in the end, they bounced back and I am very happy that they are holding up. These are people who want to work. They try, they evolve.
When I see the shutters of a restaurant open, even if it's a couscous restaurant, I'm happy.
In the restaurant business, the sun rises for all and when the sun shines, it shines for everyone.
People attract people. A crowd brings a crowd. Today the customer might eat a cassoulet, tomorrow he will have pizza or couscous. And then there is Maison Empereur, France's oldest hardware store, open since 1827, which sells kitchen utensils. There are people who come to Noailles just for this shop. You can buy everything there that you can't find anywhere else. Sometimes I go inside, I walk around, and it gives me ideas. There are knives you can't get elsewhere. It is a place that is truly part of Noailles.

When you cook for your family and friends . . .
I very rarely cook at home. I assure you. My wife does the cooking. At home, we eat pasta, *briks*, chorba [an Algerian stew] and other Algerian dishes. And couscous, I can eat it anywhere as long as it looks a bit like mine and isn't greasy. Recently I went to the Kouss-Kouss festival at Friche la Belle de Mai and I tasted one that Sébastien Richard made.
It was very, very good. Whether in Marseille, Algiers, Constantine or Paris, I can eat any dish if it isn't greasy. You add fat to cook, you need it, but when it's served, the fat must have disappeared.

How would you summarise Marseille gastronomy?
The whole world is in Marseille. You can eat all the dishes in the world here. You can eat couscous, Senegalese, Ivorian, Provençal, or at an Italian pizzeria. The people of Marseille know that in Noailles, all the world's cuisines are here. Sometimes one can be apprehensive about coming to Marseille, but once you're here, you're fine. In Noailles and Marseille, one is quickly accepted. You have to talk, chat with others. You can engage easily here.

What would the smell of Marseille be?
It would be couscous and bouillabaisse. And if you want a third, pizza. For that matter, the fishmongers at the Vieux-Port must be preserved. There are less and less of them. There are families who have been there for four or five generations. You know . . . couscous, it came through there too! It arrived by sea. Bouillabaisse and couscous arrived via the port.

So, this couscous recipe, will you give it to me?
I will give it to you, but I'll keep my secret safe. The secret is here [he taps his heart]. It's heart and passion.

BARLEY COUSCOUS

INGREDIENTS FOR 4

300g lamb neck cut into large chunks
300g barley semolina
2 tbsp olive oil for the semolina and some olive oil for the cooking
1 tsp *smen* (fermented butter)
1 glass of water (30 cl) for the semolina
50-100g lentils
50-100g each, dried white and black beans, soaked the night before
50-100g potatoes
50-100g carrots cut into chunks
50-100g dried chickpeas, soaked for 2 days before
2 onions, chopped
2 celery stalks, finely diced
2 red peppers, finely diced
4 tomatoes (not canned), diced
2 whole garlic cloves, peeled
A few sprigs of coriander
Ground paprika
Ground cumin
Salt and pepper

Couscous is made in several steps. Don't hesitate to start making it the day before. It has to simmer for 3-4 hours.

1. Moisten the barley semolina with water and olive oil and finish with a bit of fermented butter (*smen*). Keep some olive oil, water and *smen* for later.
Work the grains between the palms of your hands to separate them.
Pour water into the base of a *couscoussier* (large double boiler). Once boiling, put the barley semolina in the colander of the *couscoussier*. Steam for around 5 minutes. Rinse the semolina with water. Drain. Add a little olive oil and work the semolina with your hands. It will fluff up. Steam it again for 15 minutes. Repeat the process, adding more water and olive oil. Steam for 20 minutes. Add salt and the rest of the fermented butter to the semolina and work with your hands.

2. Cook the lentils, white beans, black beans, potatoes, carrots and chickpeas separately in boiling water until tender. With couscous, you should never cook all the ingredients at the same time. It's a mistake everyone makes. The ingredients don't all have the same cooking time – between 30 and 45 minutes, depending.

3. In a large, heavy-bottomed pot or *couscoussier*, heat a bit of olive oil and brown half the onion, celery, red pepper and garlic, then add half the coriander and tomatoes, together with some salt and pepper.
Next, add, in this order, the chickpeas, lentils, beans, carrots and potatoes, and let it simmer.

4. In another large pan, brown the lamb in a little olive oil, with the remaining onion, celery, red pepper, garlic, coriander and tomatoes. Add salt, pepper, paprika and cumin. Cover with water to let simmer as long as necessary – 3-4 hours – like a Provençal *daube* (beef stew).

At the end, mix the two preparations and serve on top of the semolina in a shallow bowl.

Lilian Gadola

MÄNNEDORF-MARSEILLE

Cheffe Marine Crousnillon from the excellent La Fabriquerie (the gourmet market, wine shop, and delicious takeway) strongly advised me to climb the steep Cours Julien stairs to Limmat where, according to her, I would find the true Marseille cuisine of the moment: generous, full of flavours and colours, seemingly simple, and so lively! I did not hesitate for two seconds, and I went back several times, including one unforgettable Kouss-Kouss festival day when I ate bowls of couscous one after the other in many restaurants. All the dishes are spot on. And what's most impressive is that this Swiss female chef, like so many women who cook, whether professionally or not, is a force of work ethic and organisation. Often the only one in the kitchen, Lili stays calm and even finds the time to greet customers at the tables. I can think of a few male chefs that should follow her lead. Her partner supports her and often pitches in in the early morning to spiff up the place after the quarter's late-night festivities. It's worth mentioning that there aren't many people who would dare open a restaurant in the middle of this stairway. But Lili did!

Mediterranean cuisine, light, generous, and veggie-friendly

41 Rue Estelle
13001 Marseille

I grew up in Männedorf, a village on the shores of Lake Zurich in Switzerland. I arrived in Marseille in 2017. I spent two months here in 2014 and since then, I wanted to move here. I adored this city, its joyful atmosphere, the laid-back people, the cultural and culinary richness, the sea, the sun, the light. Cours Julien, where I opened Limmat, is a popular neighbourhood that is lively both day and night, showing both the good and bad sides of Marseille. This city is like a promising cocktail, I see so much of its potential that isn't (yet) discovered! The culinary scene is diverse, enticing, bubbly. I like to go to little Maghreb, African or Asian restaurants. Fish, couscous, *fleur d'oranger* [orange-flower water], spices, fresh herbs . . . so many ingredients embody Marseille!

Originally, my cooking did not have many ties to the city because I grew up in Switzerland with a lot of butter and cream! My *omi* [grandmother] made the best cakes, but I've found they are even better with less sugar! Mediterranean cuisine suits me better, it's lighter, but just as delicious. I love cooking fish, anything from the sea in general, good fruits and vegetables from the region, selecting products from sustainable farmers and fishermen, and respecting seasonality and local distribution channels. People often tell me that I cook 'just like at home'. To me, that's a nice compliment! I cook simple and comforting food. I like traditional dishes, whether it's a potato dish from the Swiss mountains, a Sicilian pasta, or a Tunisian couscous. More and more, I'm discovering how to cook with spices, which I rarely did before moving to Marseille. You inevitably create a bond with this city when you are curious!

VEGETARIAN COUSCOUS

1. For the butternut and potato balls: preheat the oven to 180°C/gas mark 4. Peel the potatoes and cube into 1cm pieces. Do the same with the butternut.

2. Mix the butternut and potato cubes in a bowl with a bit of olive oil, salt, pepper and cumin. Spread them out on a baking sheet covered in parchment paper. Bake in the oven, stirring regularly, until the veggies are soft and golden brown, around 30 minutes. Let cool.

3. Chop the onion, garlic, parsley and coriander. Mix all by hand in a big bowl with the cooked vegetables. Add a bit of lemon zest and juice, then more cumin, salt and pepper if you like.

4. Shape the balls in your hands, about 5cm in diameter, and place them on a baking sheet covered in parchment paper. Drizzle with olive oil and bake at 180°C/gas mark 4 for around 20 minutes until they are browned and crisp.

5. For the couscous: peel the potatoes and carrots. Cut the potatoes, carrots, squash and courgette into large chunks.

6. Caramelize the onions and garlic in a large saucepan (*une marmite*) with olive oil. Add the spices and whole pepper (the pepper can be removed when you want) and lightly salt. Add the potatoes, carrots, squash, and enough water to cover the vegetables.

7. Grate (or finely chop) the tomatoes and add them to the pan with a bit of chopped coriander and dill for even more flavour. Let simmer. After 10 minutes, add the chickpeas and courgettes. Let simmer until the vegetables are softened and the stock has been reduced. Adjust the seasoning and add fresh herbs to serve.

8. Prepare the semolina shortly before serving. Place in a large saucepan with a lid. Boil 300ml of salted water separately. Mix with the garlic and olive oil. Pour the hot mixture on top of the semolina. Let rest for 5 minutes. Fluff gently with two forks.

INGREDIENTS FOR 4

For the butternut and potato balls:
300g butternut squash
300g floury potatoes
Olive oil
1 tbsp ground cumin
1 yellow onion
1 garlic clove
1 handful of parsley
1 handful of coriander
1 organic lemon
Salt and pepper

For the vegetarian couscous:
2 potatoes
2 carrots
1 small piece of squash
1 courgette
2 onions, chopped
2 garlic cloves, chopped
Olive oil
1 cinnamon stick
2 tsp ras el-hanout spice mix
1 tsp caraway seeds
1 tsp ground cumin
1 mild green chilli pepper
3 tomatoes
1 handful of dill
1 handful of coriander
100g chickpeas, cooked

For the couscous:
300g fine/medium semolina
1 garlic clove, crushed
3 tbsp olive oil

Sarah Chougnet-Strudel

LA NOUVELLE STAR

It was Chef Emmanuel Perrodin who introduced me to Sarah Chougnet one summer day in 2020 at the Grandes Tables de la Criée (the restaurant at the theatre of the same name). The two chefs were cooking that evening on the terrace alongside the Vieux-Port. The second night I saw her, she was a cooking duo with Cheffe Georgiana Viou, then a third time for a 'four-hands' with Cheffe Laëtitia Visse of La Femme du Boucher. Freshly landed in Marseille with the desire to stay here, Sarah immediately threw herself into the deep end with all her concentration, precision and seriousness. It's true that you learn to tame Marseille on the job, by practising here, and at the same time Marseille cuisine needs top talents to grow (Sarah was head of her class at esteemed Parisian culinary school, Ferrandi).
Sarah passed her integration year with flying colours, so was able to open her own restaurant very quickly here. With the complicity of her partner Lucien Salomon, an ex-Parisian who I find is always in a good mood, Sarah has hidden her bistro behind the bustling La Plaine square, on a street where, yet again, no Marseillais would have imagined one day going to dinner. Regain's immediate success allows me to say, 'Now, Sarah and Lucien, it's time to take a deep breath because a Michelin star is not far off. Relax.'

Original bistro cuisine

53 Rue Saint-Pierre
13005 Marseille

MY FIRST STEPS
My father arrived in Marseille in 2011 [*Author's note: Jean-François Chougnet was the president of Mucem, Museum of European and Mediterranean Civilisations, from 2014 to 2022*]. I fell in love at first sight with Marseille. Nine years later, it was my turn to settle down.

MY FIRST CULINARY MEMORY
Panisses at the end of the afternoon in L'Estaque.

MARSEILLE'S APPEAL
It's bursting with energy.

MY DESIRE TO COOK IN MARSEILLE
To be closer to ingredients, between land and sea.

MY FAVOURITE QUARTER
Noailles, without a doubt, for the omnipresence of all things food related: the scents of herbs and spices, and the temptation, at each store, to stop and taste new things.

A RESTAURANT THAT HAS PARTICULAR MEANING TO ME
La Boîte à Sardine, where I discovered rouget [red mullet] *à la marseillaise* (just grilled whole with its liver.) Their chef, Céline Bonnieu, cooks it like that.

AN ENCOUNTER
For his essential role that he played in my move to Marseille, Emmanuel Perrodin, the most Marseillais of roving chefs, who impresses me with his incredible knowledge of the city, but also by his utterly personal cuisine that is so imbued with his relationship with art.

A DISCOVERY
Ourea, on Rue de la Paix-Marcel-Paul, an enchanting cuisine with marvellous wine.

A SCENT THAT SYMBOLISES MARSEILLE
The scent of fig leaves that accompanies my ambles in town.

A CULINARY CLICHÉ THAT I ADORE
Pastis. I love it!

MY PROJECT IN MARSEILLE
Regain, a place that pairs wine with local ingredients that I opened in October 2021, on the Rue Saint-Pierre, with my partner Lucien Salomon, a natural wine specialist.

MY RECIPE FOR THE BOOK
A couscous created for the 2020 Kouss-Kouss Festival that marries two emblematic Mediterranean ingredients (clams and bluefin tuna) with couscous classics (semolina, bouillon and spices).

COUSCOUS WITH BLUEFIN TUNA PASTRAMI, CLAMS, CHERMOULA SAUCE, CARAMELISED TOMATOES AND RAW COURGETTES

INGREDIENTS FOR 4

For the pastrami:
60g fine salt
65g brown sugar
200g bluefin tuna loin
2 bay leaves
3g pink peppercorns
2 cloves
2g coriander seeds, crushed
2g fennel seeds, crushed
2g black peppercorns, crushed
10g ras el-hanout spice mix
1 bunch of rosemary

For the broth:
Olive oil
1 onion, cut into chunks
1 garlic clove, cut into chunks
20g fresh ginger, cut into chunks
1 tbsp tomato purée
Vegetable scraps: carrot peel, green part of leeks, fennel stalks (or 1 good-quality vegetable stock cube)
1 bird's eye chilli, cut into thirds
1 tbsp ras el-hanout spice mix
200g fishbones
A few stems of parsley and coriander
Harissa (optional)

For the chermoula sauce:
1 soft-boiled egg
2 garlic cloves, chopped
10g fresh ginger, chopped
2 preserved lemons, roughly chopped
1 tsp cayenne pepper
1 tsp ras el-hanout spice mix
2 pinches of fine salt
200ml grapeseed oil
¼ bunch of parsley, coriander and mint
Juice of 1 lemon

For the garnish:
250g cherry tomatoes
Olive oil
1 tbsp caster sugar
2 yellow courgettes
1 bunch of spring onions
1 garlic clove, finely chopped
1 preserved lemon, finely diced
Juice of 1 lemon
600g clams
Fresh herbs

For the couscous:
300g semolina

1. The bluefin tuna pastrami must be made at least 5 days before. It can be replaced by slices of beef pastrami.
To make the brine, whisk the salt and brown sugar to dissolve them completely in 1 litre of water. Place the tuna loin in a shallow dish with the bay leaves, pink peppercorns and cloves. Cover with brine, and leave in the refrigerator for a minimum of 40 hours.
Drain the tuna loin and roll it in the spices. Place the rosemary in the base of your *couscoussier* (large double boiler), then the tuna loin in the upper section. Light the rosemary and immediately cover with a lid. Leave the tuna all afternoon, you can re-ignite the rosemary every half hour or so.
The ideal is to then let the tuna dry in the refrigerator wrapped in a tea towel for 3 days. On the couscous day, finely slice the pastrami with a knife.

2. For the broth: heat a little olive oil in a pan and brown the onion, garlic and ginger, tomato purée, vegetable scraps, bird's eye chilli and ras el-hanout. Add the fishbones, cover with water, bring to the boil, then let simmer for 30 minutes, skimming regularly.
Add the herb stems, turn off the heat, and let infuse for 20 or so minutes. Strain the bouillon through a fine strainer, then season with fine salt, plus harissa if you like things spicier.

3. For the chermoula sauce, put the egg, chopped garlic and ginger, spices, the fine salt and the preserved lemons in a blender. Blend at high speed. Gradually add the oil and emulsify the sauce like a mayonnaise. Lastly, add herbs (coriander, parsley and mint leaves) and the lemon juice. Adjust the seasoning and refrigerate.

4. For the garnish: caramelise the cherry tomatoes over very low heat in olive oil with the salt and sugar.
Cut the courgettes into small 2cm cubes. Finely chop the spring onions. Dress the raw courgettes like a salad, with the chopped garlic, preserved lemon, spring onions, a drizzle of olive oil, the lemon juice and some salt.

5. Prepare the couscous: put the semolina and some salt in a large bowl, moisten with 5 tablespoons of broth, stir, then add 1 tablespoon of olive oil and mix until the semolina is moistened. Pour the grains into the upper part of a *couscoussier* or steamer, cover, and steam for 5 minutes. Pour the partially cooked semolina back into the large bowl, fluff up with a fork, and moisten again with 5 tablespoons of broth, toss, add 1 tablespoon of olive oil and toss again. Put back in the steamer and cook for 5 minutes. Remove the semolina, fluff up, and serve hot.
While cooking the semolina, open up the clams in heavily salted boiling water, remove them onto a plate, and cover to keep warm.

6. Serve immediately in shallow bowls, putting the courgette salad in the bottom of the plate, then covering it with couscous, arranging the pastrami slices, a few caramelised tomatoes, clams, a tablespoon of chermoula sauce, and finely chopped fresh herbs. Serve the broth on the side.

Claire Lombard, Annaëlle N'Kaoua, Estelle Billet, and Laura Guemeche

EN BANDE ORGANISÉE

(AS IN MARSEILLE'S FAMOUS RAP TITLE)

Mediterranean lunch canteen

9 Rue d'Aubagne
13001 Marseille

'*Nine*', pronounced '*neeneu*' is an unambiguously affectionate way to address girls in Marseille. Just as '*minots*' or '*pitchounes*' mean 'kids'; '*ma gâtée*' means 'my darling'; '*peucheure*' is 'poor thing' . . . and so on. We have our own language around here, a mix of Provençal, Italian, Arab and the local creative extravaganza that Marseillais have a lot of fun with.
Les 4 nines here come from Aix (that's it, the world has gone pear-shaped, and pigs are flying if Marseille's southern rival has landed here), Grenoble, London and even Lourdes. They got around before choosing Marseille.
Their freshly refurbished nest (Maison des Nines) in the heart of Noailles first gave everyone a fright, then we went in there, we asked questions, we had lunch there, we discovered what a real perfume bar could be . . . and finally we adopted this lively place where you can pass by and chat without necessarily having to open your wallet. At the start of the adventure, there was Claire, Estelle, and Annaëlle but recently Annaëlle has decided to forge her own path. Meanwhile, Laura joined the band along the way as their chef. These sunny, neo-Marseillaises (aka the new kids on the block) speak with everyone without being 'know-it-all, been there, done that' types, which is very rare lately, especially in the district of Noailles.

Who are you?
I'm Claire, born in Paris. I lived in Toulouse then in London where I worked in finance. Here, I'm in charge of the canteen. Coming from London, where I lived in Brixton, a vibrant cultural, artistic, multi-ethnic neighbourhood that is very Caribbean, I had a particular predilection for coffee shops, finger food, delicious affordable restaurants, global cuisine . . .

I'm Estelle, born in Grenoble. I lived in Paris and then abroad a lot before coming back to Marseille. I worked for ten or so years in the perfume business. In Marseille, I began with a pop-up dedicated to perfumes, that's how I met Claire, and at Maison des Nines, I run the shop, a selection of brands spread between niche perfumes, eco-friendly clothing, and jewellery.

I'm Laura, the chef here, born in Toulouse. I lived near Lourdes, where I did a professional baccalaureate in tapestry, then I landed in Nîmes to study applied arts at university, but I didn't like it. I decided to get a vocational certificate in cooking. I apprenticed in Nîmes, then I took a chef job for four years at Maison Villaret, a renowned boulangerie-patisserie there. For the last two or three years I've lived in Marseille.

I'm Annaëlle, I come from Aix-en-Provence. A few years ago, if you lived in Aix, you never came to Marseille. Not much was happening here before 2013. It was the Marseillais who came to see us in Aix. Restaurants, parties, nightclubs were all in Aix (*Author's note: for a Marseillais, Aix is Paris of the South meaning a snobbish town where people behave as if they have richer blood*). I did part of my studies in Lyon in management and communication, then I went to work in Paris in a communications agency, then in events. For Maison des Nines, I organised offsite events, welcomed guest chefs once a month, like Simon Auscher, Delphine Roux, Thomas Graham…

Why Marseille?

Claire: Because of Brexit, I was sent to Frankfurt in Germany, and at that point, I preferred to return to France and not necessarily Paris. I came very often to see friends in Marseille and it was love at first sight. I fell in love with my boyfriend here, too, and he adored Marseille. It was head over heels for him as well. In London, there is a strong sense of freedom, you can be who you are, have many personalities, and I found that again in Marseille, this mix. And here, the principal activity, the sea, is free. Everyone meets up on the rocks by the sea. Third reason: in England, you put the emphasis on projects. If a project doesn't work, it's a step, it's not viewed as a failure. In France, it isn't like that but in Marseille it is. The rents are less expensive, the investments are less sizable, so you take less risk. All this really spoke to me in relation to my personal/life-changing project. Here, I didn't feel judged if it didn't work. The first time that I came here, I bought an apartment. I still had a job in London and came here every three weeks. I immediately met artists who launched projects and who said, 'we try and we'll see.' The city is changing but there are still so many things to do! I'm very optimistic. The city of all possible, it's here.

Estelle: I wanted to go to business school. When I came to Marseille to do my interviews at the local renowned business school, KEDGE, I said to myself, 'Oh la la, Marseille, no way.' I really wanted to go to the one in Bordeaux, but I didn't get in. So, I came to study in Marseille instead in 2014. The school is right above the Calanques! I lived in four different districts, I saw the city really change, under construction, and in the end, I adored Marseille. Then, I left to work, mainly in Paris. When I asked myself about leaving the world of perfume, and luxury – which didn't suit me because we didn't talk at all about the product – I mused about which city I'd like to live in. Marseille is the second-largest city in France and there isn't a benchmark parfumerie. There are two in Bordeaux, one in Toulouse . . . there wasn't any reason that Marseille didn't have one. I saw an opportunity. The city is becoming more and more attractive but the businesses in Noailles remain independent, and there are a lot of female entrepreneurs . . .

Annaëlle: I landed in Marseille a bit by accident, and I didn't like it at first. When you come to Marseille, you ask yourself, 'WTF?'
In all other cities, you have a city centre, but note here.
Then, people in Marseille aren't ashamed of saying that they work a little or not, that they take advantage of life, that they live by doing small jobs. It's cultural here to say 'let's take it easy' and enjoy the day to day. In Paris, you must show that you start early and you finish late . . . that you have a relentless rhythm.

Vérane: I am sure people here tell you that you work too much . . .

Annaëlle: And they are right! Today, I love this city, I feel integrated in Marseille life, integrated in the circle of Marseille business and restaurant owners. We've had really cool encounters, there is mutual aid. There is a network that came to us, and that was brilliant. Marianne Tiberghien, the true godmother of local businesses around here, comes to see all of us, gives us news . . .

Vérane: Today, can you say, 'I'm Marseillaise?'

Annaëlle: Yes! I feel way more Marseillaise than Aixoise! But here, as in Aix, anonymity is impossible. When you leave your house, you can't go 2 metres without encountering an acquaintance or someone who knows someone who knows you.

Laura: After Covid, I found myself working as a pastry chef at Pâtisserie Villaret in Nîmes and I had to wake up at 4am. It didn't suit me at all! My friends had gone to Marseille. I was going back and forth to see them . . . it was time to make the leap to Marseille. The first time I came here, I thought it was a bit of a mess! Everything is jumbled up, it's not coherent, there's a Louis Vuitton store next to a tiny Chinese restaurant, but because of that everyone mixes. I love it. I have never seen such a dirty city, but I don't care. And I have never seen a neighbourhood like Noailles anywhere else. People recognise you, know you, and I think it's great.

What dish has wowed you since you moved here?

Claire: The vitello tonnato at Il Capriolo, it's delicious. The pélamide carpaccio that Lili makes at Limmat, which I fall for every time, and Emki Pop's black sesame ice cream that I eat with a little cake.

Laura: The first time I came to Marseille, I got an aioli sandwich at Pain à l'Ail, which does Provençal street food, and it was incredible. I had never eaten aioli in my life. Since then, I go twice a month, at least. And I love the aubergine Parmigiana at Chez Étienne. They bake it in a wood-fired oven. I can't do the same!

Annaëlle: You're right, it's insane!

Laura: And then, just next door at L'Idéal, I ate an ice cream that they made themselves with Roellinger spices [Roellinger is a top quality spice mix made by Breton chef Roellinger) and it was *trop bon* (so good), served with caramelised focaccia French toast . . . just incredible!

Estelle: My favourite is the restaurant l'Arôme. You won't be disappointed by it, ever, especially in winter.

What is missing in Marseille?

Claire: A real cultural calendar that brings together all the events that are so numerous today.

MY FAMILY'S COUSCOUS

BY CHEFFE LAURA GUEMECHE

'At my house in the morning, it smelled of crepes, of waffles, there was always a cake to snack on. We ate all kinds of food. My mum is Kabyle and my dad is Lebanese. We didn't eat Algerian or Lebanese all the time, but, in the end, these two influences were quite similar. As for me, I like cooking with coriander, harissa, but I also like cooking Asian dishes.'

Laura plays with an original global cuisine. Very diverse flavours and proper seasoning distinguish her dishes. The Turkish egg on labneh with paprika butter or the Iranian pancake with herbs, cranberries, nuts, bread and eggs are part of the team's top 10. It's a generous cuisine with a bonus, a love for patisserie and a passion - chocolate! Her mum forbade mass-produced supermarket biscuits and cakes at home. We are so lucky!

For the 2022 Kouss-Kouss Festival, Laura served her family's couscous.

'Couscous is my great-grandmother's dish. I can still see her making it. Then, it was my grandfather's, then my mum's . . . I'd watch them make it. We had a family home in the Pyrenees, where my grandfather, my uncle and my great-grandmother lived. I lived 50 metres away.
The village had a population of 250 people, of whom 40 were part of my family! For the festival, I recreated the flavours of this couscous thanks to my mum who made me a spec sheet! I don't know what's special about it because I've always refused to eat couscous anywhere else.
I know that normally in couscous, you only put one kind of meat, but we also add merguez sausages in my family. Once my grandfather even added kidneys cooked in butter, it was *trop bon*.'

MY GREAT-GRANDMOTHER HADDAH'S BOUILLON

INGREDIENTS FOR 4

300g lamb neck
200g rack of lamb, separated
2 onions, chopped
1 red pepper, coarsely chopped
80g butter
4 tbsp olive oil
1 can tomato paste (200 g)
1 tbsp yellow ras el-hanout
1 tbsp red ras el-hanout
1 tsp allspice
1 tsp paprika
1 large, long turnip
4 carrots
2 celery stalks
2 large courgettes, cut into rounds
1 medium can chickpeas (100g-200g)
1 bunch of fresh coriander
Salt and pepper

280g medium semolina
Olive oil
140g butter
Sultanas (optional)

1. For the bouillon: in a *couscoussier* (large double boiler), brown the meat, onions and red pepper, with some salt and pepper, in the butter and olive oil, until everything takes on a nice golden colour.

2. Once everything is well browned, add the tomato paste and all the spices (toast them in advance for more flavour!). Moisten with 4 litres of water. Bring to the boil, add the turnip, carrots, then celery, all cut into sticks (3cm wide and 2 finger knuckles long). Leave to simmer for 3 hours.

3. After 2½ hours of cooking, add the courgettes and chickpeas. Continue to cook for 30 minutes. Finish with a bouquet of chopped fresh coriander!

4. How to cook couscous semolina: place the uncooked semolina in the *couscoussier* basket, moisten to the top with water, strain, add a drizzle of olive oil and some salt, and steam for 8 minutes.

5. After 8 minutes, put the semolina in a large bowl and break it up by adding cold water and rubbing the grains together in your hands, then steam again for 8 minutes. Put the semolina back in the bowl then add the butter and break it up again by hand. You should end up with a fluffy couscous. At this point, you can add sultanas. I love them!

MY MUM'S LAMB AND MINT MEATBALLS, SAUCE BLANCHE WITH DATES AND CORIANDER

INGREDIENTS FOR 4

For the meatballs:
400g minced lamb
1 red onion, thinly sliced
1 bunch of mint, chopped
1 tbsp cumin
3 garlic cloves, crushed
Salt
Flour for dusting
Olive oil for frying

For the sauce:
200g Greek yoghurt
3-4 Medjool dates
½ bunch of coriander
1 tbsp sumac
Juice of 1 lemon
Salt

1. For the meatballs: mix all the ingredients together and shape into 30-40g meatballs. Dust them in flour. Brown the meatballs in olive oil. Me, I don't like to cook them too much so that they remain moist!

2. For the sauce: blend all the ingredients until they are a beautiful green. Set aside. Eat the meatballs dipped in the sauce. A delight!

3. A little tip: my mum prefers meatballs cooked in olive oil then simmered in a saucepan together with 2 ladles of broth, a can of crushed tomatoes and chopped coriander.

4. Add the 'Meatballs of my Childhood' to your couscous!

MY UNCLE KARIM'S CARAMELISED CHICKEN WINGS

INGREDIENTS FOR 4

8 chicken wings
1 tsp sumac
1 tsp cumin
1 tbsp paprika
1 tsp turmeric
3 garlic cloves, crushed
Salt
Olive oil
Juice of 2 lemons

1. Marinate the chicken wings with the spices and garlic, without oil or lemon juice. Mix well and leave in the refrigerator for at least 2 hours (the night before is always better!). Once the wings are well marinated, add the liquids, then bake at 120°C/gas mark ½ for 3 hours. Feel free to baste during cooking. After 3 hours, you will have chicken wings that melt in your mouth. Pure pleasure! Eat them with your hands, it's the best!

2. The rest of the recipe is to be eaten with a soup spoon!

3. One last thing. My grandfather's instructions: 'Laura! You are surely not going to drink water while eating couscous! It makes your stomach swell and in 2 hours you'll be hungry!' And he was right: 2 hours later my mum would make me a bowl of semolina with sugar . . . delicious . . . the choice is yours!

EAT FOR YOUR COUNTRY!

Attention! When in Marseille, don't go looking for the Luberon, the polished Provence with pristine villages where rich Parisians decorate their holiday homes as if Condé Nast Traveller was planning a photo shoot there. Marseille is Marcel Pagnol's Provence. Quite a different story. Think Peter Mayle mixed with Elena Ferrante's Neapolitan Italy.

First rule: we speak loudly at the table, all at the same time. In between bites, we fight over French politics or football and one must take sides. I think that's what I miss the most in my London life – the fact that no one argues around the table, no one is for or against tea. British people all seem to agree that tea is lovely.

Second rule: we eat our weight in food to be polite, though hardly ever manage to finish off the dishes. The home cook prepares too much food as over-budget generosity is ingrained in our Mediterranean DNA when catering for family or friends. Then we usually eat the leftovers for days until vastly bored with that menu.

And if your Marseille host feels at ease having you at the table, the one detail that will signify the intensity of your friendship is the table layout. If not one plate matches another, nor the chairs, the glasses, the silverware . . . you're definitely part of the family! It's got nothing to do with a fondness for antique fairs. It's simply that our cupboards are filled with a mix of what our grandmothers inherited from their grandmothers. Nothing goes to the bin ever and beautiful brand-new plates and glasses are kept for special occasions that never happen or for foreigners we want to impress.

The following recipes are a very personal selection, memories of my childhood Sundays or, particularly, festive family lunches where after the meals while the grown-ups would take their *sieste*, I trudged for hours with my cousins and my sister in the hills of Allauch around the Garlaban massif.

There we swam in old rainwater basins and ate fruit from the trees. The grandmas would starve petit-gris snails to prep them for cooking or prepare rabbits, and Grandpa Dédé would set traps for thrushes, the small game birds adored by local hunters. I can just hear fans of vegan honey crying foul, but if we don't contextualise Provence, it becomes a fictitious postcard like in American films.

My Provence, she is indeed real.

It's Provence, Marseille-style . . .

04

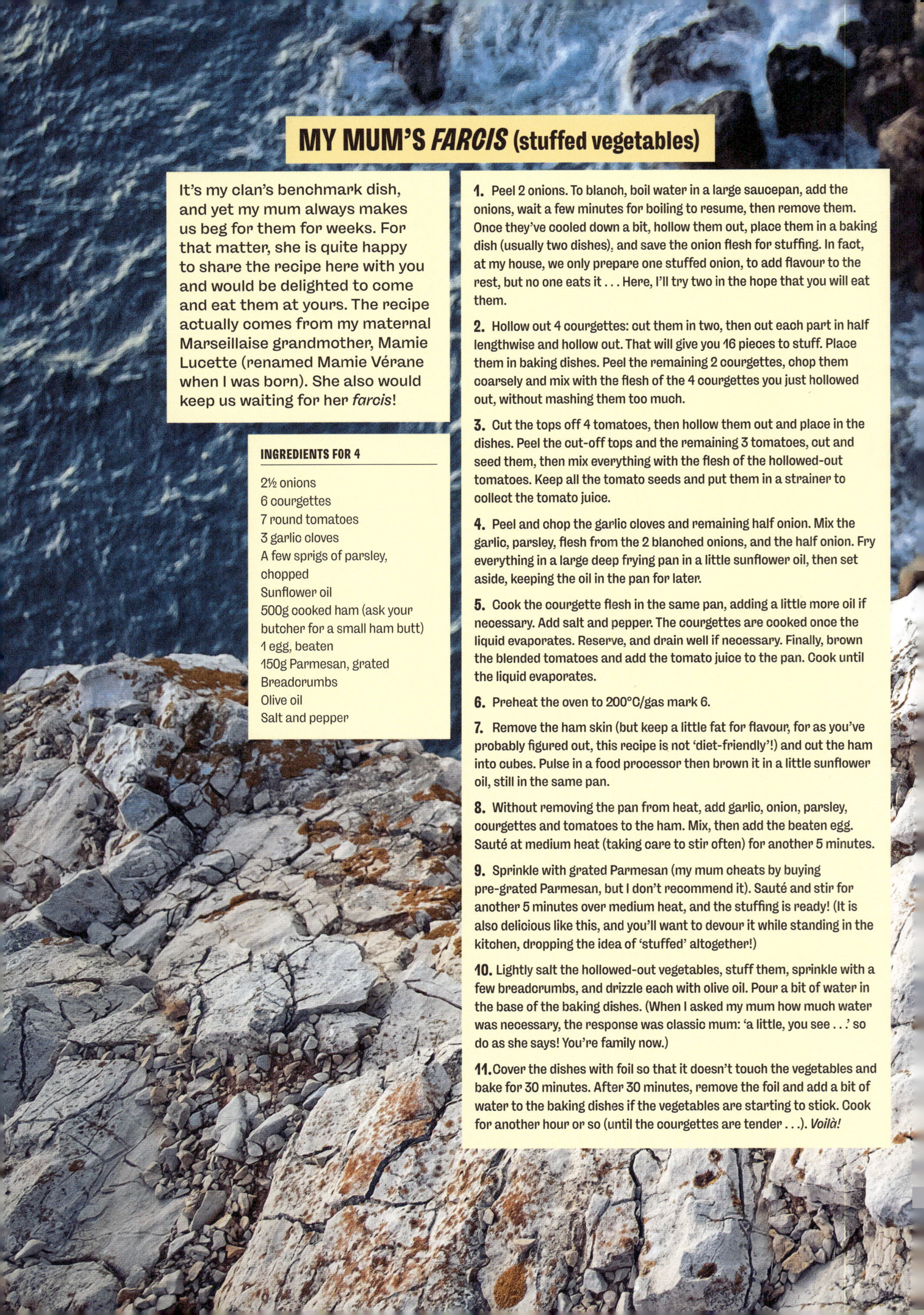

MY MUM'S *FARCIS* (stuffed vegetables)

It's my clan's benchmark dish, and yet my mum always makes us beg for them for weeks. For that matter, she is quite happy to share the recipe here with you and would be delighted to come and eat them at yours. The recipe actually comes from my maternal Marseillaise grandmother, Mamie Lucette (renamed Mamie Vérane when I was born). She also would keep us waiting for her *farcis*!

INGREDIENTS FOR 4

2½ onions
6 courgettes
7 round tomatoes
3 garlic cloves
A few sprigs of parsley, chopped
Sunflower oil
500g cooked ham (ask your butcher for a small ham butt)
1 egg, beaten
150g Parmesan, grated
Breadcrumbs
Olive oil
Salt and pepper

1. Peel 2 onions. To blanch, boil water in a large saucepan, add the onions, wait a few minutes for boiling to resume, then remove them. Once they've cooled down a bit, hollow them out, place them in a baking dish (usually two dishes), and save the onion flesh for stuffing. In fact, at my house, we only prepare one stuffed onion, to add flavour to the rest, but no one eats it . . . Here, I'll try two in the hope that you will eat them.

2. Hollow out 4 courgettes: cut them in two, then cut each part in half lengthwise and hollow out. That will give you 16 pieces to stuff. Place them in baking dishes. Peel the remaining 2 courgettes, chop them coarsely and mix with the flesh of the 4 courgettes you just hollowed out, without mashing them too much.

3. Cut the tops off 4 tomatoes, then hollow them out and place in the dishes. Peel the cut-off tops and the remaining 3 tomatoes, cut and seed them, then mix everything with the flesh of the hollowed-out tomatoes. Keep all the tomato seeds and put them in a strainer to collect the tomato juice.

4. Peel and chop the garlic cloves and remaining half onion. Mix the garlic, parsley, flesh from the 2 blanched onions, and the half onion. Fry everything in a large deep frying pan in a little sunflower oil, then set aside, keeping the oil in the pan for later.

5. Cook the courgette flesh in the same pan, adding a little more oil if necessary. Add salt and pepper. The courgettes are cooked once the liquid evaporates. Reserve, and drain well if necessary. Finally, brown the blended tomatoes and add the tomato juice to the pan. Cook until the liquid evaporates.

6. Preheat the oven to 200°C/gas mark 6.

7. Remove the ham skin (but keep a little fat for flavour, for as you've probably figured out, this recipe is not 'diet-friendly'!) and cut the ham into cubes. Pulse in a food processor then brown it in a little sunflower oil, still in the same pan.

8. Without removing the pan from heat, add garlic, onion, parsley, courgettes and tomatoes to the ham. Mix, then add the beaten egg. Sauté at medium heat (taking care to stir often) for another 5 minutes.

9. Sprinkle with grated Parmesan (my mum cheats by buying pre-grated Parmesan, but I don't recommend it). Sauté and stir for another 5 minutes over medium heat, and the stuffing is ready! (It is also delicious like this, and you'll want to devour it while standing in the kitchen, dropping the idea of 'stuffed' altogether!)

10. Lightly salt the hollowed-out vegetables, stuff them, sprinkle with a few breadcrumbs, and drizzle each with olive oil. Pour a bit of water in the base of the baking dishes. (When I asked my mum how much water was necessary, the response was classic mum: 'a little, you see . . .' so do as she says! You're family now.)

11. Cover the dishes with foil so that it doesn't touch the vegetables and bake for 30 minutes. After 30 minutes, remove the foil and add a bit of water to the baking dishes if the vegetables are starting to stick. Cook for another hour or so (until the courgettes are tender . . .). *Voilà!*

This is a recipe from the cooking heroine of my childhood, Aunt Yvette, an excellent cook with a solid reputation in the village of Allauch. Custodian of our grandmothers' recipes, Yvette is the only one to have them all down on paper. But, for the book, it was my husband who put himself up to the challenge to cook my grandmothers' famous stuffed artichokes. Yvette was on the phone to guide him. I was in charge of photographs and eating them! I feel the recipe is in safe hands now.

ARTICHAUTS FARCIS

(stuffed artichokes)

INGREDIENTS FOR 4

8 medium purple artichokes
1 lemon
3 slices of ham (jambon de Paris)
200g pork belly or unsmoked bacon, diced
300g white mushrooms, cleaned and chopped
2 garlic cloves, finely chopped, germ removed
10 stems of flat parsley, chopped
1 egg
Whole nutmeg, for grating
2 onions, sliced
200ml white wine
Olive oil
Salt and pepper

1. Remove the toughest artichoke leaves, leaving only a few leaves to hold the stuffing. Snip off the top of the leaves, hollow out the heart with a small spoon, removing the fuzzy centre (choke). Immediately squeeze lemon juice over the inside and outside of the artichokes. Set aside.

2. Mix the ham, pork belly or bacon, mushrooms, garlic, and parsley. Mix in the egg to bind the stuffing. Add salt, pepper and grated nutmeg.

3. Fill the artichokes to the brim with stuffing. Save the remaining stuffing.

4. In a flameproof casserole dish, brown the onions in a little olive oil then add 200ml of water, the white wine and the rest of the stuffing. Mix the sauce well and place the artichokes in the casserole. Cover and cook for 1 hour.

5. When my husband tried this recipe at our house, he blended the sauce just before serving. It was . . . such a pure delight that I sopped up every last drop with bread, as the French like to do.

MY AUNT LUCIE'S STUFFED AUBERGINES

Serious cooking began in my family via my maternal Marseillaise great-great-aunt, Aunt Lucie, my great-grandmother's sister. She was the one who really knew how to cook, I was told! Easy-going is not how my mum describes her. This strong old maid ruled the working-class neighbourhood of La Barasse, and local families would hire her to cook their festive dinners. Now, her stuffed aubergines will be made in your kitchen . . . who would have thought it?

INGREDIENTS FOR 6

6-8 aubergines, depending on their size
6-8 garlic cloves
4 tbsp olive oil
1 bunch of parsley, chopped
8-10 ripe tomatoes
About 12 pitted black olives
1 bunch of basil, finely chopped
1 egg, beaten
Breadcrumbs
Salt and pepper

1. Cut off the tops of the aubergines and scoop out their flesh. Peel 1 clove of garlic per aubergine and finely chop.

2. Heat the olive oil in a pan and brown the garlic, aubergine flesh and some of the chopped parsley. Add salt and pepper.

3. Blend 2 or 3 of the tomatoes and add them to the pan with black olives (use 1 or 2 olives per aubergine) and finely chopped basil. Add the egg to bind the mixture together.

4. Preheat the oven to 225°C/gas mark 8. Stuff the aubergines and arrange them in a well-oiled gratin or baking dish.
Cover the stuffed aubergines with tomatoes *à la Provençale* (tomatoes cut in half and topped with a mixture of garlic, parsley and breadcrumbs). The tomatoes need to cook on top of the aubergines. Pour half a glass of water in the bottom of the dish.

5. Cover with foil (be sure the foil doesn't touch the vegetables) and bake for 1½ hours.

R
M S

Endoume,
Les Cinq Avenues
Le Cabot

Clément Higgins

Clément is an inventive pastry chef who, with his partner, Aurélie Pauletto, is leading the dessert revolution in Marseille. The couple opened several sugar-coated boutiques around town and yet, when asked 'What recipe would you like to share in this book?', Clément responded without hesitation, 'My grandmother's, Grandma Armande, recipe for *pieds paquets* [stewed sheep's feet and tripe]!' What else?

LE CHOUCHOU

Neo-patissier

223 Rue d'Endoume - 13007, Endoume
35 Boulevard Philippon - 13004, Cinq-Avenues
53 Boulevard du Cabot - 13009 Le Cabot
Marseille

Which neighbourhood did you grow up in?
By the sea, southern Marseille, in the La Grotte Rolland neighbourhood, right between Montredon and La Madrague, en route to Les Goudes.

Which ingredient reminds you of your childhood in Marseille?
Olives cassées [broken green olives, left to lose their bitterness, washed with water, put in a brine solution and seasoned with fennel seeds, flowers and stalks]. When I was little, I would always have breakfast with my maternal grandfather who lived below my parents. On the menu, *olives cassées*, cured sausage, and lemonade with a splash of rosé.

Would you go out to restaurants with your family when you were little?
Yes. Chez Aldo in La Madrague was where we'd celebrate with my family.

How old were you when you started cooking?
24 years old.

What training did you do?
None. I'm self-taught. I have a Master's in business law.

Which district do you live in today?
In La Grotte Rolland, where I grew up. My partner, Aurélie, and I lived for a few years in the 7th before returning here. I love the small village aspect away from the city and the proximity to the sea and the coves. My parents have lived there for over 40 years and know everyone. I have always found this neighbourhood family-oriented and very pleasant to live in.

Which district do you work in?
We started in 2015 in the Vallon de l'Oriol. Now we are in Endoume, in Cinq Avenues and in Le Cabot.

How have your feelings toward Marseille evolved?
Despite recent developments in the urban planning of certain areas (like near the Mucem museum and the massive Euroméditerranée urban renewal project), I find the northern and southern districts more separated from each other than ever. I also find the north/south divide is particularly exacerbated in the minds of many people I meet, and that's a shame. That said, nothing is being done one way or another to make things better. Lastly, compared to other cities that I've had the opportunity to visit (Bordeaux, Lyon, Lille), I feel that Marseille is quite behind in many sectors (green spaces, nightlife options, cleanliness, etc.). But one must acknowledge that these cities have all had brilliant mayors, which was not the case for us for many years.

What is the link between your food and Marseille?
My pastries are quite atypical and advocate the mixing of flavours and genres. I like to make the great classics as much as very modern pastries. In one sense, they resemble the city: cosmopolitan.

What is the scent or the flavour that symbolises your Marseille today?
The scent of the sea in my favourite season, winter (very different from summer).

Who are the people working in food or catering that you admire in Marseille? Those who intrigue you, or with whom you have a particular bond?
There are too many, I can't list them all. I will only cite two of them: Lionel Levy and Rodolphe Bodikian. Rodolphe was my first chef, at the L'Eau à la Bouche pizzeria, where I worked and where I took on every job in the kitchen. He gave me an appetite for catering. He's someone I am quite fond of. Lionel welcomed me to Gourméditerranée [an association that promotes key players in the Provence food scene] when I was only self-employed and made cakes in a tiny atelier at my parents' house. I presented my work to him in the kitchens at

My pastries are quite atypical and advocate the mixing of flavours and genres.

the fancy Intercontinental Hotel, he trusted me and introduced me to many people in the local food sphere. Then a few years later he did not hesitate to ask me to chair the club of pastry chefs within Gourméditerranée. He's someone I have tremendous respect for. On the supplier side, there are quite a few too! Gilles Baille, who is a farmer and cheesemaker in nearby Trets and with whom I work a lot. In particular, he makes us fresh cheese for our Chizeucake [a Marseille-style cheesecake] and raw milk for our ice cream. His products are phenomenal, and he's a great guy. I'd also mention Alexandre Corsiglia, head of Maison Corsiglia, local Master Confectioner since 1896. Alexandre is a remarkable person who knows his products and the history of his family company by heart. He talks about it with passion. I'm fascinated by this family's history with chestnuts.

Where do you eat in Marseille today?
At Sépia, I love Paul Langlère's cuisine. At Saisons, the plates have a real signature, a cuisine that cannot be found elsewhere – and the price-quality ratio is incredible for a Michelin star restaurant. Chez Paul, Auberge du Corsaire, in Les Goudes, I have been going there for many years. I live right next door. I like the atmosphere and how they serve everything simply without fuss.

Three words to describe Marseille's food scene today?
Dynamic, cosmopolitan, underrated.

According to you, what do people generally overlook about Marseille gastronomy?
That it will become a reference in the same way as Lyonnais or Parisian gastronomy.

What are the Marseillais themselves unaware of in regard to their gastronomy?
That it is no longer necessary to travel across France to discover great restaurants, starred or not.

What do you like to cook for your family?
I'm not a great cook, while Aurélie, my partner, is really talented. But lately I've been experimenting with things, including the latest: a chilli con carne that's way too spicy!

What do you like to cook for your friends?
Cakes! I often use them as guinea pigs to test new things. Otherwise, I like to share a good barbecue with fish that I catch or a nice cut of meat.

Is there a recipe that you and a family member disagree over?
Yes, Aurélie and I don't agree on her favourite patisserie, tarte Tatin. She advocates the use of Canadian Reinette apples on puff pastry while I support the use of golden apples on a shortcrust pastry. That said, she's the one who always bakes it because it is a dessert that I mess up every time!

***Pieds paquets* are my favourite dish, a dish that my grandma makes for each big family event.**

It is a dish that has disappeared in favour of ease and 'trendiness'. However, this dish survives in the nostalgic hearts of many Marseillais and reminds us that one should eat the whole animal if one is eating animal at all.

FOCUS

Battle of the *pieds paquets*

Let's end this chapter with the longest and most complicated recipe, the ultimate Marseille dish . . . and one of my favourites: *pieds paquets*! *Pieds* = sheep feet and tripe; *paquets* = packages.

Popular in Marseille since the end of the 19th century, the recipe was invented in 1880 in the once-rural La Pomme district, at Louis Ginouvès' *restaurant-auberge*. I have serious doubts that this man really invented this hearty labourer's dish, since his restaurant's kitchen, Le Chalet de l'Huveaune, was run by a female chef, Mère Maurel, and we know that creative women have long been erased from history, particularly from the history of French gastronomy. However, what makes these *pieds paquets* so exceptional, was that they were cooked in a wood-fired bakery oven. Now, I can only dream of that!

Why a battle? Because several people that I interviewed for this book spontaneously offered me their *pieds paquets* recipe and I found it surprising, even touching, given that this dish is only very rarely found on the menus of restaurants in Marseille and the region. It is a dish that has disappeared in favour of ease and 'trendiness'. However, this dish survives in the nostalgic hearts of many Marseillais and is here to remind us that one should eat the whole animal if one is eating animal at all.

Since I am one of those people who love the stories behind recipes as well as the recipes, I have decided to share two *belles histoires* (tales) about *pieds paquets* here. The first recipe, I owe to Clément Higgins, renowned co-owner and pastry chef of the Bricoleurs de Douceurs patisseries. I asked him, 'What is the aroma that reminds you of your childhood?' and his response was clear: 'The smell of *pieds paquets* simmering in my maternal grandmother's kitchen. It's my favourite dish that my grandma (Mamie) still cooks for Christmas each year!' I am so honoured to be able to print Mamie Armande's recipe here.

During my cinematic adventure, filming my documentary *À la Recherche des Femmes Chefs (The Goddesses of Food)*, I discovered the names of two iconic female chefs whose restaurants were both on Marseille's Rue Sainte across the street from one other: Suzanne Quaglia, who ran Le Patalain at Nº 49, and Jeannine Moréni, who helmed Échevins at Nº 44 (now the 44 bistro). In the 1980s, 1990s and 2000s, these two self-taught chefs shared the admiration of Marseille gourmands, each in their own restaurant across the street from one other. It turns out that Cheffe Suzanne Quaglia's *pieds paquets* even once won first prize in France!! That just goes to show how precious this recipe is. Her two sons kindly sent it to me. Incidentally, I feel that archiving chefs' and cheffes' recipes in France would be deserving of funding a museum, or something!

MAMIE ARMANDE'S (AKA MAMINOU) PIEDS PAQUETS MARSEILLAIS

INGREDIENTS

1 piece of sheep or lamb tripe will make around 15 *paquets* (packages)
Allow at least 2 sheep feet per person
2 slices of pork belly or unsmoked bacon for each piece of tripe, plus a little extra for the pan
Garlic
1 bunch of parsley
Olive oil
Onions
Carrots
Tomatoes (or tomato purée)
1 bouquet garni (fresh parsley, thyme, bay leaf sprigs)
Freshly grated nutmeg
Juice of 1 orange
Salt and pepper
Boiled potatoes, to serve

1. Rinse and thoroughly dry the tripe then cut into 15 x 8–10cm squares. To each square, add salt, pepper, 2 slices of pork belly/bacon and 1 teaspoon each of chopped garlic and parsley. Make a 'buttonhole' in a corner of each square and pass the opposite corner through it, or tie the packages together with fine string.

2. Put the rind from the pork belly/bacon together with a few pieces of pork in the bottom of a large saucepan and brown in a little oil.

3. Neatly arrange the sheep feet in the bottom of the pan then place the packages on top. Add thinly sliced onions, a few carrots chopped in large chunks, well-ripened tomatoes or tomato purée, the bouquet garni, a little grated nutmeg, and the orange juice. For the first round of cooking, simmer for 2–3 hours over low heat, then cover and let cool.

4. For the second round, you can wait until the next day. You need to cook it for 2–3 hours more and thin down the sauce a bit.

5. You can either now serve your *pieds paquets* with boiled potatoes, or put them in the freezer and bring them out for the holidays. If that's the case, cook the *pieds paquets* for a little longer. They will just get better!

The feature of Armande's *paquets* is that they are very small.

CHEFFE SUZANNE'S
PIEDS PAQUETS MARSEILLAIS
(written by the chef, in 1980s style)

INGREDIENTS FOR 6

2 pieces of sheep tripe, sliced and cleaned (makes 4 packages per person)
6 or 12 sheep feet, well cleaned and flambéed

For the stuffing:
200g tripe trimmings
200g bacon lardons
4 garlic cloves, chopped
4 tbsp chopped parsley

For cooking:
100g salted lard, cut into cubes
2 leeks, sliced white part
200g onions, thinly sliced
1 bouquet garni (sprigs of fresh bay leaf, thyme, parsley, celery)
1 onion, studded with 4 cloves
Optional: 1 pinch of cayenne pepper, 1 piece of dried orange rind
1 head of garlic, cloves peeled and crushed
200g carrots, sliced into rounds
400g ripe tomatoes, roughly chopped
1 tbsp tomato purée
1 litre white wine
2 litres veal stock (make the night before)
1 small glass of Cognac
Salt and pepper

For the veal stock:
1 veal foot, split in two
1 veal hock
1 leek
1 celery stalk
2 carrots
1 onion, studded with 2 cloves
1 bouquet garni
Salt and pepper

1. The night before, cook all the stock ingredients in 3 litres of water for 3 hours over low heat. Let cool, then refrigerate. Skim off the fat with a slotted spoon before using. If the stock doesn't get chilled, the fat can be skimmed off with paper towels.

2. Make the packages: cut each piece of tripe into an 8 or 9cm square. Make an incision in a corner. In the middle of each square, put a spoonful of the stuffing ingredients. Fold the sides over the stuffing and roll into a package, passing the opposite end of the incision through it. (You can also tie up the packages, in which case, don't forget to remove the string before serving.)

3. To cook: in a flameproof earthenware casserole or a heavy-bottomed saucepan, melt the cubes of lard. Remove any pieces of lard that don't melt with a slotted spoon. Add the leeks, some of the sliced onions, the sheep feet, the bouquet garni, clove-studded onion, salt and pepper, cayenne and orange rind (if using). Then, layer by layer, add the packages, crushed garlic, carrot rounds, the remaining sliced onions, the tomatoes and tomato purée (thinned with a little water). Cover with the white wine, veal stock and Cognac.

4. Put a piece of parchment paper and an upside-down plate on top, to submerge the feet and packages while cooking. Bring to the boil and cover to seal as tightly as possible. Cook on the hob or in a very low oven for 7 hours.

5. After cooking, take out the packages and feet, removing the central bone from the feet. Pass the cooking stock through a sieve and degrease with paper towels. If there is too much stock, reduce it a little. Serve everything in a warmed shallow bowl together with some steamed potatoes.

Photo of *pieds paquets* from Grand Saint-Antoine, reputed charcutier-deli in Noailles

Suzanne Quaglia

I would have liked to have met Suzanne Quaglia. The chef passed away a few years ago, but I tracked down one of her sons in Vancouver, Canada, where he successfully runs the Provence Marinaside restaurant. When he was younger, Jean-François worked in the kitchen with his mum, while his brother, Jacques, oversaw the dining room.

His mum's restaurant in Marseille, Le Patalain, had earned high praise from the top two French gastronomic guides: Gault & Millau and Michelin. In a 1993 article from the prominent French newspaper *Le Monde* titled 'Les Toques en pointe' ('Cutting Edge Chefs'), one could read: 'Suzanne Quaglia, owner and chef, loves hunting, which requires chance and precision. She hits the mark with Scottish grouse *à l'orange et au whisky* and a grey partridge casserole with apples and mushrooms. Cheese in two services: goat and then cow; dessert trolley and choice of the best regional wines. Décor between chic and kitsch. Reception and service are attentive. Around 250 francs.'

At the beginning of the 1990s, Marseillais journalist Alain Delcroix decided to write a book on Marseille cuisine, surprised at the lack of importance that had been given to the subject. I so understand. Seems like we're still facing the same issue 30 years later! In his work *La Cuisine à Marseille*, edited in 1991, he also praised Suzanne Quaglia: 'With her buxom figure, direct gaze, and natural and radiant smile, Suzanne has all the assets to encourage you to discover her cuisine.' His word choice aptly illustrates an era when female chefs were first considered according to their physical attributes, but has that actually changed over the last decades . . . ?

LOCAL FIGURE

Suzanne's career, for that matter, also exemplified what it was like for female chefs in France before women had access to professional culinary schools. Women chefs existed and were numerous but becoming a professional cook was a decision they made once they had to earn a living, often when their husband passed away, or when they got pregnant outside marriage, or when their husband's mum was the chef in the family restaurant that the son inherited. None of them really chose the profession freely out of passion. Evidenced by this excerpt from an interview published in *La Cuisine à Marseille*:

'I belong to an utterly Provençal family (Maurin). One of my grandmothers was already an exceptional cook. At 21 years old, I moved to the Rue de la Loubière to work as a tailor. In 1960, I married Jacques Quaglia, an interior designer and decorator, with whom I had two sons, Jacques and Jean-François. My husband died, and I ran his business until 1980. I had a big house, I loved hosting and cooking for my friends. They often complimented me on my talent as a cook . . . I "threw myself in the pots" in 1981, when I took over Le Patalain on Rue Adolphe-Thiers. I took over from the excellent chef Alain Delmas who had earned a Michelin star. I only worked at nights, which gave me the time to perfect my culinary know-how and to participate in competitions. In 1987, I decided to change my surroundings, and that's why I created the new Le Patalain, on Rue Sainte. Jacques, my eldest son, was at reception and Jean-François worked as a line cook at the Chèvre d'Or in Èze, a Michelin-starred restaurant in a 5-star château hotel on the Côte d'Azur.'

Alain Delcroix then asked Suzanne, 'How do you see your future?' Suzanne's response shatters the persistent cliché of a female chef and mother. 'I devote 24 hours a day to my job, and I don't regret it. It's not about sacrifices for me . . . On Sundays, I rest a bit and I just go and have a bite to eat at my colleagues' restaurants who are open . . . At the moment, my youngest son works in the gourmet restaurant of the Hotel Negresco in Nice, orchestrated by the talented Dominique Lestang. I hope to be able to get him back at the end of the year because his presence will be a significant support for me.'

And how did Suzanne see the future of Marseille gastronomy? 'It has strong and competent advocates, who only seek to have the opportunity to defend it, provided that the tourist outreach expands . . . In Marseille, we eat as well as they do elsewhere, and why not say we eat better here – but too many tourists aren't aware of this.'

Photos taken in Canada during one of Suzanne Quaglia's trips to see her chef son

I put my questions to her son, Jean-François:

Where did your mum grow up?
In Marseille, on Boulevard Chave.

What were your mum's signature dishes?
Pieds et paquets (they were always on her menu) and *dos de loup rôti aux épices* [spice-roasted fillet of sea bass].

What type of chef was your mum?
Passionate, extravagant, abundant.

What was the relationship between your mum and the chef (across the street) Jeannine Moréni?
They were rivals, jealous of one another, but they still had a friendly relationship.

How did you tell your mum that you wanted to follow the same career as her?
She was the one to tell me!

How was it in the kitchen?
Good. She had a lot of respect for my skills and my hard work, the long hours that I could do without complaining.

What did you learn from your mum?
In management, not much. It wasn't her forte . . . On the other hand, on a culinary level, I learned too much to tell you everything, but, when it comes to game, her restaurant was the best experience I ever had, and also for traditional dishes.

I devote 24 hours a day to my job, and I don't regret it.
— Suzanne Quaglia

When did you decide to leave Marseille?
Around 1988, I left to work on the Côte d'Azur to gain experience.

Afterwards, you moved to Canada. What opportunities did Canada give you that you couldn't have had in Marseille?
I have been the owner of my own restaurant for 18 years and I've had two for 17 years. In Canada, business has a better return on investment and profit than in France. Financially I am in a very good position. My mother always had difficulty managing her business . . .

Do you have any of your mum's dishes on your menu?
The *soupe de poissons* is in her honour. '*Mamie* Suzanne's fish soup'. And I often cook dishes inspired by my late mother.

What are the culinary clichés of Marseille that you love?
Sea urchins, grilled fish with fennel, gambas [king prawns] *à la Provençale*.

According to you, what do we generally overlook about Marseille gastronomy?
Probably traditional restaurants that make simple, tasty food.

05

'I LIVE ON GOOD SOUP, NOT FINE WORDS . . .'

. . . wrote Molière, the 17th-century playwright, famous for his mastery of the French language. In Marseille, eating soup doesn't mean that you are on a diet or recovering from a cold. *Au contraire!* Here, soup is more of a festive, hearty dish that is prepared for guests, in summer and winter alike, and with love and patience. It's not just a starter, it's the main, and only, course. Don't forget to refill your bowl several times. That's what is expected from you.

I asked Quebecoise Laura Vidal, celebrated sommelier and co-founder of the voguish restaurants La Mercerie and Livingston in Marseille, to take care of the soup-wine pairings for this chapter. I can almost hear the culinary purists claiming that soup is a liquid so it doesn't need any additional . . . but in Marseille, our soups are thick, our evenings are warm and we never go by the book.

First thing to remember: pistou is not pesto.
Pesto is Italian. Pistou is ours! Provençal, that is. No pine nuts in it and cheese is not mandatory.
I admit that as a kid, I was never a big fan of *soupe au pistou* which was one of our family rituals on Sunday nights. The other was *soupe de poissons* (fish soup), which I much preferred!
Every family has their recipe for making a *soupe au pistou* that is rather thick or quite light, and a more or less *goûtu* (toothsome) pistou, of course, but they all never use any other pasta besides spaghetti. Obviously!
Last summer I worked hard and re-tasted my mother's, her brother Guy's and my cousin's wife's soup . . . and boldly chose one for you. The latter! My cousin's wife, Céline Ferrari, is a dietician who created her precious one by mixing our two family's recipes. My mother did not understand my choice. How surprising . . .

SOUPE AU PISTOU

INGREDIENTS FOR 6

350g fresh white beans
350g fresh red beans
300g green beans
300g runner beans, sliced
300g potatoes, peeled and diced
300g courgettes, diced
60g spaghetti

For the pistou:
3 ripe tomatoes
3 garlic cloves
1 bunch of basil
50g aged Edam
50g Parmesan
3 tbsp olive oil

1. Note: *soupe au pistou* is way better when eaten the next day!

2. Sort the beans. Add white beans and red beans to a large saucepan (*marmite*) and cover with water. Cook for 40 minutes over medium heat.

3. Add the green beans, runner beans, potatoes and courgettes. Add more water until everything is covered. Cook at medium-low heat for around 1 hour.

4. During this time, peel the tomatoes. (Note from Vérane: cut the stalk off the tomatoes, make a small incision on the opposite end to peel them more easily, dunk tomatoes in boiling water for 10 seconds, then put them in a bowl of ice water for a few seconds. Now, you can peel your tomatoes without much trouble.)

5. Then, mix peeled tomatoes, garlic, basil, freshly grated cheeses, and olive oil until you get a slightly runny paste. (Note from Vérane: or else, try the old-fashioned way. Crush the garlic and basil with a mortar and pestle, then add olive oil, and lastly, the grated cheese and the tomatoes cut into pieces. I challenge you to not gobble it all up on slices of grilled bread!)

6. Once the vegetables are fully cooked, add the pesto. Gently mix. Add the spaghetti, broken into approximately 3cm pieces. Let the pasta cook gently in the pan for around 10 minutes.

7. Once the spaghetti is cooked, let the soup cool down then place in the refrigerator. The next day, reheat the soup over low heat and serve!

MUSSEL SOUP
À LA MARSEILLAISE

Yet another recipe from my Auntie Yvette, who has welcomed me with food all her life. However, she had never written this one down. Now, it's done! In my view, it's an easy alternative to bouillabaisse.

INGREDIENTS FOR 4

6 mussels per person, around 1kg of mussels
Oil
2 onions, diced
1 garlic clove, chopped
Dried fennel stalks (or fresh if you can't find dried)
2 bay leaves
1 piece of candied orange peel
2 or 3 tomatoes
2 handfuls of spaghetti
A pinch of saffron
A pinch of chilli powder
Salt and pepper

1. Clean the mussels and open them in a bit of water over high heat in a giant pan. Save and strain the cooking liquid.

2. Coat the bottom of a large saucepan (*cocotte*) with oil, then brown the onions, garlic, fennel, bay leaves and orange peel.

3. Blend the tomato flesh and add them to the saucepan. Sauté for a few minutes, then pour in the strained mussel cooking liquid and cover with water.

4. Let cook for a bit. Add saffron, pepper, chilli powder and a bit of salt. Let simmer again, then add the spaghetti, broken into pieces (it's really a Marseille thing for soup!), and continue to cook until the pasta is soft, around 10 minutes.

5. When the pasta is cooked, add the shelled mussels, and let cook for another 5 minutes.

6. Remove the fennel and bay leaves before serving. This soup can be served with small toasts rubbed with a clove of raw garlic and topped with grated cheese, usually Emmental here, and even a *rouille* (recipe later in this chapter).

MRS

Noailles

Ishak

Chez Yassine is the place to eat on Rue d'Aubagne. This familial *maison*, run by Ishak, his brother Farid, their sister Imen and her husband Yassine, existed in Tunis well before landing in Noailles in 2014. The Marseille version starts serving warm dishes from 10am and we all pop in at one moment or another, lured not by the flashy décor, but by the atmosphere, the welcome, and the tasty, stick-to-your-ribs Tunisian classics. In summer, tables sprout up all around the restaurant since the demand is great and their logo is now displayed on both sides of the street. There's even a third address on Boulevard d'Athènes near Saint Charles train station. For the sake of this book, I devoured a mega *leblebi* and *kefteji-frites* in the early morning . . . and I was not the only one!

THE INSTITUTION

Everybody has something to do on Rue d'Aubagne!

MY ARRIVAL IN MARSEILLE

Around the end of the 1990s. The call of the sea (because my family lived between Lyon and Grenoble), the hope of a new life! My father always told me that the restaurant industry was a sure thing, he sent me to work with my restaurateur cousins . . .

MY FIRST CULINARY MEMORY IN MARSEILLE

As surprising as it may be . . . couscous. They served couscous on every corner.

MY FAVOURITE RESTAURANT

It was La Bouffe Tunisienne, the first restaurant I worked at when I arrived in Marseille. (*Author's note: the Senegalese restaurant Mame Diarra replaced it.*)

A DISCOVERY

I try my hand at all the specialities, I like how Marseille is both exotic and familiar at the same time.
But, I admit Épicerie L'Idéal, in Noailles, with their creative French cuisine, enables me to travel in my own way.

THREE WORDS TO DESCRIBE THE RUE D'AUBAGNE TODAY

Convivial, lively, multicultural . . . everybody has something to do on Rue d'Aubagne!

THE CULINARY CLICHÉ I CAN'T GET ENOUGH OF

Navettes. Their *eau de fleur d'oranger* [orange-blossom water] scent reminds me of its extraction season in Tunisia. Their flavour takes me back a few years ...

MY MARSEILLE IDENTITY

Marseille is, and will remain, the city where cultures meet and get to know one another. The city is reinventing itself, revitalising, but its multicultural identity will always be its strength. This allows me to be from Marseille without renouncing my Tunisian background. In Marseille, we all come from elsewhere but we all end up sharing a common local identity.

MY CULINARY HEROES

The person I admire the most is Hicham, the fisherman, who wakes at dawn to get the catch of the day from his boat and who is content with what nature offers him. From time to time, he comes to the restaurant to offer me what he has left.

MARSEILLE GASTRONOMY

Global cuisine is certainly more authentic in Marseille than anywhere else! It's often watered down in restaurants. Here, it tastes like what you'd eat at someone's home.

WHAT I COOK FOR MY FAMILY

Mloukhiya! It's a speciality made from powdered, dried jute mallow leaves . . . A unique flavour to discover at our restaurant on Thursdays. We eat *mloukhiya* in Tunisia. Every family has their own recipe.

Tunisian cuisine

8 Rue d'Aubagne
13001 Marseille

Originally, *leblebi* was the dish that workers in Tunis ate when they got up early before starting a long day of work.

LEBLEBI

INGREDIENTS FOR 4

500g tinned chickpeas
Olive oil
4 pinches of salt
1 round Tunisian bread, stale or day-old
2 tbsp ground cumin
5 dried garlic cloves
4 tbsp homemade harissa

1. Cook the chickpeas in twice their volume of water in a large saucepan with a few glugs of olive oil to taste. Add the salt.
2. Tear up bread into each bowl.
3. Once the soup is ready, pour 2 ladles of soup into each bowl. Add cumin, a bit of dried garlic, and homemade harissa.
4. You can also serve the soup with a poached egg, capers or tuna, according to taste.

Mina Rouabah-Roux

SHARING

Mediterranean and North African caterer

In Marseille, you can eat magnificent *chorbas* at the Comptoir des Beaux-Arts in Noailles, accompanied by addictive, hot *kesra* (Algerian semolina flatbread)! While meeting Mina at MinaKouk for a dessert recipe, I learned everything about *chorba* with her and, to my great joy, picked up her family recipe.

I was born in Algiers, then lived in Marseille in the 5th arrondissement in the La Plaine quarter. I had come to Marseille at the age of 20 to continue my studies at the University of Saint-Jérôme. Since my childhood, I have been immersed in four types of cuisine: French, Algerian, Moroccan and Lebanese. I decided not to choose just one, because they are rich and very complementary. It's interesting to call the same dish by different names. For example, the samoussa is also called beurek or *brik*. The *croquant* is called *cantuccini* in Italy or *canistrelli* in Corsica.

MinaKouk's cuisine and those of Marseille are cuisines for sharing dishes, life's moments, and encounters with different generations and origins. All cuisines wish to evolve over time. It's hard to accept a chocolate *corne de gazelle* (a North African almond, sugar-topped crescent cookie). We almost cry foul. But we think it's normal to offer a lavender millefeuille . . . So, I decided to be creative and some of my culinary creations make me particularly proud. On the savoury side, the "mac kefta" (a sandwich with homemade bread + spiced kefta which replaces hamburger meat), the foie gras *pastilla* (a sweet and savoury filo-dough pastry) and the zaatar pizza. For sweets, *kadaif* (baked, shredded filo-dough nests) with berries, chocolate *corne de gazelle*, orange-blossom millefeuille, date and almond *croquant* cookies, wedding cake with Middle Eastern flavours, rose *loukoum* – Turkish delight.

Le Cloître
20 Boulevard Madeleine Rémusat
13013 Marseille

MINA'S ALGERIAN CHORBA

**INGREDIENTS FOR 6
(AROUND 3 LITRES OF SOUP)**

300g dried chickpeas (or canned)
1 onion, thinly sliced
500g beef, chopped into small pieces
Olive oil
4 tomatoes, peeled (or 1 can tomato purée)
A few stems of coriander
A few stems of mint
1 tsp paprika
4 tsp ras el-hanout (cumin, ginger, turmeric, cinnamon, black pepper, white pepper, allspice, ground coriander, cayenne pepper, nutmeg, clove)
Salt

1. If using dried chickpeas, soak them the night before in a large bowl. If you use canned chickpeas, you just need to rinse them.

2. In a large saucepan (*marmite*), brown the onion and meat over high heat with a bit of olive oil. Once the meat is caramelised, add the tomatoes (or tomato purée) and chickpeas. Add coriander and mint tied up like a bouquet garni, paprika, ras el-hanout and salt. Pour in water. The quantity depends on your desired consistency, but we start by thinning out the soup only a little bit. Let simmer, covered, for an hour.

3. This is where the three schools differ:

4. You can add vegetables: carrots, courgettes cut into small dice (aka *brunoise*), sometimes even cut-up potatoes. Purists say that we should not add these vegetables . . . but it's done. They are added at the same time as the tomatoes.

5. Another way to go: add green wheat (freekeh). Its smoky flavour will understandably be quite prominent, and its nutritional value is enormous. You must soak it in cold water before using it or else it will expand in your stomach. We add it with the rest of the ingredients. This is my favourite version of *chorba*. The flavour is very special. Best to find freekeh with yellow highlights that is on the verge of turning yellow.

6. And, then there is the 'I have teenagers at home who are hungry!' version. In this case, my mother says that the most neutral ingredient is vermicelli or angel hair pasta that you can add to make the soup more filling. It must be added 10 minutes before the end of cooking. You can also add a little chilli pepper and garlic.

7. At the end of cooking, remove the bouquet garni, and just before serving, sprinkle the soup with finely chopped coriander and mint.

'There are three schools for *chorba*. I always make it with beef, preferably cheap cuts to give a flavour like pot-au-feu. My grandmother collected the small pieces of meat clinging to the bones. The idea is that everyone has a little meat in their soup at the end.'

Marie-Josée Ordener

OUR RAY OF SUNSHINE

Marie-Josée Ordener, artist, chef, and co-director of Les Grandes Tables, the restaurant (and so much more) at the Friche la Belle de Mai cultural centre, is one of the fairy godmothers who watches over Marseille and its future. Marie-Josée creates links and builds bridges between art and cuisine, between the north and south of Marseille, between those who arrived before and newcomers, farmers and city dwellers, established chefs and migrants looking for a job in the kitchen. Her energy has no limit! Today, the Grandes Tables does the same in Calais and Clermont-Ferrand and events abroad are multiplying. She wants everyone to mingle and mix. Curiosity, culinary and artistic education are the main axes that guide Marie-Jo's unique projects. Spending a day or an evening at the Friche gives you hope in people – and confidence in yourself and your power to change the world.

Where did you grow up?
I was born in the enclave of the popes, in Valréas. This region in northern Vaucluse has the feature of being landlocked in the department of the Drôme. I grew up at the foot of Mont Ventoux. A little in Malaucène, a little in Vaison-la-Romaine. It's right in the middle of the Comtat Venaissin.

Did you have cooks in your family?
My two grandmothers, Léa and Marcelle, and my mum are all three great Provençal cooks in the most noble sense of the word. My maternal grandmother cooked only using products from the farm. My grandparents were farmers . . . they always had a vegetable garden, chickens, ducks, rabbits and a pig. I was brought up to cook seasonal food and using produce from the garden.

When did you start cooking?
At age eight, I made pizza every Tuesday night . . . Otherwise, as far back as I can remember, I can picture myself picking green beans from the garden!

What training do you have?
A plastic arts baccalaureate, then chance encounters studying humanities in Aix-en-Provence, made it possible to do my dream job very quickly: a puppeteer. From companies to creative projects, I was a puppeteer for 25 years of my life.

When did you arrive in Marseille?
In 1983, living in Aix was unbearable for us.

What did you think of the city before you came to live here?
Absolutely nothing . . . except that everything was possible here.

Were you particularly surprised by anything here in Marseille?
Nothing to do with food, although . . . our first apartment was at Place Sébastopol, and on our street, people threw their garbage bags out of their windows . . . Every evening at the same hour, we heard 'splat' . . . and the sound of their shutters closing very quickly.

What typically Marseillais thing have you experienced?
In Marseille, people have a way of meddling in your life without appearing to. People watch over each other naturally, without specific friendships per se, you just have to live on the same street. We lived in four very different neighbourhoods, and this phenomenon happened all four times. People are very attentive to others, to 'newcomers'. A kind of balance is set up, by the 'veterans' of the district, without it being intrusive.

Which quarter do you live in today?
25 years ago, we were looking in the classifieds to buy an apartment . . . the calculation was quickly made . . . The La Belle de Mai district allowed us to settle in a small townhouse with a garden . . . we do not regret this decision, which was initially economic. This district is part of the older districts of Marseille. It was built by the men and women who arrived from various countries. It is a neighbourhood in perpetual motion. La Friche, a former SEITA tobacco factory which has become the essential cultural centre in Marseille, contributes to the liveliness of this district.

Now that you live in Marseille, how have your feelings changed?
Life has made me hate Marseille as much as I love it. It is a city of

Marseille is a city of contrasts. Incredibly beautiful and incredibly abominable things happen here.

all possibilities in one way or the other. Nothing is set in stone . . . from one minute to another everything can change . . . she often frightens me, she worries me, I don't always understand her, but I know she is an incredible reservoir of hope. I am not, and do not feel like a native Marseillaise, but I do not like it when people criticise this city. Marseille invents itself every day, it saves itself every day, it destroys itself every day . . .

What is your first culinary memory in Marseille?
Couscous at *Sur le Pouce*. It fed me for the first six months of my first pregnancy.

What did you want to bring to Marseille with the Grandes Tables and all the culinary events you have organised?
In 2006, when Fabrice Lextrait and Philippe Saumande brought me aboard this adventure, our ambition was to create a restaurant with everyday and extraordinary cuisine . . . By creating the Grandes Tables, we responded to the expectations of actors and audiences from the Friche, who wanted to have access to quality food at affordable prices and to sample new experiences in contemporary culinary creation. With the Grandes Tables, we want to affirm that cooking can be an important activity alongside artistic disciplines in cultural places.
The Grandes Tables are restaurants of the possible, utopias. We like to make dreams come true.

Which quarter in Marseille has particular significance for you?
The Port Autonome, without a doubt. Marseille comes from the sea. I had the chance to be there with Armand Gatti in 1993 for his creation *Adam, quoi?*, then to work there for six months with Véronique Guillaud for her performance piece *Qui va où? Marseille un jeu de piste* [Who goes where? Marseille a treasure hunt] between 1999 and 2000, and between 2019 and 2022 with the Grandes Tables for the Dîners Insolites, a series of dinners in atypical settings.
Today, in principle, the commercial port is closed to the public but that might change . . . At the Port Autonome, we are in the heart of the history of Marseille, past and present. I am always fascinated by this place whose past has never been erased from its soil: the platforms where fishermen perch, the Arenc station which bore witness to the deportation of Jews during the 1943 round-up, but also the forced departures of young soldiers, the quays which have seen men and women disembark, lost, seeking refuge in Marseille, the detention centre, the cruise ships, the cargo ships, the containers, the 'ferry' boats between Corsica, Algeria, Tunisia, Morocco . . . social protests and strikes.
Then there is the seawall and the feeling of freedom that is palpable there . . . the light of the sea, the horizon. The commercial port is a source of creation and inspiration for artists, directors and projects. Marseille is built by the sea, the Port Autonome is a magical and unique place.

What is the dish or ingredient that symbolises your Marseille?
The *chichi* . . . How to explain the '*chichi*'? It's a beignet, that is lightly scented with orange-blossom water, that we buy and eat in L'Estaque [the Marseille district on the northern edge of the city] because it must be savoured right after it's removed from its oil bath. Careful, this isn't a churro or a doughnut! The *chichi* is a unique beignet. The recipe isn't complicated, but being successful at it is another story. A *chichi* must be crunchy and melt in your mouth at the same time. It is cooked in oil, but it shouldn't be oily when you eat it. *Chichis* are still one of those 'typical' dishes, which cannot be found anywhere else in the world. If you look carefully in the regional dictionaries, a *chichi* also refers to a penis . . . so, how can you not burst out laughing when all the information is connected in your brain, and the vendor asks you in his Marseille twang, '*Alors, il est pas bon, mon chichi?*' [Say, my chichi is good, no?]

What scent or aroma symbolises your Marseille?
The scent of the sea, the scent of the wind on the seashore.

Who are the people working in the food industry that you most admire in Marseille? Who intrigues you, fascinates you?

I am very curious about the artistic collective SAFI, run by Dalila Ladjal and Stéphane Brisset. I really like their work. I met them through projects with the Grandes Tables. They are for me the poets of the 21st century. They are visual artists, they have an incredible knowledge of the Marseille territory, of 'urban nature', and therefore of the people who live here. Dalila's foraging enables Marseille chefs to discover or rediscover flavours. They are omnipresent in the culinary landscape of Marseille.

What are your ideas or your desires for restaurants post pandemic?
Post Covid, restaurants can no longer have qualms. The food industry must do the job of sounding the alarm. Intellectually, everyone agrees on what is good or bad; the hardest thing is to stay the course, to not give in to the temptation of 'easy'. We have been feeding the kids in day-care at the Friche since it opened. We worked with Marion Latuilliere's team to obtain the '3 Carrots' certification. What is interesting about this certification is that it promotes a comprehensive effort around children. The cuisine, the supplies, the educational project, the place that welcomes the children, and the parents are all taken into account. It's sometimes disconcerting, we can no longer hide behind an 'I didn't know'. This moved us all forward towards what is best for the children. If we model this principle for more traditional catering, we can no longer have certain products in our grocery stores, our refrigerators, or in our restaurants. We can no longer say that we are unaware. I believe in the little things which, when put together, enable us to make a difference.

Three words to describe the food scene in Marseille today?
Agitated, fragile, under stress.

According to you, what do the Marseillais generally overlook about Marseille gastronomy?
That it exists.

Where do you eat today in Marseille, and why?
I like to eat at my friends' houses . . . I'm lucky to have friends that cook with passion and so sublimely! Graziella's pasta, Nicole's peppers, Philippe's anchovies, Jean-Jacques' pizzas, Isabelle's pear tart, Mohamed's mum's couscous, Claude's eggs with herring, Charles' *aligot* [cheesy potatoes]. Friends' cooking has a very special flavour.

What do you like to cook for your family?
I especially like cooking with my family, and pizza takes first place.

What recipe did you choose for the book and why?
Soupe de poissons [fish soup], and the rouille [saffron aioli] that goes with it. *Soupe de poissons* is a childhood memory . . . it's the soup of summer, of vacations. It's the only dish where both my father and mother were absolutely essential to be able to make it. My dad caught the fish, and my mum would make the soup. My dad at the mortar, my mum with the olive oil, and slowly the rouille would 'rise'. No potatoes in this rouille, but there's garlic, chilli, saffron, egg and olive oil.
I don't know if we can speak of a 'maritime terroir', but one thing is sure, the fish caught off the island of Frioul, or near the Deux-Frères rocks, or on the Côte Bleue [the 'blue coast' just north of Marseille] do not have the same taste at all. Can we say that the marine ecosystem makes it possible to bring out flavour profiles in fish, in the same way as terroirs do for wine?
The fish soup I am talking about comes from fishing off Deux-Frères island, in La-Seyne-Sur-Mer, located between the Saint-Mandrier peninsula and Cap-Sicié [south-east of Marseille]. When we talk about rock fish, we can't get any better than fishing around these two prominent rocks. Emerging from the depths, the Deux-Frères provide fish with many screes, welcoming holes and rock shelters where marine flora and fauna can develop. *Verdao, sar* [porgy], *roucaou, rascasse* [scorpion fish, the little one], *sarran, castagnole* (bream), *bogue, marbré* [striped sea bream], *pagre* [red sea bream], and of course the large family of *girelles* (wrasse), are among the many local fish that can be caught off this site.

The best fish soup in Marseille, photo taken at l'Esplaï du Grand Bar des Goudes.

SOUPE DE POISSONS & ROUILLE MARSEILLAISE

INGREDIENTS FOR 6

1½ onions, finely chopped
4 large garlic cloves, finely chopped
Olive oil
About 2kg Mediterranean fish*: 600g wrasse (for creaminess and finesse), 700g comber or grouper, roucaous, verdaos (for flavour, for the soft texture of their flesh), 700g small fish, scorpion fish, crabs, John Dory (for oomph)
2 tbsp tomato purée
2-3 fresh tomatoes, well ripened
1 large bunch of wild fennel
2 good pinches of saffron
Salt and pepper

For the rouille:
2 large garlic cloves
1 egg yolk
Tomato purée
1 or 2 pinches of chilli powder
1 good pinch of saffron
Olive oil

1. In a large saucepan (*cocotte*), gently brown the onion and garlic with enough olive oil to cover them. Lightly salt. Let simmer for 4–5 minutes, then add the fish all at once and raise the heat to brown them. The big trick is to stir vigorously so that the fish 'stick' but not too much. When they start to flake (we can almost say become mush), lower the heat, stir in the tomato purée and fresh tomatoes, cover generously with water, and slide in the large bunch of fresh fennel. Bring to the boil, then lower the heat to a slight simmer. Cook for about 15 minutes.

2. Make yourself as comfortable as possible with your food mill and start straining the soup after removing the fennel. If your mill has different size strainers, go from the largest to the smallest holes. Then adjust the seasoning, add saffron, and leave to infuse.

3. Make the rouille (all ingredients must be at same temperature): with a mortar and pestle, smash the garlic into a purée. Add salt, pepper, the egg yolk, a little tomato purée, a good pinch of chilli powder and saffron. Mix all well, then slowly drizzle in olive oil to thicken. When the rouille is done, store in the refrigerator.

4. Grill thin slices of good bread. All that's left is to enjoy . . .

Be creative and substitute with your local fish, just don't tell the Marseillais!

As with wine, your soup will have a different taste depending on which varieties or quantities of fish you add: soft and velvety with more wrasse; more flavourful and brinier with more scorpion fish, roucaous and verdaos. Avoid bogue, the nightmare of fishermen, a pretty, shiny fish that imparts a certain bitterness to the soup.

Marie Dijon

THE SCENT OF MY CHILDHOOD
Anise lollipops. The green and red ones they sold at the newsstand with wooden sticks =)

MARSEILLE'S FOOD SCENE
Evolving, no-fuss, open.

SYMBOLS OF MARSEILLE
Bouillabaisse and Ricard®. I think everyone recognises us like that. Haha.

MY CUISINE WITH FAMILY
A big plate of leftovers with pasta, but not just any kind of leftovers =)

MY CUISINE FOR FRIENDS
Bluefin tuna bought that morning at the port, a few girolles sautéed in garlic, a miso, soy, ginger and orange reduction, and lots of fresh herbs.

AN ESSENTIAL RECIPE
Vinaigrette. I find vinaigrette very personal. Everyone has their own ratio of vinegar, oil, and which oil? White or black pepper? Some mustard? Old-fashioned or not? Emulsified or not? For me, each dish has its own vinaigrette, and it is very important on the plate!

Talent is unpredictable!
But you'll never be disappointed

27 Rue Fontange
13006 Marseille

INTENSITY

A word to those who recently wrote, 'The restaurant is dead.' Marie Dijon and the duo she formed with Eugénie Cenatiempo are reinventing the restaurant. Brimming with talent and ideas, the young chef put her culinary genius at the service of reputable Marseille bistros before opening her first restaurant, Caterine, in 2021, between Cours Julien and La Plaine, Marseille's second *ventre* [colourful "fill-your-belly" neighbourhood]. Marie and her team want to create affordable menus with high-quality ingredients that is accessible in terms of price. To live up to their words, they had to make choices, opting to invest in the kitchen and the team of cooks, rather than in waiters and waitresses. The service is therefore pub-like. Very relaxed. But what's on the plates is high-end! Don't be baffled by the simple dishes' names. It's to better surprise you once they're in front of you, contrary to what is practised in a certain type of gastronomic restaurant. Cheffe Marie is no menu-bore as she likes to test her creativity non-stop. Hence the '*match aller-retour*' (a home and away game) she sets up with other Marseille chefs, and menus *de ouf* (wow) that she creates for these special evenings … like the one around sauces where terrific chefs Maëlyss Vultaggio and Eric Maillet from restaurant Cédrat were invited to compete with her. Get ready to (food) party!

I grew up here in the 5th, between Place Sébastopol, Boulevard Chave, La Plaine and Cours Ju. What I really remember as a child is school, so the ambiance of this neighbourhood with my friends, and then there were family strolls in the Calanques on the weekend, or hikes in the Sainte-Baume hills, or boat trips with my uncle. We left in the morning with a picnic, and we gathered sea urchins, my mum hunted octopus with a harpoon, and we returned at the end of the day. My mother put the octopus in the freezer, and we devoured the sea urchins right away. We also went to the Vélodrome stadium with the family to watch football games. Football is everything here.
Inside the stadium, it is a crazy atmosphere.
Huge clichés, I know, but these are true memories.
I loved my town and I still do.
I never managed to stay away from Boulevard Chave for very long. I feel good there, I have all my bearings there. My mother still lives there and her mother too. I have known all the merchants since I was little, I regularly meet the parents of students with whom I was in class, and they still live here too. It is a village-like neighbourhood where everyone knows each other, it is close to everything without being quite in the city centre. In a tram ride, we are in Noailles. And then, I have a small motorcycle that allows me to be near the water in 15 minutes.
Over these last four or five years, many merchants (a fromagerie, fishmonger, coffee roaster, neighbourhood bar, wine bar, restaurants) have set up shop on the boulevard and many people want to live here now. Chave is becoming livelier than ever and I'm incredibly happy. Well, one shouldn't be completely naive either. Marseille is nevertheless a very poor city with very significant disparities from one district to another, which can from time to time be quite disturbing.
But I was born here, I find that it creates a general atmosphere in the city which is quite racy after all, and that suits me well.
My restaurant is at the border of the 5th and 6th arrondissement. It's one of the streets with the most merchants in the quarter and runs from the Église Notre-Dame-du-Mont to the bustling La Plaine square. The commercial fabric is something that is very important to me, it creates social ties, solidarity, and it contributes to the village ambience that is so dear to the people of Marseille. In this area, there is everything you need. We work with the cheesemaker, the tea shop, the seamstress, the poultry seller, the butcher, the Lebanese grocery store, the bakers, the beer shop . . . We say hello to them every morning; some were already friends. It simply creates good vibes, a shared desire to bring our surroundings to life, to make them pretty and welcoming, for us and for others.

We are two boss ladies that cook.
We wanted Caterine to be a space of sharing and interaction, which are the main values of a meal. In addition, it was important for us to establish reasonable prices to prove that it is possible to eat healthy while having fun, discovering new flavour combinations, and ways of working. Eating in a restaurant does not mean feeling heavy when you leave!
Having lived my life here, I am naturally drawn to products of the sea, and I marry them with techniques and condiments from elsewhere. I prepare my dishes with a lot of freedom. I think I put a lot of intensity into my preparations, which some have often described as full-flavoured.
My cuisine is free, diverse and intense, and I think that reflects the city quite well..

SOUPE DE FAVOUILLES AND FOCACCIA TARTINE WITH SMOKED GOAT CHEESE, THYME, FENNEL AND ORANGE

INGREDIENTS FOR 4

For the soup:
2 leeks
2 onions
2 carrots
1 orange
Olive oil
500g *favouilles* (local tiny green crabs)
Pastis (Ricard®)
Aromatic herbs: thyme, bay leaf, sage, rosemary
½ head of garlic
Salt and pepper

For the vinaigrette:
450ml rapeseed oil
Trimmings from the leeks, carrots and onions for the soup
½ head of garlic
2 oranges, untreated or organic

For the tartine:
1 fennel bulb
1 celery stalk
1 red onion
Focaccia from PAIN PAN our favourite boulangerie in the neighbourhood

For the smoked goat cheese:
120g fresh goat cheese
Stalks from dried aromatic herbs (hay also works very well!)

1. Place the fresh goat cheese in a small strainer (*une passette*). Put the herb stalks in a large glass or stainless-steel bowl and set fire with a lighter or matches. Wait until there is no longer a flame, then place the strainer with the cheese above them. Rapidly wrap the lot with cling film to trap the smoke inside. If you have a smoker, that works too!

2. For the soup, wash, peel, and chop the vegetables into small dice (a mirepoix). Save the trimmings for the vinaigrette. Cut the orange in quarters.

3. Drizzle olive oil in a large, heated saucepan and add the live crabs. Smash them to release as much flavour as possible. Let them stick to the bottom of the pan, then deglaze and flambé them with pastis.

4. Reduce the heat and add aromatic herbs, ½ head of garlic, the orange, and vegetables. Add cold water to the top, then let gently simmer for an hour. Strain the soup. Reheat at low until it reaches your desired consistency, then season.

5. For the vinaigrette, pour the rapeseed oil into a saucepan at low heat (it mustn't boil!), add salt, pepper, the vegetable trimmings, ½ head of garlic and the zest from 2 oranges. Cover and let infuse gently away from the heat until it's completely cool.

6. Strain once the oil has cooled. You must press the solids well to release as many flavours as possible. Make a vinaigrette with your infused oil and the juice from the 2 oranges.

7. Slice the fennel super thin with a mandolin. Season with vinaigrette, add a few finely chopped celery leaves and slices of red onion.

8. Put smoked goat cheese on a slice of lightly toasted focaccia. Top with fennel salad and vinaigrette. Put your tartine in a shallow bowl, serve hot soup next to it, and that's all there is to it!

M R S
Noailles

Laura Vidal

Laura is one of the founders of now iconic restaurant La Mercerie, responsible for the awakening of Marseille's *bobo* (*bourgeois-bohème*) side that slept so deeply in us. In fact, it's still snoozing but, once in a blue moon, it does us some good to pretend to be readers of Le Fooding (the hipster, anti-Michelin dining guide . . . that is now partly owned by Michelin) and go and pick at expensive nibbles at this former knitting shop. What appeals to me at La Mercerie is the ensemble of offerings I never thought I'd see in Marseille. An English chef already, sends shivers of amazement down my spine, but with a Quebecoise sommelier in Noailles . . . *c'est hot*! Another good thing is that the team opened a hip retro-bakery next door because if you are my kind of eater, you might not bumble back out of the door wholly sated with your top trouser button loosened, as British food critic queen Grace Dent would merrily put it.

LIBERTÉ

Unique cuisine in Marseille, with Mediterranean, Asian, and British influences!

La Mercerie
9 Cours Saint-Louis
13001 Marseille

Where did you grow up?
I grew up in Montreal and I arrived in France at the end of 2010. I was promoting a Canadian ice wine made from apples, ice cider. I met winemakers and restaurateurs who made me want to stay. My mum is French, so my French citizenship made it easy to stay. Next, I worked in Paris at Frenchie for three years as a sommelière. I oversaw the wine list. They had never had a sommelier before, and the chef, Grégory Marchand, really wanted a woman to do it. He wanted someone who could create a wine list that was open to the world, because he had travelled a lot. Afterwards, I met the chef Harry Cummins, who became my partner in 2011. From 2012 on, we organised pop-up events in Paris, then we travelled for three years with our other partner, Julia Mitton. We did 35 events around the world, and in 2015 we started doing food events at Nord Pinus Hôtel in Arles in the south of France. We were anchored in Le Sud from this point on. Eventually, we launched a business, creating Le Chardon in Arles. Instead of flying, we invited chefs to do residencies with us.

What did you think of Marseille at this time?
We adored Marseille. Arles is a mini city. Marseille, seen from Arles, is a huge city. We always dug Marseille even though we didn't know it very well. But all three of us are foreigners. Julia is Canadian, Harry is English, and I'm from Quebec, so we've always had a romantic view of France and Marseille. There is a really enjoyable sense of freedom in Marseille and freedom is our main value. When we arrived here, we found the city very free, very chaotic, feverish, full of energy, electrifying, and we liked it!

And which has a huge potential . . .
Since we opened La Mercerie, five years ago, things have changed a lot, but we are still only at the beginning. The city has experienced several stops and starts but today there are a lot of people with very dynamic energy. We are not the only ones to have settled down here, we encourage others to do so . . . and we want to contribute to all of this, to keep things boiling, to support local talent . . . We opened a new restaurant and wine bar near Cours Julien, Livingston, with one of our former employees, Marseillais chef Valentin Raffali, and we now have our own bakery and coffee shop, Pétrin Couchette in Noailles.
It's true that at the beginning, we felt a bit alone in Noailles with just Épicerie L'Idéal. Marseille was a bit of a wasteland compared to what it is today.

How do the Marseillais see the very contemporary gastronomy that you serve?
We noticed those who had grown up in Marseille but live elsewhere, most notably in Paris, had heard of our restaurant before their parents who still lived here. As a result, our clientele is a new generation, who come to see us when they come to Marseille. They bring their families to us and that's how we met the older generation of Marseillais. There are also Marseillais who are more open to the world, those who have travelled a lot, people who have left – especially for their studies – and come back. And a wave of neo-Marseillais, people who moved here four or five years ago, who are huge fans of our restaurant.
The Marseillais told us, 'It's brave to settle down here in Noailles,' but we are right in the city centre, two minutes from the Vieux-Port, it's potentially the number one location in Marseille! It wasn't brave, it was strategic! Marseillais don't always have a great image of their city. They are mistaken about themselves, about their city.

And you, how have you adapted to this city?
I feel completely settled in Marseille. I made the city my own by meeting all the people who are doing good things. The good boulangerie, the good coffee shop, the good fish stand on the Vieux-Port. I have a little dog that I walk

early in the morning, so I see which stands have fish delivered by refrigerated trucks and which get fish by boat. On Wednesdays, I love strolling around the Cours Julien farmers' market, at Jamal's stand, which is one of the best, then hiking in the Calanques, going to Les Goudes . . .

Is there a quarter that you have a particular tie to?
I love the city centre because I live here. Before, I lived in front of the Palais de Justice, on the Puget hill. There are lovely little walks in this part of town. And then there is Malmousque, I spend a lot of time there with a girlfriend. We take dips in the summer. It is the best. For me, Marseille is a blue city, a city turned towards the water. In the morning, I run with my dog and in 10 minutes, I am at the waterside at the Plage des Catalans. It is an incredible luxury. In December, I say to myself, 'Wow, I'm at the water's edge, it's not cold, there's sun, there's no snow . . .!'

Do you see a link between Quebecois' and Marseillais' mindsets?
Yes! The bon vivant, benevolent and welcoming side. I feel that here. Everyone talks to each other, it's a good atmosphere. People are much more relaxed than in Paris, where it was hard. Overall, hearts are more open here. In Paris, the relationship with customers is complicated, hostile. At the same time, when I was working there, I found it funny. Hostile people who are hungry are the worst! Good food and a good glass of wine later, all the dragons turn into miaowing little kittens. Then, we had the most difficult public in the whole world, the people of Arles. That's another topic! They are so judgemental. They have super high standards. If you succeed in Arles, you can succeed anywhere. When we arrived in Marseille, we were already familiar with the Arlesians. We were amazed by the Marseillais' kindness and benevolence. Customers bring us gifts, cakes. When we opened, we had flowers and plants from all the neighbours. It was amazing. We always felt included.

Who do you feel close to in Marseille's restaurant industry?
Most of them are female entrepreneurs. Mahéva who created La Bonne Mère pizzeria, Julia from Épicerie L'Idéal, the Deep coffee shop crew and the Eclectique team; we get along well with Mathieu and Camille of Ourea, with Ben and his team at Gaspard bar, with the CopperBay bar, with distiller Guillaume Ferroni. It's like a network. We all refer clients to each other. We invite Marseillais chefs like David Mijoba and Georgiana Viou to join our events at La Mercerie. The community we belong to is an ecosystem that must be nurtured. We must interact, we can't do our own thing in our own corner, American style, in competition. Here, we must stick together.
We also work with Jean-Baptiste Anfosso in Bandol for fruits, vegetables and wild herbs. He's an expert, he has no equal in the permaculture world.

How do you build your natural wine list for a cuisine that has such a mix of influences?
The wine list here is made by feeling, it's very spontaneous, like everything we do. It was built over time through my encounters, tastings. We are rather focused on France, and mostly southern France, but the region is not an obsession for me. It shocks people, but I have yet to find a natural wine that really wows me around here. In Cassis, there is Clos Sainte Magdeleine. I am very good friends with Jonathan Sack, I try to push him to make a vintage without sulphur in an amphora . . . I choose wines in relation to the human being behind the label. Wine is not a finished product that you can put on a shelf like canned food. It's a living product. You have to follow its development.

And what soup has saved your life?
As soon as I have a cold, it's chicken soup for the soul. It fixes everything! It's a very simple soup: caramelise onions in olive oil in a saucepan, then add carrots, celery, thyme, rosemary, and a bay leaf if you have one, and a whole chicken. Cover with water, bring to the boil, then lower the heat and cook for 1½ hours. Then add leeks, turnips, or other fresh vegetables from the market and remove the chicken. Shred the chicken and add back to the broth once it has reduced a little.

I asked Laura, Gault & Millau's 2020 Sommelier of the Year, to take part in this book in a collaborative way. I said to her, 'In Marseille, you feel at home everywhere. Create soup-wine pairings with total freedom. *Blue sky is the limit!*' Laura immediately responded, 'Count me in.' Here is our original soup and wine tour.

For Marie-Josée Ordener's *soupe de poissons*: a wine with salinity and minerality like Olivier Pithon's Macabeu in Roussillon near Calce. Nervy, lively, but with a nice richness also.
For the Algerian *chorba*: a red that is a bit spiced, yet fresh, like Domaine Dufaitre's Brouilly from Beaujolais. Crisp and thirst-quenching with a bit of pepper.
For the *soupe au pistou*: a Bandol rosé, La Chance, by Jean-Christophe Comor served well-chilled. A rosé from Le Sud that is herbaceous and that pairs marvellously with pistou.
For Marie Dijon's *soupe de favouilles*: a Chenin Blanc from the Loire from Domaine Richard Leroy: les Noëls de Montbenault. Preserved lemon blended with minerality and a honeyed finish that is still dry.
For Tunisian *leblebi* from Chez Yassine: an orange wine, the cuvée Supernova from the Danjou-Banessy brothers, a dry, macerated Muscat from Roussillon, saline, but a lightly floral nose and a lively finish.
For the saffron mussel soup: an elegant and delicate Pinot Noir from Burgundy (Bourgogne). Ostrea, a Gevrey-Chambertin from Domaine Trapet. Its long finish and elegance pairs well with the touch of saffron.

My BFF in Marseille – ANNELISE'S SALADE CUITE, AKA JEWISH SALAD

A *pied-noir* tradition that has become a Marseille classic.

INGREDIENTS FOR 4

2kg red and green peppers (more red than green)
Olive oil
6 or 7 garlic cloves, finely chopped
2 x 400g cans of chopped tomatoes
Salt and pepper

1. Grill the peppers in the oven, on all four sides, until their skin is blackened. Place the peppers in a large bowl and cover them with a tea towel so that the steam loosens their skin. Peel the peppers and remove the seeds. Cut them into strips.

2. Heat 0.5cm olive oil in a frying pan with the garlic then add the pepper strips. Add salt and pepper, then the chopped tomatoes.

3. Mix and let caramelise for an hour over very low heat until you get a jam-like texture. Let cool. The salade cuite (cooked salad) is eaten cold. It's *un délice* with challah bread!

PEPPERS IN OLIVE OIL BY MY COUSIN CÉLINE

INGREDIENTS FOR 4

4 or 5 large peppers, firm and glossy
4 tbsp olive oil
1 garlic clove, finely chopped
Salt

1. Preheat the oven to 160°C/gas mark 3. Wash the peppers. Place them on a baking sheet covered in parchment paper. Bake for 1 hour, even 1½ hours. The peppers should be nicely puffed up and a little browned, but not blackened.

2. Take the peppers out of the oven and let them rest until they are at room temperature. Halve them, remove the skin and seeds by hand. Cut them in slices and place them on a plate. Add the olive oil, garlic and salt. Ideally, let the peppers marinate overnight (maybe in a glass jar). They'll be even better.

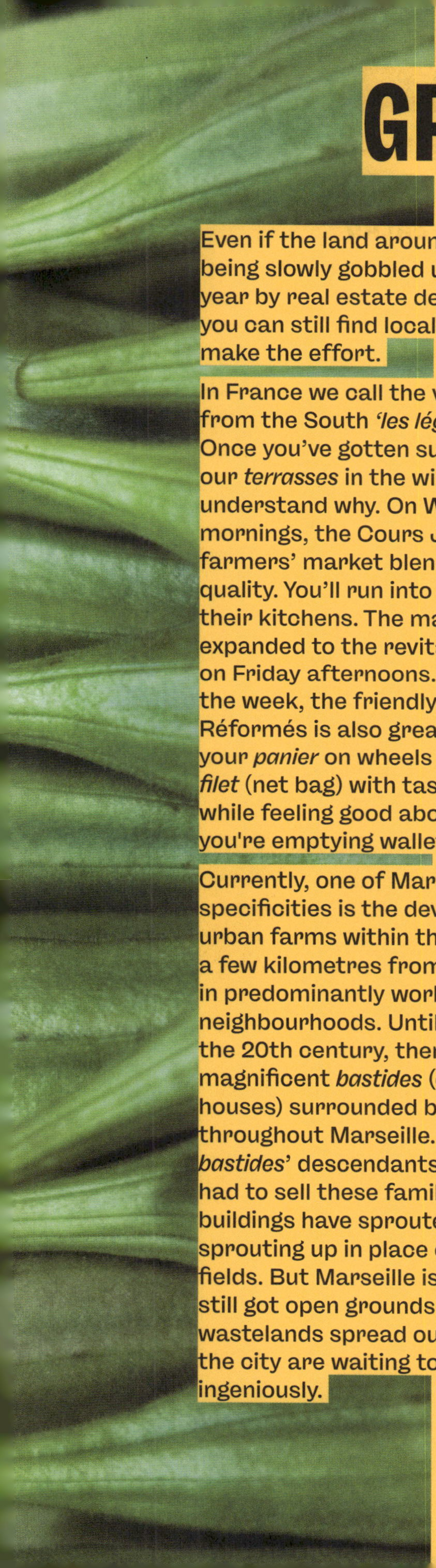

GREENS TO ENVY

Even if the land around Marseille is being slowly gobbled up year after year by real estate developers, you can still find local veggies if you make the effort.

In France we call the vegetables from the South *'les légumes de soleil'*. Once you've gotten sunburnt on our *terrasses* in the winter, you'll understand why. On Wednesday mornings, the Cours Julien organic farmers' market blends hype and quality. You'll run into chefs stocking their kitchens. The market has just expanded to the revitalised La Plaine on Friday afternoons. The rest of the week, the friendly marché des Réformés is also great for loading up your *panier* on wheels or flamboyant *filet* (net bag) with tasty local things while feeling good about where you're emptying wallet.

Currently, one of Marseille's specificities is the development of urban farms within the city limits, a few kilometres from the centre in predominantly working-class neighbourhoods. Until the end of the 20th century, there were many magnificent *bastides* (country houses) surrounded by farmland throughout Marseille. Today, the *bastides*' descendants have often had to sell these family homes, and buildings have sprouted up and keep sprouting up in place of gardens and fields. But Marseille is vast, we've still got open grounds and industrial wastelands spread out throughout the city are waiting to be used ingeniously.

And so seven years ago, farmers created Terre de Mars, the first organic, inner-city farm, in Sainte-Marthe in the Quartiers Nord (northern quarters), on the former land of the 18th-century *Mas des Gougettes* (a mas is a huge house). Their produce can be bought on Monday afternoons at l'Épopée and on Thursday afternoons at Zoomaï. Further north, between the motorways and Servières castle, there is now Capri farm whose land was provided by the city.

These new urban farmers are visible players all around town but also in their neighbourhoods, where you couldn't find healthy, fresh, local produce and where few could afford it anyway. These fields come alive thanks to educational workshops for all ages, direct sales, and also catering or convivial restaurants on the weekends. These neighbourhoods are now reviving their former role as 'weekend destinations'. We are beginning to understand that spending our Saturday with vegetables on a farm makes more sense than spending it in traffic jams at sprawling shopping centres like nearby *Plan de Campagne* – France's fourth busiest, cunningly named 'in the country'. These neighbourhoods are now reviving their former role as 'weekend destinations'.

We kick off this vitamin-rich chapter with two salads centred around peppers. The Marseillais gobble them both up.

06

In Marseille, there are as many ratatouilles as there are families. One thing is certain, since Pixar gave the très Provençal dish its very own film, we're all convinced about the recipe's emotional potential! So, get your pans ready! In my family, we don't eat crunchy vegetables. It's the secret to our ratatouille. The vegetables need to cook until softened. Less vitamins and minerals, but more sweetness . . . You can't have it all. Determine the amount of tomatoes according to your taste. For the purposes of this book, I did two attempts, one with too much tomato purée and one with not enough. My mum did not approve of either of them. The best ratatouille falls somewhere between the two!

MY MUM'S RATATOUILLE

INGREDIENTS FOR 4

2 aubergines
3 courgettes
½ small red pepper
Sunflower oil
½ onion, finely chopped
Olive oil
½ can tomato purée (100g)
2 garlic cloves, crushed
1 sugar cube
Salt and pepper

1. Wash and cut the aubergines into quite thick rounds and salt them to draw out excess moisture. Set them aside for 30 minutes on paper towels.

2. Meanwhile, dice the courgettes and cut the pepper into pieces.

3. Pour sunflower oil into a large pan and fry the courgettes at high heat for 5-10 minutes, then lower the heat, cover, and let them cook, stirring from time to time. Once the courgettes are almost cooked, remove and set aside, without rinsing the pan.

4. Put the peppers in the still-oiled pan and fry them in the same way. Once they are almost cooked, set them aside.

5. Dry the aubergines with a paper towel and dice the rounds. Add to the same pan with a bit more oil to fry at high heat for 10 minutes while stirring. Then, cover and let cook over very low heat. Once the aubergines are almost cooked, remove and set them aside.

6. In a saucepan, brown the onions in olive oil. Add tomato purée, garlic, sugar, salt and pepper and cook for 5 minutes. Then, add all the vegetables to the pan together with a little water. Let cook covered for 30 minutes over medium heat (cooking time depends on the vegetables' freshness).

7. After 30 minutes, if a little water remains, continue to cook uncovered.

Photo of the 'not enough tomatoes' version

The second Chez Yassine recipe, *kefteji* is normally a dish of leftovers: fried vegetables to which eggs are added to make a main course. Served with giant fries Rue d'Aubagne style. In Noailles, it's best to come hungry!

TUNISIAN KEFTEJI

INGREDIENTS FOR 4

- 7 long green peppers
- 4 tomatoes
- 200g squash
- Olive oil
- 4 eggs
- 20g capers
- 1 onion, chopped
- ½ bunch of parsley, chopped
- 1 handful of olives
- 1 pinch of salt

1. Cut the vegetables into pieces and fry them in oil. Chop them by hand, using two knives like scissors.

2. Fry the eggs in a bit of oil, add them to the veggies, and re-chop everything by hand. Add salt and mix well.

3. Serve with a drizzle of olive oil, capers, chopped onion, parsley and olives.

Julia Sammut and Chef Aurélien Baron

Julia dreamed of it, Noailles made it happen. Her Épicerie L'Idéal blends into the crowd as if it had always been there. And yet, the products that Julia puts on her shelves are often jewels (local, as well as Italian, Japanese...) that cannot be found elsewhere on Planet Marseille (in Marseille, we say Planète Mars after IAM's first album).
L'Idéal is also a brand that produces its own jars of chakchouka, acciugata (anchovy sauce), harissa, and preserved lemons, at a small Sicilian artisanal food company in Syracuse - just to fill your cupboards with even more addictive ammunition!
Julia definitely makes waves around here but L'Idéal is also a team, and it was a duo since the beginning - Julia behind the sourcing, Aurélien at the stoves. It seemed one could not be without the other, the serious épicerie on one side of the street and the epicurean dining room across from it, even though this daughter of a Michelin-starred female chef had dreamed of everything except running a restaurant!
Today, L'Idéal is inventing its new life without Chef Aurélien but it was relevant to have them together in the book. Aurélien will soon open his own restaurant and Julia is nurturing a new duo...

WAVE MAKERS

11 Rue d'Aubagne
13001 Marseille

How did your story start in Noailles?
Julia: In reality, my DNA is here. I had to end up here. Otherwise, I would have been in Tunis. I'm really attached to my Mediterranean origins. Living in Marseille over the years, the only quarter I went to outside of the one I lived in was Noailles. I worked in Paris, I left Lourmarin and the family-run restaurant at 16 years old. The village of Lourmarin where I grew up is my Provençal culture, but not my beacon. My Sicilian and North African roots are my foundation.
I had promised myself that I would never have a business and especially not a restaurant and, in the end, here I am. But, if I hadn't found a place in Noailles, I wouldn't have opened an épicerie nor a restaurant. For me, it was not a challenge to settle down in this neighbourhood. It was obvious.

Having grown up in Marseille, I can clearly see that, over the past five years or so, Noailles has changed and become very trendy. How do you manage this?
Julia: We don't manage it, actually! I was raised in my parents' restaurant in the Luberon and I always saw people arriving in our village thinking they would strike gold. As we say here in Provence, these people arrive with cherries and leave with grapes! So, this entrepreneurial craze around Noailles is cool and it gives me great pleasure to see a lot of people come and settle down here, but the real story of Noailles is work! There are only hard workers here. If you just want to make money, you're in the wrong place. The most annoying question is when people ask me if I was well accepted here, because in fact, here we are all judged for our work ethic. And we're all in it together. We see each other all the time.
The biggest 'ideal' story is between Tunisian restaurant Chez Yassine and us. They are our brothers. We work together. We order their dishes and eat them here. One day, my mother cooked my

grandmother's fish couscous, and we had a couscous battle with them. Having them across the street made me decide to settle down here. It was my dream to eat *kefteji* every day, since my Tunisian grandmother lives strongly in me . . .

And at the same time, all the historic shops' owners are glad that L'Idéal has opened here. They happily say that it has put the spotlight on their work.

Julia: I sourced my first products for the store in Noailles. Here, I found the same scented path my father followed at the council estates in nearby Martigues, where he ate with the Lopezes or others. Living all together is part of my childhood and it is also my grandparents' memories of Tunis 80 years ago. We ate dishes that everyone brought to the table. That's what I was looking for when I came here. I wanted to be able to sell loukoum from Pâtisserie Journo, which is a stone's throw from here, and their citronnade by the glass, on Saturdays when they're closed for Shabbat. And it was like that with everyone. I dreamed of talking about them. I stopped my job as a food journalist, but I wanted to continue talking about others. I can't ask for anything better in my life!

How did you let yourself give in to the restaurant biz?

Julia: I met Aurélien 15 days before opening. I had built out the back of the shop with a professional kitchen, telling myself that if one day my mum came to make risotto, I better have the right equipment . . . But my idea was to make sandwiches and salads at the counter for a few tables. I met Aurélien but I had never asked myself if I wanted a chef. In general, when you start this kind of business, you play shopkeeper and you don't really know what you're going to do. Your business is born out of your relationship with your customers. But, during this first meeting with Aurélien, we only talked about cookbooks. He's a book collector like me. I had met many chefs throughout my life, with my parents! Beyond the cuisine he offered, it was his personality that pleased me.

Aurélien: I had heard about Julia's project, but I came to the rendezvous quite nervous because, for me, it was the famous Sammut family, and being face to face with that was a bit intimidating. What's more, I met her for a shop assistant position, but I told her: 'I am a cook, I would like to cook.' She replied 'Okay.' I arrived here the next day, it was still a construction site! I came for a month just to understand the idea of the place, to do the opening from A to Z and to get to know Julia, to find out what she wanted. On opening day, there was water damage and, suddenly, we could not open. Except that the whole Sammut family was there, there were ten of them and I had to cook for them on the first day!

Julia: Aurélien worked with women and men alike in the kitchen. We've also hired women who just wanted to change careers; 20 years ago, French chefs would never have taken these women seriously and would have probably made them fry parsley for a year before letting them touch a pan.

What kind of boss are you?

Julia: What is good, is that I'm only the boss because I pay their wages. It is also their place. I have absolutely no desire for it to be just mine. I couldn't care less. It's way better to say to each other, 'Here, let's do this today, this month, this year . . .' For example, Jérémy Nguyen's passion is wine. He wanted to learn. So, I said to him, 'Okay, you will do the wine list.' I wanted him to bring me things, to tell me things. It is so much stronger this way.

And Sicily in all of this?

Julia: My grandfather was Sicilian and my grandmother was Tunisian. They met in Tunis. There was a huge Sicilian immigration to Tunis. The Sicilians had their quarter.

In my dream, I really wanted to create a story of production, cooking in Sicily with an eye towards Tunisia, and putting it in jars.

When L'Idéal opened, I 'hoarded' products. Next, I went to Syracuse to source, invited by the Italian Chamber of Commerce. I went with Alessandra Pierini who is like a sister to me. [*Author's note: Alessandra owns the Italian épicerie RAP in Paris and used to run Pasta e Dolce in Marseille.*]

During this trip, I tasted Maison Trimarchi's products. Sometime afterwards, I spoke to a Frenchman by phone who was doing an internship there. When he returned to France, he worked with us at the épicerie until he went back to Sicily. One day, he called me to say that Trimachi had invested in a new laboratory to fabricate products for others. So, we went with our team to create recipes together. It's such a pleasure to work with Italians in their small enterprise.

In the Sammut family, you are four strong women (the mum, Reine, Julia and Nadia, her daughters, and their paternal grandmother – now deceased – who trained Reine). However, you say non-stop that you aren't feminists . . .
Because at our house, the man's place is insane! My father, we polish his shoes all day and we are there to choose his suit with him. We have done this throughout our lives. Man is king and we manage everything. At the same time, I've never been confronted with a man that was overbearing. My father didn't show off. He said every day that he wouldn't do anything without us. And I have the holy grail of a partner, the antithesis of macho.
That being said, the team here healed me of my matriarchy.
We must all move towards our own 'ideal'! The power of this word! We set the intention, but in addition, we wrote it on the shop front. So, our only mission here is to find our ideal at L'Idéal. Me, if I listened to myself, I would do everything here, I would sweep the floor, I would clean up . . . and it makes everyone laugh. So, I try to cure myself by talking about it. The strength of this team is to be able to talk openly about things.
I say to them, 'How can I not be like my mother? Help me, I beg you!' Otherwise, I'd be working 20 hours a day here. And then there is the question of the meaning of family. Where does it fit in here? With my parents, everything is based around the concept of family, but on the other hand, where does the family fit in? Their only raison d'être is work. At the same time, Sammut in Maltese means 'he who dies at work'!
To not work on Sunday, that was a big deal for me! A novelty! The restaurant is open on Sundays but I'm not always there. For example, this morning, I stayed with my kids! I have finally accepted the fact that I do not want to have the same life as my parents. I stopped feeling guilty and yet at the beginning I said to myself, 'If I am not working, what will I do?' It is an exercise. I've trained myself to not ask myself, 'Have you finished your (to-do) list?' All you have to do is dare. Today I feel like I have an extra life, like I'm in Mario Bros and I just got a star. I was offered the opportunity to live differently and experience things I didn't know . . . Plus, I have two daughters and it's cool to pass this on to them.

My father is from Dunkerque, and my mother is from Choisy-le-Roi next to Paris. As a kid, I grew up in Essone, near Paris, and I arrived in Marseille at nine years old. It was a shock! I lived in Colbert, near the Belsunce district, when my parents were relocated here. It was incredible! When we moved in, the neighbours offered us mountains of beignets, couscous, an enormous watermelon from their village. In the building, there were Moroccans, Tunisians, Corsicans, Algerians. And at the secondary school, those were the best years of my life, even though I went to Anatole-France, the toughest one in the city centre at the time.
I went to the Bonnevine culinary school in Marseille and interned with one of the city's 3-Michelin-star chefs, Passedat, but I didn't want to stay there.
15 years ago, it was complicated to find a nice restaurant to work at in Marseille. I didn't want to go to the Michelin star L'Épuisette or to the Sofitel hotel's Trois Forts. I had a good experience at L'Absainte, a restaurant in Suzanne Quaglia's former Patalain. The kitchen that she left behind was incredible. Then, I did two years at Ventilo, five years at Pieds Dans le Plat, during the restaurant's heyday, where I learned a lot. Pieds Dans le Plat was in the same vein as Café des Épices. A novelty at the time in Marseille. We had 35-euro dinner menus and we had a hard time getting people to come. Today, Marseille's food scene has never been so rich! Also, before, people stayed in their neighbourhood.
Today, Marseillais are up for heading to different parts of town to eat out. That's new! In Marseille, you can still eat for 10 bucks and be super surprised. You have great three-course menus for less than 40 euros.
At L'Idéal, the challenge is to cook with the shop's products to showcase them and show the customers how to use them.
There are some products that I didn't know, and cultures that I wasn't familiar with, like Japan's. I have 400 cookbooks at home, so, by reading, researching, trying, and having a go, I ended up with some nice dishes. For example, I had trouble at first with mélets [preserved anchovy paste]. When I tasted it raw, I said to myself that it was going to be very complicated to integrate, to cook, and I wondered how I could avoid changing its structure. During that week, I only prepared dishes based on mélets! — **Aurélien Baron**

Today, Marseillais are up for heading to different parts of town to eat out. That's new!

11 Rue d'Aubagne
13001 Marseille

LE CHOU-FLEUR BALLON

INGREDIENTS FOR 4

1 cauliflower
100g pitted black olives
10 anchovies in oil
50g capers
250g feta, crumbled
500g cottage cheese
300g breadcrumbs
Dried oregano
Olive oil
Fresh parsley
Citron sublime condiment from L'Idéal (optional!)

1. Preheat the oven to 180°C/gas mark 4. Remove the cauliflower's leaves and core. Poach the whole cauliflower in boiling water for around 15 minutes until it is *al dente*! Set aside.

2. Chop the black olives, anchovies and capers. Add the feta and mix all with the cottage cheese. Mix in the breadcrumbs and some oregano until you get a paste-like texture.

3. Put the cauliflower in a baking dish. Liberally cover with the paste, a good layer about 1cm thick. Drizzle with olive oil and roast for 30 minutes.

4. Serve sliced with olive oil and fresh parsley, and if you're in the neighbourhood, the citron sublime condiment from L'Idéal.

Sylvie Sy and Co

THE FAMILY

Sylvie and her brother Rémy in the shop

An épicerie, a greengrocer, and a deli, Tam-Ky gathers Asian, West Indian and African products, fruits and vegetables all under one roof. It is a unique stop in Marseille. Going to Tam-Ky market is like taking a trip around the world at a square where one of Marseille's two famous fish markets once stood. The Halle Delacroix ended up being demolished in 1981, but the vocation and atmosphere of this square has not changed much since the 19th century. The Vietnamese Sy family, five brothers and five sisters, deploy their boundless energy to keep it as alive as it was back then. And speaking of atmosphere, let me introduce Sylvie! I don't think there is anyone in Marseille today that is more Marseillaise than her. Sylvie alone symbolises local eloquence and our talent for jubilant exaggeration. Surrounded by seven of her brothers and sisters, Sylvie has worked tirelessly for years in this modern-day shop while two of her sisters run Lôc-Nam, a little further in Noailles on the Rue de l'Académie. It is also the Sy clan that took over the famous Lebanese bakery Le Cèdre, on Rue d'Aubagne, to turn it into a Vietnamese restaurant called Gingembre with Chef Pham Duy. It's surely the most beautiful restaurant in town. That's where you'll find Sylvie these days and if you're lucky enough to have her waitering on you at lunch, calling you *'mon coeur'* or *'mes bébés'* . . . enjoy the lesson, her Marseillais style is the best you'll find in town.

World market, Vietnamese cuisine

5 Rue Halle-Delacroix
13001 Marseille

SYLVIE: When I started at the Tam-Ky store, I was 19 years old. I'm 50 today.
RÉMY (ONE OF HER YOUNGER BROTHERS): And me, I've been working here for 25 years.
SYLVIE: I was born in Vietnam, as was Rémy. My family is from Dà Lat. In fact, only the youngest two kids were born here in France. My sister in Salon-de-Provence, and my brother, Philippe, is a true Marseillais. He was born in the Belle de Mai neighbourhood. My parents took over the shop at the end of the 1980s. It already existed. A Vietnamese man and a Spanish woman ran the shop, and before them, it was an Asian family, way before the 1970s. When I saw the kids of the first owners again, they told me that originally it was a butcher's shop.

How old were you when you arrived in France?
SYLVIE: We arrived in France in April 1979, in Sarcelles near Paris, then Miramas, near Marseille. I was nine years old. Rémy was little. It was the first time I saw snow. And little blonde kids with blue eyes . . . They did'nt have either in our country! We didn't speak French. We lived in a hostel in Miramas for a year. They enrolled us in school, and they put me in Year 4. I didn't know how to read or write in French . . . I still made it to Year 10. Not bad! Then, my father found work in the vines in Courthézon near Châteauneuf-du-Pape, where we moved. The Town Hall found us a house and the residents really helped us. We were the only foreigners, a big family . . . The people were incredible, some came over to help us read and write French. They gave us clothing because we didn't have anything! We were truly lucky. We stayed there for four years.
Next, little by little, my father found friends in the Asian community, most of whom had settled down in Marseille. There was a wire factory in the Saint-Louis quarter, his friends got him work there, and we moved to Marseille. We settled in La Savine, so we grew up in the Quartiers Nord. My mother stayed at home to raise us, she had 10 kids! On the weekend, we'd often go swimming in Fos-sur-Mer, and en route, there was an old Asian farmer couple in Gignac-la-Nerthe, the countryside, who grew Asian vegetables like cabbages and mint. They were the first to do so in the area. We would buy our veggies directly from them. They became friendly with my parents. One day, they retired, and they offered their land to my parents. This, also, was a stroke of luck because they gave my parents a loan. So we moved to Gignac.
My parents began growing vegetables and we delivered them to all the shops. This is how my parents knew that the Tam-Ky store was for sale. And when they bought it, we all came to work for our parents! At first, it was really small. It was the four eldest children – my older brother, my sister, one of my brothers, and

I were in the stockroom. The little ones, they went to school. After five years, my parents were exhausted and wanted to retire. So we took it over, we expanded, we took over the first floor . . .

What are your first memories of Marseille?
I grew up in the Quartiers Nord and I had a blast! They were my best years! We didn't have the means to leave our neighbourhood. As an adolescent, I only knew this part of Marseille. You lived in your quarter; you didn't go anywhere else. I got to know the city centre later on, when I was around 16 years old. When my parents bought the shop, I came to live in the city centre, but every weekend I was in my quarter because all my friends were there. By working here, I discovered the centre, the movie theatres. Then, when I met my husband, he had a little motorboat, so he showed me the Calanques!

What do you think about the evolution of Rue d'Aubagne today?
Frankly, it's the best. It changes everything. Maison Empereur and Épicerie L'Idéal have done lots for the street. It's partly pedestrianised, there are less cars. On the weekends, there are some *beau monde* [jet setters]. We've even opened our own restaurant there, Gingembre [Ginger], but working in a restaurant is so much harder than working at Tam Ky!

Where is the Vietnamese community in Marseille?
Asians own many of the restaurants, and all the restauranteurs know each other. So, at night, when they finish service, they meet up in each other's restaurants and play cards. After service, they also go do karaoke, they eat, and they sing together. Every Asian has a karaoke machine in their restaurant's cellar.

Your brother David is the business manager of the family . . .
Ah, my brother David, he's too serious. He bothers us at the restaurant. Here, it's familial, we laugh with the customers, they adore that but when he comes, he greets them with a formal, *'Bonjour, Madame . . .'* Fortunately, he has a brain. In business he's good. We must recognise that. When we arrived in France, even though we wanted to go to university, we didn't have the money. My brother, David, was able to go when we took over the shop. Thank God, we worked and made money, so we paid for David's studies, and we sent him to Paris where he went to a good university! He also went abroad and now, it's his duty in return to give us a hand. He knows everything better than us, so it's fitting that he manages Tam-Ky. When David returned, he also helped us to build up our assets. Well, he has some brothers and sisters that can be good-for-nothings . . . so he freaks out a bit!

How was David's path decided?
He's the only smart sibling. He met Gaston Defferre! You remember, this former illustrious mayor of Marseille? David was top of his class at La Savine [housing estate] and he received a book from Mayor Gaston Deferre's hands, who congratulated him because he was a simple foreigner who worked super hard at school. *Eh oui!* Once I began working, I wanted to live in the centre, not in Gignac. I rented an apartment near the Opera, and, inevitably, my brothers and sisters came to live with me. They didn't want to be in the countryside any longer. From secondary school on, my brother David lived with me. When he passed his baccalaureate, he didn't know what to do. He was really good at drawing, he loved it since he was little. We passed by the fashion school on Rue Saint-Fé [Férreol] and I said to him, 'Why not this school?' and we signed him up. He passed all his exams, then he went to study in Paris. He had to rent an apartment, he had to eat. He worked at Ungaro. Remember Lady Diana's pink dress? Well, what do you know, my brother had his hands on it!

And who will take over?
Today, my parents have 13 grandchildren. *Les petits* come to eat here between noon and two. My daughter comes from secondary school at noon to eat, there are three or four of them who come from *le lycée*. They go to the office upstairs, they have a blast, they laugh. For me, my daughter was essentially born here! She is 15 years old, but at the beginning, when she was a baby, I put her in a baby seat in the kitchen upstairs and told the team to keep an eye on her. All my brothers' and sisters' kids grew up here. Now, I have my niece at the cash register downstairs, my nephew drives the truck, his father can no longer do the markets . . . and we hope that they will take over the shop. Well, they don't like that idea very much because it's a lot of sacrifices and a lot of hours . . . Me, I spend

Chef Pham Duy arrived in Marseille in 1993. He then left to work on the Côte d'Azur, in Monaco and Saint Tropez, and worked many years in Italian restaurants. Duy came back to Marseille to cook his Vietnamese cuisine.

Mondays to Saturdays here. On Saturdays, when I work at the shop, I return home at 21.30 or 22.00. They're long days! And young people don't want that.
I'm at my house only on Sundays. So, I didn't see my daughter grow up. At three months old she was at daycare, and she had a nanny, the activity centre. At 10 years old, she said, 'Mum, stop. I don't want to do anything. I just want to stay at home.' She is closer to her father than me. It's symbiotic with her father. But, when we arrived in France, we had nothing. Once we saw that by working, we earned money, we were eager to keep at it, for we wanted lots of beautiful things. We wanted so many things we didn't have when we were young. Now, we have less kids, we make more money, and what do we do? We give it all to our kids. We spoiled them too much; we corrupted them, and they don't want to work anymore. It's the truth! We were 10 children, and my dad was the only one who worked. We didn't have anything. Already, he was feeding all of us, which was huge. We couldn't ask for more. We didn't even think about it. It never crossed our minds. It was not even worth asking. The answer was no. We longed to have everything we saw at others' houses! So, I always said to myself, the day I had a child, they shouldn't miss out on anything. When I had my daughter, I was 34 and I had everything; I had my situation, she lacked nothing. But maybe that's not good. As a child, I missed everything so much . . . I think that's what gave us the drive to work. Now my niece, at 18, when she got her driver's licence, her father had already bought her a car! And then she quit school.
Even my own daughter, when I ask her to give me a hand, she tells me she is tired. But it's like that. Their generation is different. At the beginning, when the four of us took over the shop, when my parents couldn't work anymore, we worked seven days a week. It was morning to night. The banks didn't want to give us a loan.
We had to work, we were young, we didn't have partners, nor kids, and we were desperate to succeed! On Sundays, we came here, we set up shelves, we tore down walls . . . we transformed the place with my brothers. For five years, we only lived for our store. When we had our kids, we calmed down a bit, we closed on Sundays, but, well, every morning, we are still here today!

5 Rue Halle-Delacroix
13001 Marseille

BÒ TÀI CHANH 5 FLAVOURS (Imagined by Chef Pham Duy)

INGREDIENTS FOR 2

1 shallot
Fresh ginger
Vietnamese coriander
Thai basil
2 garlic cloves
1 onion
50g white rice
Sunflower oil
A few sesame seeds
1 rump steak – 300g
1 green mango (have fun trying different varieties)
100g rice vermicelli
Vegetable broth (optional)
Chives, finely chopped
Soy sauce
1 lime

1. *Brunoise* (finely chop) the shallot. Peel the ginger, cut into fine slices then into minuscule cubes. Finely chop the coriander and Thai basil. Finely chop the garlic and brunoise the onion.

2. Cook the rice in boiling water.

3. Brown the garlic in sunflower oil. Add the rice and toast it. Once the rice is hot, let it stick a bit to the bottom of the pan, but remove from the heat before it burns. Mix the rice with the sesame seeds. Leave the mixture to cool then grind into a powder.

4. Barely sear the steak before cutting into thin slices, thicker than a carpaccio.

5. Thinly slice the mango and spread out the slices on the plate. Cover the mango with the steak slices.

6. Sprinkle one-fifth of the plate with coriander, one-fifth with Thai basil, one-fifth with powdered grilled rice, one-fifth with shallots and one-fifth with ginger.

7. Cook the rice vermicelli: bring salted water to a boil over high heat. Once boiling, lower heat and add vermicelli. Let cook just until the vermicelli turn translucent. This will take only a few seconds. Drain.

8. Brown the onion in a pan. You could then add a vegetable broth and let it simmer for a few minutes. Add the hot vermicelli, mix well, and let cook for a few minutes.

9. Turn off the heat, add coriander and chives. Serve in a bowl on the side.

10. Serve soy sauce as well on the side.

11. Squeeze lime juice over the mango-beef plate.

12. To eat, roll up a slice of beef in a mango slice and dunk into the soy sauce. Go for it with your hands. Each bite is different.

M R S
Préfecture-Opéra

Hugues Mbenda

AFRICAN NOUVELLE CUISINE

Franco-Congolese cuisine, gastronomic menu at night

10 Rue Francis Davso
13001 Marseille

We are super lucky to have Hugues Mbenda in Marseille! He's the wind in our gastronomic sails. A breath of fresh air who mixes ingredients, techniques, cultures, flavours and textures with precision. His culinary adventure is also ours. And we're happy to let him surprise us.
After making his mark in Michelin-starred establishments across the country, Hugues chose Marseille to open his first restaurant, L'Orphéon, not far from Noailles, which was quickly adopted by a band of regulars. Hugues and his partner Mathilde then landed in nearby Place de Rome where they opened the canteen Libala ('wedding' in Lingala), and there, we were served memorable brunches, among other treats. They continue their creative path today in a magnificent restaurant, Kin, on Rue Francis Davso. Calm and talent guide the chef in his desire to create a Marseillais-Congolese bistronomy.
The first time I met Hugues was at L'Orphéon, during the Covid 'non-essential business' closure. I had the restaurant all to myself, plus the chef's cooking and the welcome of his brother, Éric. We were enchanted by this moment that we got to share on a Sunday afternoon in December. It did us good. I think we all three needed to 'play' at the restaurant for a few hours.
A month later, L'Orphéon was awarded a Michelin Bib Gourmand. I wanted to clink two or three glasses of champagne with them to celebrate, but restaurants in France were still closed, I had to wait . . .
We've well made up for lost time since then. I interviewed Hugues again to update these pages and in December 2022, I accompanied him and Mathilde to Kinshasa, in the Democratic Republic of Congo. We visited his family as he searched for new culinary inspiration, but I'll save that for my next book – about African cuisine in France.

How would you define your cooking?
Hugues: One day, we got a comment on the dining website The Fork, from a customer saying that it was very good but that she thought my cuisine should be more African. It made us laugh. I arrived in France at age nine with my brother, Éric, who was 11 years old. In terms of cooking, I know more about French cuisine than African cuisine. I had only worked in Michelin-starred restaurants in France until I opened my own. I'm trying now to glean from African ingredients and make blends between ingredients and techniques. During my time at prestigious tables, I noticed that you had to show off your technique, you had to impress, but today, the criteria have changed, the Michelin Guide has been rejuvenated. You must keep it simple, use simple, high-quality products and elevate them.
Éric: What surprises me, is that when a black chef is inspired by his African roots, we find that normal, as if he didn't have to do any research on his part, whereas our culture is more French than Congolese.
We grew up in Kinshasa, then in a Parisian suburb.
Actually, the gastronomic world doesn't resemble us, in fact.
We have had to count our pennies. We don't have the means to lunch at Alexandre Mazzia's 3-Michelin-star Marseille table every day! So in our restaurants, we want a mixed clientele.
Hugues: We need sincerity. We want people to naturally come eat at our place. If they like it, they'll return. We want a genuine relationship with our customers or with food writers or inspectors from culinary guides.

Your first restaurant, L'Orphéon, was located just above Noailles . . .
Hugues: I'm not Marseillais, so I have an outside perspective. When I came here, I found that in many places in Marseille, people stay in their neighbourhood. But here, in Noailles, there's everyone, and I like that, it's an area in which many people come and mix.
Éric: We could have put our restaurant in the 7th. It's more chic. That would have also worked. But we wanted an area that was accessible to everybody. We can't forget where we came from. We left the Congo because of a civil war when President Kabila arrived in 1997.

Hugues: I try to put our identity in our restaurants. I worked at Apicius in Paris, in the 8th, with Chef Vigato. It was 300 euros per person. Me, I want to cook gastronomically at affordable prices. That's the hardest thing. Gastronomy with a courgette! Because gastronomy with caviar and truffles is easy. We try to be creative while remaining simple. The creativity is here. Without breaking the bank.

How did you choose Marseille?
Éric: My wife was born in Marseille. She's a nurse and she worked in Paris. We met there. But in Marseille, there's an African-like chaos and I like its accessibility. We're down to earth here.
Hugues: Me, I came here five years ago, and it took a long time to acclimatise. Coming from Paris, it's tricky. But the customers made me feel comfortable. Here, people have time to talk, to discuss. In Paris, there isn't that. Sometimes, we finish service and we stay until 1am chatting with customers that we don't know. This interaction made it easier to adapt to the city.
Éric: The first time I came to Marseille, I was in an AirBnb near Place Castellane. I walked from the north to the south and I really liked the diversity, but I saw that it was necessary to create this mix. I knew many people in the northern districts where my wife comes from who had never set foot in the 8th in the south. It's more spread out than Paris, so you have the impression that it's far, but the city is one and the same.
Hugues: We now manage to get people to come to our restaurant from afar. That makes me happy.
Éric: If people don't leave their comfort zone, the mix will never happen. You must make the effort.
Hugues: The restaurant's playlist is African, we play Fela Kuti, Koffi, Fally Ipupa, Mbilia Bel, people discover them and they are ready to explore further. The craze is on and we like sharing. This work makes it easy to connect. We have friends today that we would never have had beforehand. We have created real bonds.

What are your childhood memories of dishes and ingredients?
Hugues: Rice and beans. These are the two primary ingredients of my childhood. They are the base. White or red beans. And rice is obligatory. I cannot go a week without eating rice. I've convinced my wife Mathilde now. We eat rice in a salad, as a dish, for dessert . . . I love it! I don't often cook with it at the restaurant, but I eat it all the time.
There's something important to add. When you say 'African cuisine' in France, everyone thinks of *mafé* or *tiep*, but we don't know them! We're from the Congo, in Central Africa, so we discovered these West African dishes after arriving in France.
Éric: We've discovered other African cultures in France! We eat manioc, manioc leaves (saka saka), it's the base of Central African cuisine. With manioc, you make semolina, fermented manioc paste steamed for a long time . . . we eat it from leaf to root.
Hugues: It replaces starches. It's the equivalent of a potato.

Who did the cooking in the Congo?
Éric: Our mother. She had a restaurant in Kinshasa.
Hugues: My parents came to France, first to Paris, then to Avignon, where they had Éric in fact, but they had me when they returned to Kinshasa. My father then came back to France alone, the time it took to refill the coffers, then we were able to join him much later. So, I didn't know my father until I was nine years old. When I landed at the airport in France in 1999, I didn't have any memory of him. My first reaction . . . I found him tall, like in the photos, but physically I look like my mum.
Éric: My mother had to stay with my father's family while waiting to join him. She didn't like it because her family was more upper class than my father's. But my mother was a person who didn't complain much.
Hugues: She was a woman who sucked it up.
Éric: So, she opened a restaurant to make money. Often her customers were street vendors, sellers of spare parts. She would play music. Everyone called her 'Auntie Jeanne'. People still talk about her.

And your mum taught you to cook?
Hugues: Not really. She passed away the year after we arrived in France. We are a reconstructed family, eight children in all, but from our mother, we're four. Because I was the youngest, I spent a lot of time in the kitchen with her. That's maybe where my love of cooking comes from. Anyway, who I am today I owe it to my mum. She taught me the discipline.
Éric: And me, I crushed! I ground a lot of spices, leaves, garlic…! For that matter, I burned my thigh while crushing chilli pepper. I often went to wash the vegetables too and I would go shopping with her.
Hugues: I would have loved to cook

for her. My father didn't want me to become a chef. I had to convince him when I was 15. He wanted me to go to university. In fact, I didn't choose cooking. It came naturally to me. At 10 years old, when I came home from school for lunch, I watched the French show *Bon Appétit, Bien Sûr* with Chef Joël Robuchon, then in the evening I baked bread to test myself . . . but I didn't even know that you could study cooking! I did my research about that. One day my father came to eat at renowned chef Christian Constant's restaurant, where I worked as a sous-chef. He had tears in his eyes. When he saw that people addressed me with the formal French 'you', and that they had a lot of respect for me even though I was only 24 years old, he understood that it was not just nonsense. He saw I was doing what I loved and that you did not have to have a PhD to be someone. My father and my mother went to university, they worked in a bank in Congo. In Kinshasa, in Mobutu's era, my father was a bank manager. Unfortunately, when he arrived in France, his diplomas were not valid here, and he had to find a way to support the family. He was a security guard, then in Avignon he worked in the vineyards.

Éric: In 2016, Hugues and I went on holiday for a month in the Congo to pay homage to our mother.

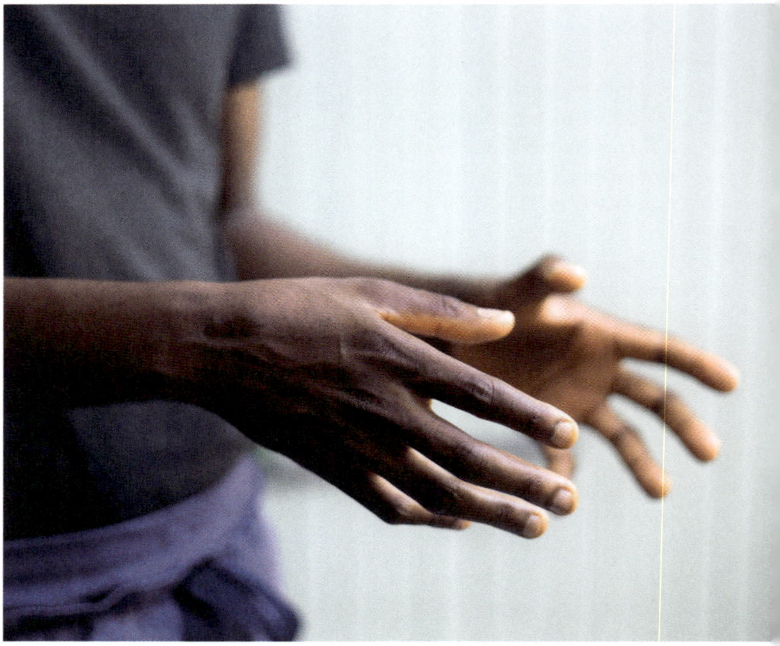

Hugues: It was important for us to take this trip. It had been 17 years since we had left the Congo. When we arrived in France, we were little. Our goal was to fit in as quickly as possible. Now, I realise that that was a mistake because we had pushed our culture aside. At school, we needed to catch up. We had to learn as quickly as possible. It was later, when I started working, around the age of 20, that I understood that our Congolese culture was so important.

Éric: For me, the thing that got me back into my culture was museums. I often went to the Musée du Quai Branly in Paris, and that's how I started to do this work of refocusing. In art and gastronomy, diversity is key. For example, we served sake as a digestif at L'Orphéon and people were surprised. But why shouldn't we? We serve many European dishes even though we are Congolese. We do not want to be limited to Africa.

Franco-Congolese cuisine, gastronomic menu at night

10 Rue Francis Davso
13001 Marseille

PISSALADIÈRE-STYLE CAKE

INGREDIENTS FOR 4

For the savoury cake:
200g flour
11g baking powder
20g Herbes de Provence
100g grated Gruyère
4 eggs
125ml milk
70ml olive oil
Salt and pepper

For the pissaladière onions:
4 onions
10ml olive oil
5g Herbes de Provence
30g anchovies
3 garlic cloves, crushed
Salt and pepper

For the garnish:
Pearl onions
Okra
Olive oil
Anchovies
Rocket

1. Preheat the oven to 180°C/gas mark 4.

2. In a large bowl, add all the cake ingredients in the order they are listed and whisk well. Pour into a non-stick 20–25cm diameter cake tin and bake for 30–35 minutes.

3. Prep the pissaladière onions: peel and finely slice the onions, put in a saucepan with the olive oil, Herbes de Provence, anchovies, garlic, salt and pepper. Sweat mixture at high heat for 2 minutes, then let cook for 30 minutes at low heat. Purée in a blender.

4. Remove the cooled cake from the tin and hollow it out, leaving a base of around 2cm. Garnish with the stewed onions.

5. Cut pearl onions and okra in half vertically, sauté for 4–5 minutes in a bit of olive oil, and place them harmoniously on the cake with a few anchovy fillets and a bit of rocket.

M R S

Vieux-Port
Rue Sainte

Charlotte Baldaquin

For a dancer and self-taught cook, being the chef at the Théâtre de la Criée's restaurant seemed logical. The military rigour and tireless physique that is necessary for a ballet career prove very useful in a professional kitchen. We all got used to meeting up at this theatre on the Vieux-Port to feast on the chef's gourmet imagination, and it's the best spot to watch the Bastille Day fireworks. But, recently, Lolotte wanted to choreograph her own spot. In 2023, she found investors for her solo performance. A new challenge for this fighter who enjoys free falls.

MY HISTORY WITH DANCE

I always wanted to be a dancer or a chef, but my mother told me that it was not possible to do both. I had been doing classical dance since I was 3, then every afternoon from age 10, the conservatory and the opera . . . so dance became the only option. I danced for the ballet in Nancy but my future husband was hired by the famous choreographer Roland Petit in Marseille three weeks after we met. It's a ballet company that I didn't want to be part of since Roland didn't like girls. Even his ballets were men first, then girls after. Nevertheless, I was 18½ years old . . . and I told myself that I was still going to audition. I was accepted, so I moved to Marseille, and it was wonderful. We were doing worldwide tours. Roland Petit was adored in Japan. The Japanese spectators hung on to us like rock stars. In Marseille, we danced at the Opera.
Afterwards, with two children, pregnant with my third, and a dancer husband who travelled all the time, the passion began to diminish. I could not do this job without passion. I stopped working for two years, I had a job in food, I conducted surveys on the street, then I was hired at the Repetto dance shop and went on the road to meet dance schools. At that point, I said to myself that I really wanted to cook.

MY HISTORY WITH CUISINE

I began to cook for others when I was 12 years old. Although I was thin, my mum forbade me to eat because the dance teachers said I couldn't gain weight. My mum didn't cook, nor did my dad. So, I got used to cooking. My mum made frozen food, Royco instant soup, but she had every issue of Elle and on weekends I organised their recipes. My brother also cooked. It was a fight between us. By contrast, I saw my grandmother cook, she was the daughter of a butcher-charcutier and made terrines. My sister-in-law and Julia Sammut had a good friend in common who told me about Julia's new project – Épicerie L'Idéal in Noailles. I met Julia and joined the team 15 days after its opening. It's there where I discovered high-quality ingredients. I waited tables and worked in the épicerie. Julia wanted us to give customers a taste of all the products.
La Mercerie, the fine-dining restaurant near L'Idéal, had not opened yet, so I was very happy that we were across from the Chez Yassine eatery in the winter when it got dark early. The Tunisians always kept a kind watch on us.
At L'Idéal, I met Chef Emmanuel Perrodin, who was a customer.
I told him that I wanted to cook and he advised me to put my hands in it, even without a diploma. After two years at L'Idéal, I lent a hand to Chef Christian Qui when he was cooking in Les Goudes for the popular food show on France Inter radio, On Va Déguster, then on his boat. One Saturday morning, Emmanuel sent me a text, 'Do you have anything against being a dishwasher?' and at the tender age of 42 years, I told him, 'No, it doesn't scare me as long as I can see the kitchen because that's how you learn.' He gave me an appointment at 6pm with Marie-Jo Ordener at the Friche la Belle de Mai, a place where I did not go often. I had never eaten at their restaurant, Les Grandes Tables. Marie-Jo told me, 'I don't need your CV.' I said to myself, 'She's cool.' It was the end of June, Saturday night, and there were people partying everywhere at La Friche. Marie-Jo had been ditched by the Friche's child nursery's cook. She said Emmanuel had told her I'd do the job. 'You have three children, that should work. You start Monday.' She came with me for the Monday meal. I had a chef's coat that I had bought for a week of patisserie training at Bricoleurs de Douceurs. On Monday morning, I arrived with my very thick uniform, Marie-Jo showed me the nursery. I read the nurse's folder that night to find out who was allergic to legumes . . . and to learn what a legume was! The next day, she left me on my own. I ended up soaked from my neck to my knees, a mixture of water and sweat. I did the two summer months all alone and helped Marie-Jo at Grandes Tables events, particularly the Kouss-Kouss festival.
Six months later, I found myself working my first service as head chef at the Théâtre de la Criée's restaurant, run by Les Grandes Tables. I was replacing the chef on maternity leave; 40–170 covers each service.

Mediterranean cuisine
in constant exploration

39 Rue de la Paix Marcel Paul
13001 Marseille

DISHES BY MARSEILLE CHEFS THAT HAVE LEFT THEIR MARK ON ME

The first time that I tasted Emmanuel Perrodin's oyster with Comté cheese, that left its mark. And the tuna pastrami with an emulsion of just-grilled onions that Cheffe Sarah Chougnet (restaurant Regain) made, just because she wanted to make a couscous with it. She graduated top of her class at the prestigious Ferrandi culinary school. She has the most insane technique. With her and chef Laurent Mercier who just took over from me at la Criée, I've shared the most and I've grown the most as a chef.

Marseille's food scene is evolving. For chefs that are doing well, I think the trend is to come back to showcasing the ingredient because today's customers are asking, 'where can I eat a good bouillabaisse?' and not just 'a bouillabaisse'. The right ingredient is an affordable luxury.

AUBERGINE PLEASURE

'It's a dish inspired by a photo of Florentine aubergines and leftover Comté.
I created it for the 4 As (Aces) summer pop-up and everyone liked it.

INGREDIENTS FOR 4

340g whipping cream
70g Comté, diced
1 tbsp of artisanal pastis like Ferroni's Château des Creissauds
2 small Italian aubergines (Violetta di Firenze)
Olive oil
2 small yellow or green courgettes (the small ones have less seeds. The younger and fresher, the better)
1 preserved yellow lemon (buy ready-preserved or preserve a fresh lemon in salt)
Chervil or fennel fronds (chervil has a nicer taste)
Small shiso leaves
Young mint shoots
Salt and pepper
A small siphon (500ml)

For the blackberry pickles:
12 blackberries
1 espresso cup sugar
1 espresso cup cider vinegar
1 espresso cup red wine vinegar
3 espresso cups water

1. To make the blackberry pickles, rinse the blackberries with clean water, dry them and let them finish drying for a moment. Place them in a deep, narrow jar.

2. Boil the sugar, vinegars, and water together. Pour the hot mix over the blackberries and let cool for at least 40 minutes in the open air.

3. For the Comté emulsion, heat the cream and the Comté in a small saucepan, stirring with a spatula to help the Comté melt. Let the mixture boil until it thickens slightly. Reduce the heat, keep stirring to make sure the cheese has fully melted. Add pepper and a tablespoon of artisanal pastis. Cut the heat and let it cool down.

4. Strain through a fine strainer before pouring in a siphon with a gas cartridge. You need to keep the siphon at room temperature. (If you put it in the refrigerator, you will need to put it in a hot water bath to reliquefy it.)

5. Prepare the aubergines: preheat the oven to 175°C/gas mark 4. Wash, dry, and cut off the pointy part of the heads, keeping their pretty purple frocks intact. Halve lengthwise. Now you've come to the delicate part.

6. Take a small paring knife (*couteau d'office*) and slice diagonal lines (1cm apart) onto the aubergines' flesh, then turn it 90° to make a grid pattern. Make sure not to let the tip of the knife sink in. The knife just caresses the aubergine flesh.

7. Drizzle olive oil on the flesh. If you have a pipette, that's ideal. You don't have to drizzle on that much. What's important is that it's everywhere. Season with salt and good-quality pepper.

8. Bake for 15–20 minutes, depending on the oven. The aubergines should be light golden brown and the flesh should be tender to the touch.

9. The courgettes stay raw. They must be young courgettes. If freshly picked, even better. Quarter them lengthwise then horizontally. It's a *brunoise* in fact!

10. Halve the preserved lemon, remove the pulp, only keeping the rind, and cut into a mini *brunoise* (dice). Add to the courgettes. Salt and pepper the mix then drizzle with high-quality olive oil.

11. Plating time! Remove the herbs from their stems. Put an aubergine half on each plate. Put some courgette tartare on top, slightly drained. You don't need too much oil. Next, the Comté emulsion, then the herbs. Place 3 blackberry pickles around each aubergine half. Finish with a drizzle of olive oil.

2e Arrt
MONTEE
des ACCOULES
"Aujourd'hui ma bibliothèque est fermée.
Ou peut-être hier, je ne sais pas"

FOR THE LOVE OF SPICE

The title of this chapter could have been the book's title for it sums up everything I'd like to tell you about Marseille. Many mistakenly think Marseille lacks subtlety and security, but Marseille is one of the few cities that makes sense in today's France, if not the world. Marseille's chaotic nature is natural, it awakens our senses, and makes us question our usual ways. One must admit this irreverent behaviour is not just refreshing, it brings us together instead of us staying stuck in different social strata. The world isn't bland and smooth, nor is Marseille or cooking. Thank goodness for that!

As for spice, and chilli, in cuisine, retro-French bons-vivants still have a long way to go to understand the beauty of them . . . African, Asian and South American chefs get tired of explaining that their cuisine is spicy but won't tear our throats out. Many of them have reduced their recipes' heat and spice for local or novice palates who remain biased against them. Wake up, France! And retrain your taste buds.

07

Magd, Mohaned, Feras, and their mum, Majda

RESILIENCE

From left to right:
Mohaned, Magd and Feras

Unpretentious Ashourya opened in April 2017 with Majda, chef and mother of three grown boys, in the quarter between Saint-Charles train station and the Palais Longchamp that is becoming an unexpectedly appealing culinary crossroads. The success of this talented and resilient Syrian family gave a real boost to the neighbourhood. Today, the three brothers work together in the kitchen. Their mum runs it all from afar, and the family opened a sprawling, second location in Cours Julien.
When I came to the restaurant to photograph their recipe, Feras was cooking a snack for his kids before fetching them from school and Magd cooked a flavourful *safarjaliyé* with me while answering my questions.

When did you arrive in Marseille?
At the end of 2013 after first passing through Turkey. We arrived in Ankara by car, and we went to the French Embassy. I have cousins who walked two and a half months to go to Germany. Some countries like Saudi Arabia closed their borders and kicked out those who were already there. They were afraid that the revolution would spread there. My parents had studied in Toulouse between 1980 and 1987. My father has a PhD in agronomy and my mother a masters in agronomy. My brothers and I were all born in France at that time. So, it was logical for us to flee to France, but my brothers and I didn't speak any French.

How big is the Syrian community in Marseille?
There are 50 or so families.

What jobs did you and your brothers have in Syria?
Two of us are petroleum engineers and Mohaned is an agricultural engineer. I also have a degree in life and earth sciences from Saint-Charles University in Marseille. Today it is difficult to work in petroleum because of our Syrian nationality. People are afraid. But recently I have had new offers.
In Syria, we had import–export stores. We sold everything, computers, clothes, accessories, lingerie, and we had a café. We also had a two-storey department store in Raqqa, which was the capital of jihadism, and the building was bombed. We lived in Deir ez-Zor, a big city. There, everything is organised in clans. It is very different from Damascus where everything is a bit more impersonal.

How did you all learn to cook?
We all three knew how to cook because we always helped our mum out. Arriving here, we didn't have a choice. Catering or opening a restaurant was a necessity.
My mum got a professional certificate at the state-run culinary lycée in Marseille, via their job insertion programme that is devoted to adult women, *Des Étoiles et des Femmes*, where Michelin-star chefs welcome a female trainee in their *brigade* (team). The celebrated chef

Alain Ducasse is one of the sponsors. Today, I often bring back the restaurant's dishes to my home. So we don't have to cook twice.

What is your perspective on your arrival in Marseille?

We arrived with just a receipt for a residence permit application which meant we couldn't rent an apartment, nor work. So, like many others, we first landed in a 30-square-metre place in Noailles. The rent was 850 euros a month. We were five inside. Then, we were able to find work in restaurants. I was also a security guard in Marseille and Nice. I was even part of President Hollande's security detail when he came to the Vélodrome Stadium in Marseille. In my opinion, the problem with integration in France is the language. We made the effort to learn French, but up to now no one forces you to do so. In Germany, anyone who comes to live there must study German for two years and there is a test. It's controlled. In France, people don't learn French! As a result, no one talks to each other because no one understands each other. We lack a common language.

Who are your restaurant's customers?

International and local. The customers are curious. In general, they know Lebanese food since the Lebanese arrived here well before us. Actually, Syrian cuisine is broader than Lebanese cuisine because, in the past, Lebanon was part of Syria. Lebanon became independent in 1943. But often Syrians prefer to open Lebanese restaurants. It's easier in terms of marketing.
Our cuisine has points in common with Turkish, Armenian, and even Indian food (spices, cooking techniques, the use of yoghurt . . .). These are influences from the Silk Road. In Syria, we eat a lot of meat. Hence my choice of recipe for this book.
Here in Marseille, we lack certain ingredients. We had to be inventive, especially for desserts. For example, for *knafeh*, we make our own *crème de lait* [fresh milk cream] with local ingredients.

Is there something that has surprised you in Marseille?

The roasted chestnuts seller in winter on La Canebière with his little fake train. It's great! And the *savon de Marseille* when it is good quality. It's like Aleppo soap. The Marseille mindset is close to that in my country. But what is the most surprising, is that everyone thinks that here. Everyone says Marseille resembles their country!

What quarter do you like to explore?

With my wife, we like to walk along the Corniche or go to

La Pointe Rouge to eat and have a coffee. I ate bouillabaisse one time in Vallon des Auffes in 2014. It was totally new for me. I went with my French professor and other students in my class.

'The Marseille mindset is close to that in my country. But what is the most surprising, is that everyone thinks that here. Everyone says Marseille resembles their country!'

SAFARJALIYÉ (veal with quinces)

INGREDIENTS FOR 6

- 1.2kg veal, cut into large chunks
- 2 cinnamon sticks
- Red, white, black pepper
- Jamaican pepper
- Ground cardamom
- Ground ginger
- 500g tomatoes
- 2 quinces
- 5 garlic cloves, chopped
- 50ml vegetable oil
- 2 tbsp sumac
- 1 tbsp paprika
- 2 tbsp tomato purée
- 1 tbsp dried mint
- Salt

1. In a large saucepan (*cocotte*), boil the meat in water with the cinnamon sticks, a pinch of each pepper, cardamom, ginger and salt for 1½ hours (more or less, it depends on the calf's age). Once the meat is cooked, discard the cooking water.

2. Cut the tomatoes and quinces, without peeling them, into medium-size pieces, and soak them in water to avoid browning.

3. In another large saucepan, brown the garlic in a bit of vegetable oil. Add sumac, paprika, 1 tablespoon red pepper, 1 pinch of ginger, black pepper, white pepper and Jamaican pepper (add peppers according to your taste, they are spicy!).

4. Add meat to the mix then let cook over low heat until the meat takes on the spices' colour and absorbs their flavours.

5. Add the chopped tomatoes and tomato purée. Without waiting, slowly pour in 1.5 litres of hot water to make a sauce. Let simmer for a few minutes, then add the quinces. Don't add salt before they are done cooking. If you add salt at the beginning, it will harden everything, the quinces as much as the meat.

6. Cover and let cook for 10 minutes until boiling. Once boiling, add dried mint and salt.

7. This is when you add the *kebbés* (see following recipe). Let cook for another 15 or so minutes over medium heat. When the quinces are soft and the sauce is well incorporated, but not too thick, it is ready.

8. At the restaurant, we serve this dish with bulgur and meat *kebbés*. They don't have the usual 'rugby ball' shape. These *kebbés* are round, smaller, and more compact.

INGREDIENTS FOR 6 (30 KEBBÉS)

For the filling:
300g minced beef
Vegetable oil
Red, white, black pepper
Ground cinnamon
Ground cardamom
1 onion, quartered
1 handful of pine nuts (optional)
Salt

For the shell:
500g bulgur
Ground cinnamon
Ground cardamom
Ground coriander
Cumin
Red, white, black pepper
1 onion, cut into wedges
250g lean minced beef
Salt

KEBBÉS

1. For the filling, brown the mince in vegetable oil. Once the meat is cooked, add spices and salt. Mix in the onion last. If you want to use pine nuts, brown them in a separate pan for a few minutes, then add to the meat once the onion is cooked. Leave to cook for another 2 minutes, then let the filling cool before using.

2. To prepare the shell, rinse the bulgur with water in a strainer, add spices, peppers and the onion. Add salt, then mix with the minced beef.

3. Form the mixture into little balls with your hands. Put a ball in your palm, make an indentation with your thumb, and turn the ball around it to form an empty shell.

4. Fill the shell with filling. Tamp down the filling well inside so that the *kebbé* doesn't fall apart during cooking, then close the shell by rolling it in the palm of your hand to seal the ball. (Wet your hands to make the assembly easier.)

5. Fry the *kebbés* in vegetable oil in a big pan or a fryer until they are beautifully browned, around 5 minutes. Place them on paper towels to absorb excess oil.

6. To serve, first put the meat and quinces from the *safarjaliyé* on a plate, then its sauce, and, lastly, place the *kebbés* on top.

'In Syria, we prefer to make this recipe with lamb, but here, we noticed that our restaurant's customers prefer veal. So, we adapted it.'

Najla Chami and Serje Banna

Najla and Serje will adopt you within one minute of knowing you. And you'll do the same with them. This director by training and her DJ/photographer husband left Lebanon eight years ago to write a new chapter in their creative lives. And, pow, they came up with Mouné, the Lebanese restaurant that Marseille had been waiting for . . . a long time!
Cheffe Najla shares her modern, festive, and enveloping cuisine (yes, it sticks to your ribs, and we ask for seconds!), all with an Armenian touch, as chatty Serje likes to remind you, for it is he who works the room with gusto. Serje is a huge fan of his wife's cooking and that of his mother's, an Armenian who is a fantastic cook also (a tautology!). Let's eat! And before leaving, be sure to drink a bit of Jermuk, produced in the Armenian city with the same name, a sparkling water that will rattle your nostrils. You'll think of me half an hour afterwards . . .

SAHTEIN! BON APPÉTIT!

NAJLA: With Serje, we want to introduce people to real Lebanese food. We're from Beirut, our families are from Beirut, but I know all of Lebanon well. My father went on many hikes. I often accompanied him, and I really got interested in each region's specialities. I realised what culinary diversity this small country has.
The problem is those who make food incorrectly and say that it's Lebanese food. Recently, an Instagram blogger explained that you must peel chickpeas before making hummus. I went crazy and messaged her, 'Are you mental?' And one must learn where the dishes come from. For example, there are so many ways to make *kebbés*. My recipe comes from the north of Lebanon. Normally, we serve only one giant *kebbé* on the plate and it isn't fried. It is baked. My *kebbé*, I make it lighter, smaller, but in the same spirit. Even in Lebanon, there are different ways of making it.
In Palestine, they also make a lot of *kebbés*. In fact, I think they come from there.
My cuisine isn't rigid. I adapt my recipes all the time, which are, ultimately, quite personal.
I make a lot of creations, with fish for example. I also learned tips and Armenian recipes from Serje's mum. Armenians eat more spice than Lebanese do. I always liked spices but now I use them even more, and I make Serje taste everything. I trust his palate.

How does one define Lebanese cuisine?

SERJE: The region was part of the Ottoman Empire for 450 years. Now, we're divided between Lebanon, Palestine, Syria, Armenia, Jordan, and Greece also . . . But the foundation of our cuisines comes from the Ottoman Empire, from Turkey. For example, it was the Ottomans who invented *mezze*.
NAJLA: And yoghurt for cooking, that comes from the Turks.
Lebanese cuisine is wonderfully flavourful, a blend of all the countries that surround us. Some dishes have an African influence, others are influenced by Moroccan or French dishes that we adapted. The Lebanese have always travelled a lot and brought back ingredients and ideas to Lebanon. We have dishes that are influenced by Palestine and Syria, even if we don't use the same spices or cooking methods.
SERJE: Israeli cuisine is more recent.
NAJLA: Jews who lived in Lebanon, Syria and Palestine had the same cuisine as ours – and we had the same cuisine as them. Then, some Russian and French Jews settled down in Israel and brought other culinary influences there.

Why did you choose Marseille?

NAJLA: I am Franco-Lebanese, and my father has Italian roots. I really liked Marseille when I was a student in France. Then in 2013, Marseille was the European Capital of Culture. Serje and I came to visit and it was amazing. There were new restaurants everywhere.
SERJE: We fell in love with the city. There were so many people . . .
NAJLA: Now, we don't know if we'll stay here all our lives, it's a complicated city, a special one. Over the course of the first two years, some neighbours would pass by the restaurant every day, read the menu, but never walk inside! People here take a long time to adopt a cuisine they don't know.
SERJE: Actually, all Mediterranean cities live in their past, culinarily speaking. In Greece, in Italy . . . each country thinks that they make the best food in the world!
NAJLA: Fortunately, we have the *bobos*, the hipsters . . . and Marseillais culinary websites like Le Grand Pastis, which have helped put us on the radar. Many of our clients are female. Marseillais men eat pasta and pizza. When a man dares to dine here, he usually tells us afterwards, 'Wow, it's actually really good and hearty!'

Do you feel Marseillais today?

NAJLA AND SERJE: (laughing) Yes and no.
NAJLA: It's a city that clings to you, but it's not an easy city to live in. She's endearing, but difficult. But I prefer to live in Marseille over Aix or Nice. Marseille has character and a strong identity.
I would like to tell Marseillais to be more curious. Restaurant food does not stop at bouillabaisse. The only one I've eaten, by the way, I ate at Chez Fonfon, I paid a fortune, and it wasn't that special. It's become a luxury good even though it was a simple fisherman's stew. Fishermen no longer make bouillabaisse.
In Lebanon, there are little stalls where you can eat hummus at 3 in the morning. Why can't you find little fishermen's stalls that make a good, fresh bouillabaisse that isn't expensive and at any hour?
SERJE: For our fish, we buy it at Laurence Ciccarelli's Poissonnerie du Golfe, a tiny little fishmonger that is one of the oldest in the city.

'Lebanese cuisine is wonderfully flavourful, a blend of all the countries that surround us.'

It's just next door on Rue Dr-Combolat. Laurence is super friendly, and her fish are high quality. You must check out this colourful poissonnerie!
NAJLA: We work with local small producers. As a result, at the beginning, our clients told us that our menu was expensive. Me, I don't find it expensive compared to what we cook! Our accountant scolds us about it! But, in Marseille, if you're too pricey, you won't have any clients, especially for lunch. The restaurants also adapt to French tastes. Lebanese in France serve vermicelli rice with *brochettes* [kebabs] because they know the French like that. In Lebanon, you'd never eat *brochettes* with vermicelli rice. It's a sin! When someone asks me for them, I say, 'No, you need to eat *brochettes* like we do in Lebanon, with hummus and potatoes or grilled tomatoes, and onion salad.' You can't eat rice with something dry. It's not logical. The Iranians do it, but they do it well. They put an egg in the rice . . .
SERJE: It's the same with Coca-Cola. We don't sell it. Drop it. End of discussion. We have other drinks, Lebanese beers, artisanal lemon soda, teas . . .
NAJLA: For the épicerie, we work with Terroirs du Liban, who exports fair-trade products from small Lebanese producers, NGOs, associations for women in need . . . We wanted to sell Lebanese products but not just any. These products are really good, and we are starting to sell quite a few.

Lebanese kebbés

Over the past few months, a lot of mezze bars have sprung up in Marseille. Asabiya in Cours Julien stands out due to their desire to develop a real cultural and music space. Najla and Serje endorsed it immediately.

What is the ingredient of your childhood?
NAJLA: Coriander.

The scent of your childhood?
NAJLA: Garlic mashed with fresh coriander that we sauté. It's a base of Lebanese cooking when making sauces. This aroma makes me immediately think of my mum. When I was little, I would spread this mix on bread.

Did you go to restaurants when you were a kid?
NAJLA: In Lebanon we often eat out. Every Sunday, we go to restaurants with our family. Sometimes 20, 30 people, the whole family! We've had insane tables with 150 mezze, we can eat for four hours in a restaurant. Here, it's the opposite. On Sundays, families gather at home.

What link is there between your cuisine and that of Marseille?
NAJLA: A lot of the ingredients are the same, notably vegetables and chickpeas. Speaking of which, I buy dried chickpeas and they are grown near Marseille, in the Bouches-du-Rhône department. That's rare.

What do you cook as a family?
NAJLA: There are many fights with my mother over her recipes. At the beginning, she came to help me at the restaurant, and we fought every day. She wanted me to make them like her, by intuition. I changed the recipes, and it was a battle over everything. For her, nothing could be changed. If there are tomatoes in a recipe, you must add tomatoes even if they aren't in season. Me, I wanted to find an alternative.

Who are the people you admire most that are working in Marseille?
NAJLA: Chef Matthieu Roche at Ourea restaurant and Guilhem Malisson at Le Bec du Coq restaurant. Both are neighbours of Mouné. And we love Sophie Lovergne, pastry chef and founder of Encore un Morceau in Endoume. She is a friend now.

SAMKÉ HARRA BEL TAHINI (FISH WITH SPICES AND TAHINI)

This dish is a classic of Lebanese cuisine, some make it with tahini, others without. It's a holiday dish in Lebanon. My version is quite sour. I often serve this at the restaurant, to my customers' great delight. Traditionally, you grill a whole *daurade* (sea bream), you debone it, and then you cover it with the famous sauce, but at the restaurant, I serve the fish as fillets.

INGREDIENTS FOR 5

1 glass tahini (sesame purée)
½ glass lemon juice (or more according to taste)
5 medium garlic cloves
2 tbsp ground coriander
1 tsp chilli powder (if you don't like chilli, you can omit or reduce the amount)
1 tsp sumac
½ tsp ground black pepper
1 medium onion
Olive oil
3 tbsp pine nuts
5 sea bream fillets (or cod loin), about 150g each
1 glass walnuts, finely chopped in a processor
A few microgreens of coriander or fresh coriander
Salt and pepper

1. In a large bowl, mix the tahini and lemon juice (the mixture will thicken, that's normal), slowly pour in 2 glasses of water, and whisk until you obtain a very smooth texture. Add salt and set aside.

2. Peel and smash the garlic in a mortar, then add the ground coriander, some chilli powder, sumac and black pepper.

3. Peel and finely chop the onion, brown in a pan with a bit of olive oil over low heat until it becomes translucent. Add the mix of garlic and spices, sauté for a few minutes, keeping watch so as not to burn the garlic. Set aside.

4. Preheat the oven to 220°C/gas mark 7. In a small frying pan, brown the pine nuts in olive oil for a few minutes and set aside.

5. Put the fish fillets on a plate, season with salt and pepper, sprinkle with a pinch of chilli powder, and lightly drizzle with olive oil. Bake for 12–15 minutes, just until the flesh is pearly white, and not transparent.

6. Meanwhile, pour the tahini sauce into a saucepan and constantly stir over low heat for 5–10 minutes until the sauce begins to thicken and little bubbles start to form on the surface. Mix the garlic-spice blend as well as the walnuts into the tahini sauce and stir another minute over the heat. Adjust the seasoning.

7. Serve the fish on plates coated with the sauce. Sprinkle with pine nuts and coriander. You can also serve the fish with wild rice from the Camargue. *Sahtein*! (Which means 'Bon appétit' in Lebanon!)

Nadjatie Bacar M'ze

Nadjatie is a radiant soul whose spirit wanders between the Comoros and Marseille. Her creativity in the kitchen invites you to let yourself go. You must be curious and attentive, so that you're open to a sensitivity, a biculture, a hope (*l'espoir*, in French, the name of the cocktail that Nadjatie will happily serve you), a spicy sweetness, and a surprising personality. Each recipe has a story, you must take the time to understand it. Nadjatie's culinary universe can be discovered at pop-ups or art galleries, like Les Grands Bains Douches in La Plaine or Jeanne Barret; you can be inspired by her pickled lemon and pepper achar sold at the Fernand et Lily épicerie beside City Hall; and you will probably run into her in Noailles. Go ahead and strike up a conversation.

AN ARTIST

The famous Comorian dessert, goudou goudou

Why did you settle down in Marseille?
I came here when I was 13 years old. I didn't know anything about Marseille, I arrived at the Marignane-Marseille airport in flip-flops, and the escalator actually worked! And I said to myself, 'I've changed worlds . . .'
When I landed in the city, it was dirty, it was violent, but I was privileged. I had a roof over my head, I went to school, I lived on Rue de Lyon in the 15th arrondissement with my mum.
My mum was a seamstress, she welcomed many people into our home, it was noisy. I had a hard time doing my homework, I went to school on foot because we didn't have enough money for bus tickets. I didn't yet have my official ID. But it wasn't difficult. I'm used to adapting. I knew I had changed worlds. No one asked for my opinion, but I was here.
My mum brought me to France. For her, it was a gift. To bring people to France was a gift. It's a poisoned gift, but it's true that when I returned to the Comoros to see my little sister, where her husband had taken her child to give it to his second wife who couldn't have any . . . I told myself that every situation has advantages and problems.
If I had stayed there, I probably wouldn't be a chef or a cook, but I surely would have done something because I'm stubborn and I got good grades in school. But today, here, I am happy. It is another lifestyle. I made the choice of my life. What I do is my choice. The pressure I put on myself is mine. In France, there is this freedom and France, today, is my country.
In the end, I love living in Marseille. People accept the problems here. We say, 'Come on, tomorrow, we'll see. It doesn't matter. *Inch'Allah* [if Allah wills it].' And besides, I love the sea.
My family, here, I chose them. They are friends, my sweetheart, Jean-François, and my son that I had when I was very young, 18 years old.

How did you start cooking professionally?
I was a saleswoman, then at the employment office, Assedic, they talked to me about cooking thinking that I would never try it. I think they wanted to get rid of me. But I went for it! I had the opportunity to work and train in many brasseries, there was mutual aid there. It was welcoming. That comforted me. Because, at that time, I took care of my son all alone. And that world did me good.
The only hierarchy in the kitchen is know-how. A 20-year-old chef can give orders to a 40-year-old cook because he knows.

Local épicerie

45 Rue Coutellerie
13002 Marseille

How did you open your first restaurant in Le Panier (which is now closed)?

By chance. My partner Jean-François and I moved into an apartment in Le Panier neighbourhood. At that time, I was a personal chef. One day, I saw that there was a space for rent. The place appealed to me. I didn't have a lot of money saved. 3,000 euros. But I didn't dwell on my lack of means. I was lucky. My bank adviser was on holiday, and a woman, Fatima Menaï, who was the same age as me, had replaced him. When I presented my project to her, she said to me, 'Go for it!' She helped me submit my project, she saw that my personal cheffing brought in a bit of money anyway, and, in 15 days, I borrowed 30,000 euros. I was oblivious at the time!

I was so enthusiastic.

Since the beginning of my restaurant, I've changed a lot. I've opened up. Before, I wouldn't give bread to clients, nor salt. When someone asked me for salt, it annoyed me. I had seasoned it! Comorian cuisine is delicate. You must find the precise and correct taste of each dish. Now, I tell myself it isn't so dramatic if someone wants to add salt . . . But, my cooking is my identity. Before, I didn't add that much chilli pepper. Now, I dare to cook the spicy cuisine that I love.

How would you define your cuisine?

My cuisine is wild, concretely wild, or more accurately, wild but logical. My cooking has evolved with my self-confidence. I have grown a lot personally. Today, to get inspired, I look at fashion photos. That seems superficial, but, in fact, the creations are very structured and that helps me to create.

What ingredient reminds you of your childhood?

Fish. My father was a fisherman, he had a little dugout canoe. He fished for his four kids. It was his way of showing us that he loved us. I remember the smell of tuna and shark guts. He dried them in our home. It was sickening. The Japanese would come to buy them at the house. Now, I'd happily eat them.

How would you present Comoros cuisine?

It's close to Indian cuisine. In the two families that I've had in my life, the cuisine was very different. One was vegetarian because we didn't want to spend a lot on food. In the other, in the fishing village Iconi, where I was born, food was the priority. We didn't think about school a lot, but on the other hand, we had to eat well.

My mum entrusted me to friends when I was eight years old. It was, incidentally, thanks to this host family that I began to imagine what my life could be like. My parents were fishermen, and the father of my new family was a doctor. He made us play charades at the table. This family influenced me. I was privileged, so I couldn't do anything wrong. I had to do well in school.

Who do you work with in Marseille? Who are the people in the food industry with whom you have a particular bond?

I work with Jamal who sells vegetables at the Wednesday morning Cours Julien farmers' market. For years, I've bought my small kilo of cocktail tomatoes from him. Today, everyone helps themselves at his stand, including the trendy Le Mercerie restaurant. He sells a lot, but for me, he sets aside my little kilo of tomatoes, and he picks nettles for my 'hope'

'I put a photo of my grandmother on the wall of my first restaurant. I was closer to my grandmother than my mother.'

cocktail. He doesn't really have time to do it anymore, but he brings me some anyway. It's really great.

I'm also close to my fisherman as well. He taught me how to fillet skate. It's a fish that I had never seen before in the Comoros, I never dared to buy it. It's an impressive fish for me.

I also work with Fabienne Völlmy at Microcosmos, an intra muros winemaker in Le Panier that blends her wine in the heart of Marseille. She taught me how to taste wine. With her, I discovered something that I never dared to utter aloud: that red wine pairs really well with chilli and the fish dishes that I make. It's logical that I went to see her, because Microcosmos is located near where I had my first restaurant, but I did not expect this woman to give me so much love. Her wine has become high-end today and she puts pressure on me. She has customers who come from all over the world and she used to send many of them to eat at my restaurant. So we're going to open a new creative cooking space together.

I also love Marie-Jo Ordener. She's a marvel! She does so much for young chefs. I worked with her at Les Grandes Tables at the Friche la Belle de Mai where I met a lot of different people, including Comorians in the restaurant industry, like the excellent Yassine Siradji, who we call Yass. We have

become very good friends. They had also a young Comorian intern, born in Marseille, who told me she couldn't roll samoussas. I told her, 'That's not possible. Come here, I'll teach you,' and I taught her how to roll this Comorian classic . . . in Marseille. There was also a young Afghan chef in training who was extraordinary. He lived for cooking; he was interested in everything. He wasn't rigid about his origins. He's a future star.
Among the Marseille chefs, I adore David Mijoba and Alexandre Mazzia. David Mijoba is Venezuelan and one day, for an event, he created the perfect sauce to accompany my favourite Comorian dessert, the good good or *goudou goudou*. He impressed me with his accuracy for a dessert that he didn't know. The good good comes from the English influence in the Comoros.

What ingredient symbolises Marseille for you?
The colour in the morning. It reminds me of the Comoros. The light. There's also the people's laughter. It's not necessarily a scent that reminds me of Marseille. Smiles and laughter come easily here. It's something that does us good.
And then the ingredient I really learned to master in Marseille is olive oil. I had to find my identity in it, to integrate it into my cooking. It must be fruity, light and young.

How would you describe Marseille cooking today?
Marseille cuisine is the ability to mix ingredients and customs . . . we can dare to do anything. Now I can use soy sauce on fish. Well, it took me a long time to use canned coconut milk. When I was little, my grandmother massaged me with coconut milk. I recognise its smell and its different textures. I prepared it with her. In a can, it smells like nothing, and the taste is not the same . . . But you adapt.
For me, the ultimate Marseille dish is aioli. I really like it. It's strong. And anchoïade, I love! I worked for a long time at Bar de la Marine on the Vieux-Port. They were the ones that trained me. Every Friday, as is tradition, it's aioli there. That is also part of me.

How have you seen Marseille gastronomy evolve?
Marseille is evolving in the right direction in gastronomy because there is no longer room for mediocrity. As there is not a lot of money in Marseille, the little we spend at a restaurant, it must be good. That's what 30-year-olds want now, to eat well, more than to sit in a fancy restaurant. They are more respectful of the ingredients.

What do you cook at home?
I cook simple things, with good products and good seasoning that doesn't distort the ingredients.
I make traditional Comorian dishes for my son. He asks me for them, he has never been to the Comoros. Then again, things have changed a lot in the Comoros. The Emirates have come and imposed their wealth and their system with certain conditions. In the Comoros, we had never been forced to put a shawl on our heads and now we are obliged to. On the other hand, behind that, in certain parts of Comoros, the people drink a lot of alcohol. Hidden of course. Me, I drink because I find it good. It's part of my identity. Moreover, in general, when the Comorians here die, they have their bodies repatriated there. But I'm okay being buried here, I'm comfortable with that. I said this to my father, in a very calm, simple way, without arrogance.
Marseille has the largest Comorian community in France . . .
In Marseille, we have a Comorian star, Saïd . . . the rapper Soprano. I like him a lot, I like his energy, his way of evolving. It's thanks to him that the Comorian community appeals to children.
The youth are very closely-knit, there is mutual aid. We aren't a community that rebels. We are a calm community, without violence. Recently, I went to the beach, and I saw seven Comorian women chatting together. I was happy to see that. There is solidarity among the men also. For that matter, I'm more friendly with men than women. Comorian women must sacrifice for the family, for others, for everyone. And me, I think I've done enough.
Also, women don't cook professionally in the Comoros and, consequently, we're killing our gastronomic culture. The dried cakes for weddings are made by machines now and not at all by hand. It's disheartening.

The last word . . .
Me, I'm Marseillaise. We are here, so we are all Marseillais. To those who ask me where I'm from, I respond, 'And you, where do you come from? Were you just in L'Estaque?'

Local épicerie

45 Rue Coutellerie
13002 Marseille

'In 2013, a handsome man with a guitar sat down in my restaurant one day and asked me for a vegetarian dish. At the time, I made little salads to accompany my dishes. So, I made one for him as a main course. He ordered seconds, then thirds! I said to myself: "There is a flavour in this salad that I must keep!" Then, one day, Arnaud Carton du Grammont, who now runs Ciao Marcello pizzeria, tasted the same salad and liked it. That really touched me because he is a chef I really admire. Ten years ago, he invented Marseille *bistronomie* on his own at the late Café des Épices.'

— Nadjatie Bacar M'ze

THE MUSICAL SALAD OF 2013

INGREDIENTS FOR 4

500g dried red beans
2g turmeric root
1 head of fresh garlic
3 white onions
2 chilli peppers
Juice of 1 lemon
Neutral oil
1 beetroot, grated
3 pomegranates
1 handful of redcurrants
1 head of Romaine lettuce, chopped
A few sprigs of coriander, finely chopped
Salt and white pepper

1. Soak the beans the night before.
2. The next day, drain the beans. Peel the turmeric root and garlic. Cut the onions and chilli peppers into big chunks.
3. In a blender, mix the beans, turmeric, garlic, onions, chilli, lemon juice, salt and white pepper to a paste and let rest for 20 minutes at room temperature.
4. Dip a soup spoon in water and shape beignets with the help of your wet spoon. Heat neutral oil in a big saucepan and fry the beignets. Remove them and put on a paper towel-covered plate.
5. Prepare a light vinaigrette and add the grated beetroot. Strain it through a sieve and leave to rest for 10 minutes.
6. Tap on the pomegranates, open them in half, and remove the seeds. In a salad bowl, mix the pomegranate seeds, redcurrants, chopped Romaine and finely chopped coriander.
7. Add the vinaigrette or keep it in a small bowl on the side so that one can add it to their plate according to their taste.
8. Put the beignets on top or crumble them over the salad.
9. Depending on your taste, the chilli and turmeric can be optional. Depending on the season, you can substitute strawberries, those from the beginning of the season, for the redcurrants and pomegranates.
10. *Bel appétit!*

'Douceur piquante' vinaigrette

INGREDIENTS FOR 6

1 small red beetroot
⅓ white onion
1 small mild chilli
Juice of 1 lemon
1 tbsp neutral oil (like grapeseed)

1. Cut the beetroot into small dice, finely chop the white onion and chilli pepper, and add to a blender with the lemon juice. Blend with a glass of water. Then strain through a sieve and add the mixture back to the blender. Slowly, add oil to emulsify. *Voilà*, it's ready!

SELF LOVE
CLUB

FISH MECCA ON THE VERGE

Fish and Marseille have a complicated story. 'Fish is expensive,' the Marseillais complain. As for bouillabaisse, we are proud of it, but we can no longer afford it in the restaurants that make a decent one. So, we talk about it, but rarely eat it as we wearily watch tourists fill their bellies with both bad and good versions at seafaring tables.

One way to get more on board with fish is via fishing poles and harpoons. The Mediterranean isn't totally empty yet, we can save it and she belongs to all those who want the best for it.

Another solution would be to expand our knowledge of Mediterranean fish. The Japanese-Marseillais chef Ippei Uemura told me, 'All the fish aren't overpriced, you just have to know which ones to buy.' 'The fish that our grandmothers cooked hardly exist anymore,' explains Chef Christian Qui, 'so let's reinvent our bouillabaisse with the fish that are here now.'

I can easily write that we are super attached to the *poissonniers* and *poissonnières* at the Vieux-Port, but actually we don't know much about our *poissons*. This chapter is also here to shed light on the subject for us locals.

08

R
M S
Vallon des Auffes
La Corniche

Ippei Uemura

'TO COOK IS TO TELL YOUR LIFE STORY'

Local Japanese cuisine

165 Corniche Kennedy
13007 Marseille

Otaku friends, get off your screens, and come and get some fresh air in Marseille! Our tip of France is twinned with the port city of Kobe, Japan. The intense Ippei is here to remind us of this and put fish back in the heart of the Marseille diet. When I landed in this outstanding restaurant, facing the sea above the postcard-esque Vallon des Auffes port, I did not know what to expect. I had shot several documentaries in Japan. I can't say that I understood everything about its culture but, like a good chunk of my generation, I'm genuinely a fan (except for the gender roles of women).
That day, Ippei, a Japanese chef who has become very Marseillais, was teaching his apprentice how to sharpen a knife. Two hours later, they were still at it. Which is normal . . . since in Japan, it takes about ten years to master the technique. Well, I decided to take root and stayed there all afternoon. I really enjoyed getting a glimpse of the delirium of this Japanese chef, who keeps live moray eels alongside flags of the local football club, Olympique de Marseille, in his pantry.
Of course, Ippei is not the only Japanese to serve Nipponese delicacies in Marseille. The family-run Hako in the Roucas Blanc neighbourhood is a must, and everyone swears by Takosan in Le Panier. But I had to choose and Ippei's crazy side put a spell on me. Everything I tasted in this restaurant was haute cuisine that I had never eaten anywhere else, not even in Japan. Ippei likes to challenge himself and innovate. He nails it.

Where did you grow up?
I was born in Kyoto and I grew up in the centre of Kyushu, Japan's third-largest island.

What is your training?
There weren't any chefs in my family. I began cooking in 1995. I was 15 years old. I had wanted to be a chef since I was three. My dream was to either be Superman or a chef! Because I liked everything that was manual, the meticulous manipulations. I like the fabrication aspect, and even today, it's the part that I most like. Since I was little, I dreamed of coming to France. I was a fan. Before I was 10, I had books by great French chefs like Paul Bocuse, Joël Robuchon, Alain Ducasse . . . When the restaurant where I was working in Japan closed down, I had job offers in Japan, in the US, in England, and one in France! I didn't hesitate and arrived in Cannes in 2003. But I didn't like the atmosphere there. Like a luxury store that lacked typical culture. You find these types of stores everywhere. At 20, I didn't want to settle down in Paris. Capital cities are the same everywhere, they're full of people, full of buildings, people walking fast . . . So, after a few months, I decided to go back to Japan. I bought a ticket: Marseille-Paris, Paris-Japan. And before leaving, I had a week to spend in Marseille. I didn't know anything about it, yet, in the end, I've been here for 20 years. I immediately fell in love with the city.

What are your memories of this first week in Marseille?
The people! They are a bit crazy. Exactly like in Osaka, Japan, and I love Osaka. Lire here, people talk with their hands and they don't know how to drive in the rain. In Marseille, we have the football club, OM. In Osaka, it's a baseball team. When we win, it's the same story . . . cars and scooters honking.

They're good teams, but not always in first place.
I arrived in Marseille around Christmas. I was invited to someone's house. That night, the woman who was cooking opened the oven to show me what was inside . . . and there were tiny quails! I said, 'Madame, I cannot eat that!' but now I love them.
It was the same with rabbits. In Japan, rabbits are animals in the countryside. We don't eat them! And here, I've seen rabbits sold at the supermarket chain Carrefour! I looked up the translation on my phone and I said to myself, 'Ohhhhhhh.'

How has your vision of Marseille evolved since then?
Marseille has changed over the past 20 years. Actually, I think that the city had stopped growing for 30 years or so, and for the past seven to 10 years, it has resumed its evolution. There is huge potential in this city, at a tourism and industrial level . . . but there hasn't been a strategy nor organisation. At the culinary level, Marseille is the second-largest city in France and only has six or seven starred restaurants, for example. That's not normal. There are many chefs here who don't know what is fished in the Mediterranean. Instead of sourcing fish locally they buy fish from Brittany in the north. We must start all over again. I'm also a fisherman, I have boarded fishing boats here and I learned that they toss a lot of fish back (*chinchard* [horse mackerel], *rascasse blanche* [white scorpion fish] that we call '*boeuf* [beef]' here, *mostelle* which is Marseille cod . . .). In Spain or Italy, you eat horse mackerel. In Japan as well. It's so good. The problem is that in Marseille, no one buys it! *Sériole* [amberjack] costs a fortune in Japan. No one buys it here.
So, the fishermen don't keep it, everyone catches the same fish, and of course, there are fewer and fewer of them. It's like how eel is disappearing from Japan. Here, in the nearby town of Saint-Chamas, we have France's capital of *anguilles* [eels]! Each year, I take part in the *Anguillades* de Saint-Chamas. In my opinion, we don't have a fish culture in Marseille. There should be more signature dishes with fish. The chefs need to lead by example.
I've also trained some Marseillais fishermen at *ikejime*, the Japanese technique of killing fish. It makes fish taste better and allows them the chance to mature. Plus, you must never grab a fish directly with your hands. The water temperature is 13–14°C and your hands are at 37°C. If you touch fish when they've just been caught, you'll hugely stress them out. You must grab fish with both hands in a towel moistened with sea water and you must not let them die alone. They must be killed. At first, Marseillais fishermen didn't believe me, so I offered to pay for the fish in advance, and added a tip, so that we'd go fishing together and I'd kill them with my method. Nine or 10 years ago, I became known for this technique that allows you to conserve fish longer. I'm happy that others use these techniques today since my dream is that Marseille becomes the fish capital of France.
I was trained in Japanese cuisine, which has centuries of history. I master Japanese techniques, theories, detailed work . . . I studied traditional Japanese cuisine for 20 years. It takes 20 years to learn how to sharpen knives. And it's never enough time! I could still advance, but I've changed. Today, I do contemporary cooking. It took me 20 years before I dared to, before I tried.

Le Vallon des Auffes

Why did you dare here, in Marseille?
I met so many fantastic producers. We have wonderful herbs, incredible tomatoes, beautiful aubergines, amazing fish . . . so I said to myself, 'why import Japanese ingredients?' That's what I did at the start. When I became a bit known, thanks to the Gault & Millau *Jeunes Talents*/Young Talents award in 2017, I began to travel a lot. And each time I travelled with two suitcases stuffed with Japanese ingredients to cook on site. One day, I was over it. It was in Croatia in 2017, for the Taste of Mediterranean festival. I decided to only go with my knives. Since then, I've done nomadic *kaiseki* dinners. I use Japanese

techniques with local ingredients. So, in Marseille, I no longer serve wagyu beef, wasabi . . . I serve the story of my life. Cooking is telling your life story. My cuisine is unique. I don't call it fusion cuisine because I want to highlight a culture. It's very technical. For example, I make tuna tartare, *nakaochi* style. It's an ancient technique by Japanese fishermen. You scrape the tuna with shells to remove the tendons and nerves without imparting the taste of stainless steel as knives do. I've used this method with scallops. I learned this from fishermen in my homeland. My grandfather did it like that. But, with all of this, I want to compete with other chefs from the same culinary scene, the French scene. I want to be number one in French gastronomy. It's different from many Japanese chefs who settle down in France. Often in Japan, they study French techniques and they come to France to perfect them. Me, I learned Japanese techniques.

How would you define Marseille's culinary scene?

Today, there are talented chefs like Coline Faulquier (Signature), Frédéric Charlet (Foud.com), Vanessa Robuschi (Question de Goût), who is too humble. She deserves a Michelin star. There is a dynamic new generation. And me, I want to add another star to Marseille, for Marseille and for Japan. Before, I never thought like that, but thanks to Chef Lionel Levy at the Hotel Intercontinental, I learned that if you are well known, you meet people who give you even more motivation to move forward. Thanks to all that has happened to me, I met my idol: Alain Ducasse.

Also, Marseille is a mix. I'm Japanese and I'm part of the city's delegation! They send me all over the world to represent Marseille talents. That's Marseille, and it's indie like Osaka!

What crazy thing has happened to you in Marseille?

There are too many to mention! I had an employee who asked to take a cigarette break and, in fact, he went home and never returned. Another employee told me he was taking out the garbage and he had put all the bottles in the wine cellar in garbage bags. He left with them and never returned. But, the worst story, was the night that I was having a party with my team in my former restaurant. We drank a lot and I fell asleep in the restaurant. When I woke up, my phone and the restaurant's computer were gone. I no longer had the restaurant's keys, my car keys, nor my car. It wasn't one of my employees who had taken everything. It was just someone who had passed by. Everything has happened to me in Marseille, like in the movies.

The craziest positive moment was the big article on my cuisine in *À Table*, the supplement to *La Provence* [the local newspaper]. It was this article that lured Lionel Levy here.

I don't have sushi on my menu. For business, it would be good, but it would be too easy. I could do 200 covers with sushi. Why do something else? For Marseille! And for me! At the beginning, Marseillais didn't understand my cuisine in this restaurant. They said it was too expensive and then, *boom*, from the first year of Tabi, I was rated 15/20 in the Gault & Millau guide and 3 toques [chef's hats]! Suddenly, tourists came, I did a few TV shows, and now we're busy all the time.

The recipe I offer here isn't a wow dish, it's a palate cleanser. But it's one of my signature dishes. And it's thanks to this dish that I was one of Gault & Millau's *Jeunes Talents*/Young Talents in 2017. Each year, I do a new version.

To create this one, I put peaches everywhere at my house, in my bedroom, in my bathroom. I bought white peach shampoo, peach toilet paper . . . everything peaches! For inspiration.

Finally, I made a Provençal tomato water using a Japanese method: to remove things from ingredients to construct a taste. I began with a red tomato, and I managed to remove its colour without removing its taste. Naturally. Without chemical products. And, what we do in Japan with plums, I did with a Provençal peach. I fermented it.

165 Corniche Kennedy
13007 Marseille, France

TOMATO WATER
(the one with salted peach candy)

INGREDIENTS FOR 2

1 firm white peach
20g kombu (kelp)
1 dried medium shiitake
25g dried bonito flakes
1 large cherry tomato
Basil
Black pepper (I fermented it with salt water at the restaurant, but here we'll stick to black pepper)
Fine salt

For the nori chips:
50g flour (plain/T55)
100ml egg white
2 leaves of seaweed (nori)

1. Make the salted peach candy: 48 hours beforehand, moisten the peach with water and sprinkle with fine salt. Put the peach in a plastic bag and sous vide at around 40°C for 48 hours. You can use a food warmer, too. You can also keep it at room temperature, but it takes a bit longer. For this, wrap the peach in cling film and suck out the air around the peach with a straw. The peach must not be in contact with the air so it can ferment.

2. Prepare the nori chips: mix the flour with 50ml water and the egg white. Let rest for 6 hours in the refrigerator to thicken the dough.

3. After that, remove the dough from the fridge. Cut the nori leaves into 10 x 4cm long strips (adapt size according to the glasses used). Preheat the oven to 150°C/gas mark 2. With a brush, spread the dough over the cut nori pieces. Bake in the oven for 19–23 minutes (don't let the chips burn).

4. For the dashi (1 litre), soak the kombu and shiitake in 1 litre of cold water for 20 minutes in a saucepan, then heat until the kombu floats and the shiitake sinks. Remove kombu and shiitake. Add the dried bonito flakes. Turn off the heat and let rest for 5 minutes. Strain the broth and save the dashi.

5. For the tomato water, put a tea towel over a fine strainer and press the tomato through the strainer. Mix the tomato juice and the dashi together: the same amount of each. Pour the mixture into two tall glasses.

6. Once the peach is fermented, hollow out a big ball of flesh without removing the skin. Balance a nori chip across the top of the glass and put the peach ball on top. Place a basil leaf and peppercorn on top of the peach. Repeat for the second glass.

7. Drink the tomato water like a margarita!

Christophe Caïola

For children, in France, from 1970 to 1990, films were American, but television was Japanese. Many generations grew up with the Jeanne and Serge, Albator, Goldorak, X-Or series . . . then Japanese animation films even came to the cinema, with Totoro and Ponyo. Today, still, the ever-popular Pikachu imprints Japan in the imaginations of both young and old. And that's how Caïola-san decided to cook Japanese street food in Marseille without having ever set foot in Japan!
We met one night where, as it often is, his shop was packed. Customers even offered to come with their own table to dine on the pavement in front of the restaurant . . . *C'est Marseille, bébé!*

I grew up in Marseille, in the 13th arrondissement in the Quartiers Nord [northern districts], Saint-Just, Corot, Le Merlan . . . I began working in restaurants quite late. In 2009. I was 29 years old. Before, I was a graphic designer. I didn't cook at all. I'm a self-taught chef. I began in a Brittany *crêperie* in Marseille. I was a dishwasher. At the beginning, it was mostly just for money, but they finally gave me more and more tasks in the kitchen and in the dining room. I liked the chef *métier*. Cooking, interacting with customers, the atmosphere, the moments when you're slammed, the speed . . . I enjoyed it all. I don't claim to be a gastronomic restaurant, but I think we are all working in the same direction. We try to do the best we can and help customers discover something new, to share. My passion for Japanese street food began in my childhood with the animé that I watched as a kid, in which you'd always see crazy dishes. The characters eat all the time! Even in Japanese films, cuisine takes up a lot of space. In Japan, there are small, specialised *izakaya* taverns everywhere, and you can eat anything at any time! And you eat very well for cheap. Here, we are often sold sushi and the refined, precious side of Japanese cuisine, which is eaten in silence . . . but in fact, in Japan, they also like to party, eat small plates, drink beer, and share moments together.
One day, I felt like I had made the rounds at the *crêperie* and I wanted to create my own place. I first wanted to make ramen. A very good friend, who had a network in Japan, introduced me to a Japanese cook who advised me to make *okonomiyaki* [savoury pancakes], *takoyaki* [fried octopus balls] and Japanese street food instead, which is not widely known here. Plus, *takoyaki* are an Osakan speciality, the Marseille of Japan. In Osaka, the Marseille of Japan, there are rules, but one always tries to somewhat avoid them. Like here . . . and you eat really well. This cook showed me the foundation of all this street food in 2013 and I opened my shop in 2014, all by myself. I cooked, washed dishes, served, and was at the cash register . . .
I wanted to show the Marseille community this Japanese way of eating in little shops, essentially *izakaya*, which are always very personal and resemble the chef. Each shop has its own identity and Ko Ishi is Christophe's shop. It's part of me. It looks like my teenage bedroom!
I went to Japan for the first time in 2015. I hallucinated! I had already opened my restaurant. Since then, I try to go every two years to improve. Now, I cook many more things. For example, I just succeeded in making *œufs parfaits* (*onsen tamago*), which are eggs that are cooked halfway between soft- and hard-boiled. I'm pretty happy with them! And on Saturday nights, I make ramen.
I opened my *izakaya* on Rue Sainte, THE gastronomic restaurant street of Marseille. I must admit . . . I'm a UFO on this street!

UFO MARSEILLAIS

ABURI SHIME SABA

INGREDIENTS FOR 2

2 whole mackerel
Rice vinegar
Kombu
Caster sugar
Chives
Salt

1. Clean out the mackerel by making an incision in their belly from the tail to the head. Rinse the fish. Make incisions at an angle with a small knife towards the head, behind the fin, to the central bone, then direct the blade of the knife towards the tail and separate the fillet from the bone (by placing a hand flat on the fish).

2. On the other side of the fish, pass the blade flat under the central bone, turn the knife to loosen the bone, then separate the second fillet by moving the blade flat towards the back of the fish. Detach the fillet from the head.

3. Trim the fillets, removing all the bones. The subtlety is there is an almost-transparent film on the mackerel skin that you must remove by pulling it with your fingers. Every now and then, little worms hide between the film and the skin. You could also just remove the skin.

4. Salt the fillets to firm up the flesh, then chill for 1 hour.

5. Prepare the marinade (amount depends on the number of mackerel): pour a glass of rice vinegar into a pan, add a small piece of kombu and a bit of sugar (very little), then bring it barely to the boil. As soon as it starts to simmer, turn off the heat and let cool.

6. Once the marinade has cooled off, take the fillets out of the refrigerator. Rinse them to remove the salt. Pour the marinade on top, then marinate, chilled, for 1–2 hours. The longer you let them marinate, the better they will be.

7. Grill the fillets, your choice, on a charcoal fire or on a small rack on a ceramic board, with a blowtorch (like they do in Japan). Only grill the top, the flesh will cook as we have removed the film, and the sugar will caramelise. Some chopped chives on top and *voilà*!

Aminati Halidane

Cheffe Aminati is the current fairy godmother who handles the daily lunch, by herself, at the Friche la Belle de Mai's community nursery, for 50 children that range from three months to three-and-a-half-years old. In Marseille, school canteens are served by the sole central Sodexo kitchen that prepares 50,000 student meals daily. Only nurseries can slip through their industrialised net and some even cook on the premises. The Friche's nursery, Marie Jo from Les Grandes Tables and Aminati work together and pushed the envelope to obtain the organic Trois Carottes (Three Carrots) certification. All the nursery's vegetables are sourced from Marseille urban farm Terre de Mars. The cheffe grew up in Île de la Réunion (the French overseas department and islands in the Indian Ocean) and throws herself wholeheartedly into educating toddlers' palates to blends of flavours and cultures - to the great joy of parents. They admiringly look at this cook who manages to feed everything to their wee ones.

BABY'S FIRST CHEF

I love when I pass by and the kids tell me, "It's soooooooo good." I like the way little ones express themselves this way. It makes me very happy. In the morning, they see me in the kitchen and they call out, "Aminati, Aminati!" I open the window to say hello to them, I tell them what we're going to eat and they are all delighted. Also some parents have asked, "Don't you want to open a restaurant?
We would come and eat there because the aromas coming from your kitchen call to us."
I was born in Madagascar. My parents were Reunionese. My father was in the military, he was sent to Mada, and he brought my mum there. Two of their kids were born in Madagascar and three in Île de la Réunion. I came to mainland France when I was 24 years old, with the future father of my children. I went to my mum's who had lived in Paris for a long time, and he went to his family in Marseille.
In Île de la Réunion, I already worked in canteens. But there, we cooked. When I came here, I worked in a Marseille school, in the Felix Pyat housing estate (*une cité* in the Quartiers Nord), and I saw that they were just reheating dishes. I said to myself, "Why can't children eat well?"

Marseille-Reunionese nursery chef

41 Rue Jobin
13003 Marseille

How did you go from Paris to Les Grandes Tables in Marseille?
In Paris, I found the city too cold. It rained all the time and I wanted to return to Île de la Réunion. My husband, who is now my ex-husband, said to me, 'Come to Marseille, the weather is not the same here.' Once I landed here, I thought to myself, 'I'm staying in Marseille.' Here, even if it is cold out, there is always a bit of sunshine. The cold weather is not that cold!

What was your first impression of Marseille?
I had the impression that I was in Île de la Réunion. The first thing that I did was to go to the Vieux-Port. The smell of fish and the sea, it was like being on the island. And the people! In Paris, no one says 'Bonjour' to you but in Marseille, people talk to each other all the time, they smile. And me, I like to talk.
I came here in 1987. That's over 30 years ago. My three children were born in Marseille, three lads. Now men. The oldest is 24 years old.

Do they cook?
No! Only the middle one cooks a bit. Simple things. Pasta, steaks and *cordons bleus* [chicken stuffed with cheese and ham]. They say to me, 'Mum, it's better if you do it.' When I return home, they say, 'Mum, I'm hungry! Uber!' but I tell myself, 'You know, Aminati, chefs never cook at home.'

You no longer cook at yours?
On the weekends, I make them whatever they want, but during the week, they cook for themselves. I showed them how to use the oven, the cocotte for rice… I taught them how to do little things.

Have they ever cooked for you?
Petit déjeuner on the weekends. Coffee, because they know that I love coffee. And the middle one makes good crêpes. Me, I am not good at it. My batter always sticks. So, he makes the batter and I cook the crêpes.

When did you decide to get a professional cooking certification?
I worked at the Paoli Calmettes Institute, Marseille's centre for the fight against cancer. After a while, I couldn't work anymore, the atmosphere was too painful, so I left. I cooked at home, and I told my kids, 'Bring your friends,' so that I'd know if it was good. It's with children that you learn. And they told me, 'Auntie, you can cook things and we'll sell them!' I told them no, it's too much work by yourself. But the idea to get a professional certificate came from there. I first looked for a kitchen job, in restaurants, at city hall, in schools. The day that I went to the social centre to photocopy my CV, a woman who was accompanying me on my job search said, 'If you want to cook, come tomorrow, there will be someone who can offer financing for a vocational certificate.'
I came and chanced upon Rebecca Gaillard, who presented the *Des Étoiles et des Femmes* [Michelin-Star Chefs and Women] programme, started by the Table de Cana in Marseille. She came to the La Castellane cite social centre to entice women to get trained in cooking. Many of us in the neighbourhood were interested, but when the time came to take the exams, there were just three of us left. The others had dropped out. We did the first course, the second course, and at the end, I was the only one in the neighbourhood to go to class. The two others had also dropped out. The reality is you must want to do this. If you don't want to, there's no point.
On the third day, we began to meet

chefs, and they asked us questions. There was one that pushed us down, another that lifted us up, but I didn't let them get to me. In fact, they test you because they know that the job of a cook is not easy. I wanted to do this job and I fought for it. When they asked me how I was going to keep up with the course, I always had a response. Because of this, they offered me the opportunity to continue the studies even further. With all the neighbourhoods combined, we were 20 women in the end. We met new chefs with the same questions . . . it was always about our kids and our husbands! Often, they said, 'If your husband doesn't want you to do this, how will you?' I told them, 'I don't have a husband!', so they asked me a lot of questions about my kids. I said that my children were older, that I could continue my studies.

How old were you at the time?
48 years old. At the end of this selection process, I was on the bus when they called to tell me, 'You're one of the 12 women that have been chosen.' I screamed with joy!

Then what happened?
My first day as a proper culinary student at the Bonneveine lycée, I said to myself, 'Well, my life starts now.' We were 12 women, we were like kids. At the start, we were stressed out, we didn't have confidence in ourselves, we were afraid we weren't going to manage, but we had a psychologist who coached us. One day, he put me in front of a mirror, and he asked, 'Look at yourself, what do you see?' and I said, 'Nothing.' I saw nothing. After several sessions, he put me in front of the mirror again and I told him, 'Now, I see me.' And it was true. I said, 'I'm courageous, I'm dynamic, I see that I will make it, I see my professional certificate being handed to me. I don't think anyone can put me down like before. No man can walk over me anymore.' He looked at me and he said, 'Yeah! I'm proud of you.' Before, I didn't speak up, I kept everything to myself, and I would cry a lot when my emotions exploded. But, at that moment, I told myself that I wanted to cry for joy. At the social centre, there are people who give classes to kids, and I went to see them to take maths, French and English, private lessons that I paid for.
On Saturdays, I practised there for two hours so that I'd succeed. Each week, we spent two days in the kitchen and three days in class. For nine months. To be able to transport my huge bag of knives and kitchen utensils, my kids brought me to the bus stop every Monday. On Fridays when I returned with my bag, they picked me up at the bus stop. During the week, I dropped the bag off at school. I wore loafers, a jacket, and pleated trousers. In La Castellane cité, they said that I gave the impression that I worked in a bank. On graduation day, Chef Laurent Mercier from Les Grandes Tables (I had the great opportunity to do my professional internship with him at Les Grandes Tables de la Friche) and my children came with me. My kids encouraged me, the neighbourhood women, the social centre also. The local *boulanger* started offering me bread and now, I have my photo in the La Castellane social centre (*Author's note: La Castellane is also the estate where Zinédine Zidane, the famous French football player, grew up*).
The first time I saw all of the photos on the wall of my culinary lycée, I realised that gastronomic cuisine is an art. But I don't see myself in gastronomy, I see myself more in day-to-day cuisine instead of the extraordinary. That said, at Les Grandes Tables, we do both.

At the start, who did you learn to cook with?
With my grandfather. My sister was in charge of the housekeeping, but me, I liked to be in the kitchen. That's where I learned how to make a true *rougail saucisse*, the Reunionese classic. When I make it at the nursery, I make it like my grandfather did, but without chilli pepper.

ROUGAIL À LA SARDINE

INGREDIENTS FOR ROUGAIL WITH ABOUT 30 SARDINE 'MEATBALLS'

3 slices of white bread
Whole milk
800g sardines
Curry powder
2 red onions, finely chopped
Coriander
4 garlic cloves (to divide between the sauce and the sardines)
Juice of 1 lemon
Olive oil
3 small orange peppers (sweet) or 1 large one
2 shallots, finely chopped
Curry powder
Tomato sauce (2 big ladles or 10 tbsp)
Salt and pepper

1. Soak the bread slices in a bowl of whole milk.

2. Make the meatballs. Use the freshest sardines possible, clean and dry them. Add a good pinch of curry powder and the red onions. That adds a sweet flavour. For kids, it also mellows the strong taste of sardines.

3. Add some chopped coriander and 2 finely chopped garlic cloves, together with a bit of salt and the lemon juice. Mix everything by hand.

4. Remove the bread from the milk. Crumble it over the sardines, mix everything together, and form small balls by hand. Drizzle with olive oil.

5. For the sauce, chop 2 garlic cloves and put in a food processor. Chop the peppers and add to the food processor. Process until very finely chopped.

6. Add olive oil and the shallots to a pan and brown them. Add the garlic and peppers. Sauté everything.

7. Add a bit of curry powder. Then pour in the tomato sauce and a glass of water.

Simmer gently over low heat for an hour or so. My grandfather always told me to cook over low heat to mix the flavours together well, and to stir regularly so that the bottom doesn't burn. Once the sauce is well simmered, add the sardine meatballs. I let them simmer a bit, for 15 minutes, so that the meatballs absorb the sauce well.

If you had made a *rougail saucisse* (sausage), how would the recipe be different?

You don't add curry, nor black pepper. Just onion, garlic, salt and tomato sauce. You might add the pepper. In Île de la Réunion, I put the sausages in a pot of boiling water for 15 minutes and when they're done, I strain them, and that way, they stay juicy in the tomato sauce. If you put them in the oven, they will become dry. At the nursery, I do as my grandfather showed me. I boil the sausages, I cut them in small pieces, and I simmer them in the sauce.
I let the rougail simmer so that the sardine meatballs, the sausages, or the cod soak up the sauce . . . When you say 'rougail', it must be well coated . . . When you say 'rougail', it's thick. When you say 'cari' there must be some sauce (*Author's note: the Reunionese Creole 'cari' derives from Indian and South Asia Tamil 'kari' which British language transformed into curry*).

M R S
Le Prado

Coline Faulquier

A MARSEILLAISE STAR

Driven and brimming with talent, Coline Faulquier is my darling. The first time I met this strong-willed woman was in 2017, at the Lot of Saveurs Festival in Cahors where Coline attended the screening of my documentary, *À la Recherche des Femmes Chefs (The Goddesses of Food)*. At the time, Coline had toiled in many Michelin-star kitchens, given birth to a little boy, reached the finals of the Top Chef cooking show, and opened a restaurant with her boyfriend in the Quartiers Nord of Marseille. Already, it was a hit.

We met again in Marseille a year later for my book *Elles Cuisinent* (*Women Are Chefs*). We were on a terrace in Les Goudes, the boyfriend had left, and Coline was thinking about standing on her own two feet. It was there that she told me, 'I want to be the first female chef in Marseille to get a Michelin star.'

I knew she would get there. Everyone believed in her, with Lionel Levy at the lead.

At the beginning of 2019, Coline opened her new restaurant on her own, a few minutes as the crow flies from Alexandre Mazzia's place . . .

And since January 2021, the deed is done: Marseille has a Michelin-starred female chef.

This Bourguignonne from the Vaucluse has written a new chapter in Marseille gastronomy. Coline, you have my utmost admiration. Thanks to you, many female line cooks, sous-chefs, and chefs know that the rules of the game have changed and that women now have a place at the table of French gastronomy. We need these female talents to push professional cooking towards new horizons, to renew our creativity, and diversify conversations and points of view.

At the beginning of 2023, a new baby boy completed Coline's galaxy.

The stars will not change Marseille but Marseille will change the stars.

1 Michelin Star

180 Rue du Rouet
13008 Marseille

WHERE I GREW UP

In Burgundy until I was seven, then in the Vaucluse (in Vaison-la-Romaine and Avignon).

THE INGREDIENT OF MY CHILDHOOD

Thyme . . . my little house was in between vines and the *garrigue* [scrubland] and there was thyme everywhere! The scent of thyme is the one that reminds me the most of home.

MY START IN COOKING

When I was little, a bit with my mother and my father who liked *'les bonnes choses'* (good food) and who ran *tables d'hôtes* in Burgundy. Then, as a teenager, I began taking it seriously. I was 15 years old.

MY TRAINING

I got a hotel and restaurant baccalaureate in Avignon, then I did a vocational certificate independently, then an advanced certificate as part of a work/study programme in Montpellier, a diploma from the private Ferrandi culinary school in Paris, and a stint on the *Top Chef* TV show, which confirmed and validated my determination (lol!).

MY ARRIVAL IN MARSEILLE

I arrived in 2012 to join my then-partner in *Le Sud*. But I especially wanted to leave Paris and the 5-star Le Bristol brigade for an establishment where I would have fun professionally. I made it happen at the luxury Hôtel du Castellet near Marseille, during Michelin-star Chef Christophe Bacquié's era.

MY IMPRESSION BEFORE I SETTLED DOWN HERE

When I was little, my sister lived in Marseille. During weekend visits, I said to myself, 'One day, I will live in this city because it is different!' Due to its culture, its citizens, its location, its atmosphere, its climate . . . Marseille always made me dream.

MY IMPRESSION NOW THAT I LIVE HERE

I'm learning to discover Marseille, and I appreciate it more and more. Its gastronomy and those that have pushed it to evolve and change. Everything is here and anything can be done!

MY FIRST CULINARY MEMORY IN MARSEILLE

Pieds et paquets [stuffed sheep's feet and tripe] that I learned how to make, by the book, with a butcher friend. I had never seen them before . . .

A SCENT THAT SYMBOLISES OUR CITY

The aroma of spices, and aromatic herbs . . .

A DISH OR AN INGREDIENT

For me, aioli is the dish that most represents this city! Pure, colourful, zesty, and gourmand! Vegetables, fish, garlic . . . the most beautiful ingredients we have in Marseille.

A gathering with female Marseille chefs for the release of the guide *Cheffes* that I created with another Marseillaise, Estérelle Payany, in this photo on the left

A QUARTER THAT I ADORE
I particularly like Les Goudes . . . we meet up there with friends and family to share moments untouched by time. It once was a fishermen's village, its soul is still there . . . and time actually stops when you are there. The scents of the sea and the rocks are soothing and here, at the end of the world, nature reasserts itself. This is where I like to take the time to relax, to contemplate the sea, and get lost in my thoughts.

THE MARSEILLE CULINARY SCENE
Dynamic, ambitious, cosmopolitan.

THE LINK BETWEEN MY CUISINE AND MARSEILLE
The ingredients, eating locally . . . the influence of the sun and this city of many colours which I also find in my dishes.

WHAT I COOK FOR MY FRIENDS
Grilled fish with a good aioli!

WHAT WE GENERALLY IGNORE IN MARSEILLE GASTRONOMY
We ignore that our terroir is strong and that professionalism (when it comes to chefs and restaurants) is more and more present! The level is rising in Marseille and the local supply chains are way more important than people realise . . .

WHAT WE GENERALLY OVERLOOK IN MARSEILLE GASTRONOMY
Every day, customers tell me, 'We don't know where to eat in Marseille.' What we overlook is that Marseille doesn't just have big touristy restaurants, but many lovely little restaurants with chefs, real ones! We don't realise that Marseille is also all about diversity and quality! That there are not just lazy folk in Marseille

'Good ingredients, a lot of work and passion, and a bit of folly!'

PAELLA-INSPIRED RED MULLET

INGREDIENTS FOR 10

10 red mullet
Salt and piment d'Espelette

For the blanquette-style fish emulsion:
Red mullet heads and bones
3 shallots, finely chopped
1 sprig of thyme
150ml white wine
100g fresh ginger
1 bunch of coriander
1 lemongrass stalk
400ml double cream
Zest of 1 lime
Zest of 1 lemon
Salt and pepper

For the chorizo-mint cream:
100g spicy chorizo
200ml double cream, 35% fat
½ bunch of mint

For the saffron arancini:
1 white onion, thinly sliced
Olive oil
200g arborio (risotto) rice
150ml dry white wine
80g taggiasche olives
20g piquillo peppers
½ bunch of basil
15g ground saffron
100g grated Parmesan
200g flour
3 eggs, beaten
400g breadcrumbs
5 litres oil for frying

For shellfish and condiments:
1 shallot, finely chopped
20g butter
A few sprigs of parsley
100ml white wine
200g raw clams
500g raw mussels
10 cherry tomatoes
5 mini courgettes
3 kumquats
Olive oil
Wild sprouts
Fleur de sel

1. Fillet each fish by slicing down the backbone (2 fillets per fish, keeping the tail attached), remove any bones, and place on a baking sheet covered with parchment paper. Season with salt and piment d'Espelette and refrigerate until use.

2. Soften the fish heads and bones with the shallots and thyme. Deglaze with white wine, add water to cover, and simmer for 20 minutes. Skim off the fat regularly. Reserve a third of the fish stock for the arancini.

3. Soften the peeled ginger, coriander and lemongrass in a sauté pan. Pass the fish stock through a fine strainer, then add to the sauté pan. Heat until reduced by half. Add the cream, salt and pepper, and lemon and lime zest. Keep your blanquette-style fish emulsion in a bain-marie.

4. For the chorizo-mint cream, slice the chorizo in rounds and brown in a saucepan. Before they are fully cooked, add the cream and mint. Let infuse for 30 minutes over low heat, then blend. Pour into a container and chill for at least 6 hours.

5. For the arancini, soften the onion in olive oil. Add the rice and sauté until it becomes translucent, then deglaze the pan with white wine. Add all the condiments (olives, piquillos, basil) finely chopped beforehand, then the saffron before moistening with the fish stock (that you set aside) and a bit of water. Cook until the rice grains are just softened, then add the Parmesan to bind it all together. Season and let chill on a baking sheet.

6. Cut out 10 x 3cm rectangles and bread them English-style (flour rectangles on all sides, dip in beaten egg, then in breadcrumbs). Fry and set aside.

7. Cook the shellfish in a marinière style: in a large saucepan, soften the shallot in the butter, add parsley, then pour in the white wine. Add the rinsed and cleaned clams and mussels, mix, cover, and let cook. The shellfish are cooked once they open. Let cool and remove the clams and mussels from their shells. Set aside 10.

8. Slice the cherry tomatoes in half and roast them quickly in the oven. Cut the kumquats in thin slices and heat them at 70°C in olive oil. Cook the courgettes *à l'anglaise* [English-style, or blanched] – in a large pot of boiling salted water, then plunged in an ice bath. Slice diagonally.

9. Sear each side of the red mullet on a hot griddle or pan, then quickly broil them for a minute in a salamander grill or under the broiler. You want their flesh to have a pearly sheen.

10. Put arancini on the left side of the plate and garnish with shellfish and condiments. On the right, add a quenelle of chorizo-mint cream, then a red mullet fillet. Sprinkle with fleur de sel and finish plating with the blanquette-style fish emulsion and sprouts.

'For me, this recipe, and the strong flavour of red mullet, represents Marseille and me well, as does the rich flavour of the chorizo with the Mediterranean spices. The shellfish are the sea, the brininess that I love. The fish stock is a choice to use the entire fish, to respect the product, the terroir, and what this city offers to us. This dish reflects the love of good things and the generosity that Marseille gives us!'

R
M S
Opéra

Romain Chartrain

LA VIE EN BLEU

In today's massive Parisian exodus, or invasion, as some might say, my favourites are the team from Azul, a concept store that brings together the best of Mediterranean craftsmanship, including local ones, without falling into clichés. Tea from the Greek mountains, chocolate from Marseille's La Baleine à Cabosse, terracotta cups and plates from Portugal, Moroccan glasses . . . and, at lunchtime, Romain introduces us to dishes from the South and shares his recipes. 'Azul' means 'blue' in Spanish and Portuguese, and 'hello' in Kabyle. In Marseillais, it could mean: Time to eat!

Mediterranean concept store and southern European cuisine

73 Rue Francis Davso
13001 Marseille

How did Azul start?
The concept stems from a friendship between Élise and Hélène, who finished their studies together, and I'm Élise's partner. All three of us were dreaming of a change of lifestyle. We were fed up with our respective jobs. We decided to work with craftsmen and designers from the Mediterranean basin. We each went on a trip on our own to meet artisans, to see how things were done elsewhere . . .
At first, we set limits in terms of products, and then, eventually, we decided on ceramics, carpets, tableware, cosmetics, textiles and a delicatessen. We are guided by our encounters with interesting people who have savoir-faire and with whom we want to work. I focused on the café and deli part. I was always behind my mother or my grandmother watching what they were cooking. I loved to eat, taste many things and, as I got older, cooking became an escape from the daily stress of work.
I'm still learning every day! I try, I fail, I start again. When you travel, sometimes you eat better in a B&B or a homestay with garden-grown ingredients than in restaurants. So, I thought, 'I'm going to do home-style cooking.' I brought back recipes from my travels by eating with locals. We make a Tunisian lemonade that is a hit, the Portuguese pastéis de nata . . . So, when my customers ask me for a recipe, I give it to them in turn.

Why Marseille?
All three of us are Marseillais by adoption. When we started talking about the project, Hélène was already in Marseille and we were in Paris, but we knew that we were going to come and live here. We were looking for a big city where we could have culture, sun and the sea. There aren't a lot of options on the map, and we had friends here. We knew it was going to be a good match. A Mediterranean project fit perfectly with Marseille, and we've been here for five years and we just opened a new store in Aix-en-Provence.

Your first memories when you arrived in Marseille . . .
What strikes you at first here is the light and the colour of the sky. You don't see that anywhere else. You can see the sky, whereas in Paris, you don't due to the tall buildings and the bad weather. And then, it's a city at the beach. It's a big city with little neighbourhoods. It's small village life in a big city. In Paris, you don't know your next-door neighbour!

Not all Parisians can be exported to Marseille . . .
Marseille is particular . . . but after the Covid-19 lockdowns and curfews, people think differently. That said, my feelings vis-à-vis Marseille have evolved. We have returned to a daily working life, but it is a super pleasant city which is progressing enormously. There was a boost in 2013, the year Marseille was the European Capital of Culture and with the opening of the Mucem. It's now developing a lot. The Opéra district, where we are, has really changed. It has become a large pedestrian area; we can put tables outside and customers won't be grazed by scooters. The façades have been cleaned.
Many Marseille residents who no longer came to the city centre are starting to realise they can come back, there are plenty of new shops, concepts, restaurants. The co-working space Babel Community has taken over the former Galeries Lafayette shop on Rue Saint-Fé with a great rooftop restaurant – Ciel! The problem is that downtown rents have remained high while foot traffic has fallen. We need the Marseillais to come to the centre at night as well so that neighbourhood restaurants can remain open.

Where do you live in Marseille?
We live in Endoume and Vauban. We hang in our neighbourhoods, we head down to the little Malmousque port, we're quickly at the seashore. We go out to eat in Le Panier, in Noailles, in Cours Julien.

What Marseille clichés do you adore?
The chichis in l'Estaque, with Nutella on top. It's a real experience, it's hallucinating . . . The prevailing chaos of the city, it's teeming everywhere, nothing is respected, it's all over the place. And, in the end, you get used to it because it's part of the city's identity. You end up doing the same, like parking anywhere *(Author's note: In Marseille we call it 'creating your own parking space.')*. It's shocking at first . . . As for the dirty side of the city, it's both true and false. It's not dirtier than Paris. Well, except for the cigarettes thrown out the window . . .

PORCO A ALENTEJANA (PORK WITH CLAMS)

Marseille likes to mix surf and turf. You can find this on the plate, and Romain's Marseille-Portuguese recipe perfectly sticks to our mindset of marrying extremes, even opposites.

'The Alentejo is a rural region in south-eastern Portugal. In Portugal, this recipe is their *bœuf bourguignon*. They don't necessarily make it with clams and there are two schools: lean or fatty pork. Me, I'm a bit in the middle.'

INGREDIENTS FOR 4

800g medium clams
1 tbsp coarse salt
800g potatoes (Miss Blush, or waxy potatoes if not in France)
800g pork tenderloin
80g butter
2 onions, thinly sliced
1 tbsp paprika
350ml dry white wine
3 bay leaves
2 garlic cloves, finely chopped
1 tbsp tomato purée
Olive oil
1 bunch of coriander
Salt and pepper

1. Put the clams in a large bowl with 2 litres of water and the coarse salt.

2. Peel and quarter the potatoes and put in a large saucepan with cold salted water. Bring to the boil, then let the potatoes cook for 5 minutes.

3. Cut the pork tenderloin into 3–4cm pieces.

4. In a cast-iron saucepan, melt the butter then brown the onions with the paprika. Add the meat, and let cook for 4 minutes over medium heat.

5. Put the clams in fresh water.

6. Add the white wine, bay leaves, garlic and tomato purée to the pan. Let simmer over low heat for at least 1½ hours (ideally, let the pork cook until it shreds easily).

7. Put the potatoes in a baking dish. Drizzle with olive oil, salt and pepper, and bake at 180°C/gas mark 4 for an hour.

8. 6 minutes before the potatoes are done, add the clams to the saucepan. Serve topped with fresh chopped coriander.

Gagny Sissoko

A RARE GEM

La Cuisine de Gagny is ultimately a typical Marseille story. A Malian born in the Ivory Coast, Gagny spent his first springs in Sinfra. Followed by a few years in his father's village in Mali, which he finally left at around age 15 to build a life on his own . . . Today a Marseillais, the radiant Gagny has set up his kitchen in a former butcher's shop, in the family-friendly neighbourhood of Eugène-Chave. With his ace partner Julie, they hit the road to the restaurant world through sheer hard work. Consequently, a loyal clientele of all ages comes to pick up lunch at their eatery each day.

Eat-in or takeaway lunch

153 Boulevard Chave
13005 Marseille

When did you start cooking?

We were blacksmiths in my family, and we made everything used in African kitchens. Cooking came from there since I was eight years old. I also cooked because as children, we stayed with our aunts and mothers, and we saw them doing it. Afterwards, I found myself all alone in Bamako, the capital of Mali, and the first job I got was with a family that cooked food without a permit, the kind that is sold on the street. I was a salesman. We made pasta, pastries, juices . . . I stayed with this family for 13 years. Then one day, I met Julie, who was a cultural attaché in Bamako. She invited me out for pizza. It was the first time I ate it and I thought to myself, 'This is exactly what I want to do.' Make pizzas. I wanted to learn how to make them, but I didn't have the means, I wasn't from a family that could pay for school. Julie told me, 'If you really want to do this, I'l pay for your cooking school.' There was a school in Bamako but you needed to have your degree, and me, I had never gone to school. I didn't know how to read or write.

At the culinary school, they told me it wasn't possible, but I finally convinced the school director. I told him that I loved cooking, that I had to try and that I'd make it work. He said to me, 'Let's try for a month.' It worked and after three months, I even had replaced their pizzaiolo. I worked for them, and I asked to be paid but they didn't want to. So, I stopped. I tried to build a pizza oven. I made it myself, but it didn't work. It took 40 minutes to bake a pizza . . .

At that time, I got lucky and met people who worked at the French Consulate and the United States Embassy in Mali. I made them pizzas and they paid me. Since I didn't have the right ingredients, like mushrooms, I invented pizzas with bananas, cassava . . . These were pizzas that had nothing to do with what we know here. Thanks to this, I met a stage director in Bamako, Eva Doumbia, whose theatre company *La Part du Pauvre* is based in Marseille. She tasted my pizzas and she was about to create a show in Europe.

She asked me to join her and act in the show as a cook. I cooked on stage. I had the opportunity to travel with her. I also worked in circuses, then I catered at theatres, for weddings, birthdays . . . I had the chance to meet people from all over the world. Every time I cooked, someone told me it resembled something from where they were from. So, I listened to how they would do things in their homeland and then I mixed things up. That's why it's hard for me to give recipes. They are always blends. That's what defines my cooking.

Do you feel Marseillais?

With Julie, we have two kids who have never been to Mali. They only know Marseille and the Auvergne region, because that's where their mother is from. My eight-year-old son, he's often at the restaurant because he has a lot of food allergies. Since he was born, he has never eaten out. At school, he brings everything, even his knife and fork. And now, the parents, who are customers here, would like me to cook for the school!

As for me, in my head, I'm Marseillais. Like my Armenian friends. They came here four or five generations ago. The Italians, the Corsicans . . . In my group of friends, that's how it is. People know that I'm Malian, I know that I'm Malian, but apart from my mum, I have everything here, my business, my kids, their school, Julie. My mum, she's in Mali. She's never come here. Visas are complicated. In any case, I feel Marseillais. Marseillais . . . but I'm not really a big fan of l'OM. I sort of like . . . the Parisian football team PSG. In fact, I don't have a preferred club or country when it comes to football. I only like the players. Before, in Paris, there were players I liked a lot. Less now. And with l'OM, there isn't a player that I like.

What is your first memory of Marseille?

Before coming here, I said to Julie, 'If I must go to France, I will go to Marseille.' She had never come here. She is from Auvergne in the centre of France. She was in Mali for her studies. She then left for Grenoble in France to finish school and later returned to Mali to work in the Centre Culturel Français. So, we arrived in Marseille at the same time.

My first Marseille memory dates back to 11 December 2009. It was cold. When I landed at the airport, I thankfully saw Julie or else I would have returned directly to Mali.

I knew Marseille from its football club. I was surprised by the city because it didn't resemble what I had seen on TV. It's the same for Mali, on television they only show the misery. For Marseille, I only knew of TV antennas on every roof, or laundry hanging from the windows to dry. That's what I saw in Marseille rap videos.

What scent reminds you of your childhood?

A memory from childhood . . . it's complicated because my childhood had many highs and lows. Life changed quickly. My father passed away in 1991, we found ourselves living with my dad's brothers who were very mean. Before that hell, I had a happy childhood, I was good. I have memories of the Ivory Coast with my dad and my mum from when I was little. I remember really large escargots. I wanted to try to cook snails here, but they are little and frozen. There's nothing to eat inside. You only have the taste of butter that you put in them. I remember one day my father arrived on a moped with a 10-kilo sack of giant snails. He gave them to my mother who prepared them. You need to clean them well, remove everything, chop them, and I don't know how they were cooked, but they were delicious. I've tried to research the foundations of African cooking, I even went to Haiti for this. I'm interested in slave cuisine. I went to Cape Verde as well for this project, but it did not come into fruition. I couldn't find funding. However, there are plenty of ingredients that are said to be African but which in fact are not. For example, before, there was no rice in Senegal, so why is the fish, tomato and rice dish, tiep, Senegalese? When I was little, I didn't eat rice. In the village, we ate it only once a year, on the feast day of Ramadan. It was truly exceptional, a luxury.

All the African coconut countries, Gabon, Congo, Cameroon (not Mali which has very few trees), have roughly the same climate, the same vegetation, and therefore similar cuisines. And there are also links with Latin America, Brazil particularly, in terms of climate. If I had the means, I would have continued my research. One year, the Grandes Tables de la Friche invited Colombian chefs. I found that their recipes were no different from mine, I just noticed small differences in the techniques.

The base is the same, with peppers for example. Even when using ingredients like yams, cassava and bananas, there are links with South American cuisines. And for fruit also.

Today, I like all ingredients. I don't eat chicken or pork, but I cook everything. I particularly like spices and herbs. And also, I eat a lot of seafood. When I tasted it here, I was transported back to my childhood with my father.

At the beginning, I didn't realise how expensive it was here. In the Ivory Coast, you eat seafood all the time. My dad wasn't a millionaire, but it's cheaper there.

Is there a Marseille personality that matters most to you?

Marie-Jo Ordener and Chef Emmanuel Perrodin, they are family! Chef Bernard Loury whose restaurant was next to the Vieux-Port is also someone I adore. He's a part of my life. It was people like him who gave me strength in Marseille. If I have anyone to thank, it's him. When I arrived here, I had to cook for an event at Waaw in Cours Julien. I also did workshops there and Loury signed up. I had just arrived, I spoke French badly, I cooked in my delirium.

I invented dishes in my head. I told my group, 'Cut what you want,

The duo Gagny and Julie work with the PPL co-op (Plateforme paysanne locale - Local Farmer Platform) which brings together organic and eco-responsible farmers and manufacturers in the region. Even their beef is organic. On the day we made this recipe, the octopus came from the Frioul Islands, just across from the city, where fishing for this genius of the seas is prohibited between June and September. It was March.
Vital info: At La Cuisine de Gagny, everything is made in house. And, when I say 'in house', that means on Wednesdays, burger day, Gagny cuts potatoes by hand until 11pm the night before so that no one will miss out on *frites*. I've only seen that in the best *estaminets* in the north of France. Marseille has found a rare gem here, a luxury for neighbourhood cuisine for top eaters who, even for lunch, want high-quality grub. Such beautiful plates are unusual for a lunch counter. Make good use of it . . .

as you want,' and then I orchestrated a dish. This is how I work in the kitchen. So, Chef Loury and his server were in this group. They are open-minded people.
A young Malian arrives, without speaking French . . . I am doing a cooking workshop and he, Loury, is attending it. At the end, he gave me his card and he told me to come and see him at his restaurant.
For one year, I didn't go. I crossed paths with him, he again told me to come see him. Another time, I ran into his server who told me that his boss was still waiting for me. Finally, I went there to eat, and at the end of the meal, he told me that he didn't want me to pay for it. He told me, 'It's been four years since I invited you!'
At that time, I left to work in Paris for two months. When I returned, I wanted to open my own restaurant. So, I asked Loury if I could come and work for him. He said to me, 'With pleasure, come as much as you want.' He taught me everything, he showed me everything. People who eat at my restaurant tell me I make some of the best fish in Marseille. This is thanks to Bernard Loury.
The problem is that I don't know how to read. I don't know how to write. I can read a few words, but I don't retain what I read. And Loury, since he does everything himself, he showed me his techniques; I observed, and I remembered them. I loved it. *(Author's note: Loury decided to retire a few months ago.)* I had started classes in an association to learn to read and write French but quickly found myself organising cooking workshops for the other students. I transformed the class! There were people who came from all over, Syrians, Algerians, Chadians, Russians, Comorians . . . I brought them to the market, telling them, 'Everyone choose a recipe, and we'll do it my way.' No one spoke French, they didn't know how to read or write. So, I made a graphic cookbook, with drawings. I could publish it. Now, my son is learning to read. I'm going to learn with him.

Do you, in turn, try to help young people when they come here?
In the kitchen, it's complicated. I'm practically alone, I don't have a lot of time to explain what I'm doing. I tell them that you must love this métier. 'If you don't love it, I can't help you.' There aren't miracles. It's difficult. I tell them, 'It will serve you. If you know how to cook, you will find work.'
And then, there's the issue of alcohol. Even though I'm Muslim, I drink it and I sell it. I don't criticise other people's choices, I do not ask them to taste my bouillons, but they cannot refuse to serve them to customers. There are also people who want to come and work here but ask me if it's halal. I tell them no. I'm not halal here.

How would you define Marseille cuisine?
Marseille cuisine is a *mélange* (a mix). In Marseille, there are 70 countries represented by a consulate. In fact, Marseille is not bouillabaisse, it's couscous. Before, I made couscous at the restaurant, but I stopped. I have a lot of grannies and grandpas as customers and if I make couscous, they only want to eat that. They won't even look at the rest of the menu.

What are your plans?
My dream would be to open a restaurant with modern African cuisine. Nothing like what I do here. A restaurant for people who know Africa, or Africans themselves, a cultural centre with a restaurant. It's truly what I'd like to do now, with African chefs, who went to African culinary schools and can work with African cuisine, to prepare dishes that we eat in the heart of Mali.
In my restaurant, I want to cook what I love. There aren't recipes, nor names of dishes, it's my cuisine. Sometimes, I make African *yassa*, when I get onions delivered. But I told myself when I started off that I didn't want to be pigeonholed. That would have limited my clientele. Even so, my customers are often afraid that my cooking will be too spicy. However, there are lots of cuisines that are spicier than African food.

Eat-in or takeaway lunch

153 Boulevard Chave
13005 Marseille

LA DAUBE DE POULPE
(octopus stew)

INGREDIENTS FOR 4

1 leek
3 turnips
3 carrots
¼ cabbage
3 onions
6 garlic cloves
2kg fresh octopus
50ml olive oil
Thyme
Bay leaves
1 litre full-bodied red wine
1 large can chopped tomatoes
Salt and pepper

1. Peel the leek and slice it into thick rounds. Peel the turnips and carrots and cut them into rounds. Cut the cabbage into chunks. Peel and finely chop the onions and garlic.

2. Put the leek in a saucepan filled with salted water. You can also add the carrot, onion and cabbage peelings. All of them will add flavour to the bouillon and the octopus. Bring to the boil.

3. Once boiling, dunk the octopus in the bouillon for 4 minutes, remove, and repeat the operation twice. Then, let the octopus rest in the bouillon until it cools. If necessary, once cool, you can even leave the octopus in the bouillon in the refrigerator for a few hours.

4. In a saucepan, soften the onion and garlic in the olive oil for 5 minutes. Season with salt and pepper, and add the carrots, cabbage, turnips, thyme, bay leaves and octopus. Pour in the wine and bring to the boil.

5. Add the chopped tomatoes, the strained bouillon from the octopus, and pepper. At this time, Chef Gagny often adds a bit of *bissap* (hibiscus-flower juice). Let simmer over low heat for at least 1½ hours until the octopus is really tender.

6. Serve the octopus with the vegetables and sauce over a bed of rice (the chef uses rice from the nearby Camargue) or creamy polenta.

R
M S
Les Goudes

Christophe Thullier

The inhabitants of Les Goudes have got into the habit of stopping at L'Esplaï du Grand Bar des Goudes for l'apéro at any time during the day but they also like to pick up bottles of fish soup *(soupe de poissons)* there for takeaway. Christophe's recipe is universally adored!
As for the restaurant, it is always full, and the owner, Didier, takes as much pleasure in chatting with holidaymakers as with the locals. Here, you're sure to be well received, and you eat well. When you add that to the magnificent view, who could ask for more?
When I sat down to eat at the Grand Bar des Goudes, Didier said to me, 'I am Goudois, and you?' I replied, 'I am from Marseille,' but that didn't suffice. 'From where in Marseille?' he asked me, and, at that moment, I rattled off all my origins and he his. We discovered we have a lot in common!

THE BIG BLUE

Let's get one thing clear. We are all welcome in Les Goudes, but we must respect the little fishing port and arrive by foot rather than by car. Come by la *navette* boat, by bus, or bike from the Vieux-Port. Come to fish, swim and eat . . . but don't pay 1 million euros for a *cabanon* (beach shack) just to transform it into a boutique-studio with a bay window and a rooftop terrasse – a stupidity that proves that some have not understood the spirit of the place today. Les Goudes during 1990–2000 had a taste of Ibiza. For 20 years, we all tried to get into the Maronaise, the disco-cabanon where we partied under the stars. In 2010, the building was demolished following a court order. Times have changed. The recent opening of the hotspot Tuba restaurant with its St.-Tropez-like deco and the 20,000 Lieues Sous la Bière pub is reviving a certain sunset party atmosphere . . . but the time has come for calm and to protect the coast.
Now, back to the talented chef at the Grand Bar des Goudes, the warm and enthusiastic Christophe Thullier, who took his afternoon off to make this recipe and pose for this book. I tasted his bouillabaisse, excellent, his red mullet ceviche, excellent, and his sea bass tartare pleased me just as much.

What is your relationship with Marseille?
I came to Marseille when I was 10 years old. I came from Lille. I followed my parents. My mum is from Oran. My parents landed in Marseille in 1962 when Algeria became independent from France after the Algerian War. My mother went to Lille in the north to work at the post office. What a change of atmosphere! My father, a *Lillois*, was a plumber and heating engineer; he travelled a lot in the South, and he realised that there was a lot of work here, mainly with the petrochemical plants. In the end, the whole family settled down here. So, my main childhood memories are from Marseille.

What are your culinary memories of Marseille as a child?
The giant paellas in the field with family, friends and my parents. Catalan gazpacho, that is not at all like Andalusian gazpacho. The Andalusian version is a cold soup, the Catalan one is made with stale bread that you soak in a very tomato-y mix. My paternal grandmother, Jiménez, is of Spanish heritage, and on my mother's side, they were called Cruz. My childhood aromas are tomatoes, *gambas à l'armoricaine*, all Spanish cuisine. Or more aptly Maghreb [North African] Spanish. I have this culture in my head. Couscous as well.

What is your Marseille?
I grew up in the Quartiers Nord in the La Castellane housing estate. Home of the famous Marseille-born, Franco-Kabyle footballer, Zidane, who scored two goals for France's 1998 World Cup victory. I got to play football with him and his brothers *(Author's note: many Marseillais from Algerian descent are Kabyle, proud of their Berber ancestors who pre-dated the Arab invaders in Algeria)*. In my time, the northern part of Marseille was very united regardless of the different communities. We helped each other out, we did favours for each other. There was a lot of sharing. We invited each other over for meals. We gave each other cakes. It was good to live there. Today there are no more stores, it has changed a lot. It's less pretty. I now live in Vitrolles, a small town north of Marseille. I knew the little harbour of Les Goudes because there were nightclubs here. Particularly the famous Maronaise! My vision of Les Goudes has not changed. Life is good here. I like Les Goudes off-season, like all the very touristy villages.

How would you describe your cuisine?
At L'Esplaï, I cook from my childhood. That's why it works. Here, we invite customers into our universe, and our universe is Marseille. When I came here, the menu was already established. The restaurant was 20 years old.

Fish & seafood

28 Rue Désiré Pelaprat
13008 Marseille

I just brought my own touch to the menu, like my father's fish soup, which is very thick. I added fish fillets and used less pastis and its strong anise notes to bring out the flavours of the fish. Customers quickly noticed the change. I also reduced the garlic in the *rouille* [traditional saffron aioli] since I find it masks the fish's taste and erases the flavours. For example, *panisses* should not be served with a super-garlicky aioli, otherwise you no longer taste the chickpeas.

Today, what are Marseille's culinary symbols?
Bouillabaisse, but also Mediterranean cuisine, and *les légumes du soleil* [vegetables grown in the Provençal sun]. Fish, certainly, but we're evolving. Very good chefs have changed Marseille. For example, Laetitia Visse, who makes pâtés and terrines to die for. What's more, she had the nerve to open a Marseille restaurant that uses offal. I admire her. In fact, 90% of the great chefs here are not from Marseille. They all come from elsewhere and they consider themselves more Marseillais than the Marseillais. They dare to show that in Marseille, we know how to work with tripe, beef and lamb. They have brought it back in fashion. And the Marseillais have become gourmets. The whole culinary scene is changing, thanks to the chefs and the *Gourméditerranée* association of which I am a part. We want to show that in Marseille, there is not only the cuisine for tourists.

What aren't the Marseillais aware of in their own food scene?
That we know how to make great food with great ingredients! They were always the first to critique us and they were often right. In Marseille, the restaurant industry was either low-end or high-end. We had no in-between. It's changing today. We are developing a cuisine in the middle, a good cuisine with fresh, local ingredients and we showcase it. As for tourists, they don't know about *sardinades* or *oursinades* [sardine and sea urchin festivals] . . . because they happen off-season.

What do you cook for your family?
I cook other things besides fish! I love milk-fed lamb, to spend hours at the stovetop. Make a good stock. Forage for herbs or small, wild onions in the hills. Otherwise, I go fishing like my father did. After the Covid lockdowns I wanted to eat trout and I didn't want to buy them. So, I spend my days fishing!

SEA BASS TARTARE

'For the tartare, I try to make the sea bass as simply as possible so as not to alter it. I want to keep the fish natural and, even for the garnish, I don't put much. No lemon, no soy sauce. I season it with salt and pepper, then onion or shallot, tomato, chives and olive oil.'

INGREDIENTS FOR 4–6

1 sea bass (*loup*), about 1kg
1 tomato
1 large shallot
6 chives
60ml olive oil
1 lemon
Salt and pepper

1. Scale and clean the sea bass, remove the fillets and the skin (but keep the skin), take out the bones, remove the belly. (Raw, you lose 40–50% of the fish.)

2. Preheat the oven to 180°C/gas mark 4. Put the skin on a baking sheet covered with parchment paper, season with salt and pepper, and drizzle with olive oil. Put another sheet of parchment paper on top for pressure, then bake for around 40 minutes to make chips/crisps for the garnish.

3. Finely dice the fish fillets into approximately 0.5cm pieces, and set aside in a large bowl.

4. Wash and quarter the tomato, deseed, and finely dice, then add to the fish. Peel and thinly slice the shallot and chives. Mix with the fish and tomatoes. Season with salt and pepper according to taste. Add the olive oil and mix together.

5. Plate as you wish, be creative, and add a bit of lemon juice to your liking.

Christian Qui

In a way, Chef Christian Qui is the Richard Olney of today. With him, you quickly lose track of time.
It was Chef Emmanuel Perrodin who put me on the trail of this artist-chef. Of Vietnamese descent, Christian works by instinct and by whatever is inspiring him at that moment, without precise measurements. The result is unexpected, balanced, and authentically tasty.
I first met Christian in Cours Julien on a Wednesday, farmers' market day, and we toured the farmers and vendors together.

BACK TO LIFE

Christian knows them all, he has visited each of them to see how they work. Then, we cooked in Les Goudes. The chef had settled down for a while in this fishing village neighbourhood, facing the wind and the big blue. Passionate about the sea and fish, Christian wants to and will save the Mediterranean's biodiversity and artisanal fishing. I believe him. He is capable of it. The way he cooks leftovers is an education. Chefs and journalists love to come and eat at his place and get inspired. With me, he immediately displayed his collection of fish eggs that he dries himself. 'Grated over mashed potatoes or pasta, it's delicious,' he shared. Here, too, I believed him.
His association Bouillabaisse TURFU wants to believe in a FUTURE of artisanal fishing and its cuisine. 'The fishermen of Marseille, I love them despite them, because bringing them together . . . It's like assembling mushroom pickers. Nobody wants to let go of their know-how!' This future (or *turfu* in French slang) of Christian's is today taking shape in a small address close to the Vieux-Port where he's inventing street food from the sea and picnic fare for takeaway on the seaside rocks. And via the maritime shuttles (*la navette*) that embark from the nearby quay to Les Goudes or the Îles du Frioul. The shop is unconventional . . . and a huge success! He also organises tours of the fish market and seafood cooking workshops so that everyone can master basic techniques. Educating the Marseillais about fish so that they stop buying and cooking the same species over and over again is a good debut in this fight against the depletion of living things. Sharing knowledge is a priority for Chef Christian. He takes the time to reunite scientists with fishing historians, fishermen with farmers who usually don't really speak with each other . . . Notably in a podcast on Fréquence Mistral. Excuse his French, it's a must listen.
At the end of 2020, the hipster Le Fooding guide, loyal fan of Qui, awarded him the 'Table of the Year'. The blue revolution is upon us . . . but make no mistake. Christian Qui isn't into trends. He's the real deal.

You grew up in Marseille?
No, in a Parisian suburb. I arrived in Marseille in 1995 as a landscape architect to work on public space development in the Quartiers Nord. As a result, I have a view of the Quartiers Nord, of the friendships that I have been able to create there. I have seen problems too. Marseille lured me in. It was the only truly cosmopolitan city in France, apart from Paris, that was open to the world. My father had arrived in Marseille from Vietnam at the end of the 1950s, then he left for the Parisian suburbs because he couldn't find work here.

Your first memory of Marseille in 1995?
It was a period when I discovered things . . . and mentalities that, at first, I did not understand! Once I went to a café and started reading the free local newspaper on the counter, and they took the newspaper out of my hand because a guy who had just arrived would read it at that time every day. At the beginning, you do not belong to this place. It's a very Mediterranean city, macho. In bars, people look down on you if they've never seen you before . . . It takes time. And then one day you're part of the thing and the projects happen. This mentality is changing though.

What are your memories of the Quartiers Nord?
When I stopped working for the city, I started the association Téléscopage. We did brilliant artistic projects with the residents of those districts. For example, we brought kids to a contemporary art festival to build Comorian huts. When you're proud of an object that you make aesthetically and that creates encounters, it makes sense.

Sustainable seafood & fish and picnic fare

1 Rue Pythéas
13001 Marseille
(in front of Place du Général de Gaulle)

When did you start cooking?
At one point, I saw that I was not going to solve much in the Quartiers Nord. I saw the limits of my actions. When I arrived, under Mayor Vigouroux, there was a real policy to be present and reclaim public spaces in these districts. Then came the era of Mayor Jean-Claude Gaudin.
I was in the department of urban planning, and I saw the turnarounds happen. The city split into two blocks. Mayor Gaudin focused on the city centre to give it a more glamorous side and the county council, Mr Guérini and his band, took care of the Quartiers Nord. Social centres were shuttered, including the one at the Cité des Rosiers housing estate, even though the bonds it created were enormous. In this housing estate, there are many illiterates who do not know how to fill out forms, write cheques . . . They could do so there; their children could do their homework there. There was a room for martial arts, a nursery, speakers, and parties . . . it had an incredible vitality. Me, I took care of the children on the street, who were 90% Comorian because here they live like in the Comoros where everyone takes care of everyone's children. After that, I wondered what I really wanted to do. Before coming to Marseille, I had lived in England for 10 years, in London. I had worked in kitchens, in restaurants like Pizza Express, in bars like all the French do in London! Then, I went to Leeds to study.
I knew the stress and the struggle that comes with being a chef, but I told myself that I was going to do it my way and try to dismantle the system. I trained at the Bonneveine culinary lycée in Marseille and then I went to work in Los Angeles with some Japanese cooks. When I came back, I set up a very small thing, SushiQui, near Boulevard Chave before the neighbourhood became trendy.
At first, I was not sure of myself, so I wanted to remake all the beautiful things I had learned

with the Japanese. I wanted to be professional, I wanted salmon, so I went to Métro, the wholesale supermarket, and Saumaty, the wholesale fish market near L'Estaque. It took me a while to send all that packing. I had my experience as a landscape architect where I let inspiration arise, I met people, I took photos, I dreamed before making a project a reality . . . One day, I told myself that I was going to work like that with cooking. I threw all my menus in the trash, I went to the Vieux-Port, and I started buying local fish. Le Fooding, with Julia Sammut who wrote for the guide, came, they said it was great and put the spotlight on what I was doing by naming me 'best raw feast' in their 2013 guide, and off we went! Julia was my fairy godmother.

Your ideas about the TURFU (future) of the dining scene?
1. The restaurant model is dead. We just witnessed it with the pandemic. If the rent isn't paid, you can't make use of your place of work. We only own our ability to work hard, nothing else. Most chefs do not own their cooking equipment. Before, in Marseille, this was not the case, but today, we eat more and more at tables funded by investors, not the families of the restaurant owners.

It is when things are going badly that we realise the faults in the system.
2. Globalised food is not expensive and, in fact, nobody can afford local craftsmanship. In a short time, people could change their manner of consumption, but they do not have the means.
3. The plankton in the Mediterranean is affected by pollution. Many species have disappeared, which I've witnessed in the markets over the past 10 years. *Saint-Pierre* [John Dory], *galinette*, *violets* [sea squirts], you barely see them anymore. There are even less sea urchins and octopuses. It must be said that everything in the sea is precious. Chefs must use their growing media presence to set an example.

However, how do you think and act if you don't have the knowledge? The reality is sometimes counter-intuitive. Sardines have decreased in size and there are less sea urchins . . . because the water around Marseille is too clean. Wastewater treatment plants do not discharge enough organic matter into the sea, so the phytoplankton are less nourished. On the other hand, these plants don't filter out chemical products and release them into the sea, which is very harmful.
4. Conviviality, that's what Marseille must safeguard.
Here, people talk to each other . . . So take time to do your food shopping, stop for a coffee, go to the market with your children . . . All this must be a nice moment where you pause to observe the beauty of the world. Then go home to cook and the next day share your cooking with friends. It is this culture that Marseille can lay claim to. Now on the escalator that leads to the Saint Charles train station, I am asked to stick to the right to let those in a hurry pass! That's not good.

Sustainable seafood & fish
and picnic fare

1 Rue Pythéas
13001 Marseille
(in front of Place du Général de Gaulle)

SEA URCHIN BOUILLABAISSE OF TOMORROW, AKA SUSTAINABLE SEA CUISINE

n Les Goudes, Kim, the local isherwoman, brings sea ırchins to the chef when she finds them. Szechuan ɔuttons (*brède mafane*), found n Noailles, has a flavour that esembles Sichuan pepper, t's electric in a way . . . The sea urchin provides a lot of at, the *brède mafane* then ɔrings a freshness which counterbalances this fat. As for pink peppercorns, they can be found growing wild all over Marseille. For the fish, Christian chose the moray eel, which fishermen's wives here call the "Louis Vuitton".'

INGREDIENTS FOR 4

1 dozen sea urchins
2 egg yolks
Olive oil
1 soupe de poissons with saffron (the recipe is earlier in the book)
1 moray eel
1 monkfish head
Mussels (a few)
Potatoes (a few)
Butter
Ground mild chilli pepper
Szechuan buttons, leaves and flowers
Pink peppercorns
Coarse salt

1. Dunk the sea urchin tongues in the egg yolks to make a hollandaise-like sauce. Add a bit of olive oil.

2. Beat the mixture and put in a heatproof bowl. Christian put his bowl in the soupe de poissons and used the heat of the soup to whip up his hollandaise-like sauce. Whisk until it's light and creamy.

3. To infuse the soupe de poissons, put the sea urchin shells and their 'juice' in a fine strainer and dunk into the soup. Break down the shells a bit to release their flavour. You can also put the shells directly in the soupe de poissons, then strain the soup through a fine strainer.

4. Prepare the moray eel. You must remove the head and all the tail, which has too many bones. Cook the rest of the moray for 10 minutes in the soupe de poissons.

5. Prepare a stock with the monkfish head. Cook the mussels in it.

6. Bake the potatoes with their skins on in the oven or in a wood-fired stove, then peel them. Mash with butter, olive oil and coarse salt. Add the mussels and a bit of chilli pepper. With a soup spoon, form quenelles with the potato-mussel mixture.

7. Garnish the soup with some Szechuan buttons and pink peppercorns.

8. You can eat moray eel skin, according to Christian. I tried it. I wouldn't go overboard.

FOCUS

Memories of bouillabaisse

Bouillabaisse was a fishermen's dish that became a *cabanon* dish on the weekends, well before it was a dish served in restaurants . . . Nowadays, the Cabanon de Jean, in the Calanque of Sormiou, is surely one of the rare places where the bouillabaisse, and the *cabanon de mer* (beach shack), have retained their spirit of yesteryear. Part of Marseille's intangible heritage lives in this bouillabaisse.

Chef Emmanuel Perrodin penned the collection *La Bouillabaisse, Ten Ways to Prepare It*, by Éditions de l'Épure, so I knew he was the man for the job for this mythical recipe. But guess what? There are more than 10 recipes for bouillabaisse and thanks to Emmanuel Perrodin, here is *le*, or *la*, 11th!

We don't all agree on the gender of this dish, 'Le' or 'La', masculine or feminine . . . No one is sure. We do know that *lou boui abaisso* was of ancient Greek origin . . . Which gave us time to change a lot of things. For that matter, we continue to do so these days. Christian Qui et Lionel Levy have brilliantly tried their hand at it.

Emmanuel Perrodin, meanwhile, is hard to reach and always overwhelmed. Everyone knows it and we don't mind. He's an artist and a savant. We insist, we call him back, we corner him at an event, and we end up getting what we want: authenticity and realness, with a good dose of culinary culture and sincere simplicity. Everything a bouillabaisse needs.

THE BOUILLABAISSE OF HENRY V

by Emmanuel Perrodin

'The 'bouillabaisse of Henry V', they called it in Marseille. *'Aigo-sau'* they said across Provence. That is, water and salt. A remembrance of the times of Lent, when we reject meat and overly refined cooking, this recipe would almost be a bouillabaisse. The preparations are sisters: however, they don't use either saffron or scorpion fish (*rascasse*). This is about fish, especially white fish. Let's begin.'

Soften 1 finely sliced onion, 2 crushed garlic cloves, half of a fennel (minced), and two coarsely crushed tomatoes in a bit of olive oil. In a large saucepan (*cocotte*), brown a few Jerusalem artichokes. Let's be clear, no potatoes here! We can tell you all the grandmothers' stories and the grandfathers' tricks . . . the potato was looked upon with a certain dose of suspicion in Provence until the beginning of the 20th century. French people in the north of the country ate potatoes while we in the south didn't. It's the same division as with *'cuisine au beurre'* and *'cuisine à l'huile'*. So forget potatoes for now!

Then, add 4 nice slices of each whiting and monkfish, 4 pieces of *galinette*, and, if you're lucky, small fillets of John Dory and 4 red mullet. Cover with water, enough to submerge the fish, but not too much! Do not drown the fish nor drown out the flavour of the broth. Add the zests of 2 oranges and 1 lemon, 1 bay leaf, 2 sprigs of thyme, salt, pepper and 1 bird's eye chilli. Boil over high heat. Lower the heat. Let simmer for 8 minutes.

Gently remove the fish. Strain the broth and adjust the seasoning. Add the juice of a lemon for some punch. Serve hot with slices of stale bread. And a nice aioli, of course. Don't even think about a *rouille* (saffron aioli)! We told you this bouillabaisse was white.

THE MISUNDERSTANDING

'I only ate bouillabaisse once. It is a dish that is too rich for me. I'm a fan of *soupe de poissons* (fish soup). Speaking of which, is a problem. There are foreign tourists who believe that bouillabaisse is *soupe de poissons*, and I mention this because my mum and I witnessed a cultural dispute in a Cassis restaurant where Germans asked for bouillabaisse believing it was *soupe de poissons*. They saw I don't know how many fish arriving . . . red mullet, sea bream, etc. The fact that they didn't want it was problematic in itself, but the bill was a source of great conflict between the restaurant owner and them.'

— Nicole Ferroni

CATCH OF THE DAY

'I must have been 12 years old when I had bouillabaisse for the first time. It was my dad who made it, and yet, he's a *Chti* [a native of northern France]! He took the recipe from a book. My father loved fishing, he went out in the evening, and we ate the fish that he caught. We didn't buy fish. We ate what he brought back home, conger eel, octopus, moray eel, dogfish, porgy, sea bass, sea bream . . .'

— Christophe Thullier (L'Esplaï du Grand Bar des Goudes)

A GRANNY, A BOUILLABAISSE

'My first bouillabaisse was the one my maternal grandmother made. It is a dish that she loved to prepare for special occasions. One day, the poor thing even poisoned herself with a thorn from a scorpionfish while making it for us!'

— Jérôme Raffaelli (Oh Faon !)

MADE IN SÉNÉGAL

'Bouillabaisse isn't Marseillais. For me, it's Senegalese! We eat it in Mali but it comes from Senegal, which is on the sea. When I ate bouillabaisse in Marseille, I recalled the fish soup of Mali. It's exactly the same.'

— Gagny (La Cuisine de Gagny)

THE SETTING

'We went to the Cabanon de Jean (Paoli) in the Calanque de Sormiou. Here, you eat very well, without fuss. Plastic tables, plastic chairs, paper tablecloths. What matters is what you eat. There are only a few tables. It's casual, it's good fish. You eat a simple bouillabaisse there. That's more than enough to have a great night out.'

— Romain Chartrain (Azul)

THE BIRTH OF A FRIENDSHIP . . . AND A SIGNATURE DISH

'In my former restaurant, Une Table au Sud, I didn't want to make bouillabaisse. I'm not from Marseille. I didn't want to tackle a dish so well made by grandmothers on Sundays. It is a dish that evokes a lot of childhood memories and emotions. For me, it was a losing battle. A Parisian client who arrived from New York convinced me to serve one. I didn't know him at the time, we talked until 4 a.m., and he kept telling me that I had to make a bouillabaisse. I went home, showered, slept for an hour, then went back to the restaurant thinking about New York and, there, I created the bouillabaisse milkshake. I didn't want to make it a main course, I made it a starter because I wanted customers to discover the rest of my cooking. In one morning, it was done. We have become very good friends since.'

— Lionel Levy (Alcyone)

THE DAY WHEN I DIDN'T EAT MY FIRST BOUILLABAISSE

'You will laugh . . . I was 8 years old, I think. We were visiting an old aunt with my family and my parents wanted a bouillabaisse. My brother and I had no desire to eat this fish soup which seemed so foul to us, so we bought kids' menus at Quick [the French fast-food joint] and ate them in the restaurant which served bouillabaisse. My God, I'm so ashamed just thinking about it . . . !'

— Marie-Christine Aractingi (ex-Dame Farine owner, the first boulangerie in Marseille to make artisanal bread, now called Miches et Baguettes . . . and it's still just as good!)

Lionel Levy

After a stint in Paris at the musketeers of French cooking, Éric Frechon, Yves Camdeborde and Alain Ducasse, Lionel Levy set sail for the Bonne Mère 20 years ago and sounded the alarm amid the tourist traps of the Vieux-Port.
Today, you can say that this Toulousian is a true Marseillais. Lionel doesn't still walk around with his shirt unbuttoned, but he has become a unifying, uniting chef who co-created and chairs Gourméditerranée, the local association of chefs. The last election was in March 2021, and the campaign was worthy of a mayoral battle. After all, we are in Marseille, land of clans, rivalries, and egos . . . In short, now officiating at a magnificent monument in the heights of Le Panier that has become a 5-star hotel, chef Lionel Levy remains close to his followers and maintains his role as the MC of Marseille gastronomy.
He has seen a slew of young chefs pass through his Michelin-star kitchens who are a hit on the local scene today: Vanessa Robuschi (Question du Goût), Camille Gandolfo (Les Bords de Mer), Georgiana Viou (Rouge in Nimes) . . . and he is one of the most fervent fans of Coline Faulquier (Signature). So, lots of female chefs.

LEADER OF THE PACK

1 Michelin Star
Chef at Alcyone and
Executive Chef of the Hotel Interocontinental

1 Place Daviel
13002 Marseille

Where did you grow up?
In Toulouse. I went to culinary school there, then my first job was with Gérard Garrigues at Pastel. He's my mentor, he means a lot to me. He helped me when I started out, and he was the one who told me about a business for sale in Marseille. He said to me, 'Come, let's take the car and go see it. I'm sure it's for you.' That's how I discovered the first floor of the La Samaritaine brasserie that had been totally abandoned. I went up to the first floor and saw the view on the Vieux-Port, the Canebière, the Bonne Mère. These were the only things I had heard about. And that's where I created Une Table au Sud in 1999. I didn't know Marseille, I had never set foot here. I had no family, no contacts. I fell head over heels in love with this city, the light, the scents, the noise. It blew me away. Afterwards, I realised that it wasn't as easy as that. In 1999, it wasn't a gastronomic city, and nothing of that ilk happened on this side of the Vieux-Port besides the Minguella brothers' Le Miramar. And here I was, a young 26-year-old cook arriving from Paris to open a restaurant on a first floor, without a terrasse, and with a gastronomic menu . . . I think it was 160 francs [25 euros then, 40 euros today] for a set menu. I had a lot of intimidation, anonymous letters, little messages written on toilet paper that were sent by mail, phone calls . . . But, hey, I have a pretty strong character and I like challenges. Today, I can talk about it with a grin. It was just their way to test me, to know if I was capable of staying in Marseille.
In 1999, there were few gastronomic restaurants, few high-quality suppliers who offered original ingredients. My first winter, I ordered *potimarron* [chestnut squash] and the next day my vegetable supplier brought me a bag of chestnuts and he said, with his Marseillais accent, 'Here you go, *petits marrons* [little chestnuts].'
I do not have an oversized ego and I know where my place is, however, I firmly believe that I was one of the trailblazers on this side of the Vieux-Port. I made traditional recipes, modernised with my personal touch, an identifiable signature cuisine [*cuisine d'auteur*]. My bouillabaisse milkshake, we are still talking about it! But when it comes to managing staff . . .
I had to change. I had just left Chef Alain Ducasse's kitchen where there is almost a military rigour. Here, on Saturday nights after service, I got angry. I was very bad-tempered at the time, young, and therefore quick to get angry. I kicked everyone out because it wasn't going well, and I found myself alone in the kitchen with an apprentice. At 26, you don't know how to manage a team!
With Ducasse, Camdeborde, Frechon, it's this way and only this way. And me, I didn't bat an eye with them.

How much time did it take to get away from all that?
I quickly realised when I arrived here that I had to change how I worked. The blow of cleaning the kitchen from floor to ceiling at 2am Saturday night after service . . . you do that at Ducasse but not here. Here on Saturday nights, after service, we gather around the table and have a drink. We must try to detach ourselves from what we learned. I had a lot of conversations on this subject, in particular with Coline Faulquier, with whom I am

quite close, with Vanessa Rubuschi and Georgiana Viou.
Maturity and reflection in the kitchen arrive at 40 years old.
I didn't cook the same at 26 as I do today.
I remember having an interview with Chef Alain Passard when I arrived in Paris, and he asked me what I wanted to become. I said, 'I want to be a chef.' He replied, 'You will not be a chef until you are 40 years old. Before 40, you are not a chef.' I left the interview telling myself that I would be a chef before that! But he was right. Cooking is done by humans. We cannot separate what we are in life from what we cook.

You created Gourméditerranée. Why?
The idea came to me in 2012, the night before Marseille was nominated as the 2013 European Capital of Culture. We were 5 or 6 local chefs, and we realised that a lot of events planned for that year were with Parisian and Lyonnais chefs who would come to Marseille to cook. We called the Region's officials to tell them that there were many Marseille chefs and that they had to do something with us, that they had to showcase us. So, we created the association one evening at my previous restaurant, Une Table au Sud, and it's something fabulous. We have plenty of great projects. Thanks to them, we have made others want to come and settle down here and take over the city. The more of us who make quality things, from pizza to kebab to 3 Michelin stars, the better. As Lyon did in the past. Will we be smart enough to do as well as them with our differences, our rants, our passion, our spirit? That is the question. But this typicality must be found in the Marseille cuisine.

What are the ingredients of Marseille cuisine?
I have trouble with the term 'Marseille cuisine'. For me, it's Mediterranean cuisine. Marseille is the crossroads of the Mediterranean. There is olive oil, garlic, herbs, and spices. If there are no spices, it is not Marseille. On the other hand, we must make better use of our terroir. I try to use the least number of products that are not from here. I make scallops because it's a top ingredient that sells well, but I don't cook langoustines, even if I adore them. At the Intercontinental, when they chose me, it was a topic of discussion. I told them that I was coming with my attributes and my faults but that I was not going to do international hotel cuisine.
I wanted to keep the pissaladière, the milkshake, the *farcis* [stuffed vegetables], the *pieds et paquets* [stuffed sheep's feet and tripe].
We have a barbecue picnic every Thursday evening in the summer. We put out red checked tablecloths. When I proposed this to the management, they winced, but it's a hit.

How would you define the food scene in Marseille?
It is being feminised, that is obvious. One of the latest is Cheffe Laëtitia Visse, she is great. Today Marseille is uninhibited. A few years ago, we said to ourselves that we were not Lyon, that we were not Paris, that we did not have the well-being of the south-west. Today, you can eat well in Marseille for 30 euros. And we also have 3-star chef Alexandre Mazzia. There is a certain generosity here that should not be forgotten, and not just on the plate.

What are your neighbourhoods?
Le Panier, where the Intercontinental is located. It is not a tourist cliché. It is of its time. The Vieux-Port, early in the morning, is unforgettable. And, I would add the fishermen, Jean, Christian. It's part of the city's identity.
I live in another district, the 6th, near Castellane, Rue de Lodi, Rue d'Italie. This neighbourhood is becoming really pleasant. There are great boulangeries.

What are Marseille scents?
The morning brininess on the port. Roasting coffee is also emblematic of Marseille. We don't talk enough about it. There is notably Café Debout behind the opera house. Citrus, because I really love to use it in cooking. The scents of my childhood are spices, cumin and harissa. These aromas I find again in Noailles. My granny had a tiny apartment in Asnières, a Paris suburb, and when she made us *briks* and couscous, I was already in Noailles!

Do you feel Marseillais?
Totally. 110%.

BOUILLE-ABAISSE MILK-SHAKE
by Lionel Levy

INGREDIENTS FOR 6

For the rouille:
See recipe in chapter 5

For the egg cappuccino:
10 eggs
20g butter
50ml olive oil
125g mascarpone
Salt and white pepper

For the fish soup foam:
2kg rock fish
Olive oil
2 celery stalks
2 carrots
1 onion
2 fennel bulbs
1 leek
Pastis
1 orange, unwaxed, quartered
2 heads of garlic, halved
100g tomato purée
Thyme
Bay leaf
4 litres fish stock
2 pinches of saffron
50g grated Parmesan

1. Prepare the egg cappuccino: whisk the eggs with salt and white pepper, scramble in a sauté pan with the butter and olive oil, remove from heat and add the mascarpone. Blend. Pour into a syphon, then foam with two cartridges.

2. For the fish soup foam: brown the fish in olive oil in a large saucepan, add the aromatic garniture (celery, carrots, onion, fennel, the leek sliced into 3cm pieces). Deglaze with pastis, add the orange quarters, the garlic heads, tomato purée, thyme and bay leaf. Pour in the fish stock. Bring to the boil then skim. Let simmer over low heat for 2 hours. Add the saffron. Reduce by half and adjust seasoning.

3. Sprinkle grated Parmesan on the bottom of a pan, let it melt without browning, then roll with a small cylinder to create a straw.

4. To each glass, add the rouille, egg cappuccino, then fish soup foam. Finish with the Parmesan straw.

'I need to be by the sea, to see the horizon. I said to myself, "If one day I manage to settle down in Les Goudes, I will have succeeded."'

'I think Marseille will continue to surprise me, by what she's become, by what she is, and by what she will be . . .'

— Chef Alexandre Mazzia

Alexandre Mazzia

Marseille finally has a second restaurant on the gastronomic world map. It's not that we're tired of admiring sunsets from Passedat's 3-Michelin-star Petit Nice, but the second-largest city of France could not continue with just one high-flying address.
What's more, the two chefs get along well and complement each other.
Congratulations, guys, you are leading by example. At the end of the day, we all win, even those of us who do not get to pull up a seat at a Michelin-starred table often. Why? Because the stars lift a city up, it opens doors, it puts us on travellers' maps and suddenly the field of possibilities becomes wider . . . Now in Marseille, even street food is putting pressure on itself to taste better.
Let's come back to our new star. Alexandre Mazzia grew up in Africa, in Pointe-Noire in Congo-Brazzaville. Arriving in Marseille, he first sharpened his knives in the restaurant at Le Corbusier's Unité d'Habitation. For all Marseillais, the architect Le Corbusier was *un fada*. In our local slang, it's an affectionate nickname for 'crazy'. Alexandre is, when you think about it, downright *jobastre*, crazier than *fada*. No worries either, we love him for it.
The chef and I met in December 2020, when the Michelin team asked me to make a video about him a few weeks before Restaurant AM was to be awarded its third star. I had to lie and pretend I was there to film a video about Marseille and how Alexandre Mazzia and his cuisine were inseparable from it. This 'foreigner' had adopted our unknowingly brilliant food city in just a few years. The filming was easy and joyful.

'The city of Marseille welcomed me; she opened doors for me. She is generous, she is joyful, she is luminous. Her multitude of energies transport me. This city is fabulous. I love the voices, the laughter, the excessive side at times. In Marseille, we exaggerate everything, we make everything bigger because it's generous. It makes me laugh. I like the smells, the shadows, the light that is unprecedented, and the magic that it creates. In Noailles, the scents and the African dialects that I hear everywhere remind me of my childhood in the Congo.'

Alexandre is in his restaurant every day. He doesn't miss any service.
'I try to take a step back from production. It's difficult for me. The team tells me, "Chef, stop doing our work."
For me, cooking is a strong form of expression. I try to understand who I am through what I do. Because now we also operate a food truck, Michel par AM, I'm trying to let go, let the team share their ideas and take initiative. For me, it's an experience . . .
It's interesting to see people reveal themselves in their creation, their vision. I wanted to accentuate communication between them on a common project. I wanted to show them that there was a trust that we had built. It's super rewarding.
It allows me to understand their way of seeing things and to see them grow, but I don't let go completely. It's a necessary step but . . . it's hard for me! [laughs]'

In December 2020, the future third star could not yet be mentioned to Alexandre. I played the game. We filmed in Les Goudes before daybreak (Alexandre likes to meet early!), in the morning in Noailles and at Maison Empereur, shared a melt-in-your-mouth *meloui* (Moroccan crepe) on the Rue Longue-des-Capucins, and talked about cooking with the merchants of the Saint-Giniez quarter in a café that was officially closed (due to Covid). I also interviewed Marco Altenburger, a Marseillais, a pastry chef, and an essential teammate

Cuisine de fada,
3 Michelin Stars

9 Rue François Rocca
13008 Marseille

in the success of Alexandre's cuisine for over a dozen years. Marco left Mazzia's adventure in October 2022, to write a new chapter of his culinary journey in Mauritius. This was an important move for him. He wanted to reclaim his freedom and succeeded. Sadly, he passed away in April 2023.
With a heart as wide as the Porte d'Aix and a talent that could clog the port of Marseille, Marco had crossed the chef's cluttered path at Le Corbusier. 'We worked from 7am to midnight. In this historic building, the restaurant's kitchen had been refurbished, but it was still an apartment kitchen, so . . . to send out the 15 or so dishes that Alexandre wanted was a challenge! Many at the time said that his cuisine would work in Paris but not in Marseille. He was told that no one would ever come see him here. But Alexandre has a game plan, and he sticks to it. He has a point to reach and until he reaches it . . . in fact I don't even know if he will ever reach it! He's never satisfied. Even if you tell him in meetings that the clients' feedback is good, he will find a little thing to keep you working. It's constructive, it's to encourage you, so that you look further. He says, "To stagnate is to retreat." The chef takes the time to do everything thoroughly. There are so many things in his head. He is spellbound . . . and he is always one step ahead.'

The team follows captain Alexandre. 'The service is a festive moment. If you keep me away from the restaurant's kitchen, what will I do? During the Covid lockdowns, I would pretend to do service with my kids.'

On 17 January 2021, we went to Paris for the Michelin ceremony at the top of THE Eiffel Tower, which was empty because of Covid. The moment was surreal. Great French chefs Pierre Gagnaire, Hélène Darroze, Pierre Hermé and David Toutain surrounded this

Marco Altenburger, second from the left

strapping, 1.90-metre-tall man who burst into tears like a little boy at the announcement of his third star. At that moment, I understood that Michelin stars will never go out of fashion. I believed it for a while, but that day, I saw what the Golden Boot for food represents in the life of an artist, for a team that gives their all, and for a city that does not often see cameras come to film positive stories.
Marco and Anne, the chef's wife, arrived at the Eiffel Tower a bit after the announcement. They didn't know anything and thought that the chef had been invited to the ceremony to talk about Marseille. When they saw the chef's jacket, brand new with its three stars, they collapsed. No photo could have captured the emotion that the three of them felt at that moment.
A few days later, to his close-knit team celebrating around him, Alexandre Mazzia said, 'Don't listen to anyone. When you have a direction, something in your sensitivity, in your heart, listen to your instincts and your dynamism.' A great chef and a great team that allow us to open the doors of our imagination and to be proud of who we are. Thank you and I raise my glass to the future of this adventure!

FLEUR D'ORANGER SEMOLINA, HORSERADISH CREAM, SPIDER-CRAB-SHELL EMULSION

For the fleur d'oranger semolina:
250g medium semolina
55g salted butter
1 capful of fleur d'oranger (orange-blossom water)
50g browned butter
Zest of ½ lime
Zest of ½ lemon
100g hard taco shells, ground
Salt and pepper

For the horseradish cream:
50g crème d'Isigny (*crème fraîche*)
50g grated horseradish

For the garum:
100g spider crab heads, scraps and bones (or langoustine heads)
Fermented rice vinegar and soy sauce or 100g katsuoboshi (dried bonito flakes)
1g agar-agar or 1 gelatin leaf

For the spider crab-shell emulsion:
Spider crab shells
Sake
Spices (vanilla, 1 piece of orange peel, clove, ginger, cumin, turmeric, star anise . . .)
Vegetable bouillon
Milk
Cream

Start with the semolina. Boil 250ml of water, then pour over the semolina, salted butter and fleur d'oranger. Stir the semolina with a fork to aerate it well. Cover with cling film and let it fluff up. Strain, then add the browned butter and citrus zest. In a saucepan, dry out the semolina with the ground taco shells, salt and pepper over high heat. The semolina should almost stick to the bottom of the pan for it to be crispy.

For the horseradish cream, blend the *crème fraîche* and horseradish together.

Prep the garum: grill the fish heads, scraps and bones on a barbecue, then let them macerate for 24 hours in fermented rice vinegar and a bit of soy sauce or infuse them in 100g dried bonito flakes in water. After 24 hours, add the agar-agar or gelatin to get a somewhat elastic batter.

Put the horseradish cream and the garum in two separate piping bags and draw zigzags on the plate or make dots.

Finish with the shell emulsion: brown the spider crab shells to make a shellfish broth. Crush the shells, flambé with sake, then lower the heat and add the spices. Moisten with vegetable bouillon and let cook over very low heat for 7 hours. Then let it rest overnight.

The next day, cook again for 6 hours. Strain through a fine strainer, then reduce it. Finally, add a bit of milk and cream and emulsify with a hot syphon. The final texture should be airy.

GAMBERO ROSSO, MATCHA GREEN TEA, TANGY BUTTER

For the tangy butter:
100ml double cream
1 organic grapefruit
½ shallot, chopped
100ml sake
100g salted butter

For the gambero rosso:
2 gambero rosso (giant red prawn)
50ml lemon juice
50ml fresh-squeezed ginger juice
Fleur de sel and freshly ground pepper

For the plating:
½ kale leaf
Clarified butter
Chilli oil
Matcha green tea
Dried gambero powder

Reduce the double cream with the finely grated grapefruit zest. Sweat the shallot in a separate saucepan. Deglaze with the sake, reduce, then moisten with the grapefruit juice. Be careful not to reduce too much and pay attention to the bitterness. Emulsify with the salted butter. Gradually add the reduced cream for consistency. Strain.

Cook the peeled gambero drizzled with a mix of warmed lemon and ginger juice (50–60°C) for 2 minutes in a 170°C/gas mark 3 oven. Drizzle the gambero again when you remove them from the oven and blowtorch them. Season with fleur de sel and freshly ground pepper.

Dunk the gambero shells in a light warm simple syrup, either plain or citrus-infused, and let the mix cool. Then, dry in a 60°C/lowest gas setting oven overnight or for 2 hours at 100°C/gas mark ¼. Powder.

Wash the kale and roast in clarified butter in a pan.

On the plate, put a dot of chilli oil on the tangy butter. Sprinkle with the matcha green tea and dried gambero powder.

A.M.'S MARSEILLE RECIPE

This recipe and its three plates illustrate above all the spirit of the chef and his work. It's a playground on which to flex your Marseille creativity. Everyone has their own path; everyone has their own canvas. Go for it . . . and enjoy. The chef can't see you!

CRYSTALLISED KALE, CITRUS BEURRE BLANC WITH COFFEE AND PLANKTON

For the beurre blanc with coffee and plankton:
100ml double cream
½ shallot, chopped
10 gambero rosso heads, grilled
100ml sake
500ml grilled fish-head bouillon
100ml warm espresso
5g plankton

For the crystallised kale:
Kale leaves
Clarified butter
Salt and pepper

For the citrus:
1 organic grapefruit
1 organic lemon
1 organic lime
1 organic orange

Reduce the double cream. Sweat the shallot in a saucepan and add the previously grilled gambero heads. Cook until they redden, then crush.

Deglaze with the sake, reduce the sauce, then soak with grilled fish-head bouillon. Progressively add the reduced cream to add consistency, then strain. Add the warm coffee. You can play with the beurre blanc's flavour according to what kind of espresso you choose. Finish with the plankton.

Wash kale leaves and roast them in clarified butter in a pan. Cover to flatten them a bit and to also make them crispy.

Overlay 3 kale leaves on top of one another to resemble coral. Season.

Zest the grapefruit, lemon, lime and orange to give a 'sandy' look to the plate.

FOCUS

Fast social food

L'Après M. is a symbol that is placing Marseille once again at the forefront of those who are preparing for tomorrow through cooking. This McDonald's (McDo) in the heart of the city's Quartiers Nord was owned by a franchisee who went out of business. Fired employees united with non-profits to requisition it during the first Covid lockdown in 2020 to feed the city's poorest and give another meaning to the popular yellow M. Since 2022, the food bank is financed by the new project: a fast-food restaurant for professional training and integration that happily fosters humane working conditions. Set in the former McDo's, L'Après M slings burgers with local-slang-inspired names like Maouss Costo ('meaty whopper'), Pescadou ('fisherman'), or Ovni (U.F.O.) and they taste really good.

Since Marseille is a hub for social innovation, it's not surprising that the city's eating-well ecosystem participated in this major initiative. Fast food as a place of interaction, of social mixing, and solidarity, Marseille believes in this and is making it happen. It's the only way to ensure the city stands on its two feet. Le Coco Velten in Belsunce, La Casa Consolat in the Longchamp district, La Marmite Joyeuse on Boulevard National and 'Le Rep' are other examples of wholesome eating for the greater public. These places mix dining, culture, job training, and mutual aid. The fundamentals for a new equitable, inclusive and participative society are being written here, using forks instead of pens.

'This place, L'Après M., isn't an "after McDo", it's what the world can become afterwards. I come from a neighbourhood in Les Quartiers Nord which, for me, is one of the most beautiful in the world, La Savine. This district exudes diversity. I grew up with the Chinese, Spaniards, Italians, Senegalese, Jews . . . all origins, and we managed to find how rich diversity is. And this richness, I have found again in this project. We are on a roundabout, where lots of people point at us and we say to them, "Stop pointing at us, give us a helping hand." In our neighbourhoods, there are not only thugs, drug dealers or people who sell their dignity. We want this restaurant to be a place of diversity, outreach, and mutual support. Here, it's a void, we will have to help these young people to come out of the void.'

'In our hospitals, there are emergency services; well, here also, in this small Gallic village, we offer emergency services, social emergency services. We respond to those who are suffering the most, the homeless, the people who have been beaten up by life. In this fifth- or sixth-largest world power, we can't ignore each other and do nothing.'

'In my district, La Savine, I went to my Asian friends' (*collègues* as we say in Marseille) homes and ate their cuisine. We'd dine at the homes of Comorians, Senegalese, Arabs and Italians . . . That's our identity. We have lost the notion of eating together, we are focused on appearance instead of concentrating on being. In my little family, certain ideologies or political ideas have caused fractures, so imagine with the size of a neighbourhood or a district like here, it's even more violent. We must try to give joy to the people and tell them that we are here to help each other and live together. And let's try to make this city shine! Marseille is not a city like the others. It is a metropolitan city, it has a history and the fruits of this history are us.'

'Michelin-star chefs like Gérald Passédat came to give us a hand, cooks came to reteach us how to eat. At 39 years old, I just learned that you can't eat tomatoes all year round. We want to make this place a "fast social [impact] food" restaurant in which we work with seasonal products to re-educate the public. We can be autonomous in our neighbourhoods, there is a lot of concrete but there are also plots that are useless. How could we reclaim these plots, break through the concrete . . . and plant seeds? The people who work at the Talus urban organic farm are our comrades, they are extraordinary. They bring a huge contribution to what we are trying to build here. From all neighbourhoods, from all walks of life, we are a force. We must come together and move forward together so as not to be destroyed.'

— Kamel Guemari,
key figure in the struggle and the hope that the former 'McDo of Saint-Marthe' gives us

'As you are, you come'

Kamel Guemari in front of the former McDonald's that has been transformed into L'Après M.

09

Grannies tell me, 'Careful, you're going to cut yourself' and one day a client said when she saw me coming out of the back room: 'She's a little skinny for a *charcutière*!' That was funny.

— Marie Caffarel, charcutière

MESDAMES CARNIVORES

Marseille cuisine owes a lot to women. It is a matter of Mediterranean fact. But today the mamas are going pro, opening their own restaurants, and mixing cultures and traditions and inventing new ones. Two Marseillaises have just earned a Michelin star: Cheffe Coline Faulquier and Cheffe Georgiana Viou.

So, it's not surprising that, for this book, I met many more women than men. Where they amaze me is that there are so many who have arrived in Marseille without having chosen it - some for love, by following a guy - and then, ultimately, they found their true calling here. They have taken flight and, today, they really put their heart and soul in their dishes, with or without their other half to handle the toddlers. I bring this up, since the question of children is constantly put on the table by journalists and male chefs when one shines a light on female chefs! In Marseille, the history of women is moving forward and they are making great strides.

Some of them are self-taught, others graduated from the best culinary schools, but they all have important stories to share and their different paths are often strewn with the same pitfalls. In any case, in Marseille, cooking school graduates and those who learned on their own or with their family co-exist without any issues. Female chefs are considered legit and get recognition from the moment they speak up and show they aren't afraid of anything. If you are Georgiana Viou, and your creativity knows no bounds and you don't hesitate to call on renowned chefs for four-hand dinners, you have no problem getting your voice heard. On the other hand, there is no room for the shy ones who wait in the dark to be discovered and validated.

There is another cliché about female chefs that doesn't fit with Marseille: the vegetarian cliché. Many here cook red meat, and like to make their own charcuterie and sausages. Fittingly, these bold, vocal ladies cook with balls and tongues . . . no part of the animal is off limits and they cook them to perfection. This deserved a chapter.

M R S

Entre Préfecture et Castellane

Marie Caffarel

Charcutière-caterer, Marie Caffarel is an amazing woman who started cooking pâtés and duck confit in Australia at 18 years old to cure her homesickness for French cuisine. Back in France, the enthusiast thought for a moment that she would take a CAP (vocational degree) in cooking. Always eager to learn more, Marie preferred to specialise, to get a less common training, and finally enrolled in a CAP for butchery. Today, she's at the head of Maison Payany, a historic Marseille address between the Prefecture and Vauban, known to all four corners of town. The interior of the shop dates back to 1810–20.

PAPA DON'T PREACH

In 2022, Marie published *Le Grand Manuel du Charcutier*, a precise 'how to make charcuterie' book and signs it willingly for her loyal customers. As focused as always, Marie dreams that one day her clients will be able to devour her creations on site.

Where did you grow up?
In La Grande-Motte, near Montpellier.

Do you feel Marseillaise?
Profoundly.

Why did you choose charcuterie as a métier? At what moment in your life did you make this decision?
After my studies in human sciences, and a few years working in offices, I wanted a more tangible job. I chose charcuterie, allowing me to combine the noble work of meat and cooking.

Is it still hard for a woman to enrol in vocational training (CAP) for butchery? How was your experience?
Registration was easy. However, the CAP year was one of the toughest of my life. Between the prevailing misogyny, working in the cold, and getting up every day at four in the morning, it was not easy. In 2015, I realised that I did not want to become a butcher. I didn't like the butchery business. And my first passion was cooking. So, I had the idea of shifting to charcuterie.

How would you describe the job of a charcutière today?
Charcuterie is a story of cooking, creating, and meticulous presentation. This work allows us to carry on the tradition while having fun reinventing it.

How did you decide to take over Maison Payany?
I lived nearby and I fell in love with this tiny neighbourhood charcuterie, with its marble and its ancient mirrors, its fridge from the 50s. And its owners, father and son charcutiers, made all their charcuterie in house. I told myself this place was meant for me.
I asked the veteran charcutier to train me and he said no. Then, when he was looking for someone to take over, I offered myself up. He wasn't thrilled by the idea. He told me he had a lot of offers, but, in the end, he ended up passing on his *maison* [business] to me . . .
So, I worked with him for a while. We woke up at 3.30 to buy meat at the wholesale Arnavaux market at 4am, and we finished at night at 22.30. I thought that I wouldn't last. After two months, I told M. Payany that I wanted to close the shop on Monday to sleep and take care of paperwork! He had a wife, but I didn't!

What is your greatest professional memory since taking over the shop?
A customer, a 90-year-old granny, a former singer in a bar that had married a baker and had sold bread all her life. She was there for me since the beginning, and she always supported me. This woman was tremendously kind. At the beginning, she was my breath of fresh air.

What are the joys and the difficulties?
For the joys: the customers' receptiveness to new flavours. The new techniques that allow me to improve the recipes and save time. The difficulties: managing a business alone.

As a kid, did you go to the charcuterie regularly?
I went to the charcutier in my grandmother's village.
Every Sunday, we'd buy head cheese, pork feet, sausages. And I'll always remember that beautiful jellied pig's head in the window.

Chacuterie-takeaway

72 Rue Breteuil
13006 Marseille

Which Marseille quarter do you have a particular attachment to and why?
La Treille, for my childhood memories linked to the iconic films of Marcel Pagnol, and the Garlaban hills. They taste like *civet* [rabbit stew] to me.

What surprises you still in Marseille today?
The lack of vegetation in the city.

The Covid era was particular in Marseille (lots of people and restaurateurs didn't follow the social distancing measures). What will you remember?
Marseille is much more beautiful when she is free.

Which people who work in the food industry do you admire in Marseille?
Cheffe Laëtitia Visse, who spotlights charcuterie and offal in her restaurant, impresses me. She dared to put a picture of a pig's head on her Instagram account. Me, I never dared.

What ingredient that you use symbolises, for you, Marseille today?
Fleur d'oranger [orange-blossom water], abundant and present in dishes from here and elsewhere.

What is your 'signature' recipe?
Pork belly confit caramelised with orange and star anise *(author's note: the customers adore it as do I).*

Have you kept the recipe book from the previous owner?
Yes, but he made *courgettes farcies* [stuffed] all year long. Me, I said, 'stop' and in the winter, I make potato, onion and mushroom *farcis* instead.

LES FARCIS D'HIVER (STUFFED WINTER VEGETABLES)

INGREDIENTS FOR 3

3 potatoes
3 onions
3 large mushrooms

For the stuffing:
100ml whole milk
80g stale bread, crumbled
800g sausage meat
1 bunch of chopped parsley
15g chopped garlic
1 egg
1 tsp Épices Rabelais (this mix of African and Asian spices and Provençal aromatics is part of Marseille's culinary heritage. The unique and secret formula was developed in Marseille in 1880 by Raynaud de Mazan . . . It is widely used by charcutiers, you can buy it in Marseille at Maison Empereur)
Salt and pepper

1. Steam the potatoes, onions and mushrooms until they are fork tender.

2. Remove the stems from the mushrooms and gently hollow them out. Whatever you remove can be added to the stuffing. Cut the base of the onions and cut off a cap. Gently hollow out the onions and add what you remove to the stuffing. As for the potatoes, you can hollow them out a bit more, but their flesh isn't part of the stuffing. You could also sauté what you hollow out of the potatoes, together with what's left of the mushrooms and onions after stuffing.

3. Preheat the oven to 180°C/gas mark 4. Heat the milk and add the crumbled stale bread, then strain the bread and purée it with a mortar and pestle. Reserve the milk for the stuffing.

4. In a large bowl, combine all the stuffing ingredients and mix by hand. Add salt and pepper. Generously stuff the potatoes, onions and mushrooms. Sprinkle some breadcrumbs on the potatoes and mushrooms to dress them up and give them a bit of crunch. Top the onions with their caps.

5. Bake the stuffed vegetables for around 30 minutes.

MANTOUS
AFGHAN MEAT RAVIOLI

INGREDIENTS FOR 4 (OR 2 PEOPLE WHO ARE HUNGRY!)

For the dough:
600g flour
1 tsp fine salt
3 egg yolks
2 tbsp vegetable oil

For the filling:
1kg onions, chopped
1 garlic clove, chopped
500g minced beef
½ tbsp ground coriander
Ground cumin
5 sprigs of fresh coriander
Vegetable oil
Salt and pepper

For the tomato sauce:
1 onion, chopped
1 garlic clove, chopped
1 small can tomato purée
Vegetable oil
Salt

For the yoghurt sauce:
125g yoghurt or cottage cheese
1 garlic clove, finely chopped
Dried mint
Salt

1. Mix the flour, salt, egg yolks and oil and work into a dough just until it is mixed well and not sticky. Slowly add 400ml room-temperature water, bit by bit. Let the dough rest for an hour in a dry, warm place.
2. In a pan, brown the onions and garlic in a bit of oil, add the ground meat and spices, and let cook for around 10 minutes, uncovered, over medium heat. Finish with salt and pepper, and sprinkle with finely chopped fresh coriander.
3. Roll out the dough with a rolling pin or pass it through a pasta machine until it is thin. Cut the dough into 10cm squares.
4. Put a bit of filling at the centre of each square. Bring together the four corners to the centre to make them into little packages and seal them by moistening the dough with water.
5. Steam the ravioli for 15 minutes. Sometimes, it is necessary to brush the bottom of the steamer basket with a few drops of vegetable oil to prevent the ravioli from sticking. Otherwise, once cooked, carefully remove them with a spoon.
6. For the tomato sauce, brown the onion in a pan with a bit of oil, then add the garlic, tomato purée, salt and a bit of water. Cover and let simmer for a few minutes.
7. In a bowl, mix all the ingredients for the yoghurt sauce and add a little water to thin it a bit.
8. On the plates, put the ravioli on a bed of yoghurt sauce. Cover with tomato sauce, then put a bit more yoghurt sauce on top.

'I feel neither Marseillaise, nor Afghan, nor French, I feel earthbound. But I wouldn't leave Marseille for anything. This is the problem with uprooting. Even to go to another city in France, I couldn't. It's impossible unless my kids leave Marseille . . . Then I'll see.' — Myriam Rahman Ebadi

M R S
Longchamp
Les Cinq avenues

Myriam Rahman Ebadi and Romain

MOTHER AND SON

Afghan cuisine

58 Bd de la Libération
13005 Marseille

I popped into this family-run address on a whim, after spending the morning at Chez Yassine tasting their leblebi and kefteji. Suffice to say that my appetite, at around 1pm, was rather understated. But as a good Italo-Corsican-Marseillaise, I am used to eating my weight and this restaurant intrigued me. I was honestly delighted to be here and meet Romain, a three-star Marseillais. He, our football club l'OM, and Marseille are one. In the kitchen, his mother Myriam opens our eyes to the country she had to leave 40 years ago. Meanwhile, Romain, in the dining room, strikes up a conversation with everyone.

Myriam, where did you grow up?
I was born in Kabul, in Afghanistan. I celebrated my 19th birthday in Marseille in 1981.

Did you know Marseille?
Not at all. I didn't know France. It was one of my dreams to come to France, but not like that. I have an Afghan dad and a French mum. I wanted to come and study in France and holiday at my grandmother's. But to stay in France, that wasn't planned. I didn't intend to live here.

You came with your parents?
With my mum, my brother and my sisters. My dad stayed behind, at first, so that we could leave. A year later, he was able to join us. We left an astronomical sum as a guarantee, to prove that we were just going on holiday, that we would not stay in France. My father had come to study in France, and he met my mum here. Then, they left to live in Kabul. When we came to Marseille, we first lived with my grandmother, on Rue Neuve-Sainte-Catherine, near the Vieux-Port. Then, we moved to the northern districts [*Les Quartiers Nord*] of Marseille. I am happy to have landed here in Marseille.

Your first impression . . .
I had my first impression through the eyes of my mother, who had left a France that was cleaner, better organised, and more chic. I saw this in my mother's face, she was so sad. She had left France in 1958. She had returned in the 60s with my father for a holiday. On holiday, it isn't the same. In Kabul, she was a medical secretary. And when we fled here, she couldn't find anything except work as a cleaning lady. That also was an enormous blow for her. In Kabul, we had a 10–12 room house. Here, we lived in a two-room apartment. But anyway we had to leave. It was that or die. My older sister had been arrested. She was at an age where she didn't accept the injustice. Luckily, we were a known family and my father and uncle were able to get her released.

Some friends remained in prison. That's when my parents said, 'It's not possible anymore.' So, we left and never went back. Since it became possible to go there again (despite all the risks), I haven't had the courage. I cannot make up my mind. But, to close the loop, I would have to go there.

Where did you get the idea to open a restaurant?
When we arrived in France, it was difficult to learn French, we wondered how we would do it and we heard about three sisters who had a restaurant in Nice. I wanted to do like them. What's more, we were four including Mum. But my sisters refused, afraid that it wouldn't work. Then, I married an Afghan who cooked divinely well. I told him the same thing: 'Come, let's open a restaurant,' and he told me, 'No. If it doesn't work, what are we going to do?' And that was that. Seven years later, I divorced, and thought, 'I prefer to tell myself one day that it didn't work but I tried, rather than telling myself I should have, I should have.' I got my vocational certificate, and I opened my restaurant in 2006.

Today, you work with your son . . .
My daughter Marion lives in Marseille, but she doesn't work at the restaurant. She never wanted to. Whereas my son Romain always came to help me when he passed by the restaurant and saw it was busy. Romain, he likes that. Romain has always cooked a lot. He never wanted to eat in the school cafeteria. Today, he works with me here, he takes care of the dining room. Sometimes he is a little lazy and lacks punctuality, but he makes up for it with many other things! I still tell him once a week, 'You're lucky to work with your mother, otherwise you'd have been fired a long time ago!'

The ravioli recipe you share in this book, it's a common dish in Afghanistan?
Ravioli is for special occasions . . . wedding parties, birthdays or guests. It isn't an everyday dish. Everyday cuisine is palaw, tchalaw, and spinach. Simple things. We often do meatballs also. I realised when I opened the restaurant that there were lovers of Afghanistan here. And it even makes me mad because there are customers who know much more about Afghanistan than I. Sometimes I feel ashamed *(Author's note: Myriam says this with a smile).*

Romain, what do you think of the food scene in Marseille?
It is interesting, exciting. There are lots of different things, like Marseille in general. It's a city that is catching up, partly thanks to non-Marseillais or thanks to the many Marseillais who left and returned.

Marseille is very working class and you can find everything. Me, when I go to eat somewhere and I'm really hungry, I eat Tunisian at Chez Yassine. I also go to Mame Diarra, a Senegalese restaurant on Rue de l'Académie. I feel good there. You have a guy the size of a mountain who runs the dining room, and in the kitchen, you have three mamas who cook and chat non-stop.

Do you have a typical Marseille story to share?
One day, I refused entry to a child who was wearing a Paris Saint-Germain football jersey, our biggest rival. No way, I couldn't serve him! His mother insulted me. His family, his cousins, his friends, the whole clan insulted me on social media. Normal. With little racist jabs. Not normal. Okay, I shouldn't have done it. But, in a panic, I went to a lawyer from Marseille to look into it, and he told me that not only did I have the right to refuse whoever I wanted, but, that in addition, in Marseille, no lawyer would go out on a limb and work on a nonsense case about a Parisian jersey!

R
M ✕ S

Between Préfecture and Castellane

Laëtitia Visse

Laëtitia Visse has opened the restaurant we had been hoping for in Marseille: a paradise of aged-meat, tasty sausages, terrine to die for . . . and offal. Not many people remember or realise it, but Marseille and lamb's offal have a long history! In fact, this history is Mediterranean, from Italy to Algeria. *Pieds paquets* (stewed sheep feet and tripe), the Marseille invention that sustained workers at the end of the 19th century in the La Pomme district, call to mind the Algeroise *bakbouka* or *stigghiuole* in Palermo.

Laëtitia makes sausages, terrines . . . she does it all! The menu at La Femme du Boucher is a rare treat! Having shot four documentaries about meat, one of which was called Steak *(R)évolution*, you can take my word for it. Go dine at Laëtitia Visse's place as soon as you can. All the flashy, fake steakhouses should follow in her footsteps!

UNIQUE

The chef is also one of the first women to have condemned harassment in the kitchens of renowned restaurants in France and rung the alarm on the stasis of cooking schools on this matter. Like many great chefs, her disappointing start to her career quickly galvanised her to leave the haute cuisine circuit, then open her own address. I believe that women who follow this path deserve a medal. To open a restaurant so young is to have a hell of a lot of . . . talent and ambition. Hats off, ladies!

Laëtitia loves collaborations and new challenges, which has made her a key player in Marseille's food scene. You often find her in others' kitchens and at Marseille events, like during the *CHEFFES* guide launch with all the female Marseille chefs.

Crowned Gault & Millau Young Talent during Covid, the chef recently offered us *Les Couilles, La Langue, Le Jus: 10 Façons de les Préparer (Balls, Tongue, Gravy: Ten Ways to Cook Them)* from Épure publishing.
End of the story. I think you understand who you're dealing with. The butcher's wife (*la femme du boucher*) is one of the female chefs who dare. Now the trend is in full force, new addresses are following Laëtitia's trailblazing meaty menus: the oh-so-pleasing Bouillon restaurant in Marseille, and a crazy American-style barbecue named The Badass in the middle of nowhere near Aubagne.

I was born in Paris, in the 14th arrondissement. I came to Marseille by accident in 2018. It's an outstanding and brutal city. A city that has so many differences. Grandiose and dirty. An eclectic, multifaceted city, rich in colours and in diversity. The first place I discovered when I arrived here was Les Délices Pâtisserie d'Aix. This café is run by Nabil, and when I landed, lost, he gave me numbers to call to find an apartment. I didn't know him, and now I see that his benevolence and his kindness are the same for everyone; he has a sense of hospitality, Nabil! He made me love Belsunce, thanks to his smile, his sfenj and his mint tea.
I also remember my beginnings at La Relève, discovering the offbeat "character" Greg Hessmann and the encounters that ensued.
But I believe that the first service that really marked me was the one where I was a cook for Chef Emmanuel Perrodin on the esplanade of Fort Saint-Jean, on 15 August 2018. Magic! Captivating, stunning . . . Emmanuel Perrodin is the start of everything, and without him I might not have stayed in le Sud. I admire his complexity and his enormous soul. He is cultured and funny. When he speaks, you want to listen. It is also reassuring. His kitchen looks like him. He doesn't try to be someone else, and his cooking is his own.

When I arrived, my cooking had no connection with the city. Then, little by little, I integrated the local ingredients. Anchovies, for example, pair perfectly with sausage.

I think that there are a lot of great recipes that are getting lost. We only talk about bouillabaisse and pieds paquets. And when you want to cook them, traaaaaaagedy, you're attacking an institution! My grandmother this, my grandmother that . . . Argh! So, not having a Marseille grandmother, I can't tell you what I don't know about Marseille cuisine.

Savvy carnivore cuisine

10 Rue de Village
13006 Marseille

PORK, DUCK, PISTACHIO, FIG AND PURPLE GARLIC TERRINE

INGREDIENTS FOR 8

250g pork shoulder, minced (see below)
250g smoked pork belly, minced (see below)
200g duck breast fillet
350g chicken livers
35g dried figs
20g purple garlic
40g pine nuts
1 egg
13g fine salt
4g white pepper, freshly ground
40ml cognac
10 slices of bacon
1 large rectangle of caul fat

1. The quality of your ingredients is vital for a good terrine. Ask your butcher to use the large setting on the meat grinder for the pork shoulder and the nice and fatty pork belly.

2. Dice the duck (without removing the fat), chicken livers and dried figs into 1.5cm cubes. Chop the garlic after removing its germ.

3. Toast the pine nuts in the oven (around 10 minutes at 150°C/gas mark 2, tossing from time to time.)

4. Mix all these ingredients, then add the egg, seasoning and cognac.

5. Put the mix in a terrine, or, if you don't have one, in a large cake tin. Carefully arrange bacon slices horizontally to cover the entire terrine (leave 1cm between each). Cover with caul fat and delicately tuck it in (with a flexible spatula, for example).

6. Bake at 160°C/gas mark 3 for 45 minutes, covered, and finish at 180°C/gas mark 4 for around 10 minutes, until you get it nicely browned, without the caul fat splitting.

7. Let the terrine chill. Then, you can keep it in the refrigerator for 24 hours. It's easier to cut the following day.

R
M ╳ S
Vieux-Port

Delphine Roux

Delphine is the essence, she is family to all of us. *'C'est le sang'* ('we share the same blood') as we say here. Her style and cheek embody the Marseille we cherish, the one we fantasise about; but this *galinette* (a Mediterranean fish, the cut of beef used in Provençal stew, and a local term of endearment for a girl) is quite real, and hard at work. Julia Child would have loved Delphine Roux.

THE BASE

The daughter of André – a hearty eater and colourful wholesale butcher – Delphine first earned her law degree before enrolling at the state-run Bonneveine culinary lycée in Marseille. Since 1995, this hearty eater is the colourful chef/owner of one of the rare restaurants on the Vieux-Port that dishes out Provençal tradition without taking us for a ride.

Bouillabaisse, pasta with clams, an authentic soupe de poissons, *sardines à l'escabèche*, *pieds paquets*, *alouettes sans tête* made in house, alibofis (lamb testicles) that cause a stir, and even panisses . . . Some trendy eaters prefer La Caravelle nearby on the weekends, but the chill ones, those who look at the bright side of life and like to stain their shirts with thyme-scented clam sauce, have carved their names in Chez Madie's tables. I find Madie is perfect for lunch and La Caravelle is well-suited for dinner. Marseille's mayors, Gaudin and Payan, validate this lunch spot, as has the sun. It never leaves the restaurant's terrasse. A delight!

'All day, I hear Marseillais say that they no longer come to the Vieux-Port, but me, personally, I tell myself daily that I'm lucky to work here, with the light that we have on this side of the port and the view of the Notre-Dame de la Garde basilica. Back in the day, the old merchants grumbled when City Hall decided to add terraces here – "if they remove the parking, there will be no more customers!" – but I was thrilled. When I started, I was putting a four-top or two tables of two on the narrow sidewalk and I had cars parked at an angle in front. You ate with views of the wheels. There also were four traffic lanes and a parking lane on the other side. They made the terraces for football's World Cup in 1998. We were summoned a bit beforehand with the old bosses of the Vieux-Port bars, the betting shops, Le Miramar, and the now-closed Italian, Caruso, and they presented the project to us, with white awnings replacing our cheap Orangina umbrellas and beautiful planters. When they asked who approved of the project, only two of us were for it! Fortunately, they had never planned to listen to the merchants' point of view. 24 years later, City Hall decided to totally cut off summer traffic on this side of the port. Well, that also caused complaining. But, how magical to lunch without cars! Plus, each night, we had joyriders on the port . . . now we can have musicians serenade with Notre-Dame de la Garde in the background. Marseillais aren't used to walking. Me neither. But I'm evolving.'

Delphine opened her restaurant when she was 24 years old, had her kids after she turned 30, and got by with au-pairs until she finally agreed to take on a manager and a few evenings off.

'I think that was the hardest step for me at the restaurant! The restaurant started off very small. I was alone in the kitchen with an apprentice, a dishwasher, and a waiter. Sometimes, I'm nostalgic for this time. So is my sous-chef. And at the same time, it's because the restaurant has grown that I'm able to escape at nights and on the weekends. But leaving the restaurant was hard. The regulars asked, "Isn't Delphine here?" sometimes not even acknowledging the waiter that had welcomed them. It's true that I do the same when I dine out at my friends' restaurants. But, not having a day off for 11 months out of the year, psychologically, I wouldn't be able to do it anymore. When the restaurant next door went up for sale, I couldn't pass up the opportunity and suddenly we got bigger. We had to hire people because it was busy. And you never turn back. This is something I tell my son. "Be careful before expanding your future business! You will not earn more by growing it, you will have more worries, but you will be free." For years, I would plan to go see my sons' father in Mexico twice a year, but until the last minute, I knew that if one of my waiters got sick, I wouldn't leave. I had two waiters and two cooks. It was so much anxiety! Now, I can leave in peace.

My son is in his first year of his professional cooking certificate. He got his baccalaureate and then went into cooking professionally. That's different from what French male chefs would do in the past. He did a cooking internship at my friend Cheffe Georgiana Viou's restaurant in Nîmes, he loved it. He adores cooking. At 11 years old, he told me, "On the Chez Madie les Galinettes sign, there's room to add 'and

Traditional Provençal Cuisine

138 Quai du Port
13002 Marseille

son'!" I didn't want to put that in his head, so that he could change his mind. He can take over my restaurant or we can help him settle down elsewhere. I'm afraid that here, he'll always be the "son of" and that people will say to him, "You don't make alouettes? But your mum made alouettes!" or "Your mum would give me coffee on the house." I'm afraid that he won't be able to have fun and enjoy himself. Anyway, stopping for me isn't on the table now.

By popular demand, here is the recipe for alouettes sans tête!' (from Belgium to Switzerland, we give the name of headless birdies to rolled-up bundles of beef. *Les alouettes* are larks in French.) 'I didn't have any butcher's string this morning, so I took my grandmother's sewing thread. I tried several to find one that did not break, and several colours…and the plate is also my grandmother's. I love it.

ALOUETTES SANS TÊTE

INGREDIENTS FOR 6

3 garlic cloves, peeled and finely chopped (don't forget to remove germ from centre)
1 bunch of parsley, stemmed, washed, dried in a kitchen towel and finely chopped
300g salt pork, cut in 2cm cubes
800g chuck steak, thinly sliced
1 onion, coarsely chopped
3–4 carrots, cut into rounds
3 tbsp olive oil
2 glasses of dry white wine
Vegetable bouillon made from 1 stock cube and water
Bouquet garni (thyme, bay leaf, rosemary)
2 tomatoes, chopped
100g tomato purée
Salt and pepper

1. In a mortar or blender, mix the garlic and the parsley to make the *persillade*.
2. Put a cube of salt pork and a spoon of *persillade* on each slice of beef.
3. 'I put a good amount of *persillade* in my alouettes. Since I cook them a long time, it melts.'
4. Roll up the alouettes and tie with string.
5. In a cocotte or a large saucepan, brown the onion and carrots in the olive oil. Put the alouettes on top and brown on all sides. Deglaze with white wine and cover with vegetable bouillon.
6. Add the bouquet garni, tomatoes and tomato purée. Let cook for a minimum of 1½ hours. When it's done cooking, season with salt and pepper.
7. 'It tastes even better reheated the next day!!!'
8. AND we like to serve it over pasta.

Served on a plate that Delphine adores, her grandmother's plate.

Maki Manoukian

I met the talented food photographer Maki Manoukian thanks to Cheffe Georgiana Viou. Georgiana definitively remains an essential comrade and player in the current Marseille culinary scene although her restaurant now is in nearby Nîmes. *Marseillaise un jour, Marseillaise toujours!*
A few years ago, we had a rendezvous at the Vieux-Port for my book *Elles Cuisinent* and Georgiana brought Maki along. At that time, the two friends used to work together in the kitchen, but since then Maki, a Bulgarian-Armenian Marseillaise, has listened to her heart and soul by becoming a food photographer and videographer. Her creations in this sphere are like her cuisine, sublime and moving. Logically Maki took the photographs for Georgiana's very personal book that is dedicated to the cuisine of Benin, her homeland.
As for me, I asked Maki to dive back into her family's recipes. Armenian refugees arrived in Marseille in the 1920s. This community, one of the most sizeable in Marseille, has brought its touch to the local gastronomy as well. Each pizzeria offers an Armenian version with meat. Épicerie Mayrig, near Avenue du 24 Avril 1915 (commemorating the Armenian genocide), sells a multitude of Armenian ingredients and dishes. The Nouchig dragées (sugared almonds) sold in the city centre are worshipped . . . In Maki's case, it was during the Covid lockdown that she and her husband returned to cooking Armenian food at home. It's true that, in general, Armenian recipes take a while to make!
Hence the revival of Armenian cuisine at the Manoukians in 2020. I went to taste mantis at their home on a Sunday, and, indeed, what painstaking work! And what a delight!

LENS AND SENSIBILITY

MY ARRIVAL IN MARSEILLE

I grew up in Sofia in Bulgaria until I was seven years old. I arrived in Marseille in September 1989 because my parents wanted to come and live here. We immediately settled down in Beaumont, the Armenian neighbourhood. For me, this city is especially a place where there was candy and Barbie dolls . . . things you couldn't find at that time in Sofia.

THE INGREDIENT OF MY CHILDHOOD

Tchoubritza. It's a spice whose aroma is engraved in my memory. It's a mix of savory, paprika, fenugreek seeds and *samardala* [Bulgarian honey garlic]. My little *Madeleine de Proust* (Ratatouille moment) is buttered toast with a few pinches of tchoubritza.

MY FIRST CULINARY MEMORY IN MARSEILLE

It's super cliché, but it's bouillabaisse. My uncle, who was a born and bred Marseillais, was a really good fisherman, and he quickly introduced us to fishing and bouillabaisse.

MY FAVOURITE NEIGHBOURHOOD

I love Noailles. I have great memories from my first visit to the outdoor market there, I must have been seven, and I didn't know where to look since there were so many things to see. It was something very new and very different to what I knew: a market with fish, meat, vegetables, spices, all the stalls in the street . . . Today, I still love to go there. It's a bit like my Ali Baba's cave.

MY COOKING AND MARSEILLE

What's really fantastic in Marseille, is that there is everything everywhere. You can find all you need to cook Asian, Middle Eastern, African . . . For me, who loves mixing, it's a godsend.

IN MARSEILLE, I WILL EAT AT . . .

I truly love La Mercerie, because it is both simple and refined, and often spot-on. And the person who fascinates me is Chef Alexandre Mazzia because he brings cooking to the level of a sensorial experience.

THREE WORDS TO DESCRIBE THE MARSEILLE FOOD SCENE

Youth, originality, diversity.

@makimanoukian

MANTIS
Armenian ravioli

INGREDIENTS FOR 4

For the dough:
500g flour
1 pinch of salt
20ml vegetable oil
60ml warm water

For the filling:
250g finely minced beef
1 small onion, finely chopped
1 garlic clove, finely chopped
10 sprigs of coriander
5 sprigs of basil
3 sprigs of mint
1 tsp smoked paprika
½ tsp pepper
1 tsp salt
1 tsp zaatar
½ tsp piment d'Espelette

For the yoghurt sauce
200g yoghurt
10ml olive oil
1 garlic clove, crushed
A few sprigs of finely chopped mint
Salt and pepper

For cooking:
250ml chicken or vegetable stock

1. In a food processor or by hand, mix the flour, salt, oil and water to create a firm dough. Divide the dough in two, wrap the balls in cling film, and let rest for 1 hour at room temperature.

2. Dust your countertop with flour and roll out the dough into two large rectangles. Cut into 3cm-long strips, then recut each strip to get 3cm squares.

3. In a bowl, mix the beef with the onion, garlic, chopped herbs and spices.

4. Put 1 teaspoon of filling in the middle of each dough square and pinch the edges to create a small 'boat'.

5. Preheat the oven to 180°C/gas mark 4. Place the mantis on a lightly oiled baking sheet and bake for 15 minutes.

6. Make the yoghurt sauce by mixing all the ingredients together in a bowl.

7. Heat the chicken or vegetable stock, submerge the mantis for 5 minutes, then drain.

8. To serve, put the hot mantis on a pool of yoghurt sauce, top with a few mint leaves and a drizzle of olive oil. This dish can also be eaten with tomato sauce.

FOCUS

Corsica on the plate

Marseille is the capital of Corsicans. Legend even says that sailors from the Island of Beauty guided the Phocaeans from Ancient Greece to our shores, around 600 BCE, where they founded their colony, Massalia. The Corsican stranglehold was upon us long before Napoleon!

My father is from Castagniccia (the land of the chestnut) ind Corsica, and I'm a carnivorous Marseillaise, a fan of charcuterie, so I liked the idea of finishing this chapter with a Corsican recipe. My *babbu* prepares it each winter around Christmas. Like so many Corsicans, he came to Marseille with a group of friends to study (or pretend to) and he fell in love with a beautiful Italo-Marseillaise. Oh my, a *pinzutu* (a French mainland inhabitant), and of Italian origin no less! A scandal at that time!
Why don't Corsicans like Italians?
Here are some clues:
Way before Jesus Christ came along, Corsicans resisted a Roman invasion for 200 years and Corsicans are a tiny bit resentful (one of the signature local traits). But there's a lot more history between the two. To make a long romance short, Corsica was sold in 1768 by the penniless Republic of Genoa to Louis XV's Kingdom of France because they desperately needed the money! Corsicans will never digest that. Later on, during World War II, Corsicans resented their fascist neighbours and when France was defeated, 80,000 Italian armed men landed in Corsica to occupy the island. That's what the Corsicans still talk a lot about today. Our grandparents and parents were there.
To add a little bit of backstory for UK ans US readers . . . From 1794 to 1796, King George III was also King of Corsica, thanks to Corsican leader, Pascal Paoli, who was looking for a true independence for his island. Famous Lord Nelson lost his right eye in a battle in Calvi in 1794, trying to defeat Corsican Republicans. The nothern city of Bastia was a Paoli and British supporter but Ajaccio, in the south, had Napoleon's family . . . who, as one can easily guess, would do everything possible for Corsica to be French and NOT British. Corsica's rebellious history touches Americans too. Paoli wrote the first democratic constitution of the modern era for a self-declared independent Corsica in 1755. This constitution inspired the American one a few years later. Paoli city in Pennsylvania - and five other US cities - was named after this enlightened son of liberty.

INGREDIENTS FOR 4

3 pinches of salt
1kg Corsican chestnut flour (AOC since 2006, AOP since 2010)
4 eggs
1 figatellu (Corsica's pork liver sausage)
1 brocciu (made from November to April) or brousse the rest of the year
And a fireplace to grill the figatellu or the figatelli . . .

In the summer of 1793, the Bonaparte family left Corsica (Napoleon's birthplace) and settled down in Marseille. In 1795, Napoleon got engaged to Désirée Clary, the daughter of a wealthy Marseillais silk merchant. Once he went to Paris, the future emperor somewhat 'forgot' his commitment . . . Her heart broken, our Marseillaise eventually became the Queen Consort for Sweden and Norway. The Désirée Clary street and metro station behind the Joliette district are here to refresh our memories.

LA PULENDA

1. Boil 2 litres of salted water in a large pot, one that looks the most like an iron kettle! Once the water is boiling, gradually add the flour en pluie (like rain).

2. Stir and rotate non-stop for 15 minutes over low heat. Corsicans do this with a solid baton of, you guessed it, chestnut. The point is to avoid lumps. Once your arms are exhausted and the mixture is hard and compact around the baton, or your wooden spoon, sprinkle flour on the rim to unstick the pulenda with the help of a spatula.

3. Sprinkle a bit of the chestnut flour on a tea towel as well. 'Unmold' your dough, close the towel around it and shape your pulenda in the form of a loaf of bread. Cut it in quite thick slices, using a cheese wire or string.

4. The pulenda is served as it is, hot, with a fried egg, a piece of over-hot-embers-grilled figatellu and fresh brocciu cheese. But you can also grill your slices of pulenda in a pan with a little oil. At home, we do that the next day with leftovers . . .

5. The best Corsican grocery store in Marseille is located on Place Sébastopol, at the start of Rue George. The Frédiani squad swears by it. Even the late American food star Anthony Bourdain set up his cameras in front of Marie-Paule Furiosi's shop, U Mio Paese, for lunch with New York chef Éric Ripert. This episode of Parts Unknown dates back to 2015 and deserves to be rewatched today. But of course, that's not why I recommend the address. *'La Corse aux Corses, l'Amérique aux Américains'*, as my father's pro-independence family always told me.

Paulette
LES BOISSONS DE PAULETTE

LE CHAMP DE MARS

RICARD

APÉRO AND MARSEILLE BY NIGHT

The heat plays a part, for in Marseille, we really tend to live just for apéros at sunset, when the temperature becomes feasible again and the sky takes on unreal colours. In recent years, some have worked hard to cultivate our Marseillais nightlife by offering festive but serious neighbourhood bars where you can drown your day's worries in real cocktails designed by real bartenders and barwomen. No need to be part of a mafia to be welcome there.

That's a big change! Now, the Marseillais are starting to enjoy nightlife again.

To feel good in Marseille after 6pm, head to La Caravelle, Gaspard, Carry Nation, Parpaing Qui Flotte, Longchamp Palace, the Lebanese Verre à Cruise, or l'Abri wine bar (more for the vibe and Chef Pierre's apéro food than the wine), but don't leave this town without steering your ship all the way to Le Bar des Amis in La Pointe Rouge for a real party, or Chez Paulette in the Montredon quarter, for the sunset swim of your dreams. Tuba Club in Les Goudes also has the two-for-one special of a drink and a dip.

Special mention for the new trend of *apéro* at-sea (on boats) and at rooftop bars. Both make total sense in a city like Marseille.

At any hour, grab a perch above the Artplexe Cinema at the top of La Canebière. The staff, the cocktails, the nibbles, the light . . . it's a real pleasure trove. You can also touch the clouds at Le Ciel ('sky' in French) on Rue Haxo. The staff are less amiable, but the sweeping view provides some distance from the fake trendiness around you.

Another more urban way to take advantage of the golden hour: the steps that lead up to the Cours Julien quarter. Continue your eve between Cours Ju, the lively Rue des Trois Rois, and the large La Plaine square. You will easily find good music, tapas from all four corners of the world, and a local beer to kick off your night in the neighbourhood that *Time Out* 2022 picked as one of the coolest on the planet – a 'creative hotbed' they wrote. Well, the Brits got a bit carried away. From now on we take a fresh look at le Cours Julien for sure, but we still don't know whether they were serious or just playing a joke on us. The reality is, if you're going through tough times and you need to regain a little hope in humankind, wander through this maze of tagged streets at dusk, chat with strangers, observe life around you, and drink and eat what your wallet can handle. Your mood will bounce back. It will.

10

Let's pause for a bit to shine a light on an increasingly rare commodity, the old *bar-tabac de quartier*, the one that is not decorated to seduce, the place where every journalist lacking good ideas and great words would come to hole up while plugging in their dictaphone. In Marseille, if you are not known in your neighbourhood bar de quartier, it's as if you don't live here.
Unfortunately, this glorious flagship of too-loud Marseille, especially after the 11 o'clock pastis the day after a l'OM football game, is becoming extinct. I will mention some here for you to look for them: Le Bar de l'Avenir with Sylvie in the kitchen, the Bar Tabac du Pharo, the Grand Bar du Chapitre, Le Paoli on Rue Eugène Pierre, the Bar de la Station D'Endoume or Le Dolce Vita, and an institution, the overly closed-off one at the Cercle Sainte-Marthe, next to the pétanque courts and the former offices of Paul Ricard. Do protect these essential pieces in Marseille's working-class puzzle by venturing in them.
While we're on the matter, dear investor friends who are coming here from wealthier lands, please spend your dough on our ideas, our local talents and our soul rather than trying to copy and paste common, trendy bling onto our rugged backs. In the long run, that won't work for anyone. Not you. Not us.
Instead, watch the Bar Tabac video by Muge with DJ Presque Waddle, read your future in a glass of Ricard, and eat *patalaï*! The garlicky pasta recipe is in the video . . . but come here for a bit of cultural immersion to understand it all!

M R S

Between Vieux-Port and Vauban

Ben Colombani

Between the Vieux-Port and the Vauban district, a real place to drink designer cocktails has revitalised Marseille by night. I had been told so, and many had written about it, so, what surprised me the most when I first went chez Gaspard was the warm welcome. Whether an unknown or a regular, you are pampered here. This warm service is rare, it immediately makes you want to take root and trust Ben and his team by ordering a 'Fais-moi rêver' ('Make me dream') off the menu . . . and I dreamed! It should be noted that Ben, the man through whom all this happened, trained at the mythical Connaught Bar in London (voted one of the top 10 bars in the World's 50 Best list).

I have problems with the term 'mixology', I don't want to rank myself in relation to other bars. I prefer the Anglicism and say that here, we make 'drinks'.

THE BEE'S KNEES

I was born in southern Vietnam but I grew up in Paris. I didn't follow the classic CAP [professional] path, but I began my career early and at des *bonnes maisons* (great restaurants). In Paris, I worked at Michel Rostand, two Michelin stars, and thanks to one of his daughters, I went to work for 3-Michelin-star Cheffe Héléne Darroze at the Connaught in London. I spent a year with Agostino Perrone, who is a cocktail freak of nature. He's one of the great names. It was incredible to be his assistant for a year.
I took a lot of time to be at ease with my métier. When someone asked me what I did, I would speak more about where I worked. The year that I was at the Connaught Bar, we were voted the best bar in the world. Then, I settled down in Arles, near Marseille, at the Hotel Nord-Pinus with Anne Igou. In 2013, I was kind of the only one to make cocktails in Arles, then I started my own company and I began to be comfortable saying I was a barman.
I don't think that we were ready for cocktail bars in Marseille. We needed to share our cocktail and spirit know-how with the customers. And in the right way. For example, here, when Guillaume Ferroni set out to restart the city's rum production (*author's note: Marseille was deluged in rum in the 19th century*) in nearby Aubagne and opened his first cocktail bar, I don't think the Marseillais were ready. He created his bar eight years before Gaspard, he didn't wait for people to be ready. His first showcase was at his Château des Creissauds in Aubagne, the precursor to Bar Dans Les Arbres, and afterwards, he started Carry Nation in Marseille. It's atypical. It's Marseille! I greatly admire his work. Gaspard would not have had this success without it; I am super grateful to him and the work he did with the Marseillais.
It took time for customers to understand our approach. Initially, at Gaspard, we wanted to make a bar with good cocktails, not a cocktail bar. So, we also served wine and beer. I manned the room, it was very hard. Nobody ordered our signature cocktails. After a while, we removed everything from the menu to focus on the cocktails. Our best customers today are people who initially asked for mojitos (what French cocktail newbs order and a bartender's nightmare), wine or beer.
The team is young, but they've all trained at the European Bartender School. We change the menu every two months, it's ambitious! Eight signature drinks, their names and universes, the ingredients. But above all, we're all physiognomists. We remember people and their faces. We like to recognise our customers, make them cosy, and take care of them. It's sincere and we want to stay laid-back, to be on a first-name basis with everyone . . .
For eating out, I am a fan of Regain and of course, Ouréa, or I stay in Vauban. I live in the neighbourhood. There I like Figure, a natural wine bar with small plates. But for two years, I lived across the street from Gaspard! I was here 24/7. I've only begun to make the most of Marseille over the past few years. I even have my first adult apartment now!
I think that Marseille doesn't use its potential, we have incredible tools, but they aren't well exploited. We need places like Tuba and Sépia . . . Gastronomy has changed a lot in Marseille, not bars. When we go out, we'd like to find more friendly bars, with hip-hop at the end of the night . . . Nightlife in Marseille is still super challenging.

A true cocktail bar

7 Boulevard Notre-Dame
13006 Marseille

COCKTAIL *FUCK DONALD TRUMP*

INGREDIENTS FOR 1 DRINK

For the drink:
2 shots of mezcal (or tequila)
1 shot of lemon juice
½ shot of agave syrup
A few pear cubes
A few sage leaves
Fresh ginger juice
1 shot of Noilly-Prat (white vermouth)

For the garnish:
1 piece of candied ginger (optional)
Cheveux du diable ('devil's hair', strands of Mexican chilli)
A few nigella seeds (black cumin)

1. Put all the drink ingredients in a cocktail shaker, muddle well, shake, then filter.

2. Serve over ice and garnish with a sage leaf or a slice of candied ginger. Add cheveux du diable and a few nigella seeds.

Martha and Takis

Marseille was founded 2,600 years ago by Greeks from Phocaea who arrived at what was then a quiet calanque (rocky inlet) looking for a new colony and trading outpost. The legend has it that Gyptis, the daughter of the chief of the native Ligurian tribe, freely chose to marry the dashing Greek newcomer, Protis. As if the feminists would believe that! Her father gave the new couple a piece of land in what is Le Panier quarter today and the Greeks called their new settlement Massalia.

MARSEILLE THE NEAPOLITAN ...

Five centuries or so later, the independent Massalia was invaded and conquered by Julius Caesar's Roman empire. Her Latin name was Massilia.
In France, we still think of Marseille as a Greek town but, for a long time now, Marseille has resembled Naples more than Athens, even if the 'Little Naples' of Marseille, which occupied the lower part of Le Panier, was destroyed by dynamite in 1943 during World War II.
Founded by the Greeks, invaded by the Romans, Marseille, like Naples, has kept a fiercely independent spirit, often turning its back on the capital and the central power. We could talk about kindred spirits although the Marseille cultural mix makes a big difference, especially on our plates.
In Marseille, if Greek restaurants are rather rare, you can find the best Greek products here and cook with them at home. That's really Marseillais! The team at Azul put me on Martha's trail and that's how I discovered the Alpha Omega épicerie. Warm-hearted Martha and her brother, Takis, unearth sublime and rare products such as Pamako olive oil, which is particularly rich in polyphenols. Frankly, I could have drunk it from the bottle!
Martha and Takis's parents ran two Greek restaurants in Marseille: Le Pirée and Les Enfants du Pirée, but now the family continues their love of good things via imports and trade. They supply the city's Mediterranean restaurants (Greek, Lebanese, Armenian) and chefs who love authentic ingredients. Alpha Omega revives Marseille's long history of importing foreign foodstuffs.
Many products landed in France, and even in Europe, via the Port of Marseille. A great example is coffee, which arrived in the 17th century. In 1669, Marseillais Pascal Haroukian opened France's first café in Marseille, then, three years later, the first café in Paris and thus began the democratisation of this beverage. He was the first to name the fruit, the drink, and its point of sale 'café'!
Today, Brûlerie Möka, Café Corto, Deep, and La Tisserie in Saint-Lambert carry on Marseille's local coffee-roasting tradition and some heritage artisans like Café Luciani, trading since the 19th century, are as brilliant as ever.

... OR MARSEILLE THE GREEK?

Greek e-épicerie
(that ships all over France)

50 Boulevard Ferdinand-de-Lesseps
13003 Marseille

Originally our grandfather left his island of Kastelorizo in the 1920s to join up with France and its ideal of freedom. As for our father, he moved to France in the 1970s to escape the authoritarian Greek regime at that time. Then, our family went into business by opening a Greek restaurant in Marseille. When they witnessed the customers' enthusiasm for thoughtfully chosen Greek specialities, our parents decided to offer their selection in stores and on the internet.

Before moving to the Sainte-Marthe neighbourhood, our family lived at Place des Grandes-Carmes in Marseille. This incredibly symbolic place, at the edge of the first port founded by the Greeks 2,600 years ago, had a large Greek population that enlivened the district. So much so that Greek was spoken in the streets when I was a kid. Beneath the city centre, under many modern constructions, there are Greek archaeological remains everywhere. Plus, Marseille, which some designate as a rebel city, was the first democratic city on our national soil. That is true Greek heritage!

Today, there is a sizeable Greek community in Marseille and its surroundings (Martigues and Salin-de-Giraud in the Camargue). Several associations, including the Union Hellénique and the Communauté Grecque, offer cultural events: language lessons, dance lessons, Greek evenings . . . We have a special connection with the Rue Grande-Armée district in the 1st arrondissement, at the top of La Canebière, and its Greek church.

Everyone knows that Greek cuisine is healthy . . .
On the other hand, not everyone knows that the meals aren't structured as we know them with a starter-main course-dessert. All the dishes are placed on the table so that the cook can sit down and share the meal with the whole family and guests.
Undeniably, the stuffed grapevine leaves ('dolmas' or 'dolmades') have coloured our family meals. They were specially prepared by our grandmother from blanched vine leaves. We tasted them with creamy and unctuous Greek yoghurt! A true childhood delight.
So naturally, to eat Greek, all the family goes to my mother's! As for me, I do not deny myself certain liberties. Regarding moussaka, I sometimes add a layer of fried potatoes under the layer of grilled aubergines. By doing this, I move away from the 100% traditional recipe.

HOMEMADE TARAMASALATA
(because you can)

Concerning Greek cuisine, Martha wanted to clear our misconceptions about taramasalata: 'Here is the recipe for homemade taramasalata like our grandmother used to make! The industrial kitchen has tarnished the image of taramasalata, which is an extraordinary dish! It speaks of the sea like no other. Natural taramasalata is not neon pink, but rather a light pastel pink. It is made from cod eggs caught in the Mediterranean. This recipe that we deliver to you is a little flavour treasure from our family!'

INGREDIENTS

Stale breadcrumbs (around 1 or 2 baguettes)
200g cod roe (you can easily find suppliers online such as Alpha Omega)
1 small onion, chopped
1 or 2 lemons
Sunflower and olive oil

1. Moisten the breadcrumbs and squeeze out the excess water. Put the bread and the cod roe into a food processor. Pulse a few times, add the onion through the lid, then the lemon (the amount depends on your desired taste).

2. While letting the processor run, pour in sunflower oil little by little, until you obtain a consistency close to mayonnaise. Finish with a good drizzle of extra-virgin olive oil such as Cretan oil from the Sitia region.

3. Chill taramasalata for at least 2 hours before eating.

That day, with this otherworldly taramasalata, we drank a Moscato from the volcanic island of Limnos, made by one of the oldest winemaking families in Greece, Tsantali. I was chuffed to bits . . .

BANITZA: BULGARIAN FETA PUFF PASTRY

INGREDIENTS
FOR 5 BANITZA

For the dough:
400g flour
1 egg
250ml oil
4g fine salt
1 tsp vinegar
For the filling:
2 eggs
125g yoghurt
250g feta

For finishing:
30g melted butter

1. For the dough, mix all ingredients in a mixer or by hand to obtain a supple and smooth dough, wrap in cling film, and leave to rest for 1 hour at room temperature.

2. Cut the dough into 5 pieces and roll out each one into a large disc that is thin enough to see through. Leave to rest while you prepare the filling.

3. Beat the eggs and add the yoghurt. Using a fork, smash the feta into the mix until it is creamy with chunks of feta throughout.

4. Preheat the oven to 190°C/gas mark 5.

5. Brush each disc with butter, spread with one-fifth of the filling, and roll the dough like a cigar.

6. Place in a small tart tin, buttered or covered with parchment paper. If the tin is rectangular, line the cigars side by side. If it is round, fan them out like a snail. Finish brushing the butter on the top and sides of the rolled-up dough. Bake for 20 minutes.

This Bulgarian recipe from Marseille food photographer Maki Manoukian (interviewed in the meat lovers' chapter) lends itself perfectly to Marseille-style apéros, the ones that allow you to skip dinner!

3 shades of blue

In Marseille, the best apéro spot is free. Perched on the rocks, especially just below Notre-Dame de la Garde. I'm putting photos here to wet your whistle. At the beginning of the 20th century, the Bonne Mère's hill almost ended up as a quarry . . The gap in the cliffs between the Vauban and the Roucas Blanc neighbourhoods, above the Rue du Bois Sacré . . . is absolutely not natural. What were their bloody industrial minds thinking?!

Nicole Ferroni

MARSEILLE OR THE ART OF CYCLICAL DISRUPTION

I am a fan of comedian and author Nicole Ferroni's humour and Pagnolesque spirit. A child of the region, the Aubagnaise regularly applies her clairvoyance to the Marseille metropolis and its political circus and, my word, it is always well-spotted and well-said. On the other hand, before embarking on this book, I had not made the connection between Nicole's brilliant mind and that of Guillaume Ferroni's, her brother, a fountain of science for all things spirits-related who is reinventing the Marseille-style bar. What a family!
Nicole is an incredibly busy woman, but she immediately said 'yes' to talk about cuisine. With a dad of Italian origin and an Alsatian mum, that gives her plenty of material! A former biology teacher in Marseille and Aix, Nicole is a hard worker so, for the book, she endearingly interviewed herself, and I faithfully transcribed the recording she sent me.

Where did you grow up?
In Casablanca in Morocco, from zero to seven years old, then in Aubagne (with a stint for a school year in Munich, Germany when I was nine years old).

What ingredient or dish most reminds you of your childhood?
'Noni's meat' (my paternal grandmother): it consisted of small strips of beef the same size as chips (so the meat is cut lengthwise), seared with crushed garlic . . . and fat (oil, I guess) in a pan.

When did you start cooking?
Um . . . late. I'd say around 25 years old. Before, I fed myself without cooking (and now, I'm ashamed of having waited so long to have paid attention to cooking).

As a kid, did you go out to eat?
Yes, to a Chinese restaurant (L'Indochine, I think).

What's your first culinary memory in Aubagne?
My first memory, not culinary but food-wise, are Les Petits-Suisses (*author's note: tiny containers of fromage blanc*). In Morocco they didn't have them. So, for me, Les Petits-Suisses had the taste of France (which is hilarious, for a product that's trying to be Swiss).

As an adult, where did you settle down?
I stayed in the area: Aubagne and Marseille (a few years in the Catalans neighbourhood).

How have your feelings for Marseille evolved?
I'm attached to Marseille and Aubagne. I'm not born here, I didn't spend my young childhood years here, but they have become my nest, and I have the feeling that I'll never fly very far from them.

What overlooked neighbourhood in Marseille do you have a particular attachment to?
I would say Les Catalans, having lived there. It's not really overlooked but I mean I knew it apart from its tourist swell in the summer. I liked it for its incredible proximity to the most urban part of Marseille (the Vieux-Port) and nature (yes, yes, once in the waters of the Mediterranean, you are already in the middle of nature). In an eight-minute walk, you can choose to go to a metro stop or find a bare rock to dive off. And then, I liked to meet night fishermen there . . . It's rare to have city centres where you meet people with fishing rods at a pedestrian crossing.

Is there a restaurant in Marseille or in Aubagne that has a particular meaning for you?
I'm going to cheat and choose a restaurant in Cassis, the Brasserie de la Presqu'Île. The view is magnificent and you won't get overcharged for it. It's a brasserie that had, as a main course, the *pieds paquets* that my mum hates

and my father loves.
This is a restaurant where I've secretly taken my father so that he, with his friend Raymond, could enjoy the *pieds paquets* without their respective wives. I should point out that having returned there lately, I noticed that the *pieds paquets* were no longer on the menu!
When talking about it with the two cooks, I understood that they disagreed on whether to leave them or keep them. It's not a trendy enough dish but there are regulars . . . ! At any rate, just let them know in advance if you want to have a go at their *pieds paquets* and they will cook them for you. This is an important piece of info!

What are things that still surprise you today in Marseille?
The politics? [laughs] What surprises me in Marseille is the consistency with which we are surprised. There is always disruption, it's the art of cyclical disruption. Like the garbage collectors' strikes.
Culinarily, it is the diversity. What I like is that you can find everything here, including Japanese restaurants. Before, you had to go to Paris to find that. Now we even have that.

Which Marseille restaurant that you recently discovered has surprised you?
This might sound a cliché, but it's a true local monument. It's Chez Le Belge, in the Calanque de Marseilleveyre. I had never gone there for dinner, but I find it brilliant that a restaurant can be fully booked even though you can't access it by car, only by foot, by walking for an hour or so, and returning in the dark, or by boat. I don't know a restaurant in Paris that is uniquely accessible by barge, unless it's already on the barge.

What is the Marseille culinary cliché that you adore?
For me, it's *panisses*. It's what I eat the most. I regret that our region doesn't cultivate chickpeas anymore. When my father was little, there was a King of Chickpeas elected in the Marseille villages of Saint-Marcel or in La Barasse. I would have liked it if our region had remained a chickpea cultivator. I like buying local and I'd have liked to buy our chickpeas.

Do you feel Marseillaise?
Yes, I have a profound geographical attachment to my region. I need to see my hills, Le Garlaban and La Sainte-Baume. I like to drive the Col de la Gineste (*author's note: the jaw-dropping, zigzagging Marseille–Cassis route that dives into the even more unique Route des Crêtes*). I'm very attached to the sea and our shores.

What do you like to cook for your family and friends?
Very simply, pasta with an onion sauce. I like to brown onions, tomatoes and garlic and toss with pasta al dente. I happily make salads; I like salads and winter vegetable soups. Cabbage, squash, I simmer everything with pieces of Morteau sausage from the Jura. It's not very Marseillais, but that's Marseille: cultural exchange.

Is there a recipe that you and the rest of your family disagree on?
In my family, there's an issue with *blanquette de veau*. My mum is Alsatian, and she has her favourite recipes, like onion tart, fleishkiechle – which are little meat croquettes made with minced beef, sandwich bread, egg, onion and parsley – and *blanquette de veau*. This latter, my sister and my mother disagree on whether you should use lemon or not.

And if your friends come to see you in le Sud, where do you bring them to eat?
In general, it's obligatory that we stop at my parents, where they'll eat fleischkiechle! But if I have to take them to a restaurant, at the moment, my heart belongs to two canteens, where you don't have table service. Like at a canteen, you get your food on a platter and you grab your cutlery. There is Caterine between La Plaine and Cours Ju and the less gastronomic Petit Dugo, on Boulevard Dugommier, between La Canebière and the St-Charles train station.

I need to see my hills, Le Garlaban, La Sainte-Baume. I like to drive the Col de la Gineste.

What recipe would you like to put in this book?
Actually, it's a good find from my dad. He makes sage-leaf beignets. Beignets are often associated with courgette flowers or courgettes, but, it turns out that with the sage leaves, I think it's great. I don't know if it's an Italian recipe, or if it just came to him. At my parents' house, there is a sage plant with fairly large leaves. My dad makes beignet batter (don't let the batter rise too much so the leaves don't get lost in the middle of a lot of batter) and he makes sage-leaf beignets.
Well, it will take a few years for your sage bush to grow, but the beignets are worth the wait!

SAGE-LEAF BEIGNETS

INGREDIENTS FOR 4

- 120g flour
- 1 tsp salt
- 1 tsp sugar
- 1 tsp baking powder
- 2 small eggs
- 24 fresh sage leaves
- Frying oil

1. Mix the flour, salt, sugar, baking powder and eggs, then dilute slowly with room-temperature water until you get the right consistency (a little less runny than crepe batter).
2. Generously dunk the washed and dried sage leaves in the batter. Fry them, leaving room between each, in frying oil (180°C max) for 1 minute on each side until they are nicely browned.
3. Drain the beignets on paper towels and serve hot.

LES BOUILLIDICES –
out of this world cheese beignets

A variation of the famous brocciu beignets that stick to your ribs even before your (Corsican) family lunch begins, boullidices are easier to digest and easier to make. Of course, half of Corsica (at least) will not agree with me out of principle, but since I learned to make bouillidices with my father's cousin in the village of Castagniccia, I have the right to have an opinion about them. Marguerite makes them without a measuring cup, that goes without saying. So for the book, I did several tests, and printed what was approved by the head taster, my dad.
Since the release of this book in France, I have had to fry bouillidices in large quantities at each *Taste the world in Marseille* (*Marseille Cuisine le Monde*) event. They were a great success, which boosted my Corsican pride, and the recipe has even improved somewhat with experience and the pressure of serving to a crowd!
So here is V2.

INGREDIENTS FOR AN APÉRO FOR 6

(or just 2 people if you're Corsican and you're used to eating your weight in beignet batter!)

250g plain flour + 50g if the batter is too runny
2 x 250ml glasses of water
1 egg
500g fresh brocciu (between November and . . . June, max. In Marseille, you can buy it at the U Mio Paese shop near Place Sébastopol) or fresh sheep, even goat, cheese. It must have the texture of ricotta
Vegetable oil
Coarse salt

1. Put the flour and glasses of water in a large bowl. Mix. If the batter is too runny, add a bit more flour.

2. Mix in the egg and stir well.

3. If you have time, let it rest for an hour or so covered with a tea towel at room temperature.

4. Coarsely crumble the brocciu between your fingers (the food critic Estérelle Payany almost collapsed when she saw me doing this amidst professional chefs), then mix into the batter, gently, not insisting too much, there should be large crumbles of brocciu in the batter. Use a large spoon.

5. Pour 0.5cm of oil into the bottom of a pan and heat over high. Once the oil is well heated, drop in small balls of batter. Immediately smash them with the back of a spoon, or even better a stainless-steel spatula (some chef friends who helped me make 400 bouillidices a night, decided that it wasn't necessary to flatten the beignets that much. It's another school of thought. I respect that).

6. Flip the bouillidices as soon as possible and fry until the edges are lightly brown. Flip a few times in the pan and flatten them each time.

7. Once they are fried, place your bouillidices on a paper towel and if you like salt, salt the beignets. Eat them without delay, they are best hot.

8. You can also serve them with Corsican or Portuguese honey or your local delicious one. Try also with a bit of chilli, like from the Pimenteraie Plein Cagnard that has sprouted in nearby Aubagne.

9. If you're not Corsican, don't ever tell a Corsican that you know how to make bouillidices. No hard feelings, it's just how it is.

R
M S

Aubagne and below Vauban, near the Vieux-Port

Guillaume Ferroni

A MEETING WITH HISTORY

In mid-August, I was looking for a birthday gift for my dad. It was five minutes before his birthday. I parked my car at a bus stop on Boulevard Notre-Dame. (Don't judge me. There is never a tiny space for properly parking up there in the hilltop Vauban neighbourhood! And climbing on foot . . . is torture! Even electric scooters refuse this climb.) I entered Les Canons de Vauban wine shop to ask for help. And there, I stumbled upon a Château des Creissauds pastis with its beautiful bottle that makes pastaga look like a distinguished aperitif. Bingo! I had a gift idea for my pop and for almost every Marseillais!
But where is this château? The shopkeeper answered, 'In Aubagne. The best spirits in the region are made there and you toast in the trees, in a cabin bar designed by . . . Guillaume Ferroni, the owner of the place.' I did not yet know this Merlin of spirits even though today he is clearly in my top three 'people who matter in Marseille'.
This 21st-century Doc Brown collects old manuscripts of cocktail recipes to invent those of tomorrow. In addition to pastis, Guillaume Ferroni bottles forgotten ancient local spirits, reuses abandoned recipes, and writes new chapters in the great history of Marseille with rum.
And that's not all. This inventor of boozy soirées re-educated merry-making Marseillais by opening Carry Nation, a wannabe clandestine bar, not far from the Vieux-Port, which quickly became the meeting place for true cocktail lovers. At the end of 2020, he once again surprised everyone by opening his Atelier du Rhum, on the Rue Neuve-Sainte-Catherine. And if pastis is your preferred poison, you can learn how to make your own directly at the château.
So, I had to meet the man behind this alcoholic wave. Since it was the middle of the afternoon, we stayed responsible, but Guillaume welcomed me with a mulled wine made with his house-made ratafia. We were off to a good start . . .

Distiller

Château des Creissauds
13400 Aubagne

How did you get into alcohol?
To explain my approach, I come from the world of bartending. Bars are my DNA. Wine and spirits are my passion. In the spirits that I produce or reproduce, there is always a historical approach.
For example, many people don't know this, but rum is a Marseille speciality. In 1720, during the Great Plague, many Marseillais sought refuge in the West Indies, in Martinique, Guadeloupe and Sainte-Lucie, which was French at the time. Before the volcano eruption in 1902 and the island's reconstruction, Martinique's architecture was very Provençal. The roof tiles came from Aubagne and travelled via boats at the bottom of the hold. In the 19th century, there were 320 brands of rum in Marseille. Gradually, either the brands died out or they left Marseille. The last survivor in Marseille stopped in 1970. I wanted to relaunch a brand with this Marseille approach and a few other brands did the same. I started with a ginger liqueur that I use often in cocktails, then I obtained my licence to make alcohol. I make rum, and rum in the Marseille style from the 19th century.
At the time, we called it 'metropolitan' rum. Nowadays, rum is aged in American barrels that are used for bourbon – they

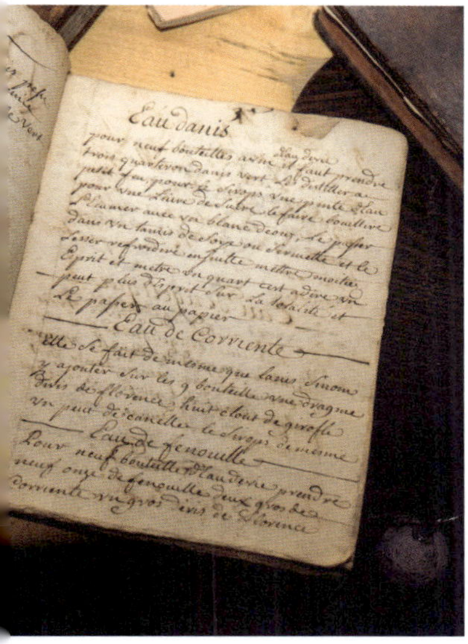

can only be used once in bourbon production. These barrels are cheap and reused for rum because they are also very aromatic, with a vanilla scent. But, in the 19th century, Marseillais used the transatlantic barrel, made of French oak, radically different in taste and up to five times more expensive. The advantage was that these barrels never travelled empty; at that time, they transported brandies, cognacs, Armagnacs and fortified, sweetened wines to the West Indies, whose quality held up during maritime transport. And on the way back we put rum in them. So, for Ferroni rums, I decided to work with French barrels used for cognac and sweet wine like Rasteau or Beaumes-de-Venise. Then, we started making pastis, our second speciality. It is not made with essences like in industrial pastis but by maceration. The plants are macerated in alcohol. It is like an alcoholic herbal tea, there is no cooking, and it is made from fresh local plants. It is domestic pastis as it used to be made. Anise-based spirits, in general, are the booze of the Mediterranean. In the south of Spain, there's paloma, in Marseille we have pastis or anisette, in Greece, there is ouzo, raki in Turkey, arak in the Fertile Crescent, mahia in Morocco, and the exception, absinthe, is an anise-based spirit born in Switzerland! That said, in Marseille, we used to have a sizeable absinthe production. It was Maison Cusenier, whose factory was on 71 Avenue du Prado, at the end of the 19th century, a competitor of Pernod-Ricard which was finally bought by the latter.

What are we generally unaware of in Marseille when it comes to alcohol?

Marseille has always been an incredibly rich city for spirits. Today, only Pernod-Ricard remains, but three recognised historic brands have Marseille origin: Saint-James rum, Noilly-Prat (a merger between Noilly, a Lyonnais liqueur maker, and a Marseille spice trader) and Picon (*author's note: a bitter orange, cinchona [quinine] and gentian aperitif often mixed with beer*). Picon had almost an entire neighbourhood between Boulevard National and the Palais Longchamp. They had made such a fortune that they bought this new district and many buildings are still decorated with oranges, one of Picon's ingredients.

Noilly-Prat is also a Marseille-born alcohol. It is a unique, dry white vermouth, the 'French vermouth', of which the secret is to roast the barrels of dry white wine in the sun for a year. Today, they do everything in Marseillan, 200 kilometres west of Marseille. In the past, the recipe was secret, they had three production sites that each made a part of the recipe. None of the employees knew the entire recipe. Noilly-Prat is the basis of the dry martini, which was the most consumed cocktail in the world for a long time. It was the 'French vermouth', white and dry. The other vermouth is Italian, red and sweet. The Noilly-Prat district was at the top of Rue Paradis in the 6th arrondissement. You still have a whole row of buildings today that have the initials N and P above their doors. Their headquarters were there. And there still is a set of offices today that bear their name. The Périer neighbourhood is now bourgeois but in the 19th century, it was a partly industrial district, with warehouses. There were a lot of brands of rum in that area. It was the new Marseille. Noilly-Prat also had a cinema and a chapel there. They're the ones who built the Château d'Avignon in the Camargue, the most modern château in France at the time, the first château with electricity and hot water.

To illustrate the link between Marseille and the West Indies, Noilly-Prat is what they drink in the French West Indies on New Year's Eve.

And the Noilly-Prat family's private chef, from 1900 on, was none other than Jean-Baptiste Reboul, the famous author of the cookbook *La Cuisine Provençale*!

Moreover, today, chefs use Noilly-Prat in the kitchen.

Many people don't know this, but rum is a Marseille speciality.

Another forgotten Marseille story is that of Chartreuse, the oldest liqueur in France. The Carthusian brothers were from Voiron, in Isère, but after the Revolution, when the State recovered the property of the Church, they were expelled from their production site. They went bankrupt and lost their brand. They took refuge in Spain, where they produced Tarragona, a green chartreuse that became the ultra-luxury chartreuse. In 1921, they returned to France, settled in Marseille, and produced a chartreuse here for five or six years. They were also based between Cours Pierre-Puget and Rue Paradis, in the Périer neighbourhood If you find a bottle from this era, you must keep it. It is worth between 12,000 and 15,000 euros. Afterwards, they managed to recover their monastery in Voiron. I recently worked with them to celebrate their Marseille centenary.

You also work with spirits that have become extinct . . .

Yes, essentially on spirits from the Age of Enlightenment. These are mainly extinct recipes that were published at that time with the development of printing. You can find lots of recipes. From then on, spirits developed until the arrival of brands and industrial bottles. At that time, the spirits that had not been supported by brands disappeared – like ratafia. In Marseille, it was made with rum, red fruits and it was spicy, which differentiated it from other ratafias in France which were made with brandies. The Marseille ratafia was drunk at Christmas with the 13 Desserts de Provence.

We also produce the Eau Verte de Marseille, a herbal green liqueur that is an ultra-menthol, bitter oddity. There's absinthe in it. It was very popular back in the day because it allegedly protected against cholera. Cholera epidemics followed one another in Marseille in the 19th century (in 1834, 1849, 1854, 1865, 1884). I found the recipe in an old Italian book. We made it but we don't have a use for it. It's not easy to drink. We are selling it as a testimonial. Some work it into cocktails . . . but it's complicated.

We also make the Élixir du Suédois by Toussaint Blaize, which for me has the most beautiful historical adventure. The Elixir arrived in France from Sweden around 1750 and was incredibly successful in Paris. Its promise was to extend your lifespan to 140 years! The recipe is public. Therefore, it was made almost everywhere in France and abroad. At the time, Père Blaize, the oldest herbalist's shop in Marseille (since 1815), had its recipe, the one I use today. The Père Blaize herbalist's shop remains a monument in Marseille. There is always a huge diversity of plants there because it is a real pharmacy, which allows them to sell herbs with active ingredients. And their homemade herbal blend recipes have remained unchanged.

PICON factory, built in 1886, on Boulevard National.

In Italy, this liqueur is the origin of Fernet-Branca. The Swedish inventor was named Hjärne, but while travelling, his name was transformed to Hierner, then Ernest, and finally Fernet, and became the Fernet Elixir that is used by Branca. It's a mentholated beverage and the first Fernet-Branca promised to cure cholera. So, I think that Branca was also inspired by the Eau Verte de Marseille. Its recipe has a lot in common with Fernet.

The Fernet Elixir's recipe is ultra-complex. There are 40 or so plants in it, and within that, another recipe for theriac, an elixir made with around 30 plants. Of course, we had to modify the recipe a bit. Theriac, originally, had opium and bits of viper. It was an anti-poison that was already talked about in antiquity, at the time of the Romans.

To find alcohol recipes, I collect books written by distillers, books about medicine, and cookbooks. The oldest I have dates back to 1738. Historically, alcohol was an integral part of cooking. The still was considered a kitchen tool. In the old 18th-century cookbooks, there's always a spirits section with recipes and, in the brigades, they always had a liquorist-confectioner in charge of preserving the fruit; they used sugar or alcohol for this. Today, that's disappeared, and the two métiers are separate. Lately, it's more bartenders who have taken on a new status in restaurants and are developing cocktail pairing menus.

How should we drink these?

The Élixir du Suédois is close to Fernet-Branca, you only need to put a few drops in your cocktails. The Ratafia de Marseille, everybody loves it. Bartenders use it a lot in cocktails. The Vespetro is good on its own and is very good in cocktails too. It is a perfect accompaniment to gin. The Eau Verte de Marseille is very complicated! It is ultra-powerful, atypical. And the last of the series is the Trappistine that we have just released and that we have not yet tested enough.

There are many products that I reissue as testimonials from the past or just out of curiosity. I make them without having in mind how you can drink them. Sometimes we figure out how to use them in cocktails. Sometimes we don't.

You're of Italian origin?

Yes, from Tuscany and Liguria and, in fact, it's an accident, but liqueur production arrived in France via Italy! It was the Arabs that mastered it and passed down the alembic and distillation. Alchemy, chemistry, and alcohol are all Arabic terms. During the Renaissance, the Arabs lost their leading role in this science, and the Italians were the first to take an interest in alcoholic distillation at the medical school in Salerno. Thus, the Italians became the maestros of *liquore* and exported them to France. Think about it. When an alcohol is old in France, it has an Italian name. And my favourite old manuscripts are often written in Italian.

À LA FRAÎCHE JUILLET COCKTAIL

You can make this cocktail directly in the glass.

INGREDIENTS FOR 1 GLASS

20ml gin (at Ferroni, we use our Juillet Gin, which is distilled in a 19th-century alembic using the London Gin method, with a base of organic alcohol and with Provençal apricots and white peaches)
20ml Vespetro (an old, northern Italian liqueur, originating from the Savoie)
20ml muscat, white Beaumes-de-Venise, or Lillet Blanc
Zest of 1 organic grapefruit
Tonic

1. **Mix the alcohol in a glass, add a bit of tonic per your liking.**
2. **Garnish with grapefruit zest. Serve over ice.**

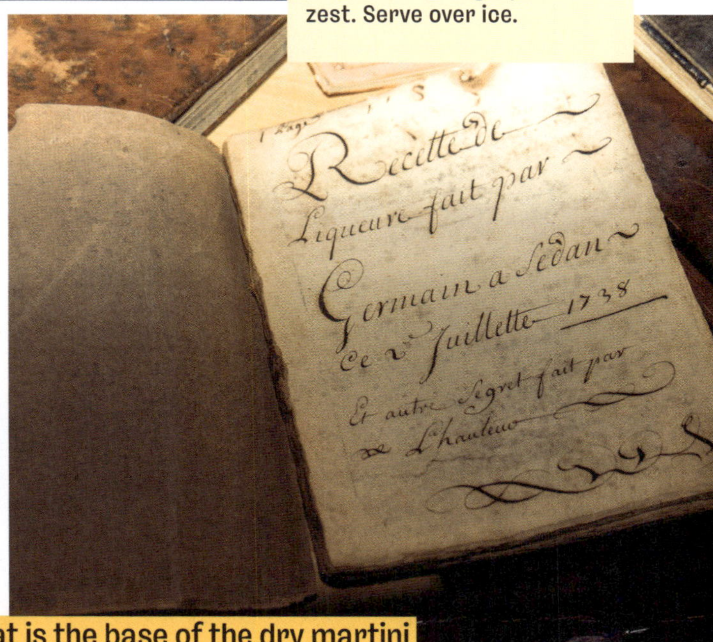

Noilly-Prat is the base of the dry martini that was the most consumed cocktail in the world for a long time. It was the 'French Vermouth', white and dry.

FOCUS

Marseille in a pint

Local craft *bières*, which have soul and flavour, are enjoying tremendous popularity today, and that is not so surprising given Marseille's brewing history. In the 19th century, independent Marseille breweries were numerous and opened or sponsored many cafés in the city centre. On this subject, Marseille journalist Horace Bertin's book *Histoire Anecdotique des Cafés de Marseille* is a marvel from 1869 that I recommend.

Names still famous today without anyone remembering why are in fact brands of bygone beers made in Marseille, such as Le Phénix, Zénith, Marx, and first and foremost, Velten. Velten was created by an Alsatian family who came to Marseille at the very beginning of the 19th century to start the Brasseries de la Méditerranée, which occupied an important place in the industrial fabric of Marseille. Part of this large factory still remains, the Grande Halle, at the heart of Coco Velten, Porte d'Aix, an ambitious experimental, cultural and solidarity tiers lieu (third place) in Belsunce.
There was also the Brasserie Suisse, which became the Brasserie et Malterie Moderne in La Valentine district in 1881, then the Brasserie Le Phénix in 1886. This same brewery was bought by Heineken at the end of the 1980s to fabricate a large part of its industrial French production. The site is still in operation! And guess what? Heineken has just relaunched the Phoenician, one of Le Phénix beers. Those cheeky monkeys!

Nowadays, as in agriculture or livestock farming, we are returning to concepts on a human scale, with a basic food-production approach. Industrialists had sucked the lifeblood out of small family breweries, but today, the French, later than elsewhere, are fighting back! In Marseille, there are now six or seven local manufacturers: La Brasserie de la Plaine which was the first, La Minotte now based in nearby Vitrolles, Les Malfaiteurs, La Brasserie Communale du Cours Julien, and, since 2018, Zoumaï in Castellane!

For 25 years, Jérôme Talin had dreamed of opening a Marseille-style pub, like an Irish tavern with local music in the background and, finally, good beer! Visiting Americans gave him samples of craft beers. 'France is 20 years behind the United States in craft microbrewing and hop development,' he explains. A trip to Ireland, then to London and Berlin finally convinced him that his idea was the right one.
'My favourites are English beers. When I went to England, a light went on in my head. Their freshly brewed beer has incredible flavours . . . And so here, we brew English-style with equipment from Manchester.' Like many, Jérôme started brewing at home, for friends. But one pivotal day, he ended up giving up his old career in graphic design to set up his microbrewery and bar. 'After 15 years in the office, I was going in circles. Me, I like messing around with things, and one day I had a wake-up call.'
In terms of location, he couldn't have asked for better. The Carroserie, in the heart of the city, was already a very convivial and well-known spot before Jérôme and his two associates, as luck would have it, took it over and transformed it into a brew pub that's ideal for hanging out. Zoumaï takes its role as public house seriously and opens its space for lectures, standup comedy, concerts, DJ nights and community gatherings, and once a week to local producers like Terre de Mars and House of Pain, an opportunity to do your grocery shopping like in Dublin, London, Berlin or Brussels, a beer in hand.

The Chez Paul restaurant team sunbathing at the Bar des Amis, accompanied by Muge, second from the right. The rapper from Endoume, Italian pride in his blood, assured me that the best pasta dishes in Marseille are the ones he cooks! Welcome to Mugeland.

MARSEILLE
CUISINE LE MONDE

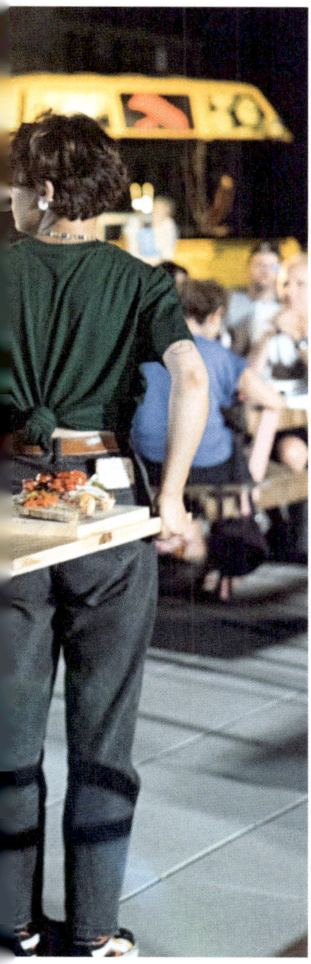

MARSEILLE
CUISINE LE MONDE
26 Mai
5 Juillet
30 Août

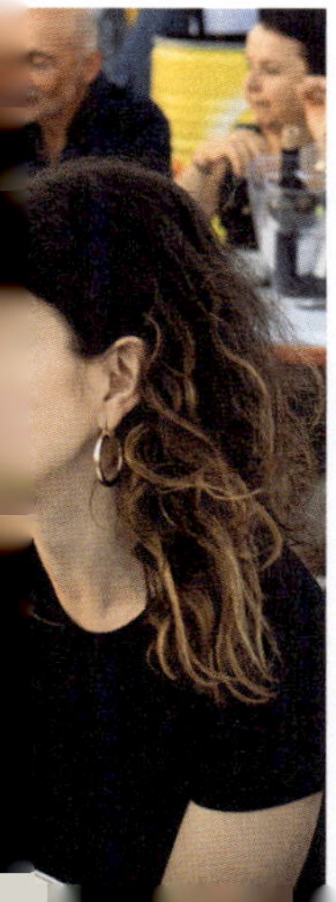

R
M S
Vieux-Port

Mayor Payan

Late-night recipe

'IL CIBO VA'

In France, this book is titled *Marseille Cuisine le Monde* and since its release, Marie-Jo Ordener, Fabrice Lextrait, Camille, Laurent, and the entire team at Les Grandes Tables have conceived and orchestrated 'Marseille Cuisine le Monde' dinners on the rooftop of Friche la Belle de Mai. I consider these as huge gifts celebrating our cultural mix that my work is all about. Chefs that appeared in the book and many others came together to concoct joyful, original and unifying menus, enlightening bridges between cultures. Marseillais and well-acclimated visitors came together and tasted these vibrant and happy marriages. In France, food is never just food. In Marseille it's 100 times more so.
With the help of three unquestionably motivated friends, Annelise Drai, Eve Richard and Estérelle Payany, we also served 400 Corsican beignets each night, my now famous bouillidices, to our guests. Chef Aminati came to our rescue, and she alone surely fried up half of them, but I almost lost my friends! Their hearts were there, but their wrists gave out . . . Even so new dinners are en route . . .

In August 2022, during one of these dinners, Monsieur le Maire de Marseille and his team joined the party and sat at one of the long communal tables. Benoît Payan had come to taste the world and the book, so to speak . . . Covered in oil and sweat to the tips of my hair, I preferred to send my daughter Valentina and her mate Rodrigue to serve Monsieur beignets. 'They are on page 213 in my mum's book,' she told him. The connection was made, we quickly found common points (of view), and that's how, a few months later, I photographed the new Mayor of Marseille (Benoît will be the 'new one' for a long time because our previous mayor had a 25-year mandate!) at the stoves of Le Fioupelan restaurant for the English edition of the book. He cooked his part of the world, a part of Marseille, his Italy. Ecco qua, here is Monsieur Payan's signature pasta recipe. A mayor that cooks, that's even better than a president that plays the saxophone, but I must say he left a real mess in the kitchen when making a plate of pasta for two!

Hôtel de Ville
Quai du Port
13002 Marseille

I heard you speaking fluent Italian with the Sicilian family who own Pizzeria Etna.
My family is from Ischia

The little island?
Little?

How did your family end up in Marseille?
Like many Mediterranean families, fleeing poverty from the south of Italy but also from the north because I also have Piedmontese origins. They escaped from the difficulties, thinking they'd leave for the United States. It's a common story; the boats at the end of the 19th century left from Naples and made a stop in Marseille before crossing the Atlantic to America. My great-great-grandmother landed here, on Rue Sainte-Françoise in Le Panier. She was illiterate, she was about 18 years old, and had five children. In Ischia, they lived like one did three centuries ago, in extreme poverty.
At some point, you had to leave, you had to leave everything, and the dream was the American dream. The French dream did not exist. So, entire Italian villages were emptied (*author's note: the exact numbers are hard to confirm but statistics say that between 1876 and 1900, a million Italians left their country. Between 1901 and 1910, 2,330,000 Italians emigrated to the United States and 573,000 to France*). Like many, my ancestors had never been to Naples. So they first did Ischia–Naples. No one in the family had ever left the island. Insularity, like in your Corsica, you know well what it implies, what it says about you, all the sediment it builds your character with, and all the anxieties and fears it creates. It's a besieged mentality. Leaving is something improbable, incredible! Therefore after five days of sailing, when she arrived in Marseille, my great-great-grandmother thought the trip was over. She had no concept of distance. She stopped here because it was impossible for her to go any further. She stayed in Marseille with her husband, her children, and her sister but the rest of the family continued on and moved to the United States. And so today, I have cousins in Boston.

Those that arrived via the road from Piedmont ended up in the east of Marseille, in the valley of the Huveaune river, and those that arrived from the south by sea landed in Le Panier, on Rue Sainte-Françoise. Then, at the beginning of the 20th century, they crossed the Vieux-Port and settled down in the 7th arrondissement. Have you seen the documentary *E il Cibo Va?* You'll definitely like it. It's the history of uprooted Italians, it asks the question 'What do we have besides our cuisine?' And, in fact, what are you left with and what do you pass on when you have left it all behind? When I came home from school, my grandparents didn't ask me what I learned. They asked me what I ate. What matters is what we eat. What we eat is who we are. This is what allows us to tell things, to share things, to do things. It is the heritage of those who do not have much. The film shows, for example, how the Italians who went to Argentina found an overabundance of meat and cows' milk there that they weren't accustomed to in their islands and their villages. Hence, this meaty Italian-Argentinean cuisine they invented.

Which Marseille districts did you grow up in?
In the 7th and the 10th arrondissements. From kindergarten to Year 10, I was at the École Pastré in the 9th, then I went to the Lycée Jean Perrin. Then, I studied law and went to notary school, and then I grew up! But cooking was always there. I grew up with my great-grandparents, my grandparents and my parents in the same house. That should give you an idea of how important cooking was!

What dishes do you remember?
Only pasta!

Did you go to restaurants as a child?
Yes, during holidays in Corsica or in Italy, but in Marseille, not a lot.

Do you ever eat Italian food at restaurants in Marseille?
I sometimes eat at Salvatore and Anne-Marie's Vesuvio but they will soon be retiring.

To be a Marseillais for you is . . .
To be a Marseillais, is to decide to be one. To be a Marseillais, that doesn't mean to be born here. That means coming here, loving this city, and feeling good here. Being a Marseillais is obviously sunnier and brinier than being a Berliner but for centuries, people did not choose this city, they came here lost. Now, for the first time, there are people who choose it and come to live here with a certain idea of the city. It's a sort of sea change. When our ancestors arrived here, they knew nothing about the city. They had to survive. Comorians, Algerians, Spaniards, Italians, Moroccans . . . they had to survive.
Wars, hunger, history brought them here. So today, we ask ourselves how our identity will evolve . . . The city has this distinct makeup. It is only an aggregate. We are the fruit of things that were put on top of each other. Here everything easily becomes your own. Why does Marseille have such a dazzling identity? Because to be able to say I am a Niçois, you need four generations. To become a Marseillais, it takes four minutes! If you live here, you are Marseillais. It can't be any other way. In our stories, we had no other choice. This identity is easy to make your own because you are in charge of it. Here, we are first and foremost Marseillais. France is a complicated identity to give oneself. To feel French and call yourself French, it's complicated. The Marseille identity is much simpler.

Le Fioupelan, glued to City Hall on the port, is a family business. The original restaurant, Au Sanglier, was created by the great-grandfather of the current co-owner – an Italian from Torre del Greco, just outside Naples – where he was a sponge and coral fisherman. His granddaughter tells us, 'At the start of the 19th century, the King of Naples gave low-income Italian families plots of land on deserted islands around Naples such as Ischia and Ventotene . . . because these were landmarks of the Barbary pirates. Our family, Sportiello, went to the island of Ventotene to cultivate the land. Part of the family returned to fishing, especially on the Algerian coast, and our ancestors finally settled in Algeria. Our family spent 100 years in Algeria, in Bône [now Annaba] and my grandfather was born in Algeria in 1908. He arrived in Marseille when he was around 12, 13 years old. He got hired as a cabin boy but his ship sank. His whole family was still in Algeria, so he worked in every trade here. He brought wild boars [*sanglier*] from Algeria which were not eaten there. He sold them to charcuteries in Marseille. It became his favourite animal. He created a small restaurant by the port, on Rue du Chevalier Roze, which he called Au Sanglier, but lost everything when Le Panier district was destroyed during the Second World War. After the war, he reopened on the port. When I was a child, there was a wild baby boar in the restaurant. We called him "sailor"! When he grew up, he started charging the customers. My grandfather wanted to eat it, but we children didn't want to kill it, so he donated it to the Marseille Zoo. My father and his brother then managed the business for more than 30 years. When my son took over the restaurant with his partner, they wanted to create a new dynamic and rename the place Fioupelan. That's what we call a big crab in Marseille – it's a tribute to the fishing past of the family.' Coincidentally, Benoît Payan – whose family also embarked for Marseille from a Neapolitan island over a century ago – is one of the regulars.

For you, is cooking political?
Anything that allows people to sit around the table and talk to each other is political. Cooking together today is political. When I tell a story, when I pass it on, it's political. It all depends on what one does with it. When it excludes, it's political. When it unites, it's political. Everything that creates interactions is political, but is cooking more political than sport . . . ?

Is it easier for you to negotiate with other politicians over a good meal?
Ahhh no, me, I don't like to do that. Cuisine is a bit sacred to me. I will not hold an important political meeting over lunch.

Where does the recipe that we're making today come from?
It is a pasta that is eaten more in southern Italy and is easy to prepare. Like most cucina in southern Italy, it is not expensive to make, it's without meat and with herbs. This is a dish that one makes here when one comes home late from a party. It's midnight, you've had a few, you pick herbs in your garden, and you put them in a pan. It is utterly simple. This pasta is very herby, very Mediterranean, and very tasty.

Is it from experience?
Obviously! I have 1,000 memories of it. When you're 18 or 19 and you come home from a party, it's not midnight but 5am and you're so hungry . . . I had friends who put ketchup in pasta at that hour but for me, that was not possible! So, instead, I would make this recipe, but with whatever I could get my hands on . . . sometimes only garlic. I would take everything I came across depending on where I was. If I was three sheets to the wind, I would make it with the lawn!

Do you remember the first time you made it?
No, but I remember this quote from Sophia Loren, 'All that you see of me, I owe to spaghetti' and for me, it's the same! Well, that could be very misinterpreted . . .
Come on, taste it!

But I'm taking photos.
This isn't eaten cold! . . . (eating) Ah, it's lacking salt and the herbs don't have the same taste in winter!

It won't show ;)

PASTA DI MEZZANOTTE
(Midnight pasta)

INGREDIENTS FOR 3–4 BOWLS

Rosemary
Fresh thyme
40g fresh parsley
40g fresh basil
40g sage
1 small dried red chilli pepper
8 garlic cloves
Olive oil
40g butter
500g spaghetti
Salt
Pepper
Parmesan

1. Think big, bring 5 litres of water to the boil. Salt the water.

2. Finely chop the herbs.

3. In a large deep pan, heat the herbs, the chilli and unpeeled garlic in a good glug of olive oil over low heat. Brown everything.

4. Remove the herbs. Press the garlic cloves, the skin will detach itself easily, the garlic is now *confit*. Keep a bit of sage in the pan for crunch. Add the butter and let it melt.

5. Dunk the pasta in the boiling water but remove a bit before it is al dente and add to the pan. Add a little pasta water and cook everything while stirring for a few minutes.

6. Serve your midnight pasta in a shallow bowl with some Parmesan.

LA
FRANCE
SAUVAGE
NAV

Marsilia Express

STREET FOOD MADE IN MARS

If your idea of Marseille *cuisine de rue* (street food) is limited to pizza slices from *les camions* (food trucks,) merguez sammies in front of the Vélodrome on match nights, and weekend chichis beignets from L'Estaque, your realm of possibilities will fatten up with the following. I'm not even going to linger on kebab sandwiches, although those at Ashourya in Cours Julien or Le Tarpin Bon on Rue de Rome are *tarpin bien* (Marseille slang for 'sooooo good').

That said, I'm not being a smart-ass. I admit to having shaken up my Marseille habits for this chapter. Without renouncing my classics!

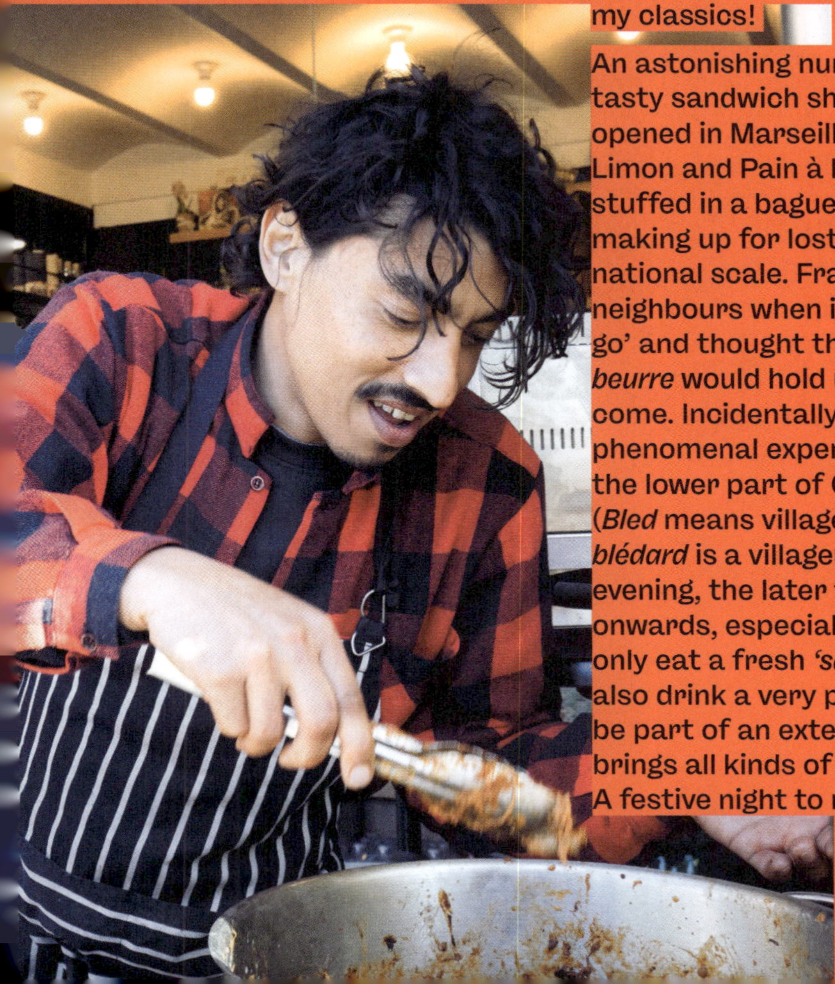

An astonishing number of brilliant and tasty sandwich shops have recently opened in Marseille (Razzia, Café Brioche, Limon and Pain à l'Ail with a classic aioli stuffed in a baguette). This much needed making up for lost time is happening on a national scale. France had fallen behind its neighbours when it came to 'lunch on the go' and thought that the industrial *jambon-beurre* would hold us over until kingdom come. Incidentally, if you really want a phenomenal experience, it awaits you in the lower part of Cours Julien at Blé d'Art (*Bled* means village in Arab and in French, a *blédard* is a villager). Hang out there in the evening, the later the better. From 11pm onwards, especially on weekends, you won't only eat a fresh *'sandiwch de dingue'*, you'll also drink a very personal *rhum dérangé* and be part of an extended jam session that brings all kinds of musicians together. A festive night to remember!

11

M R S
La Pointe Rouge

Ivan and Mélanie Sinko

It was Cheffe Laëtitia Visse who sent me to Ivan and Mélanie in the Pointe Rouge neighbourhood. When she was starting out in Marseille, she ran their kitchen in exchange for boxing lessons with Ivan, a former pharmacist who recently switched careers into the bar world. I often drove past this friends' haunt and saw a lot of people there without ever really daring to venture in, the gang seemed so close-knit. But, not closed off, it turns out, for I was adopted in less than an hour after a little control test: 'What are you drinking?'
Ivan is quite a character, like his cousin, the French actor Vincent Cassel. A Niçois who left his homeland for Marseille, Ivan longed to find a pan bagnat in the Gulf of Lion that was worthy of its name (most Marseillais serve blasphemous versions of the Niçois speciality). It's a done deal, since they now offer the best pan bagnat in Marseille at the Bar des Amis. Ivan's wife, Mélanie, is one hell of an English patissière. So the BDA cakes are also *délicieux*.
Our memorable encounter took place one sunny Saturday afternoon in December in the middle of the Covid lockdown (don't judge us now . . . you need to move on!). The BDA regulars were stopping by to pick up couscous and blanquette de veau takeaway, cooked that day by Cheffe Sabrina. The atmosphere had a 'before the pandemic' vitality. The closed-by-law terrace . . . was packed. Marseillais don't like to be told what they can or cannot do. Now you know.
Clearly, the BDA is a must-do for a convivial Sunday or a bumping night out. Both are possible. In fact, many things are possible at BDA . . .

BON VIVANTS !

Beloved bar with real food

23 Avenue de la Pointe Rouge
13008 Marseille

How did you end up in Marseille?
I moved here from Nice in 1979. I was 20 years old, and I came to Marseille for my pharmacist studies. I was a pharmacist for 30 years! In 2018–19, I took a huge leap, I sold my pharmacy. My wife was an English professor, we met at the end of the 1980s. We wanted to do something else, so Mélanie quit, and we took over this business. We live next door. It was the *bar de quartier* where I drank my *café* every morning. That said, we had no idea what we were getting into! We didn't know that authorisations were needed to stay open late, to play music . . . the *Fête de la Musique* in June was monstrous with a programme all weekend long! I spent the night here.
From the start, I insisted that we do food because we had a passion for it anyway: we were already organising chef battles at home. In fact, the Bar des Amis has become a reflection of what our home used to be. Except that now people are paying for it!
The project exploded from the start. At first, it was Mélanie who cooked, and I wanted to make Niçois dishes, socca, *pissaladière* . . . and for the pan bagnat, I really wanted the BDA one to be a Marseille point of reference, even if in winter sometimes, we stop making it because the tomatoes aren't as high quality. Very quickly, we worked with chefs-in-residence, including Laëtitia Visse. It was a great encounter. Laëtitia introduced us to the excellent Venezuelan chef David Mijoba, who had us meet Colombian chef Juan Pulgarin. Since then, the wheels have been in motion non-stop, and many young chefs do a stint in our kitchen. (*Author's note: at the time this book hit the printing press, it's Chef Mathieu Dugas who is taking our taste buds on a glorious trip in the BDA kitchen*).

It's a new way to create a restaurant . . .
Yes, however, everything we've done here was not based on a pre-thought concept. It's a gradual adaptation. I'm not an insider, I'm the new kid on the block, outside of the restaurant scene in Marseille.

Laëtitia Visse told me that you still train her at boxing . . .
I have two passions: boxing and surfing. The common thread of the atmosphere here is music, board sports, cooking, and England . . . and then there are the encounters. Rod, who creates cocktail marvels at the bar, also has a music label: Massilia Square Garden Records. Even I produced rap at one time . . . The idea was to create a lively place, so we organise readings, concerts, a Saturday street food market, DJ sets with Chris Presque Waddle . . . and we would like to start a BDA comedy club.

Which people in the restaurant industry have helped you or had an impact on you and your choices?
Amongst the people in Marseille who had a big influence, there's Pierre-Antoine Denis, the creator of the restaurants Cantinetta and Otto. He has a broad savoir when it comes to gastronomy and music. He knows all the products. He's a monster. He helped me discover a lot of things. You have to see him cook. When he lets go, when he brings it, he's a genius. He opened the world of gastronomy up to me. For example, I met the James Bond of cooking, Chef Jacques Maximin, through him.
There's also Rodolphe, the former owner of L'Eau à la Bouche pizzeria, because he worked at the biggest tables. He taught me discipline. Another person who influenced

'An insane energy, music, people galore . . . So many good things.' — Cheffe Laëtitia Visse

me a lot was Alessandra Pierini, who had the restaurant-épicerie Pasta e Dolce in Marseille. Now she runs the RAP épicerie in Paris. She was the one who introduced me to Italian products. When she left, I felt her absence big time. Today, the best pasta restaurant in Marseille is La Loco, at the Cassis train station! You can try to find better ones all the way to Italy, but the truth is, in Cassis, you have the best pasta! (*Author's note: Many restaurateurs told me the same thing.*)

As for my culinary shock, it is Chef Mauro Colagreco, 2 hours east from here in Menton, on the French Riviera. I was coming back from surfing in Italy. I crossed the border and saw this restaurant – Le Mirazur – which had just opened. It was epic. I went back in the evening, I finished at 4 in the morning. Mauro must have just received his first Michelin star at that time. He got his second star the following year. I went back, it was the cheapest 2-star table in France. And since then, I go there regularly, even today with its third star. It's really unbelievable.

And you, Mélanie, when did you come to Marseille?

I grew up in London, in Southgate, and I studied French at university. I arrived in France in 1989, in Marseille, as a student. I didn't choose Marseille, but I don't regret it! I met Ivan, we have two kids, and I had a career as an English professor here. But I always did things in the kitchen, in particular with Rodolphe of L'Eau à la Bouche for his food truck in L'Estaque.

In England, my mother always bought high-quality ingredients, she often baked cakes, and I learned the basics through her.

With Ivan, we wanted to do something else. We began looking at snack bars and boulangeries for sale, then our *bar de quartier* was put up for sale. At that time, they only offered peanuts and crisps with the drinks. We thought we would serve cheese and charcuterie boards to improve on bar snacks, but when we opened, the customers wanted to eat!

'Pan bagnat is a serious matter. There is a specific list of 14 ingredients. You can remove some, but there is a supreme ban on adding more. Otherwise, the curse will fall on you for eight generations!
And there are no cooked vegetables in it. No green beans. No potatoes. No mayonnaise. This is not a Niçoise salad in a bun. Regarding the bread, traditionally, you used stale bread from the previous day that you wet - that you bathe - hence the name (*Author's note: 'bagnar' in old Provençal = 'baigner' in French = to bathe*). Initially, it was moistened with water, later with olive oil.' — Ivan

PAN BAGNAT BY BDA

INGREDIENTS FOR 1 PAN BAGNAT

1 crusty bread roll
Olive oil
Hard-boiled egg
Tomato
Radishes
Onion
Tuna
Anchovy fillets
Celery
Salt and pepper

1. 'There are two schools, pepper or no pepper. Me, I don't add pepper. When they're in season, you can also add *févettes* [tiny, shelled broad beans]. Those are delicious. And when you find itty-bitty purple artichokes add them raw and cut into strips (just their hearts and their tender leaves).

2. Cut the bread in half and hollow out somewhat without breaking the crust. Moisten the inside of the bread with olive oil.

3. Slice hard-boiled egg and tomato horizontally and finely slice radishes. Peel onion and slice into thin rings.

4. Fill the hollowed-out bread with all the ingredients. Close the pan bagnat.'

R
M S
Noailles

Juan Pulgarin

The round-the-world-in-Marseille tour would not be complete without talking about the South American chefs that are increasingly tempting our taste buds on this new food planet. Le Bar des Amis likes to throw them in the deep end. The renowned Venezuelan chef David Mijoba cooked his signature cuisine there for a while and has now opened his own in vogue place in the Vauban quarter. Afterwards, Colombian Juan Pulgarin, a coffee roaster and chef, got his bearings there as well, going so far as to organise a world street food market on the bar's terrace.
With the same gusto, in 2023, Juan set up 'El Barrio', the first Latino épicerie in the heart of Marseille. A crazy gamble that makes sense. 'El Barrio in the barrio!' Good times, great coffee, and affordable street food guaranteed.

EL BARRIO MARSELLA

A Marseille eve can also easily whisk you away to Chile at El Santo Cachón, after having mused about it all afternoon at its cousin, La Santita, both near the crossroads of Rue Ferrari and Boulevard Eugène Pierre. After the coup d'état in 1973, Marseille welcomed a good number of Chilean refugees, and a community was born from the strong ties that already existed between Allende's socialist Chile and France. Since 2012, this restaurant has hooked loyal fans with the *pastel de choclo* (a sort of Shepherd's pie with beef and corn) and Cristobal's addictive pisco sours.

'Marseille is a choice for sun!'

South american épicerie, bar and street food

Where the Rue d'Aubagne and the Rue Longue-des-Capucins meet 13001 Marseille

Another chef forging his culinary path in Marseille is Edgar Bosquez, the newest member of our Latin American family. Edgar comes to us from Panama and the esteemed Institut Paul Bocuse culinary school in Lyon. His determination to serve us a gourmet menu is impressive but does not yet make us want to hug him. Time will come . . . For now, it is Juan Pulgarin who is the most in tune with Marseille's vibe. You'll taste his pepped-up cuisine and joie de vivre at many food events around town.
In France for almost 20 years, trained at the Médéric culinary école, this talent spent time in various Parisian restaurant kitchens before landing in Marseille in 2018. 'Marseille is a choice for sun!' he told me. 'This is my home now! It's self-organized chaos, a real barrio!'

El Barrio Marsella's tasty street food get Marseillais used to flavours from Bogotà and beyond. 'As a Colombian, I can attest that the most representative cuisine of my country is the one found on the streets.'
Peruvian, Mexican, Colombian, Bolivian, Chilean, Argentinian and Brazilian cuisines are rising in the world's restaurant rankings.
Coming from this hotbed for the renewal of flavour combinations, the *sympathique* Juan surely has a bright future ahead of him in Marseille. 'The number of pizzas that Marseillais gobble up is impressive! Latin street food did not exist here, so I took the plunge.'

'I have three adresses to recommend: Mijoba, because David's work with local ingredients is authentic, he walks in the hills to forage wild plants for his dishes. The Rôtisserie du 4ème on Place Sébastapol. Josianne, and her *pieds paquets* and *daubes*, represent a Marseille that is disappearing. And I buy all my bread at Pétrin Couchette.'

FOR A PARTY OF 6 (24 TACOS)

24 tortillas (around 12cm)
Fresh coriander
Juice of 1 lime

For the meat:
3kg pork shoulder
6 tomatoes
1 onion
Salt and pepper

For the salsa picante (hot sauce):
2 dried chipotle peppers (smoked jalapeños)
2 dried ancho chillies
2 dried guajillo chillies
2 tbsp sesame seeds
2 tomatoes

For the pico de gallo:
2 tomatoes
1 onion, red or white
½ bunch of coriander
½ bunch of parsley
Juice of 1 lime

1. For the meat: finely slice the onion and blend the tomatoes. Put the meat in a roasting pan with the onions and the tomatoes, salt and pepper, and roast for 10 hours in a 95°C/gas mark ¼ oven.
2. Prep the salsa picante: rehydrate the chillies in a bit of water. Toast the sesame seeds in a pan. Blend the tomatoes with the chillies and add the toasted sesame seeds.
3. Shred the meat and put it in a pan with the cooking juices and a quarter of the hot sauce. Reduce the sauce.
4. For the pico de gallo: finely dice the tomatoes and onion, finely chop the herbs, and mix all the ingredients with the lime juice.
5. Spread the salsa picante on each tortilla with a pastry brush and heat them in a frying pan with the sauce side up. Add a bit of meat, a bit of pico de gallo, finely chopped coriander and a fresh squeeze of lime.

TACOS DEL BARRIO MARSELLA

An importer of Colombian coffee, Juan enables us to drink better café, at a fairer wage for the families who produce it. You can enjoy a cup at David Mijoba's place.

Castellane

Yossi Teboul

Yossi's team was a little surprised when I turned up there for the book. It must be said that Au Falafel, near the Opéra, or the lick-your-lips Golda with Israeli Chef Or Michaeli are deservedly the Marseille tables we talk about when we want to seem 'plugged in' and fans of Ottolenghi. Israeli cuisine is trending and rightly so. The canteens mentioned above are cool, but I was looking for something more discreet, more hidden yet waouhhh! Marseille has the third-largest Jewish community in Europe, so, my food-guide-writing friends, we can do better than two addresses and, as it happens, I have a third one that sticks to my ribs. It's in the Castellane neighbourhood, near the historic Grande Synagogue (inaugurated in 1864, the same year as the current Bonne Mère). Yossi's owner, Yossi, calls the shots.

NOT YOUR BUBBE'S KOSHER BUT SHE WOULD LOVE IT!

Israeli comfort food

'I grew up in Jerusalem. My family, which has Moroccan roots, still lives in Israel. From my childhood there, I remember my grandmother's meatballs, Moroccan-style fish, and her famous meat cigars.

At the restaurant, I reinterpret my mother and grandmother's dishes, and I keep learning from cosmopolitan life in Israel. But I don't understand why my mother still puts garlic in Moroccan fish. Especially because she assures me she doesn't.

14 Rue Sainte-Victoire
13006 Marseille

We've succeeded in reinventing gastronomic dishes in this fabulous challah that we customarily eat for Shabbat. Kids and adults alike adore them.

The mix of cultures and scents of spices represent my cuisine well, as well as the city of Marseille, especially the Rue d'Aubagne's district, which I love for all its aromas and its flavours.' — Yossi

CHALLAH ASADO

INGREDIENTS FOR 2 – FOR THOSE WHO COULD EAT A HORSE

For 2 challah brioches:
1 packet dried yeast or ½ cube (20g) fresh yeast
300ml lukewarm water
100ml sunflower oil
500g pastry flour / T45
1 tbsp sugar
1 tsp salt
2 eggs + 1 egg yolk
Sesame seeds

For Yossi's asado:
500g meat (uncut short ribs)
Olive oil
Your preferred spices
1 tbsp date syrup
1 onion, diced
1 pinch of salt
1 pinch of sugar

For tartar sauce:
Homemade mayonnaise
Shallots
Red onion
Cornichons
White wine vinegar

For Yossi's chimichurri:
1 small red chilli
4 garlic cloves
½ bunch of coriander
½ bunch of parsley
25g red pepper
25g green pepper
150ml olive oil
Salt and pepper

To assemble:
Baby spinach
Rocket
Cornichons
Eggs (1 fried egg per sandwich)

1. Dilute the yeast in the water and oil. Mix the flour, sugar and salt in another large bowl, then add in the 2 eggs. Beat them all together.

2. Cover (the dough is sensitive to air) and let rest for 1 hour at room temperature.

3. Briefly knead the dough to release any air bubbles. Cut into two pieces.

4. Divide each dough ball into three 'sausages' and braid them into the challah. Let rest for 1 hour at room temperature.

5. Brush your brioche with the egg yolk and sprinkle with sesame seeds. Bake at 200°C/gas mark 6 for 15 minutes minimum, 30 minutes maximum. Look beneath the brioche to check for doneness: it shouldn't be white. Let the challah cool before filling.

6. Massage the meat with olive oil, spices of your choosing (Yossi brings his from Israel) and the date syrup. Roll the meat in waxed paper and close the two sides like a sweet (with a bit of aluminium foil).

7. Steam in a 120°C/gas mark ½ oven for 6 hours. Remove the meat from the oven and save the drippings.

8. Brown the onion with the salt and sugar in the meat drippings. Remove the bone and shred the meat. Mix the meat and the onions in the pan.

9. Prep the tartar sauce by mixing homemade mayonnaise, finely chopped shallots and red onions, cornichons sliced in rounds, and a little bit of white vinegar. Feel free to adjust the proportions according to your taste.

10. For the chimichurri sauce, remove the seeds and the white membrane on the inside of the chilli. Peel the garlic cloves. Finely chop the herbs, peppers, chilli and garlic, then add the olive oil, salt and pepper, and mix well.

11. Assemble the sandwich bomb: cut the challah in half, spread the tartar sauce on each side, add some baby spinach and a bit of rocket. Place the asado on the greens, add a few cornichons, then chimichurri sauce, and finish with a fried egg. Close the challah, take a bite . . . and time will stop!

We're not far from the best sandwich in Marseille! I think it might even be it, but, be prepared and come with an open-minded belly. Yossi's asado and chimichurri sauce are local interpretations.

M R S
Noailles

Sonia Illy and Raphaël Mendy

ALL THE WORLD'S A PASTEL

Noailles and Senegalese pastels are an obvious pairing! We owe this great idea to a young cooking couple – Sonia *et* Raphaël. For a long time, traditional Senegalese restaurants, among which Mame Diarra reigns queen, and African épiceries have been keeping us in the know in the upper part of Rue d'Aubagne and the neighbourhood. Pastels, or fataya, are also a good base on which to express one's creativity and a life's philosophy open to cultural mixing. I invite you to do the same, with a big glass of bissap (hibiscus juice) in your hand.

MY CHILDHOOD

Sonia: My parents are lamb breeders. I grew up in Saint-Auban-d'Oze, a minuscule village in the Hautes-Alpes. I came to Marseille for my studies when I was 18 years old. I lived at the student residence near the Timone hospital because my school was in the area.
Raphaël: I grew up in Saint-André, a small district in the north of Marseille (16th arrondissement).

THE INGREDIENT OR THE SCENT OF MY CHILDHOOD

Sonia: Wild raspberries that we'd pick in the mountains.
Raphaël: The scent of the dish of mafé that reigned in the middle of the table. We all ate from the same plate. That's my best memory. And the merguez that we'd eat at block parties, or during football tournaments.

MY IDEA OF MARSEILLE BEFORE I ARRIVED

Sonia: I thought of the sea because I only knew of the mountains.

MY IDEA OF MARSEILLE OVER TIME

Sonia: I barely ever go to the sea [laughs]! And I love the city centre. I love global cuisine and, being in Noailles, I can find every possible and imaginable ingredient. That's what Marseille is. My first culinary memory here is the couscous at the restaurant Sur le Pouce, served quickly, so good, and for a ridiculously low price.
Raphaël: It's the most beautiful city in France. I've thought so since I was a kid. The climate, the multiculturalism, the atmosphere, it's a city with personality. For me, who's rather reserved, I need these contrasts.

OUR NEIGHBOURHOOD

Raphaël: I thought I was going to spend my whole life in Marseille's Quartiers Nord [northern districts] and today, I miss it a bit, but I like the friendly side of Noailles, where we found a great location, near the market, and it's a district that corresponds with the spirit of our restaurant.

MY CUISINE AND MY CITY

Raphaël: Like everything in Marseille, my cuisine is made from 'elsewhere'.

MARSEILLE'S FOOD SCENE TODAY

Sonia: Being renewed. Innovative. Multicultural.
Raphaël: Young, ambitious, multicultural.

THE PEOPLE WHO I ADMIRE OR WHO I'M INTRIGUED BY IN MARSEILLE'S CULINARY SCENE

Sonia: I would like to eat at AM par Alexandre Mazzia.
Raphaël: The only one I admire is Sonia, it was with her that I learned how to be professional.

WHAT MARSEILLAIS OVERLOOK IN THEIR GASTRONOMY

Sonia: I'm sure that many of them haven't tried bouillabaisse.
Raphaël: I think that Marseillais aren't aware that a Marseille gastronomy even exists. As for me, I grew up with friends of all different backgrounds, and like a magnet, I was drawn to their gastronomy at first. Today, I'm lucky to be a cook and I'm taking this opportunity to make up for lost time and discover how wonderful Marseille gastronomy is.

WHAT I COOK FOR MY FAMILY

Raphaël: stews, ragouts, mafé, yassa. I love those, they are comforting, they remind me of my childhood when we all ate around a giant dish. And for my friends, the same thing. Friends are my family.

A RECIPE THAT SOWS DISCORD?

Raphaël: My cooking makes everyone agree! [laughs]

West-African cuisine

29 Rue d'Aubagne
13001 Marseille

FATAYA FROM PASTELS WORLD

'We both thought of a recipe for the book. So, we combined our ideas to create one. You use a lot of manioc leaves in West African cuisine, where Raphaël's father is from. As for me, I discovered them in Madagascar, because they're part of the national dish! I did a cooking internship in Madagascar in 2012. — Sonia

INGREDIENTS FOR 4

For the dough:
125g softened butter
250g flour + extra for your work surface
¼ tsp fine salt
1 egg yolk
Poppy seeds, sesame, nigella . . . (optional)

For the filling:
250g stewing steak (or minced beef for a faster version)
Palm oil
Beef bouillon
1 onion
1 package of frozen manioc leaves (1 bunch of fresh spinach if not available)
1 tbsp tomato purée
1 tbsp peanut butter
Salt and pepper

1. For the dough, cut the butter into pieces. Mix with the flour and salt. The mixture should become crumbly. Slowly add water just until you get a homogenous dough that is a bit firm. Cover with cling film and refrigerate.

2. For the filling, brown the beef chunks in a bit of palm oil. Once they are well browned, pour in the bouillon to cover. Let simmer over low heat until the meat falls apart (around 2 hours cooking time).

3. During this time, peel and dice onion and sauté until it is nicely browned. Add manioc leaves and tomato purée. Spoon a small ladle of beef broth into the pan. To finish, mix in the peanut butter. Let cook until you get a thick sauce.

4. Once the beef is cooked, shred the meat. Mix into the sauce. Add salt and pepper if necessary. Let cool.

5. Preheat the oven to 220°C/gas mark 7.

6. On a floured work surface, roll out the dough to a 2mm thickness. Cut into circles with a cookie cutter or a glass. Put a teaspoon of filling in the centre of each one. You have to add enough filling but not too much, so that the fataya do not break open when cooking. Moisten the edges of the dough with a little water and fold in a semicircle. Seal the edges of the stuffed pastry with a fork.

7. Brush with a little egg yolk for a golden-brown exterior and gourmand flavour. You can even sprinkle them with poppy, sesame or nigella seeds . . . Place the fatayas on a baking sheet and bake for around 12 minutes, just until they are nicely browned.

Between Rue de la République and Le Panier

Thi Hanh and her son, Jean

TO THE END!

Vietnamese cuisine

6 Rue Méry
13002 Marseille

At Nguyen Hoang, the mum is a ball of energy and a chef who never has time for anything other than cooking. Suffice to say that the Covid lockdowns and the pandemic wore out this outstanding cook's nerves. Consequently, Thi Hanh was happy to cook for me and the first edition of this book, in her usually crowded restaurant that had been closed for weeks. Then the restaurant opened again and Thi Hanh went back to crazy business as usual! For seven years now, her son, Jean, has worked with her, and not without difficulty! The fact is that, over 20 years ago, in September 2001, this Vietnamese refugee opened her own restaurant by herself at the tip of Le Panier, behind the Rue de la République. She was 45 years old.

Thi Hanh, when did you arrive in Marseille?

THI HANH: My husband and I were born and raised in Saigon.
I came to France with my eldest son in 1984, 39 years ago. I left the Galang refugee camp in Indonesia and the refugee office let me come to Marseille because my husband had arrived here in 1981. On the bus, when I saw the rural outskirts of Marseille, I thought I was moving to the countryside. I was afraid. Then, I discovered that it's a big city.
My first memory of Marseille was the Rue de la République, full of people. My husband sold fruits and vegetables at Prisunic. I spent a year learning French and then I immediately found a job as a seamstress in the Mazargues neighbourhood, with Martine Vassal, who ran her family's textile company at that time (*Author's note: Vassal is now president of the Aix-Marseille-Provence metropolis*). But childcare was difficult and expensive. Jean was always sick, so after six or seven years, when I had my third kid, I quit to care for them at home. The kids grew up, so I had the idea to open this restaurant.
I had to find something to do with my life, and my friends had restaurants. At that time, Rue de la République was home to many family-owned shops, and restaurants were part of this multicultural mix. In Le Panier, there has always been a large Vietnamese community and many Asian stores. I decided to do like my friends did.

JEAN: My mother always lived on the Rue de la République and we watched this central artery transform and empty out. Me, I was born in Marseille, I have many childhood memories of this street. I had all my addresses, the little sweet shop, takeaway chips that we bought after school . . . But, now, all our friends have had to move.

THI HANH: Before opening a restaurant, when my kids were little, one day I made traditional Vietnamese cakes and I went to sell them outside, the kids with me in their pushchair. Everyone in the community began ordering my cakes. Every day, I would leave with a bag and the pushchair. I sold my cakes on the street!

Can you imagine that? I think it took a lot of courage to do that. I watched people pass by and offered them my cakes.
When I returned home, my husband would scold me because he couldn't understand why I was doing this. In Vietnam, I was a schoolteacher, and here, I was selling cakes on the street. When I first returned to Vietnam, my father asked me what I did in Marseille, and I said I was selling cakes on the street. My dad started crying.

Where did you learn to cook?
THI HANH: I learned recipes from cookbooks. Every day I tried them and redid them to improve. In Vietnam, I didn't cook often, neither did my mother. She was a merchant.
JEAN: I'm the middle child. I became interested in the restaurant industry after my university studies. I was used to seeing my mum cooking by herself, but me, I was studying to get an accounting degree. I did a work-study programme at a hotel-restaurant in Marseille on the Corniche, the NH. It was a real eye-opener for me, a little lightning bolt! I spent more time with the front of house staff and in the kitchen than with the administrative services with whom I was doing my training.
I really didn't see where there was a rewarding side to office work.
At the time, I was shy; working in the restaurant helped me be more open with people and it opened my mind. I have become way more outgoing. So, during the last year of my studies, I decided to work in the restaurant industry. I worked in the front of house at the boutique hotel Mama Shelter in Marseille and in Bordeaux.
That enabled me to discover the world of hospitality and the profession of being a manager.
It changed me. In my youth, Mum was very strict and didn't let us go out . . .
THI HANH: Ah yes, I would go with them to school and I would pick them up afterwards. They wanted to do sports, but I didn't let them in the streets by themselves, I accompanied them everywhere.
JEAN: Then, I felt like stopping the never-ending crazy pace of this kind of working life. It's at that time I started lending a hand to my mum.
THI HANH: My son worked days and nights, he wasn't doing well. So, I told him to quit and to come and work with his mother. What's more, he ate poorly! A mum can't stand that.
JEAN: The collaboration came naturally. And now, it's been seven years since we've been working together.

How did it go at first?
JEAN: [laughs] How'd it go, Mummy?
THI HANH: I had many customers. Thankfully, Jean came to help out during service.
JEAN: It wasn't easy at first! Working with family is very, very complicated. Really! Everyone has their professional baggage. Everyone has their own way of seeing things. We say things to each other more abruptly.
We even cried at times. All of a sudden, it was Mum, then it was me . . . or the both of us!
For two years, our relationship was very complicated due to the busyness . . . We didn't have a lot of time to talk to each other. Success gradually came by word of mouth, but at some point I felt that my mum no longer had everything under control and that I had to intervene. She didn't manage the service and the crowds, she would get angry. In fact, she almost gave up on the project. That's why I came to help her.
THI HANH: The customers all arrive at the same time for lunch. They work and they want to eat quickly.
JEAN: We managed to organise ourselves so we could serve them properly within a limited amount of time. But it took us time to figure out how to work together! Family meals were explosive! When I came back to Marseille, I returned to living with her and her offices are at home . . .
It was really complicated! I saw her day and night . . . To mix your private life with your family life . . . It was a trial.

And was it difficult for you, Thi Hanh?
THI HANH: I thought about it a lot because I wanted to retire and I asked myself who would step in to cook . . . but now, I say to myself . . .
JEAN: That she'll go on to the end!
THI HANH: It's my life, and I really like our customers.
JEAN: In Asia, women cook at any age, up to 90 years old. There is no retirement. I know my mum will go all the way. I realised this during the first Covid lockdown. She was stressed, she lost her bearings a bit due to the much slower pace. The hours she spent at home felt like weeks for her! She had a tachycardia attack because of that.

THI HANH: It's true, I don't handle rest well. My heart is used to this pace. So, we restarted and took orders by phone. I would prepare them carefully . . . and customers would fetch them from the back of the restaurant.
JEAN: And you forgot to say that I was there also!
THI HANH: But you don't cook! . . .
JEAN: But, you're the one who doesn't want me to! You say all the time, 'It's not like that, that's not good. Let me do it. I will show you!' When I cook, she elbows me!

What recipes have you mastered so far?

JEAN: Bo bun, and she also taught me how to make pho soup. She took the time to teach me. You have to wrestle the recipes out of her. She has a hard time with the word 'transmission'!

THI HANH: He must watch me do it!

JEAN: Don't do, watch! That's what she says.

Is there something that your son does well?

THI HANH: Now, he knows how to roll *nems* [spring rolls]. That makes me happy! Every week he helps me roll *nems*.

JEAN: Actually, she gives me the ingredients, the recipe, but once you get to work, she's in total control! She takes the knife back and does it for me even though she has other things to do.

THI HANH: He doesn't know how to cut the ingredients!

JEAN: Well, nevertheless I have a strong sense of pride for my parents. The restaurant got mentioned in the *New York Times*. That's the Holy Grail! My parents started from nothing, they left everything behind in Vietnam. My father was able to escape the regime, but my mum's attempt failed for two years. She tried and tried again. Then, she ended up spending 10 days at sea with my big brother between Vietnam and Indonesia. Once in Indonesia, it was Bernard Kouchner [the French doctor and politician who co-founded Médecins Sans Frontières – Doctors Without Borders], who at the time was letting political refugees in, who let them join my father in France.

THI HANH: The Secours Catholique [Catholic relief service] paid for our plane tickets so that we could come to France.

JEAN: Here, in our restaurant, everything is on the plate and not in the decoration. That represents us well.

Your favourite restaurants . . .

JEAN: The Japanese Hako+ in Roucas Blanc, Ouréa near the Palais de Justice, O'Pakistan in Cours Julien, an old address on the Rue des Trois Rois and Casa Brandi, a tasty Italian on Rue Breteuil. When I want to eat pizza, I like to go to Chez Étienne for the atmosphere, and my *pizza du camion*, it's the Pizza Charly truck at Place Sébastapol. It's really good. My parents love couscous. So we go together to Tunisian La Goulette.

Marseillais are starting to understand the difference between Asian cuisines, even though when they come here, a lot of them still say, 'We're going to the Chinese.' When I hear our customers say that I tell them that they must stop! Especially when I hear them say it to their kids. There was a cultural deficit when it came to cuisine in Marseille, a lack of knowledge, but its balance has been restored. However, the French still have a rather derogatory view towards Vietnam due to colonisation and the war.

VIETNAMESE CREPE (BANH XEO)

INGREDIENTS FOR 1

2 heaped tbsp rice flour
1 tsp turmeric
3 tbsp coconut milk
Sunflower oil
30-40g lean pork
3 prawns, peeled, heads removed
1 small spring onion, chopped (both white and green parts)
A few bean sprouts or carrots, your choice
Vietnamese lemongrass leaves (kinh gioi)
Shiso leaves (trato)
A few leaves of iceberg or green lettuce

For the sauce to serve on the side:
1 tbsp fish sauce (nuoc-mam)
1 tsp sugar
4 tsp boiling water
½ tsp white vinegar
Fresh red chilli chopped into tiny pieces

1. In a large bowl, thoroughly mix the flour, the turmeric, the coconut milk and 4 large tablespoons of cold water. Chill for 1 hour.

2. Coat the bottom of a frying pan with sunflower oil, then add the meat, the prawns and the spring onion. Brown until the meat is medium rare, then add the crepe batter and let it stick.

3. Pour a little oil around the rim to gently unstick the batter. Add the bean sprouts (washed and drained) or the grated carrots.

4. When the crepe is cooked, gently fold it in two and serve with some Vietnamese lemongrass leaves, some shiso and some lettuce.

5. Mix all the sauce ingredients in a small bowl and serve with the crepe.

6. To eat, take a leaf of lettuce, put a bit of crepe inside it with some lemongrass and shiso leaves, roll it up, and dip it in the sauce.

7. Precision: my mum doesn't use any aromatic Provençal plants here. She keeps it super traditional. But, we manage to find all these Vietnamese or Asian plants here in Marseille. Some farmers cultivate them in the region or my mum grows them at her place.

'Normally I use bean sprouts, but today I used carrots.' — Thi Hanh

'I wanted to share an easy recipe to make at home. Usually, I eyeball everything, but here, I paid attention to the number of spoons of each ingredient so that I could give you the recipe.' — Thi Hanh

Le Comptoir des Beaux-arts and Louazna Ayari

In the neighbourhoods of Noailles and Belsunce, we quickly forget baguettes when we taste the piping-hot Algerian *kesra*, sesame Turkish *simits*, and *pain égyptien* (Egyptian flat bread) . . . the world of bread is vast in Marseille!
Marianne Tiberghien, the official godmother of the city centre merchants and president of the association of local traders, has made Comptoir des Beaux-Arts her unofficial headquarters. So I went there with her after hearing Chef Emmanuel Perrodin talk about it with such warmth and emotion. Each day has its plat du jour. Marianne is a fan of the *boulettes* (green olive and beef meatballs) on Mondays, Emmanuel of their chorba, but, here, I'm going to tell you about their *kesra*, a flatbread made with semolina that Madame Louazna Ayari and her all-female team bake to order in a tiny space that opens onto the Rue du Musée. It's worth queueing up to observe their craftsmanship. As for this bread, it goes wonderfully well with all the sauces and all the soups! For *petit déjeuner*, for lunch, for a snack, for *apéro*, for dinner. . .

KESRA (ALGERIAN FLATBREAD)

INGREDIENTS FOR 2 FLATBREADS

500g wheat semolina ($1/3$ fine semolina and $2/3$ medium semolina, or even coarse if you can find it in a Middle Eastern or North African épicerie)
1 tsp fresh yeast
1 pinch of fine salt
50ml fat (half olive oil, half another plant-based oil, like sunflower or palm)
Za'atar, sesame seeds or nigella seeds (optional)
250ml room temperature water

1. Mix the semolina, yeast and salt together. (A bit of yeast provides some softness and suppleness.) Add, if you want, za'atar, sesame seeds or nigella seeds. It's what Mina from MinaKouk tried and liked.
2. Shape into a mound and add the oil bit by bit. Rub the semolina between the palms of your hands to coat the grains with as much oil as possible.
3. 'When you clutch the dough between your hands and your fingers leave their imprints on it, you have enough fat in the mixture. If the dough crumbles, add a little more oil.'
4. Ball up your dough and add the 250ml water, more or less. Wet your hands with a bit of water and knead the mixture to get a thick dough that has a bit of suppleness.
5. 'It's truly a recipe that is refined by touch, not by precise measurements. And, of course, the amount of oil and water depends on the semolina.'
6. Spread out the ball of dough with your palms and gently fold it over itself.
7. It's a dough that likes warmth. It doesn't like the cold or gusts of air. Cover it with a lightweight towel and keep warm. The best is to cover it with a towel and to put a bit of wool on top. The dough will rise quickly. Let it rest overnight if you're in winter, a little less in the summer, since that's when the dough rises faster.
8. The next day, knead the dough a bit to remove air bubbles, then let rest a second time, for 20 minutes.
9. To cook, you need to have a baked clay or cast-iron dish, or a thick-bottomed pan that is super hot. Spread out the dough with the heel of your hand for a round flatbread. It also helps to use a rolling pin at the end to get it thin enough; it mustn't be more than 1cm thick. Prick with a fork.
10. While cooking, press on the flatbread with your hands and a wooden spatula for even cooking and flip the flatbread when the underside is well browned. It is better to have a flatbread that isn't too big so that you can handle flipping it and moving it.

Algerian cuisine

15 Rue Rodolphe Pollak
13001 Marseille

FOCUS

Ladies in bread

One of Marcel Pagnol's famous comedy-dramas is *La Femme du Boulanger* in which the baker's wife leaves him for another man. Times have changed and at last, we have realised that more often than we thought, the baker is a woman!

Marcel Pagnol would probably have been happily surprised to meet Nicole Baghdiguian-Wéber, Aurélie Roustan, Stéphanie Decorp, and Louazna Ayari . . . the women who are making some of the best bread and viennoiseries in Marseille today.

For the past few years, Marseille . . . – but I should really say the whole country of France – has rediscovered what it takes to make good, not so white bread and how to make a croissant from A to Z, thanks to some newcomers, who are often career-changing women and men. You may not have realised it from abroad but France had completely lost it and at some point bread was better in London or Copenhagen! Somebody French had to admit it . . .

Why? Because the price of bread in France is the most important index of our cost of living. Its price was decided by the state until 1987. Everybody had to be able to afford bread. Even today, in French people's minds, the price of bread has to stay low on principle. It's cultural. People complain whenever their baguette costs a few cents more. So the average price of a baguette today in France is 95 cents. Hence the machines, the speed and the poor quality of the wheat flour we often use to make bread and that we have a hard time getting rid of. In any case, since the end of World War II, the French government provided food security and we never let go of this expectation. Plus, in the 70s, 80s and 90s the explosion of supermarkets and industrialised food made us believe food could be cheap and money could be spent on less essential goods . . .

Fortunately, some folk are once again more willing to spend their working hours making gustatory and nutritional bread, growing healthy vegetables, raising cows in a humane way . . . and some customers are once again more willing to spend a larger part of their income on food and fresh produce. The revolution is fragile but happening. In Marseille, in various neighbourhoods, the baking teams from House of Pain, Bar à Pain, Pain Pan, Pain Salvator, Les Mains Libres, Maison Saint-Honoré, Miches et Baguettes, Pétrin Couchette and the ultra enthusiast newborn on Rue de Lodi, Ferments Bakery, all bring their mad, independent and artisanal energy to a profession that has sold out and become almost solely industrial. It's funny, or maybe sad, to realise that in the end, many of us were ready for the change!

Nicole Baghdiguian-Wéber

I breezed into Boulangerie Salvator between 6 and 7am (closer to 7am, I admit) in my usual photographer and writer mode. Nicole welcomed me with her customary huge smile and asked, 'Can you help us? We're missing someone from our team this morning.' Before I realised it, a long wooden peel was already in my hands, and I was happily pulling out *baguettes*, *miches*, and *fougasses* on the double from the oven as if I had shaped and cooked them all my life. Around 11am, when my burnt fingertips were practically smoking, I started to get tired, I had forgotten why I was there, I wanted the baguette price to climb to 8 euros (normally 1–2 euros in France) given the work it required, and I found the customers oblivious, even ungrateful, especially in a 100% organic, sourdough and artisanal bakery. This is when Nicole and I sat down to gobble up addictive *viennoiseries* and cookies, and chat without a timer!
We, the consumers, have become so used to replacing humans with unpaid machines that when perspiration comes back into the picture, particularly in the food biz, it is difficult to admit the true cost and taste of good things. Bread, our food staple since the dawn of time, had become the flag-bearer of junk food. It's nonetheless disappointing in a country that calls itself the 'temple of gastronomy'. News is we can do something about it because it isn't always a question of resources. Sometimes it's a matter of choice. Big news again, we must make choices, we can't have it all, but our generation and a few before and after us haven't learned to live in this way. A topic of heated conversations in my own *Marseillaise* family that I can't help but cite here.
So, on the slopes of Boulevard Salvator, I found a new role model in Nicole. What a great lesson in commitment!

WAKE UP!

100% organic bread

32 Boulevard Louis Salvator
13006 Marseille

How did this life choice come about?
I've been cooking for a long time. And watching my mum ageing, and getting sick, I thought to myself, 'I'm also growing old and I have to do "my thing".' Before, I oversaw training for the Chamber of Commerce, then I was a project manager there, then I hit the glass ceiling, and I was practically put out to pasture. I was given a good salary and a good job title, but didn't have much to do. That could have lasted until I retired. The Chamber of Commerce in Marseille is a man's world, and I was a woman over 50 years old . . . so the time I had doing little and being paid for it enabled me to think things through. First I wrote a cookbook, *L'Aventure végétarienne (The Vegetarian Adventure)*.
In the end, I was somehow lucky to have hit the glass ceiling otherwise I would never have started my own business. But this desire was also fuelled by my Armenian roots and the fact that I was doing a little catering alongside my work. In the eyes of my family, I had to have a higher education and have a somewhat shiny job while I wanted dough, bread, and cooking. I would cook with my grandmother . . .
I did everything right for my family but when everyone started dying, I said, 'Hold on, guys, I still haven't done what I wanted to do . . . so I will finally do it without feeling ashamed.'
I negotiated a dismissal, I trained to be an organic baker, and I put together a financing plan with my partner, my husband Étienne. Everyone found my commitment to organic ingredients brilliant, we needed 160,000 euros financing, and the bank said to me, 'Nope! You're a woman, you are old, you have no experience, and your location is really poorly placed.' This location is poorly placed but there weren't leasing rights. We only had to pay the rent. It wasn't expensive and it was big. I told myself, 'This spot is so lovely, I will manage to do incredible things inside, I'm sure that my bread will be good, I have the energy to do it, it will work, and I believe it.' I signed for the

space in mid-October, we had four months of work to do, and in mid-November, the bank called to tell me that they had refused the loan, no ifs, ands or buts. I asked them, 'Is it because I'm a woman?' and the lady responded, 'Let's just say I never told you that.'
I was in the car, and I fell apart. We had raised 28,000 euros from the local BPI [public investment bank] on the condition of this private bank loan. I couldn't help but move forward so we scraped up enough money; I had received a severance bonus, I owned my house in the Quartiers Nord, and bit by bit, we paid for it all . . . the oven, the kneader . . . and we did the renovations over three years. My two daughters believed in me. I started alone with my husband and my daughter, Axelle, selling. My other daughter, Lexane, who was studying at Paris Dauphine University, did the bookkeeping remotely. I was under extreme stress. I asked myself, 'What if the bank was right . . . ?' Where the bank was right, is that I lacked experience, so I needed 15 hours a day to get everything done.

In the banking world, algorithms rule and make the decisions, not human beings anymore.
We're told to train again, to retire later in life . . . but these are only words, truly, only words. The government doesn't provide any support for this.

How old were you when you started this second career?
I was 57 years old and I'm having a blast. I think that you can have another go whenever, regardless of your age. By becoming a baker, I liked being off hours, crossing the silent city. When you start your day, there's nobody. I wanted an open baking lab, not one in a basement. I wanted to know the customers, for people to spend time here, for this to be a story for everyone. But, anyways, it's not romantic, you have to bring it! But my company runs well, we are 11 people today in addition to Étienne and me,

and we make things that are really good, in our opinion at least. We are doing it at our scale, and I would really like us to become a destination, to host exhibitions, and to be able to show our commitment to alternative ideas for society.

What recipe could we put in the book that tells the story of your journey?
With Étienne, we lived for six months here. We were in baking mode every day. We slept in the room above, we put in a shower downstairs, we ate here, and we made focaccia with the leftover dough. It's true that these are things, like pizzas, that we toss in the oven. The reality is we put cheese and potatoes on a piece of dough and presto . . . Some nights we'd eat leftover focaccia with a glass of water at 4am.
I'm a fan of garlic, we put tons of garlic on ours whereas, when we started, I didn't put any on those we sold. Garlic is expensive, the sales price would have been too high. We started with rosemary focaccia without garlic because at first, we didn't have the clientele for it. Little by little we added garlic . . .

Marseille is the biggest Armenian city in France. Tell me about your family . . .
I'm Armenian on both my mother's and father's side. My father was born in 1920 in Cilicia, he came to Marseille by boat in the 20s, during the exodus, with my paternal grandparents, thanks to the Nansen passport (*Author's note: passports for stateless refugees between the two World Wars*). My maternal grandmother had come a bit beforehand. They weren't afraid to restart their lives. They did it. The Armenians were the '*épaves*' ['wrecks', aka the migrants forced to flee their homeland] in journalist Albert Londres' 1927 book *Marseille, Porte du Sud*.
We lived with my family in the Armenian district of Saint Antoine à La Viste. I still live in Saint Antoine in the Quartiers Nord.
Initially, I thought about opening my bakery there. I wanted to call it 'pop bread' for '*populaire* [both popular and working class in French] bread' but I couldn't sell it at a working-class price and I already had too many problems to overcome. I get along very well with the Bio Coop organic supermarket in the Grand Littoral shopping centre in the Quartiers Nord which opened at the same time as us and they sell our bread. The manager, Roustom Allali, is a Moroccan from the Quartiers Nord who fought to set up the Bio Coop there, under the giant French chain Carrefour. His Bio Coop is huge, beautiful. We deliver there once a week even if it's not profitable for us, and we buy 90% of the ingredients that I cook with from there: milk, cream, cheese, tofu . . .

Where do you eat Armenian food in Marseille?
At my house! As a kid, we never went out to eat.

Marseille is evolving . . .

Yes, when I see Cheffe Sarah and Lucien from Regain [the restaurant buys their bread from Boulangerie Salvator], they have a real desire to do something different, to share, and to have us taste good wine, good dishes, not just make money. They have high standards. It's a pleasure to talk with the chef. Sarah gives me advice without pretence. The same goes for Limmat. Cheffe Lili is so down to earth.

But now we need to start improving the city for us, for the Marseillais. We don't live in the pedestrian zones that were established for tourists in recent years. But the parts of town we live in need refurbishment as well! Next to the stairs in Le Panier neighbourhood, there are ramps that date back to the 19th century because at the time, we were thinking about people climbing up them, loaded with parcels. Now we act as if everyone lives with a car when we need benches so that grandmums and grandpas can rest. We should think about strollers, too. We put a small bench in front of our boulangerie. The number of people out of breath who ask, 'Excuse me, can I sit here for a bit?' It's unbelievable!

As a merchant, I'm happy that there are tourists here, but they should be here to shed light on our city, to bring it a new perspective. If we just make the city pretty for the tourists, that won't do. As we say in Marseille, '*on fait du genre* . . .' meaning 'we pretend to be someone we aren't . . .'

We need a real participatory democracy for the central districts. The people of Marseille have needs. There is a lack of public transport and space for bicycles, we need more green in the city centre, and we could do with a little less cars! I created an organic bakery to make a statement.

I really believe that there is a problem in this world. I grew up in the model of the 80s. For a snack, my mother would put cucumbers and tomatoes on bread and one day we discovered Mars bars and Raiders [now Twix] in lovely golden paper, they were clean, they were gems. We thought they were classy, but they are crap, including at the social and environmental level . . .

POTATO AND ROSEMARY FOCACCIA – 100% SOURDOUGH

INGREDIENTS

1kg flour
700g water (more or less, depending on the flour)
200g sourdough starter
50g olive oil
18g salt
Topping (1 glass of water, ½ glass of olive oil, 1 tsp salt – mixed)
2 large potatoes
About 10 garlic cloves
Provençal herbs, like rosemary or thyme (that I collect in the hills near St-Antoine)
Pepper

1. Mix the flour with 700g water and the sourdough starter for 5 minutes, then add the olive oil and salt. Knead for 10 or so minutes after having dipped your fingers in the topping.

2. Let the dough rise (at room temperature in a metal bowl under a tea towel) for 1 hour. Work the dough by spreading it out and gently folding it over itself, then let rest another hour.

3. At this point, you have two options: chill until the next day or with moistened fingers, spread out the dough on a baking sheet. Let rest for another hour (if the dough has been chilled, let rest for another 2 hours).

4. Thinly slice the potatoes with a mandoline, salt them (potatoes love salt), and add a bit of olive oil. Peel the garlic cloves. Remove the needles from a sprig of rosemary or any Provençal herbs you have on hand.

5. When the dough is ready, slather with a bit of the topping, and stick your fingertips in the dough to let out the air.

6. Arrange the potato slices (layered like fish scales and not forgetting about the edges. You need to be generous with the potatoes), the garlic, the rosemary (pushed down a bit in the dough with your fingers).

7. Bake for about 30 minutes in a 250°C/gas mark 9 oven. (Adjust cooking time according to your oven.)

8. When you remove the focaccia, sprinkle it with freshly ground pepper and a drizzle of olive oil.

9. Serve warm with some spicy tomato sauce or whipped feta.

BONUS RECIPE: KALAMATA OLIVE FOUGASSE FROM DAME FARINE – PROVENÇAL BREAD

As a bridge between two close communities, here is a recipe of Marie-Christine Aractingi, a *boulangère* of Lebanese roots. She was the first to plant the seeds for good, artisan bread in Marseille at her boulangerie on Avenue de la Corse. She has just handed the keys over to a team of enthusiasts who have renamed the spot Miches et Baguettes.

INGREDIENTS

500g flour (white bread/T65)
325g water
150g liquid wheat levain (liquid sourdough starter)
10g fine salt
1g baker's yeast
90g pitted Kalamata olives (large purple Greek olives cultivated in the south of the Peloponnese)
10g za'atar (Lebanese herb mix)

1. Mix the flour and the water and let autolyse for 45 minutes. This means to let the mixture sit for 45 minutes. Autolysis gives the bread a better appearance and more flavour.

2. Then, knead with a mixer at low speed (speed 1) for 6 minutes while adding the sourdough starter, the salt and the yeast, plus a few millilitres of water (called '*bassinage*') if the dough is too stiff. At the end of the kneading, add the pitted Kalamata olives and za'atar.

3. After 20 minutes, fold the four sides of the dough towards the centre. Wet your hands to do this. After 20 minutes, repeat the folding. After another 20 minutes, chill the dough overnight.

4. The next day, divide the dough into 340g balls. Shape into *bâtards* (short, wide loaves) – by folding the edges of the dough towards its centre, like a wallet, several times in a row. After 20-30 minutes, roll out the *bâtards* with the palm of your hand into a rectangle or oval shape (whichever you prefer).

5. Put your fougasse on a baking mat, floured or covered with parchment paper, and cut 3-5 slits with a dough scraper to make the traditional fougasse shape (like a leaf or a grain of wheat). Tug the dough a bit to open the slits into holes. Bake for 15 minutes at 270°C/highest gas setting.

FOCUS

Boulangerie + café terrasse

Because I spent so much time outside, in the streets of Marseille, writing and photographing this book on my own, I ended up with a very personal list of pairings: boulangerie + café terrace where time stands still and you can think while enjoying real *mignonneries*!

QUARTER: COURS JOSEPH THIERRY AT THE TOP OF LA CANEBIÈRE

Bar à Pain boulangerie + Café l'Éclectique. The best time is in the morning when it's calm. Life is good here.

QUARTER: NOTRE DAME DU MONT – COURS JULIEN – LA PLAINE

House of Pain boulangerie (incredible gluten-free bread and more) or Pain Pan! + Café la Muse or Au Petit Nice (the other one, not the Michelin-star table).

QUARTER: PRÉFECTURE

Pain Salvator (boulangerie) + Pain Salvator (café) = a real cocoon.

QUARTER: SÉBASTOPOL – CHAVE – LES 5 AVENUES

Les Délices de Granoux (a rare old-school boulangerie with the same décor since when I was a kid. Ignore the uninviting shop window and try their flan or their frangipane pastry.) + Monsieur Madame café (a real pas sympa welcome '*we don't do orange pressée, oranges are too expensive*' but vintage cups from our childhood, good food and a sunny quiet terrace).

QUARTER: CHAVE – EUGÈNE PIERRE

Les Mains Libres boulangerie + Le Georges. Pure pleasure!

QUARTER: NOAILLES

Msemen or thin crêpes from Rue Longue des Capucins + *pâtisseries orientales* from Maison Journo + Pétrin Couchette, their British barista and the terrace that successfully mixes all types. Ideal for people-watching.

QUARTER : OPÉRA

Deep Coffee Roasters + you give in and devour a burger at Howard. Made with Angus beef from the nearby Camargue with a housemade brioche bun, this is the best burger in town. Camargue is the Wild West of France and brioche buns are back in our French lives.

QUARTER: VAUBAN

Carlotta With + Carlotta With (all orchestrated by strong-minded Charlotte Crousillat).

QUARTER: ENDOUME

Pure happiness from Bricoleurs de Douceurs or Encore un Morceau + Fama for an *orange pressée* (because I am stubborn!).

A gourmet picnic option:
Boulangerie Miches et Baguettes + La Fabriquerie (a dream team that chefs in Marseille think highly of. All you need to lunch nutritiously in the sand, on the rocks, or with the wind at the Palais Pharo).

Tip: in France, it's not frowned upon to bring outside pastries into a café, as long as you order a beverage...

Malika, an excellent cook, and a piping-hot msemen, in Noailles

**‘Just eat it! What are you waiting for?
It gives you health,
It makes you beautiful, it makes you cheerful.’**

Paulette, seller at the *Foire à l’Ail* garlic fair in 1975 in Marseille (credit INA archives)

THE REPUBLIC OF GARLIC

Marseille, garlic mecca? Aye!

Marseillais still consume loads of *ail* (garlic in French, pronounced 'aye', not like the English word for an affliction), and this plant, like the olive and its oil, symbolises our history, our mix.

In 3000 BCE garlic was already grown on the shores of the Mediterranean in the fertile crescent, from Mesopotamia to the Nile via Phoenicia. Appearing in Central Asia in its wild form, garlic travelled, and everywhere it went, people quickly praised the many virtues of this universal remedy. The Egyptians gave it every day to the builders of the pyramids; Pharaoh Cheops even had a clove of garlic engraved inside his own.

The Greeks and the Romans fed it to their soldiers and their athletes.

In the Middle Ages, *ail* was used to strengthen immunity against the plague, cholera, typhus . . . and the evil eye! It kept bloodsucking witches and vampires away!

In the 19th century, renowned French scientist Louis Pasteur definitively classified it in the category of natural antibiotics.

As for its place in Marseille's culinary history, well, the oldest fair in Marseille was the one dedicated to garlic. Created by King René in 1447 as the Saint-Jean Fair, it took place from mid-June to mid-July, on the Allées Gambetta or at the top of La Canebière, or on Cours Julien, or Cours Belsunce.

Lately, local chef Emmanuel Perrodin, member of the Confrérie des Chevaliers de l'Aiet (the Brotherhood of the Knights of Garlic that preserves Provençal culinary traditions), kick-started this gathering around the Mediterranean's favourite allium.

This chapter is also a little wink to American counterculture cook Alice Waters, wine lover Kermit Lynch, the best food and wine writer Richard Olney, James Beard who was stationed in Marseille in 1945 and all their Francophile food friends in the US. Since 1976, every summer, Alice has held a Bastille Day garlic festival in Berkeley, California, at Chez Panisse.
I hope one day to party there on the 14th of July!

12

Nicolas Grégoire

AIL CARAMBA!

There are very few garlic farmers left around Marseille, or even in the south of France, as Chinese garlic has invaded the stalls of our (super)markets. Many have thrown in the towel. Today, less than 2,000 tons of garlic, not more, are cultivated on the land between Aix and Marseille. 40 years ago, about 50 farmers grew 900 tons each. The Grégoire family is from the area and have made a charming hamlet near Les Milles their own. Nicolas cultivates tomatoes and aubergines in open fields and grows garlic facing Cézanne's beloved Sainte-Victoire mountain. He is one of those young farmers who give us confidence in the future, but if you want to talk to him or write down a garlic recipe, you need to call a colourful character . . . his mum!
And that's how Hélène invited me for apéro. It was seven or eight of us. There was even Roger, a family friend and former garlic grower. As I sipped my wine, I caught a glimpse of a large, garlic-stuffed, free-range chicken cooking over a wood fire. You're getting to know me . . . of course I stayed for dinner. A delight! Joie de vivre, a love of good food, a very Marseillais gift of the gab, a playlist of the dead (dead singers, that is) . . . the Grégoires like to joke, tease, talk about everything outspokenly and put the world to rights while eating dinner. I love all that. I could have spent my summer there! The good news is that we can all go to buy our greens there in the summer on Tuesday and Thursday afternoons.

Nicolas: Today, people buy Chinese garlic! At the beginning of the season, we have a two-week lead. Afterwards, we have to deal with the influx of Egyptian garlic, then Chinese garlic. Then, later in the year, after Christmas, Argentinian garlic arrives from the southern hemisphere. There you have it! We have a window of two or three weeks to sell the local product because we have a rather special technique under mulch to make it grow a bit earlier than others. After that, it's not even worth it. The difference in price is doubled, even tripled! Even when you add in the costs of shipping from China, it's cheaper than producing it here. Well, garlic is always garlic, but the terroir does play a role in its quality. In Les Milles, in Luynes, these are the only spots where garlic has always been grown. There's a reason for this! It's what grew best here. We've always been 15 days ahead of other regions in the South. It's a matter of microclimate . . .

Chemin de Saint-Hilaire
Les Milles
13290 Aix-en-Provence

Hélène, Nicolas's mum: We were born here, and my parents were *antiquaires* [antique dealers]. But Nicolas, since the day he was born, he wanted tractors. We insisted he went to an agricultural lycée so that he got his baccalaureate, at least.
Nicolas: School bored me. It wasn't for me. I was made to be in the fields. I tried to work as a salesperson, but six months later, I quickly dropped out! My parents were not farmers. It was I who became one. My great-grandfather was. It's a beautiful métier.
Hélène: He started to farm when I stopped working so I became his sales rep and his market vendor!
Nicolas: Me, I take care of the technical and the production side. Don't ever try to call me. For that matter, on my website, it's my mother's number! Anyway, the truth is . . . on your own, you can't do this job. You can't do six farmers' markets a week (Bouc-Bel-Air, Cabriès and Calas farmers' markets) and be in the fields and on the phone.
Vérane: It's good to have a mum . . .
Nicolas: It's quite practical [laughs]. And, it's easier when you have someone you trust. And who you can whinge at too!
Hélène: I couldn't care less when he is mad at me [she says, sweeping her hand above her head]. Before, with my husband, we had a small vegetable garden . . .
Nicolas: Now, we have one that is 8 hectares! This is my family's land, plus 5 hectares that I farm thanks to Roger, a retired farmer friend who cultivated our land for years when my grandfather stopped.
Hélène: I am delighted with what Nicolas is doing! I made a lot of friends with our customers at the farmers' markets. I know them all, I kiss them on the cheeks. We've got a nice clientele. They are young people, around 30 years old. They are marvels.
Roger: Hélène is the female Pagnol!

Hélène: Of course, on Sundays, when there is a long queue, you need to know how to make customers laugh, to calm them.
Roger: The customers come for the lady that sells the vegetables!
Nicolas: You're a chatterbox! You would need 20 hours for each market but it only lasts four hours! You can't spend 10 to 15 minutes with each customer.
Hélène: I always have something to tell them.
Nicolas: The world of farmers is not an easy environment! I'm not the son of a farmer, some do not even say hello to me. The agricultural world in France is terrible. Relationships between farmers are dreadful. We're in posh Aix-en-Provence, so you can imagine that any hectare is very expensive, rare, and SAFER (*the regional rural land management office*) manages the allocation of agricultural land. When I settled down here, I was 23 years old, I was the youngest farmer in Aix. No one ever called me to find out if I needed land. Last come, last served. I don't have a problem with that. But a little consideration or help would be nice . . . because on the other hand, they like to put my photo in their marketing campaign. The young farmer looks good on a billboard. But hey, I don't care, I don't want to spend my time comparing myself to others. I try to focus on my own path. I live my life at my own pace. I get up in the morning and I'm happy to do my job.
Hélène: All they want around here is for their land to become buildable and to sell it for their retirement . . .

Hélène: Let's go, we're going to load the truck for the market tomorrow (*Author's note: it's 9pm*).

Marie Jo (a cousin): Oh! She ate it all! [referring to my plate . . .]

CHICKEN *À L'AIL*

FOR THE WHOLE FAMILY

1 large free-range chicken
Olive oil
6 heads of garlic
Salt and pepper

1. Take a good-quality chicken, brush well with olive oil and stuff it with 3 whole heads of garlic, unpeeled.

2. Season with salt and pepper. Cut 3 heads of garlic in half horizontally, don't peel them, and put in a baking dish with the chicken.

3. Bake in a hot oven for 45 minutes (a wood-fired pizza oven or as hot as your conventional oven will go).

4. Let chicken rest for a few minutes and serve.

This sauce that is made with garlic and olive oil (ail + oli), we also like to call it *'Beurre de Provence'* (the butter of Provence) and, we say 'ailloli' more often than 'aioli'. The difference between the long open o and the closed o is major for our Marseille ears. Think Italian O . . . versus Paris o.

It is said here and there that it would be good to add a few drops of lukewarm water when the mixture begins to thicken and that you shouldn't use an egg yolk to emulsify your sauce, unless it separates and a rescue is necessary. Nicolas' mum, Hélène plays it safer and chooses to start with an egg yolk. As did Chef Auguste Escoffier . . . father of modern French cookery, famous for having simplified elaborate recipes of Grande Cuisine in the 19th century.

As you can imagine, variants of this blend are found in several cuisines across the Mediterranean basin, in Spain, in Italy . . . Its origin is believed to be Egyptian.

In Marseille, the old *bars de quartier* often serve aioli for lunch on Fridays. Aioli at the Bar de l'Avenir, on the Rue d'Endoume, is strongly recommended. Cheffe Delphine Roux and *biscuitier* José Orsoni are regulars.

AÏOLI

INGREDIENTS FOR 4

800g salt cod
4 carrots
4 potatoes
½ cauliflower
200g green beans
A few cooked whelks

For the sauce:
3 garlic cloves
1 egg yolk
Groundnut oil
Olive oil
Salt and pepper

1. Soak the cod in cold water for 24 hours (or 36 hours, depending on the cod's thickness) to remove the salt. Change the water frequently.

2. For the sauce, peel the garlic, remove the germ, and smash with a mortar and pestle. Season with salt and pepper. Add the egg yolk and emulsify the sauce with groundnut oil, then finish with olive oil. Don't ever stop mixing. You can also just use olive oil, without groundnut oil.

3. Steam or boil the peeled and roughly chopped vegetables.

4. Put the drained cod in a large pan filled with cold water, bring to the boil, and let cook for 1 minute.

5. Plate everything on a large serving dish and add a few cooked whelks.

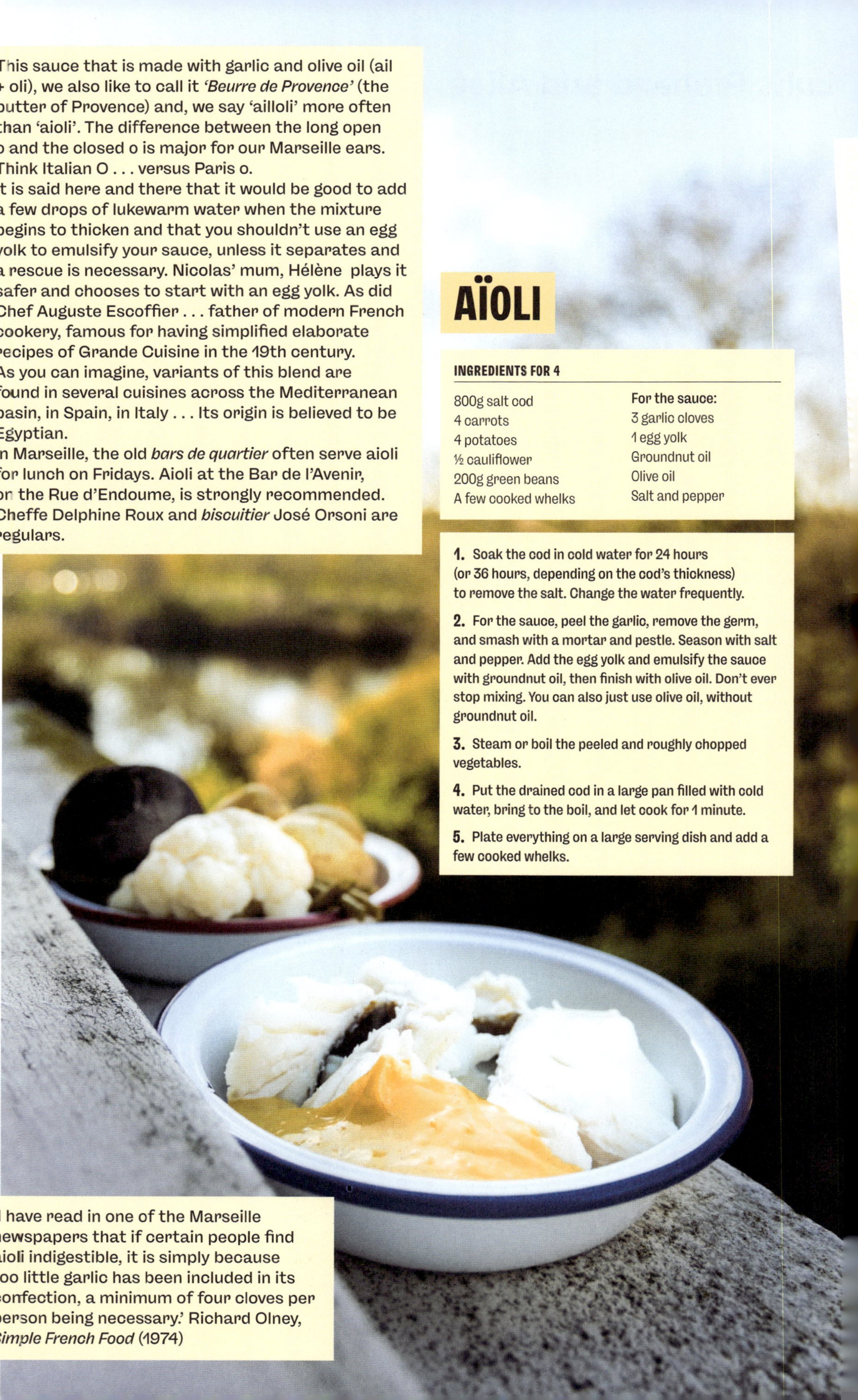

'I have read in one of the Marseille newspapers that if certain people find aioli indigestible, it is simply because too little garlic has been included in its confection, a minimum of four cloves per person being necessary.' Richard Olney, *Simple French Food* (1974)

Chemin de Saint-Hilaire
Les Milles
13290 Aix-en-Provence

Lulu, Richard and Alice

A MARSEILLAISE, TWO AMERICANS AND THE DOMAINE TEMPIER

Richard and Lulu

Born in a family of Marseille merchants, Lucie Tempier took over the family winery, in nearby Bandol, in 1940 with her husband, Lucien Peyraud. They made it one of the most refined Bandol wines that Americans adore. Sharing one of Lulu's recipes here is a tribute to this great lady of wine who left us in 2020 at almost 103 years old. She was an excellent cook. I was lucky enough to meet her a few years ago. She was 99 years old, and her energy and kindness made an impression on me. We talked about all her American friends who had so often lunched at her table at the estate. This merry band loved Lulu, especially Richard Olney and Alice Waters, who carefully compiled Lulu's best recipes in a book, *Lulu's Provençal Table*, published in 1994.

It is true that there was a time when the *crème de la crème* of American, Francophile and Francovore food writers ended up in Marseille at some point in the 40s, 50s, 60s and 70s. Even the cult Julia Child, heroine of televised cooking shows in the US, lived in Marseille in 1953–4 and later on shot an episode of the *French Chef* called 'Bouillabaisse à la Marseillaise' with the poissonnières on the Vieux-Port. I love watching the footage because it was in 1970 and I was born there only four years later. But my favourite 'ricain is the gentleman Richard Olney. He understood the essence of French cuisine better than any *Français*. A great friend of the Domaine Tempier estate in Bandol, we owe the tomes *The French Menu Cookbook* and *Simple French Food* to him. Richard gave cooking lessons and took his American students to eat *bourride* (a classic aioli-infused fish soup) at the New York brasserie in Marseille's Vieux-Port in the 1970s. As for the initiator of the delicious revolution of American cuisine, Alice Waters – who learned so much about cookery alongside Richard and Lulu – she named her restaurant in northern California after the character Panisse in the Marcel Pagnol films that she so adores. The Marseille author Jean-Claude Izzo, a great lover of garlic and Domaine Tempier, wrote: 'Garlic belongs to the gourmandise life . . . Nothing, in fact, goes better with garlic than wine, preferably red. From Bandol in particular, made from the fabulous grape variety, Mourvèdre.'

Cheers to Lulu Peyraud and her family, Detective Montale (the leading man in Izzo's noir novels), and Bandol!

And here is a garlic broth recipe inspired by those of Lulu Peyraud, Richard Olney and Alice Waters.

AÏGO BOULIDO (Garlic broth)

INGREDIENTS FOR 4

- 1 head of garlic
- 2 bay leaves
- 2 tbsp olive oil
- Thin slices of baguette, partially dried in a slow oven or in the sun or lightly grilled
- A piece of stale bread
- 4 egg yolks
- Salt

1. Peel, degerm, and crush the garlic cloves. Set one or two aside to rub on the slices of bread.
2. Add 1 litre of water, salt, the bay leaves, crushed garlic and olive oil to a deep saucepan. Bring to the boil. Lower the heat and let simmer for 15 minutes, lid ajar.
3. Strain the broth (make sure to remove the bay leaves).
4. Put a piece of stale bread in a food processor/blender to make breadcrumbs.
5. Rub fresh garlic on the slices of baguette.
6. Put a slice of baguette at the bottom of each soup plate, delicately place an egg yolk on top. Pour the broth over and sprinkle with breadcrumbs.
7. To eat it, whisk the egg yolk briefly.

Emmanuel Perrodin

IT'S NOT THE MAN WHO MAKES MARSEILLE, IT'S MARSEILLE THAT MAKES THE MAN...

For any question you have on the history of Marseille cuisine, it's best to ask Emmanuel Perrodin. This nomadic chef likes to learn it all to create better. He also likes to imagine bridges between cooking and art, between cooking and history - even prehistory - between older chefs and newcomers. He does not see a difference between female and male chefs, he likes sharing and listening, collaboration dinners with two, four, or many other chefs, pop-ups, supper clubs, *dîners insolites* in unique settings, culinary experiences of all kinds and their staging that he directs . . . Marseille, for all these reasons, suits him perfectly.

Where did you grow up?
I grew up in a little village in the Jura, Val-d'Épy, in which my brother is a producer of milk for Comté cheese, and Clermont-Ferrand, where I spent my adolescent years.

What ingredient reminds you of your childhood?
There are two. Comté cheese which is my *madeleine de Proust* [aka memory trigger like a Ratatouille moment] and pirojkis. Careful, it's the Polish recipe I am talking about, not the Russian one. It's my Slavic heritage.

When did you begin to cook?
Professionally, I began on 27 May 2003, in Marseille. I had an introduction during my studies, which I financed at the time by working in a Parisian crêperie in 1999. Another even earlier experience was from January to April 1994 at Kibbutz Kfar Masaryk. I was stuck in the kitchen because I was French. To be honest, my first memory as an amateur cook goes back to when I was nine years old. I had decided to cook beef sautéed in peppers, Hungarian style, for my Jura grandparents.

What training do you have?
For cooking, none. I learned to cook by being in contact with other cooks who were generous enough to share their know-how with me. One of the reasons why I love this job lies precisely in its spirit of mentoring and fraternity.

When did you come to Marseille and why?
I came to Marseille on 20 May 2003. My wife and I wanted to leave Paris to start a family and reinvent our lives.

What did you think of the city before moving here?
It was only clichés for me. I had heard all the *galéjades* [tall tales] about the city, but also, I had sworn to never set foot here due to a dark family history. Obviously, the city is a magnet. I know this now. This is one of its strengths.

What neighbourhood do you live in?
Today I live in the 5th arrondissement, not far from Boulevard Chave. When we arrived in Marseille, we chose to live in Le Panier. For its postcard appearance of course. Our apartment had a beautiful terrace and the light there was like no other. Then, we moved to the Chave-Eugène Pierre quarter to renovate a house. There is an ease and a unique bonhomie here.

Now that you live in Marseille, how has your opinion of it evolved?
Marseille has become my city. I truly believe that it is a global place. A place where the world can be summed up, thought of, and dreamed of. In addition, my two children were born here. My dear friends live here. And then, I admit that I love its madness, its *joie de vivre* that hides a profound melancholy at the same time. I also like that she is impolite, with bad manners. In a world where nothing should rock the boat, this city is still a place that breathes life.

Which Marseille neighbourhood do you have a particular attachment to?
I like La Vieille Charité [built in the 17th century to give poor people shelter] in Le Panier. I played there with my daughter when she was still a kid. Its museum space is incredible.
Of course, I like my quarter, Chave-Eugène Pierre. The day-to-day life is easygoing here. I also like the area around the Fortin de Corbières in l'Estaque. There, you snack on panisses while watching the city spill into the sea, it's incredible.
I also like Les Goudes, when you're in front of Île Maïre, it's both the edge of the world and the place where anything is possible. I like the Vieux-Port. Not just because I worked there, but I find that there, in particular, the city's routes meet up almost by magic. A yearning towards the heights with, stage by stage, the Abbaye Saint-Victor and the Bonne Mère, the Église des Accoules across from them, the boat masts, and Pouillon's residential buildings; and then horizontally, the Quai de la Fraternité, the mouth of La Canebière, an open door to elsewhere but also the promise of a welcome. Finally, in an even more intimate way, I love the *pierres plates* [flat rocks] between the Vieux-Port and the ferry harbour in La Joliette, with the J4, and the new Mucem museum. There exists a unique light, a unique blue, a particular breath of fresh air.

According to you, what would be the dish or ingredient that symbolises Marseille today?
I would love to say garlic. For a long time it was called 'the vanilla of Marseille'. What a beautiful expression, isn't it? It says so much about this aromatic. But I think it's the sea urchin that best symbolises the city. Beautiful, prickly, capable of regenerating its skeleton and incredibly briny, in other words, bitter, lively and marine.

What is the odour or the scent that embodies your Marseille?
Garlic, olive oil, brininess, and tripe, with a bit of spices. Impossible to respond with just one element.

4 S pop-up. Emmanuel Perrodin with cheffes Georgiana Viou, Charlotte Baldaquin and Sarah Chougnet posing for Caroline Dutrey.

What is your first culinary memory of Marseille?
I'll tell you all. Mezzes at La Caravelle and violets [a type of sea slug], which I discovered while working at restaurant Péron.

What is Marseille's culinary cliché that you adore?
Panisses, panisses and panisses, and chichis frégis.

Jean-Baptiste Reboul's famous tome, *La Cuisinière Provençale*, published in 1897, was there a time you had it on your bedside table?
Frankly, I don't really like Reboul. Actually, not at all. I've found only one great quality in him, which is that he titled his book *La Cuisinière Provençale* (*The Provençal female cook*), thus paying homage to one of the three great French regions where cooking was indisputably feminine above all. That's all. For the rest of it, it's a classic bourgeois cookbook in which Provençal recipes make up only a small part. I even think, to be honest, the book's large distribution has greatly harmed the rich treasures of our cuisine.

Jean-Baptiste Reboul was the chef of the famous Marseillais Noilly Prat family. Do you use this vermouth in your cooking?
Yes, of course. But not because of Reboul! I find it does wonders with fish.

What is the link between your cooking and Marseille?
Consubstantial.

What restaurant or chef started or caused the recent awakening of Marseille's food scene, according to you?
The real Marseille revival was born at the turn of the millennium. At that time, four chefs changed everything. Gérald Passedat took the reins of his family establishment and quickly imposed the idea of the Mediterranean Sea as a terroir. Masterstroke. Guillaume Sourrieu followed in his footsteps at L'Épuisette, and two young men revolutionised the Vieux-Port, Lionel Levy and Arnaud Carton de Grammont. Levy, now chef at the high-end Intercontinental hotel, brings with him the Parisian codes of course, but above all a real openness to the Mediterranean. Carton de Grammont, on the other hand, brought bistronomy to life in Marseille at his now-closed Café des Épices. These two chefs have a very particular point in common: they have an intuition for ingredients. All those who have settled since have deepened and followed the furrows traced by these four musketeers.

Which people working in food or restaurants do you admire in Marseille? Who intrigues you? With whom do you have a particular bond?
Impossible to answer that. I see Marseille and its various players as a whole. I find that they all bring the same great energy, precisely focused on better eating. That's why I'm part of the Gourméditerranée association, which reunites everyone from food truck cooks to 3-star chefs.

Marseille is a city of great differences.

Three words to describe Marseille's culinary scene today?
Generous, Mediterranean, and still embryonic.

What do people generally overlook about Marseille gastronomy?
That well before it was a city of seafaring cuisine, Marseille was long cited for tripe and offal. Marseille shouldn't become too polished.

What do the Marseillais overlook in their gastronomy?
Marseillais are way too unaware of the cuisines of the different cultures that irrigate their city. At the same time, they forget their classics a bit too quickly, they overlook their amazing variety of fish, so much so that they limit their expectations to six or seven kinds.

What do you like to cook for your family?
Simple things. Recipes from Franche-Comté (Comté soufflé, a savoury tarte au goumeau, Morteau sausage), a lot from here (legume soups, pastas, *pissaladières*, fougasses, many vegetables), others from Poland (pirojkis, borscht), from Japan (chirashi) or from the Mashriq (hummus, labneh, kefte). My daughter and I adore Greek salad in the summer. Sometimes grilled fish, and at least twice a year, poultry cooked in *vin jaune.*

What do you like to cook for your friends?
A lot of mezzes, tons of them. That way I can sit at the table too. And sometimes I make a bouillabaisse for those who aren't familiar with it.

Where do you go out to eat these days in Marseille?
I often go out to eat, it's true. I will only cite one name because it's my canteen: Le Comptoir des Beaux-Arts, in the Noailles quarter. The storefront says it's a snack bar. That's wrong. It's just a façade. It's a working-class restaurant where they serve chorba with a semolina galette that warms my heart.

Can you explain your choice of recipes for this book?
There is, first, a bouillabaisse recipe that isn't a bouillabaisse, because it doesn't have bitter and piquant saffron and it doesn't have scorpion fish. I really like it a lot because it's a recipe that throws a punch. For the second one, I wanted to work with *ail confit* [preserved garlic]. This recipe almost makes this pungent aromatic sensible. Almost.

In a world where nothing should rock the boat, this city is still a place that breathes life.

The *pierre plates* [flat rocks] between the Vieux-Port and the ferry harbour in La Joliette + on the left, the enchanting *digue du grand large* [seawall]

CELERIAC AND GARLIC CONFIT,
POUTARGUE, PRUNES AND BAY LEAF

INGREDIENTS FOR 4–6

125g ground almonds
10g poutargue (boutargue)
4 preserved garlic cloves
500ml mineral water
1 celeriac
Olive oil infused with garlic and bay leaf
4 pitted prunes
6 walnuts
Thyme
1 bay leaf
Salt and chilli pepper

1. The night before, infuse the ground almonds, grated poutargue and 1 clove of preserved garlic in the mineral water to make almond milk.

2. The next day, peel the celeriac, then massage it with olive oil that is lightly infused with garlic and bay leaf. Add salt. Wrap the celeriac in aluminium foil and bake in the oven at 160°C/gas mark 3 for 1½ hours.

3. Meanwhile, crush the prunes, 3 preserved garlic cloves, the walnuts, a pinch of salt and a bit of chilli pepper in a mortar and pestle.

4. Since you will still have some time, strain the almond milk after you've blended it. Reduce by half over low heat in a small saucepan.

5. Once the celeriac is cooked, hollow it out using a small spoon. Mix the flesh with the almond milk. Garnish the celeriac with the mix of prunes, garlic and walnuts. Reheat it in the oven for a few minutes with some thyme and a bay leaf beside it. When you remove it from the oven, flambé the dry herbs and serve with the warm milk.

Tao Wang and Yun Bai

GARLIC: THE CHINESE-MARSEILLE CONNECTION

Considering that the vast majority of garlic at our stalls comes from China, I wondered what place garlic occupies in Chinese gastronomy. Garlic originated east of the Caspian Sea. It spread to the west and therefore to us but logically also to the east and throughout China. This is what the Chinese-Marseille chef Tao Wang confirmed to me at Shanghai Kitchen. Garlic is a very common ingredient in Chinese cuisines.
Sino-Marseille relations go back a very long time. Garlic is not a big part of the story. Rather, it is thanks to the Suez Canal and the port. From 1869 well into the first half of the 20th century, all the Chinese who came to Europe did so by boat and landed in Marseille. Deng Xiaoping is one of the students who disembarked in Marseille's port in 1920.
Since 1987, Marseille has been twinned with Shanghai. The Chinese community grew here slowly until a wave from Wenzhou, in the Zhejiang region, arrived in 2000–2001 and gradually bought up the Jewish-owned wholesale textile businesses in the Belsunce district, Marseille's version of Le Sentier (Paris's garment district). Result: Marseille is on the way to becoming one of the largest gateways for Chinese textiles in Europe.

In Belsunce, the Wenzhou community is now diversifying its activities; we all buy our rice steamers at the Little Asia shop and the beginnings of a Marseille Chinatown is taking shape in the streets that were once only known for their prostitutes. When I was a kid, when we were told, 'You will end up on Rue Thubaneau,' it was not a compliment. The *parler marseillais* (Marseille slang) is going to have to be revised.
What about chinese cuisine in the city? Well, it wasn't always the most authentic cuisine in Marseille, as in the rest of France. But on this matter also, the times are a changin'. Some Chinese chefs have decided to break new ground.
For dumplings, we have Lilin and La Maison des Raviolis, but at Tao Wang and Yun Bai's Shanghai Kitchen, we enjoy real gastronomic dishes from Shanghai and Sichuan. There is no lack of Chinese clientele. Marseille chefs too. Harry Cummins from La Mercerie, Pierre-Antoine Denis from La Cantinetta, Lionel Levy from the Intercontinental are regulars. All that remains is for French people to value this cuisine more, and to agree to pay more for these real Chinese dishes than in an all-you-can-eat Asian buffet. The problem is global, you will tell me, since everywhere outside of China, Chinese cuisine is still considered inexpensive grub that you take-away in white & red boxes.
In our little corner of the world, a former cultural mediation student from Shanghai and his wife, a former economics student from Xi'an, tackle these preconceptions with an original menu in an almost fashionable setting. *Xie xie* (thank you).

Shanghai and Szechuan cuisine

14 Cours Jean Ballard
13001 Marseille

What kind of cuisine do you serve?
I cook Sichuan cuisine but 40% of the menu is from my region, the region of Shanghai. If I only did Sichuan recipes, I'd scare off the French! Shanghai cuisine is that of my childhood, that of my grandmothers and my parents. As for Sichuan cuisine, it's really popular in China.
I buy half of my vegetables in a farm run by a Chinese man in the east of Marseille. He grows Chinese vegetables. I rarely go to the Little Asia shop since for a restaurant owner, it's expensive. I go to an Asian supermarket called Paris Store in Plombières, they have Thai, Korean, Cambodian, Vietnamese and African products, plus fish that I've never heard of! You can find lots of things. There are also products that I still can't find in Marseille. Before, I shopped in Paris, in a Chinese supermarket owned by Wenzhou in the Arts et Métiers neighbourhood, but now I go and buy ingredients in Barcelona. I go there during my weekend, three or four times a year. I love that city!

How did you start your Marseille adventure?
Yun and I, we were two students and we met in a Chinese restaurant in Marseille, near Castellane. Me, I like to eat a lot. I try everything, but at that time, there were only a few Chinese restaurants that I liked. Even in terms of French restaurants, there weren't a lot of good places in Marseille. And in my little apartment, I couldn't cook a lot. I had planned to return to China, but I began to work in a Chinese restaurant to earn a bit of cash, and that's where I met my wife. The idea to open a restaurant followed, and we opened eight years ago.

The restaurant's decor reflects your taste in art . . .
I show local French artists because I have a good friend, Pascaline Zicavo, who has a gallery in Le Panier, the Invisible Galerie, and she lends me works. Sometimes, I also show works from young Chinese student artists from Luminy university here in Marseille. My original idea was to set up the restaurant, let my wife manage it, and open an art gallery that I would run. But a year after we started, our chef left to open his own place. I no longer had a chef. I looked everywhere, those who applied were used to cooking at cheap Asian buffets . . . These types of restaurants are, for that matter, opened by the Wenzhou community, and in the kitchen there are Cambodians and Vietnamese but not Chinese cooks. I said to myself, 'Why not me?' and I became our restaurant's chef . . . and now I have no more personal life! I'm a self-taught chef who has difficulty trusting others, but I know Chinese cooking well. That's the big difference between me and the other so-called Chinese chefs in France. Often, they never had the chance to taste great food in China. So, how could they cook it? On the other hand, I didn't have the foundation to use professional tools. I hired a retired Shanghainese chef to come to France for a month to train me.

In Marseille, there are mainly two groups in the Chinese community: Chinese students who come from all over China but who usually live far from the city centre. They don't have the means to eat out since Chinese students in France are way less wealthy than those who study in England. They chose France because studies are less expensive here.
And there are the shopkeepers who all come from the Zhejiang region. The latter don't speak Mandarin well, they speak a dialect that I still can't understand. However, their children take Mandarin lessons at a local Chinese trading association on the Rue Thubaneau that they also use for their religious ceremonies. In that region, they are Catholic and big believers. It's the same Wenzhou community that's in Belleville, in Paris. They have their own cuisine, their own flavours, they prefer seafood.
Therefore in Marseille, it's very difficult to find qualified Chinese personnel to work in a restaurant. I brought my sous-chef in from China.

How do the Marseillais identify, or not, your Chinese cuisine?
When I take orders by phone, they often ask me for spring rolls or caramelised pork. And I answer, 'I'm sorry, but I don't make that. That's Vietnamese.' Or they ask for nuoc-mâm sauce, but I don't have it! That's Vietnamese ALSO. At the beginning, the French ordered ha kao dumplings from the menu, or the Pekinese soups that don't exist in China, and Cantonese rice that is for us just rice sautéed with lots of things. It's a way to use the leftovers. And the Chinese were ordering sautéed intestines, very Chinese things. Today, three times out of four, I no longer can differentiate the Chinese orders from the French ones. We're making progress!

It must be said that in France, there first were Asian restaurants opened by Vietnamese and Cambodians who were of Chinese origin, from southern China. Often, they knew Chinese cuisine from their parents, but they had never tasted it in China.

In Marseille, there was the famous Heng Heng, run by the Chaung family, on Rue de la République. They put lacquered ducks in the window. This restaurant was packed all day. The family was evicted from their restaurant due to the street's makeover and it became a Monoprix!
I never dared to enter inside. Then, there were the restaurants opened by the Wenzhou community, but this population arrives clandestinely. They are peasants, people without a lot of means. They have never gone to a restaurant in

'Today, three times out of four, I no longer can differentiate the Chinese orders from the French ones. We're making progress!'

China. They learned the cooking of their parents, but there is Chinese restaurant cuisine, which they discover in France. And they don't know if it's good or not.
Today, we're starting to finally have good little Chinese restaurants, opened by Chinese students like me who see it as a way to promote Chinese culture and gastronomy. Of course, we want to make a living, but we also care about offering decent and authentic things with real Chinese flavours, using real Chinese products. We need to change the image of Chinese cuisine abroad. Our gastronomy is known all over the world but as a low-end cuisine. All the dishes I see in Chinese restaurants here, I have never seen in China! And with weird names . . . What is *'Les 3 Bonheurs'*? What is an 'Imperial' sauce? Nevertheless, I, too, have adapted. I have a smaller menu than restaurants in China. Such a small menu does not exist there! Because, normally, a table orders a little bit of meat, a little bit of fish, vegetables and rice and we mix it up at the table, whereas here you are used to having the dishes already plated for each of you.

What do you like about Marseille?
The weather, the climate. In my field, art, I would have had to go and live in Paris to find a job, but I didn't want to live underground . . . When I came to France, I arrived in Montpellier, then I studied for two years in Arles, then I stayed in Aix-en-Provence for a while and then I lived in Marseille. I have always stayed in the South, near the sea! Plus, the pace of life suits me more in Marseille than in Paris! I am not a very hard-working person, contrary to the image that the French have of the Chinese! Wenzhou people are. Not me! And then, we made friends in Marseille, so today it would be hard to leave.

When we met for the first time, Yun and Tao were expecting their first child. Now, their petit Marseillais is growing up in the restaurant. We discussed the future and whether it was possible to innovate in Chinese cuisine. It still seemed very complicated to imagine. Tao told me that even in the Chinese version of MasterChef, candidates are not asked to do so. That said, I hoped I had convinced Tao to start creating a Chinese-style bouillabaisse. I'm still waiting . . .

VERMICELLI WITH GARLIC AND STEAMED PRAWNS

INGREDIENTS FOR 1

1 or 2 handfuls of vermicelli (according to your appetite)
8 or 9 large whole prawns
60g garlic
1 tsp oyster sauce
Fresh chilli (optional)
10g fresh chives
10g fresh ginger
Sunflower oil

For the sauce:
1 tsp sugar
1 tbsp seasoned soy sauce for seafood (Tao uses Lee Kum Kee)
1 tsp black rice vinegar
1 pinch of pepper

1. Soak the vermicelli in advance. Mix the sauce ingredients together well.

2. Halve the prawns lengthwise but not down to the tail (it's prettier this way). Put the vermicelli at the bottom of a plate or dish that you can steam. Straddle the prawns on top of the vermicelli, their flesh towards the sky.

3. Finely chop the garlic. Fry 30g of garlic in a bit of oil just until it is browned. You really need to get a crispy texture. Mix this fried garlic with the fresh garlic. In Chinese, this mixture is called 'golden-silver garlic'. Add the oyster sauce. You can also add a little fresh chilli if you want to add a bit of spice to the dish.

4. Pour the sauce on top of the prawns and vermicelli, then spread the garlic mixture evenly over the prawns. Steam the dish or plate for 5–6 minutes depending on the size of the prawns.

5. Finely chop the chives, peel then finely chop the ginger. Sprinkle them on the prawns.

6. Heat a little sunflower oil to a high temperature, and just before it smokes, turn off the heat. Pour the very hot oil over the plate. You should hear hot oil crackling on the vermicelli. This hot oil will bring out the flavour of the chives.

'The temperature of Chinese dishes is very important. That's why I don't put tables on the terrace. Outside, the dishes would cool too quickly, and Chinese cuisine should be eaten very hot.'

FOCUS

The nougat of Allauch

You can find this little treat made from honey and nuts all over the Mediterranean, *turrón* in Spain, *torrone*, *copeta* or *cubbaita* in Italy, *jabane* in Morocco, *qubbajt* in Malta, *mandolato* in the Greek islands, *mandorlato* in Venice, *gaz* in Iran, or *djouzia* in Constantine in Algeria . . .

In France, nougat comes from the city of Montelimar in the Drôme region but not in Marseille. Provençal nougat is a descendant of the ones from the Middle East-North Africa region that have been imported to Marseille since the 17th century. During this century, Marseillais began to produce their own nougat with their own honey and almonds and added it to the 13 Desserts de Noël (a local tradition of fresh and dried fruit, nuts, *pompe à l'huile* or *gibassier* bread, nougat and chocolates. Traditionally served after Midnight Mass on Christmas Eve [or for dessert for the lot of us who put religion to rest] it represents the 13 participants at the Last Supper).

Almond trees were present in Provence long before Olivier de Serres (the father of French agronomy) decided to plant his in the Drôme region north of here.

As a result, in Marseille, our nougat helms from Allauch, the Marseillais village perched in the hills that hug the city. Incidentally, *suce-miel* (honey lollipops) and the best local *chips* (crisps) also come from Allauch! Which is no small feat!

13 DESSERTS AND THAT'S A MINIMUM

The *galette des rois* of the north will never replace the *gâteau des rois* of Le Sud, but we welcome new ideas . . .

Naturally, and on principle, Parisians' eating habits bear little resemblance to the Marseillais' but the *gâteau des rois* cake we eat non-stop throughout January (once celebrating the arrival of the three Wise Men in Bethlehem) could not be more different from their *galette*. Of course, the neo-Marseillais who recently moved down from Paris now audaciously try to impose their tradition on us!

La *galette* is a puff pastry filled with frangipane (sweet almond custard) while le *gâteau des rois* is a brioche topped with sugar and candied fruit. Both hide a *fève* inside to be found by one lucky gourmand but the gâteau also conceals a tiny *santon* (nativity figure) that the kids love. The youngest is supposed to crawl under the table to unbiasedly choose who gets each piece of the gâteau.

With this in mind, when it comes to desserts, Marseille's offerings are very eclectic, historic, often religious-based and therefore seasonal, and *fleur d'oranger* (orange-blossom water) is ubiquitous. Yet, from the Tunisian *loukoums* at Maison Journo to the whipped cream-Nutella *brioche des rois* from the Fournil du Logis Neuf boulangerie, the sugary gourmandise in Marseille must be (overly) generous and made with (too much) love. However, recently, an overwhelming desire for natural and local flavours has hooked some Marseillais and that's *formidable!*

In this vein, the world of ice cream is gaining more and more ground with new Marseille stars like Emki Pop's popsicle sticks and dips, Vanille Noire's charcoal-tinted flavour, La Mignonne's scoops and her tricycle . . . and a handful of patissiers and patissières are determined to mark their territory. Marseille now has a sweet new lexicon in a land that lends itself to it.

13

Préfecture

Jérôme Raffaelli

VEGAN PATISSERIES, NATURALLY

Jérôme Raffaelli was an assistant director who wanted to move into directing. His screenplay under his arm, he got tired of waiting for reading committees and funding. I get it, I've been there too. So he decided to re-channel his creative energy into vegan and natural patisseries. '*Oh fan*', what a great idea! My heart shouted this Marseille expression of surprise when I tasted the recipe presented in this book.
Today, Jérôme is happy, and we all get to savour his happiness! He develops his ideas and his desires as they arise and creates his sweet stories without having to wait on anyone. What a joy! With his partner, Kevin Yau, they thus run an atelier and two boutiques dedicated to pastries and biscuits that don't harm any living being. Do taste before passing judgement. A new kind of creativity has been born, and frankly, we can't help but be fans – and fawns (*faon* in French).

Vegan patisserie

2 Rue Edmond Rostand
13006 Marseille

Where did you grow up?
I was born in Aubagne and I split my studies between Marseille and Aix-en-Provence. As a child, then as a teenager, the colours of the Mediterranean and the smells of the Provençal countryside, as well as the cultural abundance of the city, built and fed my imagination. I also had the chance at a very young age to be able to travel all over the world. These trips helped to arouse my curiosity and my taste for elsewhere.

What are your family's origins?
My paternal grandfather is of Italian origin, a Christian from the region around Rome. My maternal grandmother is of Calabrian and Jewish origin. They both married children from the Aubagne region, giving birth to my parents who straddle these two cultures. I feel very close to my Italian heritage, in the kitchen of course, but also culturally, or more intimately in the ties I have with the members of my family.

What is your first culinary memory in Marseille?
It's cheese pizza! A piping-hot slice that my grandfather would buy me on Saturday mornings when we'd promenade around the Vieux-Port.

What dessert reminds you of your childhood?
I immediately think of the *tartes aux fraises* made with the strawberries from our garden, of flans, and, of millefeuille, of course, because it's my favourite gâteau since I was a kid!

What Marseille neighbourhood do you have a particular attachment to?
The Quartier des Antiquaires, near the Préfecture, which is where we were lucky to open our first shop in 2018. This quarter, and more specifically Rue Edmond Rostand, is a breeding ground for places that cultivate the *art du vivre* [the art of living], of antique shops and businesses that are still passed down between generations, and of many talented artisans and restaurant owners. It is also rich in terms of the people who visit, who live here, or who work here. At the crossroads between Place Castellane, the courthouse, Notre-Dame-du-Mont and La Canebière, it represents all the human wealth of this city. It is a very inspiring and at the same time very reassuring place.

What is the link between your sweet creations and Marseille?
Our boutique is called Oh Faon!, the popular Marseille saying with a play on words. It was super important for us to be part of the city's DNA and its cultural and artisanal affiliation. Our desserts

are inspired by the terroir, by its products like its fruits, its aromatic plants, and its flours, by the region, and by the seasons that we try to spotlight as much as possible in our creations.
We want our gâteaux to tell a story, most often ours, and through that, the ties that we have to this city.

What is the cliché Marseille dessert that you adore?
I'm an unconditional fan of the *chichis* in l'Estaque, and the *navettes* in Saint-Victor. Around Christmas, the [olive oil and *fleur d'oranger*-scented] *pompe à l'huile* and the *gibassier* are by far my favourites.

What Marseille cliché have you reworked?
There is a dessert that we created at the very beginning of the Oh Faon! adventure, which is inspired by an essential part of Marseille lifestyle: the *mauresque* [a cocktail of pastis and orgeat, almond syrup]. It is a tartlet composed of an anise-infused almond cream, a pastis and anise cream, and a pastis caramel. This creation was one of the gâteaux that made us stand out at the first Marseille Pastry Fair in 2018.

Do you eat the 13 Desserts de Noël?
Yes, of course! It's impossible not to have 13 desserts on the table on Christmas Eve. You can find fanciful desserts, but also a lot of fresh or dried fruit. At ours, there usually is a *bûche* [yule log], *pompes*, *gibassiers*, chocolates, *pâtes de fruits* [fruit paste], clementines, mandarins, apples, pears, grapes, *mendiants* [traditional chocolates studded with dried fruit and nuts], dried figs and apricots.

Are you on team *gâteau des rois* or *galette des rois*?
I'm totally for both of them!

Team *navette* (*fleur d'oranger* biscuit) or team *mouna* (*fleur d'oranger* brioche)?
Navette, for its unique taste and the magnificent story it tells.

What Marseille dessert has everyone forgotten?
The simple and gourmand *tarte aux pignons* [pine nut tart], that has practically disappeared from our patisserie shops.

Three words to describe the Marseille culinary scene today?
For me, Marseille's culinary scene is: inspired, because it willingly plays with codes and traditions; modern, through its desire for our businesses to be part of a sustainable, local and seasonal approach; abundant, because we are lucky to have a great amount of super-inspired young chefs in Marseille.

Does vegan cuisine easily feel at home in Marseille?
The region, and more broadly the Mediterranean basin, is an incredible playground for vegan creations because, historically, a great number of its dishes, often the most popular and affordable, have always been vegan!
If I mention *soupe au pistou*, ratatouille, *panisses*, and pesto, everyone loves them, but the first thing that comes to mind is not a 'vegan dish' or a dish 'free of'. Yet they are.
For a style of cookery to find its footing in Marseille, it must be good, attractive, colourful and full of character. Working with plants must be a characteristic, not a framework. For me, it is a simple component of cookery, which cannot eclipse the fact that our profession, through our savoir-faire and our sensitivity, is here to arouse pleasure and emotion in those that frequent us . . . Whatever their diet is!
We are lucky to live in a region where a great number of producers offer incredible treasures: fruits, vegetables, aromatics, oils. When we think about how to work with these products, we want to highlight them in the best possible way, and therefore considering the plants is almost a given.

'This creative work is less the fruit of the long frustration that one can encounter in the world of film.'

Is there a recipe that you and a member of your family don't agree on?
Aioli. There are so many secrets on how to make it that we can no longer get our bearings. One thing is certain, you must close the windows before making it!

A WALK IN THE GARRIGUE

FOR 1 GÂTEAU IN AN 18CM TART RING

'This patisserie pays homage to our region. The garrigue is full of bushy wild plants like thyme, rosemary and shrub oak . . . low-growing plants on chalky soil. Composed of a rosemary mousse, a pine nut praline, and a crispy *pâte sablée* (shortcrust pastry), it is inspired by Sunday walks in the Marseille calanques. I wanted to bring together pastry lovers around this memory that we Marseillais all share. The composition is simple, the decoration is natural, the textures are rich . . . just like our environment.'

FOR THE SWEET SHORTCRUST PASTRY

62g icing sugar
63g granulated sugar
62g cornflour
63g ground almonds
125g flour
2g guar gum
125g vegan margarine
20g soya milk

1. Add all the ingredients except the soya milk to a mixer with a flat paddle. Knead at speed 1 until the margarine is incorporated and the mixture appears crumbly. Once the dough has a sandy texture, add the milk, and gently knead at speed 1, just until the milk is incorporated. It is important to not knead the dough too much to avoid it becoming too sticky.

2. Roll out the dough between two sheets of parchment paper to 5mm thick. Cut out a disc of dough with an 18cm-diameter tart ring. Let rest for at least 30 minutes before baking.

3. Preheat the oven to 180°C/gas mark 4 and bake the dough for 10 minutes. Let cool before topping with the almond cream, keeping the tart ring in place.

FOR THE ALMOND CREAM

30g silky tofu
30g icing sugar
30g vegan margarine
30g unblanched ground almonds

1. Beat the tofu until it has the consistency of cream. Put all the ingredients in a saucepan and, over low heat, cook the cream while stirring it with a spatula. Stir vigorously so that the mixture is very smooth and homogeneous.

2. Leave the cream to cool for an hour. Once it has thickened, spread it over the base of the tart, leaving a 1cm margin at the edge. Bake the pie again at 180°C/gas mark 4 for 10 minutes. Let cool before removing the tart ring and decorating.

FOR THE ROSEMARY CRÈME DIPLOMATE (DIPLOMAT CREAM)

50g fresh rosemary
300g soya milk
60g brown sugar
30g cornflour
1g agar-agar
75g vegan white chocolate
100g soya cream for the whipping cream
30g pine nut praline (You can either buy it or make it yourself: roast 150g pine nuts on a baking tray in your oven for 10–15 minutes at 150°C/gas mark 2, grind them in a mixer. Put 75g sugar in a pan, cook over medium heat until you get a light-coloured caramel, spread it on parchment paper and let it cool. Once cold, break it into pieces and add them to the pine nut powder. Blend until you get a paste-like texture.)

1. Strip the rosemary of its needles and wash them in fresh water. Bring the soya milk to the boil, then remove from the heat. Add the rosemary, cover, and leave to infuse for 30 minutes. Strain the soya milk to remove the rosemary. Weigh, and if necessary, add more soya milk until you have 300g total.

2. In a mixing bowl, mix the sugar, cornflour and agar-agar. Pour in a bit of the infused milk and whisk for a slightly thick pre-mix without any lumps.

3. Put the rest of the soya milk to the boil, then pour it over the pre-mix, whisk, and return all to cook over low heat. Whisk until it forms a thick cream.

4. Put the white chocolate in a round-bottomed metal bowl (*cul-de-poule* in French). Pour the warm cream over the chocolate and vigorously stir until the chocolate is fully incorporated. Cover with cling film (so that it touches the cream) and chill in the refrigerator for 2 hours. The cream must be completely chilled and have a flan-like texture.

5. Beat the soya cream to make whipping cream. Thin the rosemary cream with the beater, it should have the texture of an unctuous cream. Delicately fold the whipping cream into the rosemary cream with a rubber spatula.

TO ASSEMBLE

Fill a piping bag with the pine nut praline and decorate the entire surface of the tart with the praline. Fill a piping bag with a 12mm nozzle for the rosemary diplomat cream. Pipe pretty spheres of diplomat cream in circles along the edge of the tart, from the outside in. Decorate with rosemary and pine nuts.

M R S
Joliette

Laura Bonnarde

Laura exudes *joie de vivre*. Having grown up in the hills of Allauch, where Marcel Pagnol spent his summer holidays, sugary Provençal recipes have a particular emotional and nostalgic dimension for this pastry chef. When you devour her *pompe à l'huile* all your senses enjoy it! This is the recipe she spontaneously suggested that I put in this book. Do not believe that Laura is confined to the classics. She masters them like the back of her hand to tease them out even better. After working in the kitchens of Michelin-starred Chef Julien Diaz in his Marseille restaurant Saisons, Laura is staying the course for her personal project: to open her own patisserie one day. In the meantime, this young talent and new mum works at the Dalloyau patisserie lab. You'll want to keep a close eye, and nose, on her . . .

NEW CHIP ON THE BLOCK

MY FAMILIAL AND PATISSERIE HERITAGE

My parents were both born in Marseille, in the 12th and the 4th arrondissements. As for my grandparents, we have Alsatian and Allaudian origins on my mother's side and Burgundian and Pyrenean origins on my father's side. I had patissiers in my family, my maternal grandfather, my godfather studied to be a pastry chef, my cousin and my grandfather's sister, Madame Michel, had a boulangerie in the nearby village of Allauch.

MY FIRST MARSEILLE CULINARY MEMORY

Pieds paquets, that my grandparents made each year on Christmas Eve.

MY CHILDHOOD DESSERT

Ah, my grandpa's *pompe à l'huile*, without hesitation! One of the famous 13 Desserts de Noël.

MY FAVOURITE NEIGHBOURHOOD

My heart beats for La Pounche quarter, in Allauch, home of all my childhood memories.

THE LINK BETWEEN MY SWEET CREATIONS AND MARSEILLE

Using Mediterranean flavours in most of my creations: *fleur d'oranger* [orange-flower water], olive oil, *immortelle* [curry plant], and many others, as well as a collaboration with the herbalist Père Blaize, a famed heritage enterprise in Marseille.

THE CLICHÉ DESSERT THAT I ADORE

Oh, the *navette*, of course! I remember that very special moment when I was a kid, we went with my grandparents to the Saint-Victor Abbey for the procession of the black virgin, and this subtle smell of *fleur d'oranger* escaped from the Four des Navettes shop, another Marseille institution.

A MARSEILLE CLICHÉ THAT I REVAMPED

Le casse-dents [Marseille biscotti]! Which I reworked for a dessert special with a pear poached in a lavender syrup, a *fleur d'oranger* ganache and a soft olive oil cookie.

DO YOU EAT THE 13 DESSERTS AT CHRISTMAS?

Oh, for sure! My grandpa's famous *pompe à l'huile* as well as his black nougat and *oreillettes* [crispy fried dough] to start. Next, we have the *mendiants*, the dates, my grandmother's *pâte de coings* [quince paste], calissons, clementines, white nougat, all kinds of candied fruit (*fruits confits*) and various chocolates.

MOUNA BRIOCHE OR NAVETTE? GÂTEAU DES ROIS OR GALETTE?

Navette, and in Provence, you eat way more *gâteaux des rois* than frangipane galettes.

THE MARSEILLE DESSERT THAT EVERYONE HAS FORGOTTEN

I would say it's *le colombier*, a dessert that is made for Pentecost with almond and melon. It's a tradition that is disappearing.

MY FIRST BOUILLABAISSE

I have never really eaten bouillabaisse, but I had a chance to try excellent *soupes de poissons* [fish soup], notably at Saisons restaurant.

HAS MICHELIN-STARRED CUISINE EASILY FOUND ITS PLACE IN MARSEILLE?

I'm torn between yes and no. I would say that convivial cuisine is much more appreciated by the people of Marseille.

Les Terrasses du Port
9 Quai du Lazaret
13002 Marseille

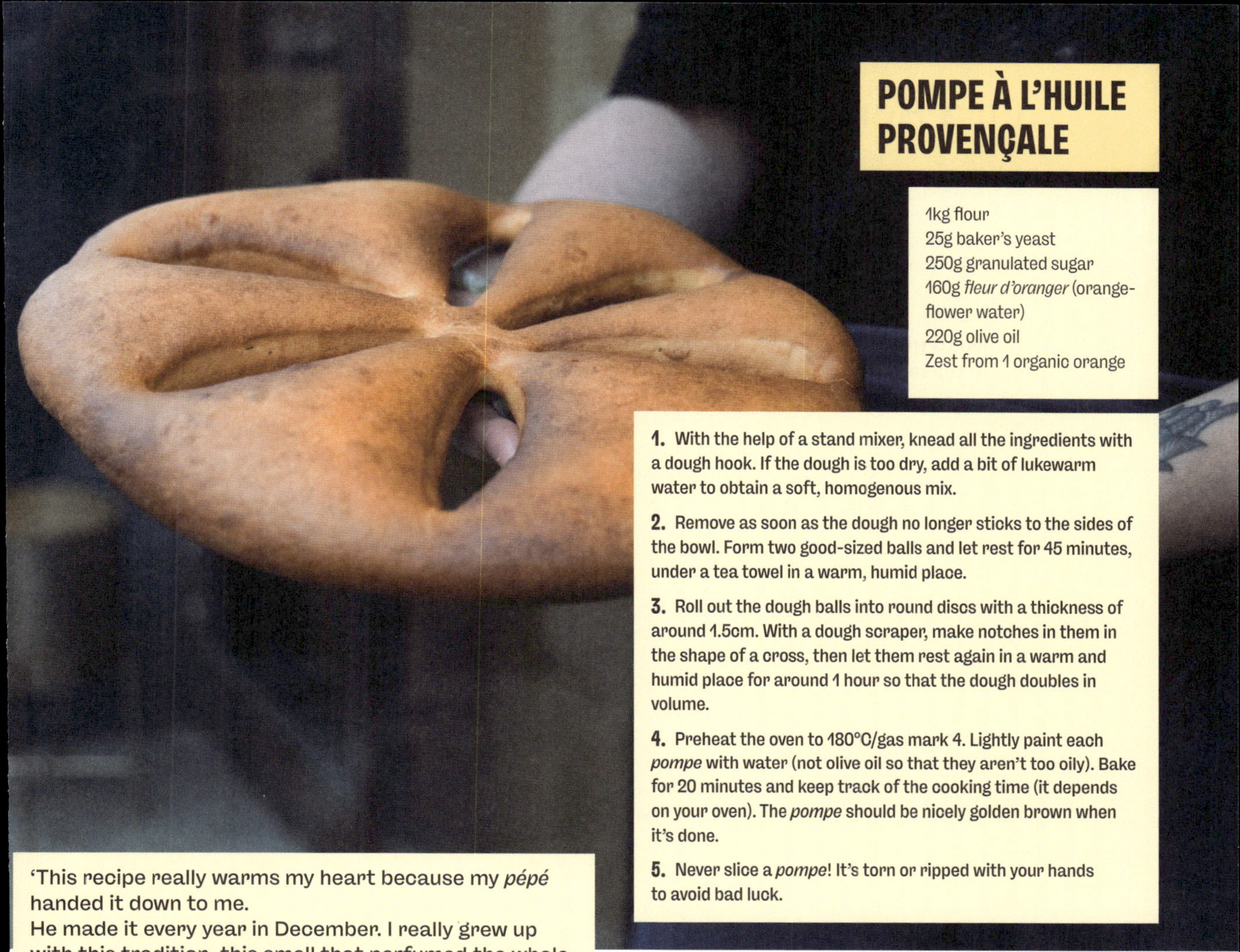

POMPE À L'HUILE PROVENÇALE

1kg flour
25g baker's yeast
250g granulated sugar
160g *fleur d'oranger* (orange-flower water)
220g olive oil
Zest from 1 organic orange

1. With the help of a stand mixer, knead all the ingredients with a dough hook. If the dough is too dry, add a bit of lukewarm water to obtain a soft, homogenous mix.

2. Remove as soon as the dough no longer sticks to the sides of the bowl. Form two good-sized balls and let rest for 45 minutes, under a tea towel in a warm, humid place.

3. Roll out the dough balls into round discs with a thickness of around 1.5cm. With a dough scraper, make notches in them in the shape of a cross, then let them rest again in a warm and humid place for around 1 hour so that the dough doubles in volume.

4. Preheat the oven to 180°C/gas mark 4. Lightly paint each *pompe* with water (not olive oil so that they aren't too oily). Bake for 20 minutes and keep track of the cooking time (it depends on your oven). The *pompe* should be nicely golden brown when it's done.

5. Never slice a *pompe*! It's torn or ripped with your hands to avoid bad luck.

'This recipe really warms my heart because my *pépé* handed it down to me.
He made it every year in December. I really grew up with this tradition, this smell that perfumed the whole neighbourhood of La Pounche in Allauch when he would make his *pompes*. He had an unparalleled savoir-faire that I'm happy to share today. He had no recipe, he made it by feel. So, I filmed him making his *pompe*. He passed away a few months later. I was so lucky to make it with him, to see it all, and to be able to jot down the quantities. '

Georgiana Viou

DANCING STAR

In Marseille, everyone loves Georgiana! This talented and spontaneous chef and mum of three, feels like a fish in water in this city that resembles her so. Georgiana's culinary career took its first decisive turn when she pushed open the door of Chef Lionel Levy's Michelin-starred restaurant to ask him for an internship. At that time, she was an amateur cook who had shone in a season of the TV show MasterChef but hadn't yet obtained her professional CAP certificate.
She then ran several kitchens in Marseille restaurants, including hers, until 2021, when Georgiana took a different kind of turn, by agreeing to become the chef of the new Rouge restaurant in nearby Nîmes. Judiciously set in a magnificent private terraced house (*un hôtel particulier*), the challenge was clear for the owners of this ambitious restaurant: to shoot for a Michelin star . . . And in March 2023, the Rouge team, Cheffe Georgiana, Sous-Cheffe Justine Mathieu, Pastry Chef François Josse and their sommelier Suzanne Cochran brought that star home. In just two years! In Marseille, we are unbelievably proud of her. This is our Georgiana. We lent her to the Gard 'region', but when the news of the star broke, Cheffe Delphine Roux brought together the world of Marseille cuisine at her restaurant, Chez Madie, to toast the talent of our friend Georgiana. For that matter, Georgie continues to joyfully take part in many made-in-Marseille festivals and culinary pop-ups, eats at all Marseille tables, drops into each new restaurant in town, and collaborates with many chefs in Le Sud, from Alexandre Mazzia to Emmanuel Perrodin, including the brilliant chef Florent Pietravalle in La Mirande in Avignon.
Georgiana remains one of the pillars of the Marseille food scene as much for her strong personality as for her cuisine.
There was a star danced, and under that was she born.

Marseillo-Gardoise-Beninese cuisine

Margaret – Hôtel Chouleur
6 Rue Fresquet
30000 Nîmes

Where did you grow up?
In Cotonou in Benin.

What ingredient reminds you of your childhood?
I would say the base of seasoning: garlic, ginger, pepper.

When did you start cooking?
I took part very early on. I would say around six or seven years old.

What training do you have?
In cookery, a CAP professional degree. Otherwise, before that, I got a bachelor's degree in LLCE (languages, literature and foreign civilisations) from the Sorbonne in Paris.

When did you arrive in Marseille?
In 2005. I joined my husband at the time.

What did you think of the city before you came?
I imagined lavender perfuming the air and cicadas singing in the streets.

What neighbourhood did you live in?
My very first place was in the heart of the city centre, Rue de Rome, in a quiet courtyard. The location was ideal since I don't have a driving licence. At the time, I worked at the Media Centre at la Belle de Mai.

How have your feelings for Marseille evolved?
There isn't the scent of lavender in the air nor the cicadas' song, but that doesn't matter. I'm very attached to Marseille. It's the second city of France in terms of its population (and yet there are less than 1 million people here) and it's the largest French city in terms of its area, but you have the impression that you're in a village. Not a day goes by without me running into someone that I know. And I really like its proximity to the sea.

What is your first culinary memory in Marseille?
A dinner at self-taught Chef Xavier Zapata's restaurant when he was running Les Pieds Dans le Plat in La Plaine quarter. A tasty and characteristic cuisine, imprinted with what I would call the 'taste of the south' . . . garlic, olive oil, spices, grilled flavours . . .

What is the link between your cuisine and Marseille?
In Marseille, I rediscovered seafood, garlic, pepper and ginger, among others. Marseille is rich in Provençal ingredients and cuisine, but also in all the ingredients brought here via the port and all the communities that have landed here over many decades. I discovered all these ingredients here and I immediately incorporated them into my cuisine.

ly cuisine is greatly inspired
/ that of my childhood and
y adolescence in Benin.

What are commonly called *les légumes du soleil* [vegetables of the sun], spices too, fish that can only be found here, seafood, poutargue, herbs from the garrigue . . .

Which quarter in Marseille do you have a special attachment to?
The Noailles quarter. It barely ever sleeps and, today even more than yesterday, there is a real mix there. All social strata, all styles, all kinds of foodstuffs and businesses coexist in harmony.

According to you, what is the dish or ingredient that symbolises Marseille today?
It's quite subjective. Spontaneously, I would say sardines.

What scent or flavour symbolises your Marseille?
I thought about saying the garbage bins, especially in the summer, when our binmen go on strike, but that wouldn't be fair. Personally, I would say the smell of a hot frying pan in which we add a drizzle of olive oil, a sprig of thyme and/or rosemary, and a smashed garlic clove.

Which people in the food or restaurant industry do you most admire in Marseille?
Out of order and for very, really very, different reasons, the bicycle delivery men (Marseille is super hilly), the market gardeners and other producers who strive to offer us their best goods, and also a great number of chefs at restaurants and catering. If I had to give just one name, I would say Marie-Josée Ordener from *Les Grandes Tables*, for her simplicity, her pugnacity, and her determination in her projects, each crazier than the next.

Which ones intrigue you?
The old lady who sells *les yeux de Lucie* [tiny good-luck shells from the Mediterranean] on the Vieux-Port . . .

Marseillo-Gardoise-Beninese cuisine

Margaret – Hôtel Chouleur
6 rue Fresque
30000 Nîmes

CARAMELISED FENNEL AND MAURESQUE VACHERIN

INGREDIENTS FOR 10

For the meringue:
100g egg whites
200g caster sugar
Fennel seeds

For the lime granita:
150g caster sugar
50ml water
30g egg whites, extra fresh
Zest of 3 non-treated limes
160ml lime juice

For the Mauresque* cream:
250g whipping cream, 35% fat
250g semi-skimmed milk
100ml orgeat (almond) syrup
Pastis (at your discretion)

For the caramelised fennel:
2 large fennel bulbs
400g caster sugar
2 pinches of fleur de sel
Pastis
2 tbsp orgeat syrup

For the oil:
Fresh lemon verbena
Olive oil
Grapeseed oil

1. Prepare the meringue: preheat the oven to 60–70°C/gas mark ¼. Put the egg whites and sugar in a saucepan and heat over low heat, stirring gently. Careful – keep an eye on it – the egg white should not coagulate. As soon as it's lukewarm, pour the mixture into the bowl of a stand mixer and whisk vigorously until the bowl has completely cooled.

2. Meanwhile, prep the lime granita. Make a 'thick' syrup with the sugar and water. Beat the egg whites until they are stiff. Remove the syrup from the stove and add the lime zest the lime juice and the stiff egg whites to the saucepan. Stir and put the mix in an ice cream maker if you have one. If not, put it in the freezer and mix from time to time with a fork.

3. Thinly spread out the meringue (as thick as a communion wafer) on parchment paper, then bake for a good 3 hours. Set aside.

4. For the Mauresque cream, mix all the ingredients together in a large round-bottomed metal bowl (cul-de-poule). Test to ensure you can taste the pastis and the orgeat. Add the mixture to the whipping siphon. Charge the siphon two times. Set aside in the refrigerator.

5. Pare the fennel if necessary and cut into cubes that are around 1cm. Put in a pan with a small glass of water and cover with the sugar. Let cook for an hour or so over low heat. Don't hesitate to pour off some of the water as it cooks if the fennel 'spits' a lot.

6. Cool the caramelised fennel when it's done cooking. Add the fleur de sel, the pastis and the orgeat. Mix and set aside.

7. Prepare a green oil by infusing lemon verbena in a little previously heated olive oil and grapeseed oil.

8. Begin the plating with the caramelised fennel. Then add the Mauresque whipping cream on top and, lastly, the meringue, arranged in a harmonious way.

*A popular southern cocktail made with pastis and orgeat syrup, believed to have been created with anisette first by French soldiers in Algeria in the 19th century, named for its colour that resembled the white robes worn by female Maures (the Moors).

FOCUS

Les Navettes: *barquette* or *foufoune*?

You'll decide when you see one... (ask French friends for a translation).

In the world of Marseille's *fleur d'oranger* (orange-blossom water) biscuits, there are two clans (are you surprised?). Each reigns on its side of the Vieux-Port, one on the Saint-Victor side, the other on the edge of Le Panier. The two recipes are different (I swear!) and the fact that the Orsoni family is Corsican naturally carries weight for me. During the first edition of this book, I had preferred to bury the case, but after two years of reflection (I eat and I write slowly), I think I am being objective or rather let's say I am comfortable with my subjectivity by immersing you in the universe of the family of the Accoules in Le Panier - José, his daughter Marie-Julie, and his son-in-law Clément.
The cheeky pater is a fan of local writer Philippe Carrèse (of famed Marseille noir crime novels), eats his aioli at the Bar de l'Avenir, and makes real Provençal macarons (with three ingredients only: almonds, sugar and egg whites. No flour, no cream, and no flavours unlike the overly fussy ones you find in the capital).

Ideal for petit déjeuner or an afternoon snack

68 Rue Caisserie
13002 Marseille

An encounter at Bar de la Place, Place de Lenche:

José Orsoni: I was born in Marseille to Corsican parents. My father was a sailor, a cook aboard ships. My paternal grandparents were the *boulangers* in my village, Carbuccia, beside the southern Corsican city, Ajaccio. My maternal grandmother was the village's patissière. She made canistrelli and would go sell them in the village three kilometres away with three platters of these biscuits on her head. We still talk about her canistrelli in the village! In fact, I have two villages: my village in Corsica and Le Panier in Marseille. I'm just as comfortable in one as I am in the other.
At first, my wife and I started a *boulangerie-point chaud* [a bakery that reheats frozen items rather than makes things from scratch] here, but little by little, I began to make my own brioches, my pains au chocolat, my *pâtes feuilletées*, by myself! I made what I loved, Corsican specialities (canistrelli, cucciole), navettes, and every morning, I would also bake fresh *chaussons* [turnovers] stuffed with Swiss chard and onions. Older neighbourhood residents would wait for them in front of the shop. Mine were really good! I fabricated a special baking tin, and thanks to that, when I put a spoonful of onions in the dough, they would get tucked into every corner!
Marie-Julie: That's when I was born and suddenly, he got tired of getting up at 2am, he couldn't see his daughter, so he had to change his pace.
José: At that time, we opened a wholesale *biscuiterie*. It has been sold since then. Later on, I felt like returning here to my old quarter where I was practically born.
I grew up in Le Panier, I knew it when it was wonderful, followed by an atrocious era. Afterwards, the neighbourhood became a bit too 'Montmartre-like' (*Author's note: referring to the picturesque and now-touristy quarter of Paris*) but nowadays we've returned to a good middle ground. However, 20 years ago, when I opened Les Navettes des Accoules, there wasn't a soul in the quarter. By the way, in Marseille, during August, you couldn't even find fresh bread. Everything was closed. It's nothing like it is now. My luck during that period was that the media already knew me and since I must be *sympathique* they talked about me. I was also aided by the folks at City

Hall who found this space for me. They took care of the rent for a bit. For me, it was a quarter within my means and where people would trust me.
Marie-Julie: Clément and I went to business school. We met in Grenoble. Then, we went to live in Singapore. We were both

salespeople and covered all of Asia. We both love food and talking to people.

Clément: We started thinking about returning to France, but to avoid feeling frustrated, we first moved to Canada. We spent a year in a van traversing the United States and Canada, then we settled down between Quebec and Montreal. We became sled dog guides and took care of 100 huskies and malamutes.

José: As for me, I was at the end of my rope! I was on my own running the *biscuiterie* shop, creating recipes, managing the staff, the accounts . . . I was going to crack. In October, when they told me that they still wanted to spend the spring in Quebec and not come back until April, well, I managed to convince them to return immediately. It was 2020.

Clément: It was a good time to return. The second Covid lockdown was coming . . .
And, there are plenty of Marseillais who are coming back to do business here. Having lived in Asia, the chaotic side of Marseille suits me. We have a small boat, we fish . . . And when you go to the supermarket here, the cashier tells you all about her life. That's funny to me. Here you can tell your life story to a total stranger.

José: My only worry now is 'Papa, the oven is broken', 'Papa, there are journalists here, come!'

Clément: And I equivocate between the daughter and the dad!

José: It's all right, Clément feels good here. But at the beginning, he didn't know anyone . . .

Clément: We came to Marseille in the middle of the lockdown. Everything was closed and we were an essential business, supposed to stay open.

José: My daughter wanted us to be open. So we opened . . .

Marie-Julie: . . . . and did 40 euros in sales. There was no one around!

José: After two days, we closed again.

Clément: As a result, our first step, was to set up an online shop.

Marie-Julie: But mail order is not our priority. The success of our shop is because our navettes are made the same day, with fresh eggs and fresh butter. We manufacture on site all morning. At 2pm, we take stock and make more if necessary.

José: Since the start, I held firm on this point. It's the same with the opening hours. I stick to them, even if it's -10°C outside.

Vérane: Why are the navettes from the Four des Navettes, on the other side of the port, really hard while yours aren't?

José: Before I made the navettes by hand. Then, I found a machine that was compatible with my dough. That's what makes the difference. Many others, not naming names, have changed their dough to suit their machine. One even removed the eggs from the recipe because they got stuck. But if you remove eggs from a biscuit that has no yeast . . . it becomes hard. Eggs have an emulsifying power. When it comes to my navettes, you can say 'I don't like them' but you can't tell me that they aren't good. Even the former owner of Four des Navettes came here to tell me that. And they came twice to chat me up so that I'd sell my business to them.

Vérane: And you? Did you offer to buy the Four des Navettes?

José: Yes, to the father, and he told me, 'No, not right now, you're too young. We'll see later.'

Vérane: Marseillais have a hard time venturing outside their quarter . . . What about you?

José: Me, I do everything in my neighbourhood, around this square (Place de Lenche). At lunch, I ate at a friend's place, a former butcher who took over the restaurant at the top of the square, the Café Théâtre. It had been ages since I'd tasted *alouettes* rolled in pork skin. Wouldn't you know it, he made them for me. Yesterday, I said to to him, 'It's the Beaujolais Nouveau, make us *pieds paquets*,' and he cooked them for me.

Marie-Julie: He sometimes crosses the port, but he doesn't go on foot. We drive him.

José: We went to the Bar de l'Avenir and they made us *vols au vent*. They were fabulous.
I went to school with the owner, Manu Montella. His son manages the bar in the afternoons, but his papa opens, and never misses apéro hour from 11:30am – 2pm. At school, he would copy my exams! Let me know when you want to go to there. We'll go together. We'll have an apéritif at the bar. Within reason! (He winks)

Vérane: Are there other places where you go together?

José: We go to eat kebabs at the tiny snack bars behind the Cours Belsunce, on Rue des Récolettes. Ilyes serves the brochettes. There is no sign but go before noon or else the queue is a nightmare. It's a really old business that's very well known. It's super clean inside and the meat is always fresh since they sell out daily. The trick is to not order a sandwich, but the kebabs in a takeaway container with harissa. When it's time to eat, you reheat the meat, and put it in a baguette . . . My word, it's delicious!

Clément: The sandwich costs 3–4 euros. The liver and lamb heart kebabs and the merguez are so tasty!

Marie-Julie: *Au village*, in Corsica, my father makes us the best pizzas in the world in a wood-fired oven!

José: The secret is to let the dough rest for three days in the fridge so that it ferments a bit.

Vérane: And your *chausson* recipe, will you share it with us?

José: I peel my onions the night before, I chop them into tiny cubes, and I put them in a large pot with salt, pepper and olive oil. Don't ever cook the onions. You must let them macerate; they cook in the salt.

Marie-Julie: That makes a huge difference.

José: Yeah, it's nothing like the others! Then I make the *chaussons* with a basic puff pastry that I prick so that it doesn't become too flaky. I fill the *chaussons*, then I cook them in a moderate oven (around 175°C/gas mark 4) for 20 minutes. *C'est délicieux!*

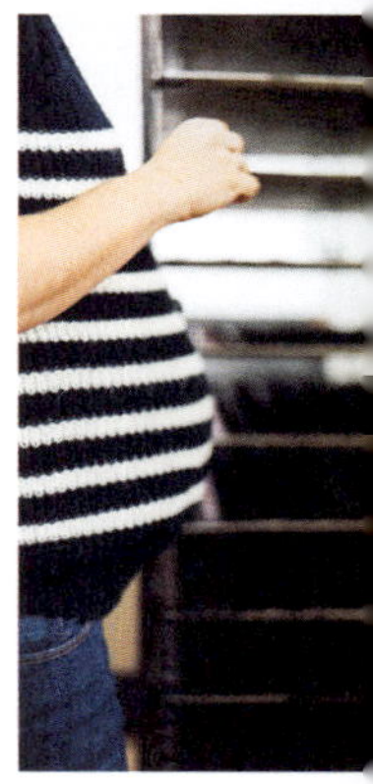

Laurent, Sabrina and Mina

ALL TOGETHER NOW

As I discussed earlier in the book, MinaKouk took part in the revival of Maghrebi and Marseille cuisine by working on a blend of genres and influences with a free spirit. In Mina's team, the self-taught pastry chef is a passionate perfectionist. Sabrina is also developing her savoir-faire by imagining one-of-a-kind wedding cakes at the crossroads of cultures.
Here is a sweet creation that they were working on when I stopped by Mina's. The pastry chef Laurent Navarro, a benchmark in the Marseille Sud'crés club, came to brainstorm with our two chums about a new dessert menu. Their session was infused with interaction and transmission. A beautiful image to end with!

AN INFUSION OF LOVE

INGREDIENTS FOR 50 BITES OR 25 INDIVIDUAL CAKES

1ST STEP

500g angel hair dough (kataifi) (1 package)
150g clarified butter
Fleur d'oranger (orange-flower water – optional)

Preheat the oven to 140°C/gas mark 1.

Fill small cupcake cups or small tins with the angel hair dough. Crush it a bit so that they fit the shape of the tins.

Soak each nest with clarified butter using a brush. If the angel hair is too dry, you can wet it a bit with orange-flower water.

Blind bake for 5 minutes. The angel hair should stay crunchy.

2ND STEP

1 high-quality black tea bag
500g Pink Lady apples (this variety is wonderfully crisp)
250g raspberries (or a mix of raspberries and strawberries or pomegranate seeds, depending on the season)
20g sugar (more or less, depending on how acidic your fruit is)

Let the black tea infuse in a large cup (300ml) for 30 minutes.

Peel and cut the apples into little pieces.

Dunk the berries into the tea and let soak for 5 minutes. Then strain in a mesh strainer or in a thicker strainer if you want to keep some of the texture of the fruit.

Add the apples and sugar to the berry-infused tea and cook over low heat, 5–10 minutes, so that the apples keep their crunchy texture. It should barely come to the boil.

3RD STEP

1 vanilla pod
600ml heavy cream
3 drops rose essence
Agar-agar (amount depending on how firm you want your ganache to be) or 2 gelatin leaves
160g white chocolate
Rose petal jam (optional)

Open the vanilla pod, scrape out the seeds, and put the seeds and the pod in a saucepan with half the cream and all the rose essence. Heat, then remove from the heat when the mixture is hot and let infuse for a few minutes.

Remove the vanilla pod from the saucepan and add the agar-agar or gelatin (both will determine how firm the ganache is). Mix, then let chill.

Grate the white chocolate if you're using a bar. Add the white chocolate and the rest of the cream to the preparation. Beat the ganache with a strong electric mixer (the fastest speed – a Thermomix works great here).

If the scent of rose is not strong enough, you can add a bit of rose petal jam at the end and remix again for a bit.

TO ASSEMBLE

Remove the angel hair nests from their tins, line the bottom with a thin layer of ganache, add a layer of fruit and top with ganache, using a piping bag or a piping nozzle.

To finish, place some fruit on top of the ganache. You can also decorate your cakes with edible flower petals.

LIBRE
PIZZA Brenda
Livraison EXPRESS 06.15.47.02.75

‘Wherever you come from, you are at home in Marseille. In the streets, you meet familiar faces, familiar smells. Marseille is familiar. From the moment you lay eyes on her.’

— Jean-Claude Izzo, French novelist who wrote the famous neo-noir Marseille trilogy in the 90s: *Total Chaos*, *Chourmo* and *Solea*

RECIPE INDEX

A

B

C

D-F

G-H-J-K

L

M

P

R-S

T

V-W

DESCRIPTION INDEX

PLACE INDEX

RESTAURANTS, CAFÉS ET BARS

BUTCHER'S SHOP, BAKERIES, ETC.

ALCOHOL, BREWERY

GROCERIES

BAKERIES, CHOCOLATE SHOP AND ICE-CREAM MAKERS

SHOPS

FARMING AND VINEYARD

ASSOCIATIONS

BIBLIOGRAPHIE AND SOURCES

Marseille, Roger Duchêne and Jean Contrucci, Fayard, 1998.

Justine Romolacci, « Dynamiques diasporadiques des Chinois de Marseille d'après leurs récits de vie », *Moussons*, 26 | 2015, 133-153.

Histoire anecdotique des cafés de Marseille, Horace Bertin, Hachette / BNF, 1869.

La Cuisine à Marseille, Alain Delcroix, Imprimerie Roche et Cie, 1991.

Marseille la napolitaine, Michel Ficetola, Massaliote Culture, 2015.

Lulu's Provençal Table, Richard Olney, Harper Collins, 1994.

Jean-Claude Izzo, « Ivresse de l'ail », *La pensée de midi*, vol. 1, n°1, 2000.

« Rafle à Marseille en 1943 : un quartier rasé et le petit rire de Pétain », by Chloé Leprince, 2019, France Culture et INA.fr

Marius, Fanny et César, Marcel Pagnol's mythical trilogy.

« Bande organisée », girls' version with Saaphyra, Veemie, Tehila Ora, Lil So, Ladyland, Léna Morgan, Mina West, Mely and boys' version with Jul, SCH, Kofs, Naps, Soso Maness, Elams, Houari & Solda.

A Considerable Town, M. F. K Fisher, Alfred A. Knopf, 1978.

Simple French Food, Richard Olney, Atheneum, 1974.

CHIFFONNIERS
MARSEILLE

L'EQUIPE
À JAMAIS
LE BOSS

ACKNOWLEDGEMENTS

Above all, my sincere thanks to Laure Aline, the editorial director at Éditions de La Martinière who listened to my long pitch and replied, 'OK! Let's do a book on Marseille's gastronomy and diversity!'

This ensemble book was photographed and written between April 2020 and April 2023, a period when restaurateurs, chefs and merchants had to, like all of us, bravely face their troubles and adapt. Merci for exerting so much energy for Marseille and this book. I ended these months of full-on Marseille with too many recipes, too many words, and too many photos. The hardest part was choosing. Thanks to Agathe Masson et Maria Notó Mora, my editors, and to Benjamin Heuzé, the magical book designer, for their precious help, their calm, and their patience!

Naturally, I took my whole family along on this adventure. My valiant partner and love, Franck Ribière, the chef in our house, made 11 of the 76 recipes photographed for the book. When her school was closed, my daughter, Valentina, tagged along with me on working days, tested many recipes, and often posed for photos. This book will be a great memory for the three of us, but I thank them for putting their lives on hold to get hitched to Marseille!

Big hugs to my mum, my dad, my granny, Lucette, who is no longer with us, my Aunt Yvette and her mum, Paulette, my godfather Guy, my cousin Céline and my childhood friend Anneu, who share their recipes with you in these pages. They are now yours, which makes me smile so.

Thanks to two enthusiasts who have embraced Marseille with every cell in their body and welcomed this project with joy and eagerness: Marianne Tiberghien, the non-stop director of the merchants' association in Marseille's 1st and 7th arrondissements and Marie-Josée Ordener, the conductor of Les Grandes Tables. Thanks to you both for your advice and your ideas.

Cheffe Laëtitia Visse and Maki Manoukian, you were the first people in Marseille who I approached for this book, and you immediately offered to help and shared addresses, contacts and phone numbers with me. Merci!

Thank you to Elisabeth Boucher-Anselin and the Michelin Guide who sent me to film Chef Alexandre Mazzia across Marseille in December 2020.
Thank you, Laurence Peyraud of Domaine Tempier for opening his mother, Lulu's, photo albums for me.
Thank you to Byron Olney, Richard Olney's brother.
Thank you to Jean-Francis and Jacques, Suzanne Quaglia's sons.
Thank you, Anne-Laure Pham, for introducing me to Nicole Ferroni.
Thank you, Zineb Torikian, Isabelle Brémond and Silvie Allemand for your support.

Merci beaucoup to my stepchildren, Thomas and June, to Marie, to Vita and Georges, to Éléonore and Louann, and to the many anonymous faces with whom I crossed paths, thanks for striking a pose.

Infinite gratitude for Alexis Steinman. Thank you for putting your heart and soul into the English translation of this massive tome. Talking about Marseille in English is one thing, but translating from Marseillais, *oh fan*, you can't be someone who gets your knickers in a twist. *Pardi*!
Thank you, equally, Nicole Foster, Estérelle Payany and Tal Bar for your proofreading.
Thank you, Mary Fitzgerald, the most *Marseillaise* Irish woman I know. You were the first to say this book should be translated into English and *grâce à toi*, I met Alexis.
Thanks to all the Marseille Believers who made this book a success.

Thank you, Bernard Tapie, for having made us Champions of Europe. You shed a unifying positive light on us. *À jamais les premiers . . .*

Merci, Marseille, for all that you are.

This new edition is dedicated to Marco Altenburger, Marseillais pastry chef *d'excellence* and Alexandre Mazzia's loyal and vital team player. Marco's kindness with many of us had no limit. *'Toujours avec le cœur . . .'* I miss you A LOT, *mon ami . . .* but you'll live in my head and my heart forever.

PHOTO CREDITS

All the photos were taken by Vérane Frédiani, except:

The photo 'Vera Pizza Napoletana' p. 20, the photo on top of the p. 199, the photos p. 28, 29, 30, 31, 40, 41, 43, 49, 62, 63, 155, 181, 233, 235 and the photo of the Nougats d'Allauch and the santon p. 264, were taken by Franck Ribière, my husband, who lent me his eye and his time when I was burning the candle at both ends;

p. 19, the photo of kids in front of Le Major was taken by my friend Vita Moltedo Samuel;

p. 85, the photo of Clément Higgins with his grandmum was taken by Aurélie Pauletto. Due to Covid, they preferred I didn't meet Mamie Armande in person.

p. 90-91, the photos were given to me by Suzanne Quaglia's son;

p. 174, the recipe photo was provided by the Hôtel Dieu Intercontinental Marseille;

p. 220-221: photos taken by Franck Ribière and Tiffany Peiry

p. 255, the photo of Lulu Peyraud with Richard Olney was found by Laurence Peyraud in a family photo album;

p. 275, the recipe photo was taken by Maki Manoukian.

MIX
Paper from responsible sources
FSC® C007507
www.fsc.org

Editorial department: Art de vie
Editorial director: Laure Aline
Publishing: Agathe Masson and Maria Notó Mora
Publishing assistant: Marine Laurençot
Production: Carine Ruault
Graphic design and production: Justeciel
Translation: Alexis Steinman
Proofreading: Nicole Foster

ISBN: 979-10-401-1213-6

Photoengraving: Les Caméléons
Printed and bound in May 2023 by Graphycems, Spain
Printed in Spain
Legal deposit: June 2023

Connect with us at www.editionsdelamartiniere.fr
Instagram: @lamartiniere.cuisine